THE CAMBRIDGE COMPANION TO JOHN CLARE

The fascinations of John Clare's life are manifold. A labouring-class poet and naturalist, he was lionized in the early 1820s but spent his final decades incarcerated in asylums. In this *Companion*, leading scholars illuminate Clare's rich life and writing, situating each within a range of critical contexts. Essays rooted in discourses as diverse as ecocriticism, aesthetics, religion, health, and time are accompanied by explorations of the construction of the *idea* (including the self-identity) of Clare through writing and images. The collection also traces influences upon Clare and considers the ways in which he has influenced subsequent poets in turn. The volume includes a chronology and an invaluable guide to further reading and provides students with a firm grounding in Clare's writings and his critical reception: this is an indispensable guide to the poet and his work.

Sarah Houghton-Walker is a fellow of Gonville and Caius College, Cambridge, a founding director of the Centre for John Clare Studies, and the author of three monographs: *Wordsworth's Poetry of Repetition: Romantic Recapitulation* (2023), *Representations of the Gypsy in the Romantic Period* (2014), and *John Clare's Religion* (2009).

A complete list of books in the series is at the back of the book.

THE CAMBRIDGE COMPANION TO
JOHN CLARE

EDITED BY
SARAH HOUGHTON-WALKER
Gonville and Caius College, Cambridge

Shaftesbury Road, Cambridge CB2 8EA, United Kingdom

One Liberty Plaza, 20th Floor, New York, NY 10006, USA

477 Williamstown Road, Port Melbourne, VIC 3207, Australia

314–321, 3rd Floor, Plot 3, Splendor Forum, Jasola District Centre, New Delhi – 110025, India

103 Penang Road, #05–06/07, Visioncrest Commercial, Singapore 238467

Cambridge University Press is part of Cambridge University Press & Assessment, a department of the University of Cambridge.

We share the University's mission to contribute to society through the pursuit of education, learning and research at the highest international levels of excellence.

www.cambridge.org
Information on this title: www.cambridge.org/9781009262576

DOI: 10.1017/9781009262583

© Cambridge University Press & Assessment 2024

This publication is in copyright. Subject to statutory exception and to the provisions of relevant collective licensing agreements, no reproduction of any part may take place without the written permission of Cambridge University Press & Assessment.

First published 2024

A catalogue record for this publication is available from the British Library

A Cataloging-in-Publication data record for this book is available from the Library of Congress

ISBN 978-1-009-26257-6 Hardback
ISBN 978-1-009-26260-6 Paperback

Cambridge University Press & Assessment has no responsibility for the persistence or accuracy of URLs for external or third-party internet websites referred to in this publication and does not guarantee that any content on such websites is, or will remain, accurate or appropriate.

CONTENTS

List of Illustrations	*page* vii
Notes on Contributors	viii
Chronology	xii
List of Abbreviations	xv

Introduction   1
SARAH HOUGHTON-WALKER

PART I   CLARE THE POET

1 On Clare and Lyric Song   17
   STEPHANIE KUDUK WEINER

2 Clare's Forms   30
   ANDREW HODGSON

3 On Clare's Translation of Perception to Poetry   46
   CASSANDRA FALKE

4 Clare and the Sublime   60
   ROSS WILSON

PART II   CLARE THE NATURALIST

5 Clare and Animals   77
   JAMES CASTELL

6 John Clare's Plants   91
   FIONA STAFFORD

CONTENTS

7   John Clare and the Community of Naturalists   106
    ROBERT HEYES

8   Clare and Ecocriticism   120
    MARKUS POETZSCH

PART III CLARE'S IMAGE

9   Self-Identity in a World of Influence   137
    TIM CHILCOTT

10 'Leading Strings': Editing and Revision in Clare's Poetry   151
    MARK STOREY

11 Constructed Image: Portraits of Clare   166
    SCOTT MCEATHRON

PART IV INFLUENCES AND TRADITIONS

12 Clare and Religion   183
    EMMA MASON

13 John Clare and the British Labouring-Class Tradition   196
    BRIDGET KEEGAN

14 The Politics of Nature   211
    TIM FULFORD

15 Clare's Health   227
    ERIN LAFFORD

16 Clare among the Poets   241
    MINA GORJI

Further Reading   257
Index   268

ILLUSTRATIONS

11.1 John Clare, by William Hilton, portrait in oils, 1820. © National Portrait Gallery, London. *page* 167
11.2 Henry Behnes [later Burlowe], plaster bust, painted, of John Clare, 1828. Photograph reproduced with the kind permission of Northamptonshire Libraries. 168
11.3 Portrait of John Clare, by Thomas Grimshaw, portrait in oils, 1844. Photograph reproduced with the kind permission of Northamptonshire Libraries. 172
11.4 John Clare, portrait by George Maine, watercolour, 1848. Photograph reproduced with the kind permission of Northampton Museums and Art Gallery. 174
11.5 John Clare, photograph by W. W. Law, 1862. © National Portrait Gallery, London. 175
11.6 G. D. Berry, pen and ink drawing, c. 1863. Image reproduced with the kind permission of Sotheby's. 176

NOTES ON CONTRIBUTORS

JAMES CASTELL is Visiting Research Fellow in the School of English at Cardiff University, where he was previously a lecturer in English Literature. He is interested in nature poetry from the Romantic period to the present day, with a particular focus on the complexity of the word 'nature', literary encounters with animals, and the role of sound. He has published on William Wordsworth, John Clare, Ted Hughes, and the relationship between science and the humanities. In 2022, he was awarded international funding for an interdisciplinary project entitled 'The Sound of Nature: Soundscapes and Environmental Awareness, 1750–1950'.

TIM CHILCOTT, formerly Dean of Arts and Humanities at the University of Chichester, has had a lifelong interest in John Clare and has written and edited several books, articles, and texts about Clare's life and work, as well as that of his publisher, John Taylor. His other major interest is literary translation, and his website, presenting some forty translations of major works in world literature, can be accessed at www.tclt.org.uk.

CASSANDRA FALKE is Professor of English Literature at UiT The Arctic University of Norway and leader of the Interdisciplinary Phenomenology research group. She is the author of three monographs and editor / co-editor of four collections. She has published over forty articles and book chapters on Romanticism, ecology, education, and representations of political violence. A new book, *Wise Passiveness: Phenomenologies of Receptivity in British Romantic Poetry*, is forthcoming in 2024.

TIM FULFORD has written many articles and books on Romantic-era topics. His monograph *Experimentalism in Wordsworth's Later Poetry: Dialogues with the Dead* was published in 2023. He has made several editions of labouring-class poets whom Clare admired: his *Collected Writings of Robert Bloomfield*, edited with John Goodridge and Sam Ward, is an open access Romantic Circles Electronic Edition, as is his *Letters of Robert Bloomfield and His Circle*, edited with Lynda Pratt. In 2023, his *Collected Poetry of Henry Kirke White* was published by Liverpool University Press.

NOTES ON CONTRIBUTORS

MINA GORJI is an assistant professor at the University of Cambridge and a fellow of Pembroke College. She has published widely on Romantic poetry, including a study of John Clare, *John Clare and the Place of Poetry* (2009), an edited collection on labouring-class poetics (2012), and essays on Romantic and contemporary poetry. She is also a published poet with two collections from Carcanet, *Art of Escape* (2020) and *Scale* (2022). She is co-founder and co-director of the Centre for John Clare Studies.

ROBERT HEYES grew up in south Lincolnshire. He studied Chemistry before becoming a teacher. He has collected books by and about John Clare for fifty years. Since retiring, he has been able to carry out research on Clare's life and work, with an emphasis on his correspondence, and wrote a PhD thesis on the provincial culture of which Clare was a part.

ANDREW HODGSON is Senior Lecturer in Poetry at the University of Birmingham. He has written several essays and chapters on Clare, including those in his monograph *Lyric Individualism* (2020). He is also the author of *The Cambridge Guide to Reading Poetry* (2021) and an editor of a new, three-volume edition of *The Letters of Percy Bysshe Shelley*, the first of which will be published in 2027.

SARAH HOUGHTON-WALKER is a fellow of Gonville and Caius College, Cambridge, and co-founder and co-director of the Centre for John Clare Studies. She has published widely on Clare and his contemporaries, including books on *John Clare's Religion* (2009), *Representations of the Gypsy in the Romantic Period* (2014), and *Wordsworth's Poetry of Repetition* (2023).

BRIDGET KEEGAN is Professor of English and Dean of the College of Arts and Sciences at Creighton University. She has written and published extensively on the labouring-class literary tradition, including co-editing with John Goodridge *A History of British Working-Class Literature* (2017). She is President of the John Clare Society of North America.

ERIN LAFFORD was formerly a lecturer in eighteenth-century and Romantic literature at the University of Oxford. She is now completing training in analytical psychotherapy at the West Midlands Institute of Psychotherapy. Her research focuses primarily on the literature of the eighteenth century and the Romantic period, and she has special interests in the representation of illness, emotion, and the environment, as well as in literary form. Much of her work in this area has focused on the writing of John Clare, but she has also published articles on William Gilpin and Dorothy Wordsworth. Erin is finishing her first book, *John Clare and the Poetry of Illness*, and is co-editor of *Palgrave Advances in John Clare Studies* (2020).

NOTES ON CONTRIBUTORS

EMMA MASON is Professor of English and Comparative Literary Studies at the University of Warwick. She has published on religion and poetry, most recently *Christina Rossetti: Poetry, Ecology, Faith* (2018). With Mark Knight, she is general editor of the Bloomsbury series 'New Directions in Religion and Literature'.

SCOTT MCEATHRON is Professor of English at Southern Illinois University–Carbondale. He has written extensively on the relationship between labouring-class poetry and canonical Romanticism and also has a continuing interest in Romantic-era painters and paintings with links to Lamb, Hazlitt, Clare, and Keats. In tandem with Simon Kövesi, he served as editor of *New Essays on John Clare: Poetry, Culture and Community* (2015).

MARKUS POETZSCH is Associate Professor of English at Wilfrid Laurier University and specializes in British Romantic literature and ecocriticism. He is the author of *Visionary Dreariness: Readings in Romanticism's Quotidian Sublime* (2006) and co-editor with Cassandra Falke of *Wild Romanticism* (2021). He has written extensively on John Clare, William and Dorothy Wordsworth, Thomas De Quincey, Leigh Hunt, and Henry David Thoreau.

FIONA STAFFORD is Professor of English at Somerville College, Oxford. She specializes in Romantic literature, including Clare, and also writes non-academic books about place and nature. Her latest book is *Time and Tide* (2024). Other recent books include *The Long, Long Life of Trees* (2016), *The Brief Life of Flowers* (2018), *Reading Romantic Poetry* (2012), and editions of *Archipelago*, *Lyrical Ballads* (2013), and *Stories of Trees, Woods and the Forest* (2012). She is a fellow of the British Academy and the Royal Society of Edinburgh and leads the Environmental Humanities Programme at the Oxford Research Centre for the Humanities.

MARK STOREY is Emeritus Professor of English Literature at the University of Birmingham. His publications include many articles and books on Romantic writers, in particular John Clare, Byron, and Robert Southey (including *A Life* in 1997); his editions include *John Clare's Letters* (1985) and the poetry of Ebenezer Elliott (2008). *Weightlifting: Selected Poetry* appeared in 2020, and *Truth and Beauty: Selected Stories* in 2023.

STEPHANIE KUDUK WEINER is Professor of English at Wesleyan University in Connecticut. She has published widely on nineteenth-century British poetry, including articles about political expression, print and oral cultures, poetic representations of sensory experience, and literary explorations of the history and multiplicity of the English language. She is the author of *Clare's Lyric: John Clare and Three Modern Poets* (2014) and *Republican Politics and English Poetry, 1789–1874* (2005).

NOTES ON CONTRIBUTORS

ROSS WILSON is Associate Professor of Criticism in the Faculty of English, University of Cambridge, and a fellow of Emmanuel College. He is the author of *Shelley and the Apprehension of Life* (2013) and *Critical Forms: Forms of Literary Criticism, 1750–2020* (2023), as well as of books on Theodor Adorno and Kant's aesthetics. He is the editor of *The Meaning of 'Life' in Romantic Poetry and Poetics* (2009) and of *Percy Shelley in Context*, forthcoming from Cambridge University Press.

CHRONOLOGY

1788	George Gordon Byron born.
1792	Percy Bysshe Shelley born.
1793	**John Clare born 13 July in Helpston, Northamptonshire; his twin sister, Bessy, dies a few weeks later.** Louis XVI executed; war declared between France and Great Britain; William Blake, *Visions of the Daughters of Albion*; *America*.
1795	John Keats born.
1798	**Clare begins sporadic attendance at schools in Helpston and then Glinton.** William Wordsworth and Samuel Taylor Coleridge, *Lyrical Ballads*.
1800	Robert Bloomfield, *The Farmer's Boy*; Wordsworth, 'Preface' to second edition of *Lyrical Ballads*.
1804	Napoleon crowned emperor.
1805	Battle of Trafalgar.
c. 1805	**Clare begins a period of working at various jobs including as a ploughboy, as a gardener, and as a labourer.**
1807	Slave Trade Act passed; Wordsworth, *Poems in Two Volumes*.
1809	**Enclosure Act for Helpston is passed, though the process of enclosure is not complete until 1820.** Charles Darwin born; Alfred Tennyson born; Byron, *English Bards and Scotch Reviewers* (published anonymously).
1811	Prince of Wales declared Regent; Luddite movement begins; Jane Austen, *Sense and Sensibility*.
1812	**Clare enlists in the local militia.** Charles Dickens born; prime minister Spencer Perceval assassinated; US declares war on Britain.
1813	Austen, *Pride and Prejudice*.
1814	Napoleon abdicates.
1815	Battle of Waterloo; Corn Law passed, leading to riots.

1817	Clare works as a labourer in the gardens at Burghley Park. Austen dies; Keats, *Poems*; Coleridge, *Biographia Literaria*.
1818	Clare works as a limeburner in Casterton and Pickworth; he meets Martha Turner (known as 'Patty'); Clare writes a proposal for publishing a volume of poems by subscription, which is printed by J. B. Henson and subsequently noticed by Edward Drury, cousin of the publisher John Taylor. Mary Shelley, *Frankenstein*; P. B. Shelley, 'Ozymandias'; Keats, *Endymion*.
1819	Clare meets John Taylor, who agrees to publish his poems. Peterloo Massacre.
1820	Clare marries Patty Turner, and the first of the couple's children is born; *Poems Descriptive of Rural Life and Scenery* is published; Clare visits London for the first time, and his portrait is painted by William Hilton. George III dies; George IV proclaimed king; Keats, *Lamia, Isabella, The Eve of St Agnes, and other Poems*.
1821	Clare's second volume of poetry, *The Village Minstrel*, is published. Keats dies; Napoleon dies; P. B. Shelley, 'Adonais'.
1822	Clare visits London again; he meets Lamb and other prominent cultural figures. Clare begins writing *The Parish* around now. P. B. Shelley dies.
1824	Clare visits London again; he meets Coleridge, William Hazlitt, and Thomas De Quincey, and consults Dr Darling about his 'nervous illness'. Byron dies in Missolonghi.
1825	Taylor and Hessey (Clare's publishers) dissolve their partnership. Hazlitt, *The Spirit of the Age*.
1827	Clare's *The Shepherd's Calendar, with Village Stories and Other Poems* appears after significant delays.
1828	Clare visits London for the fourth time and consults Dr Darling again about his mental health. The artist Henry Behnes takes Clare's bust.
1829	James Hogg, *The Shepherd's Calendar*.
1830	Swing Riots; death of George IV; William IV succeeds to throne; Tennyson, *Poems, Chiefly Lyrical*.
1832	Clare and his family move from Helpston to Northborough. Reform Act passed.
1833–4	Clare is frustrated that he cannot get a projected volume, *The Midsummer Cushion*, into print. Slavery Abolition Act passed 1833; Coleridge dies 1834.

1835	Publication of *The Rural Muse*.
1837	Clare enters High Beach Asylum as a voluntary patient under the care of Dr Matthew Allen. Death of William IV; accession of Queen Victoria.
1838	Mary Joyce dies. Dickens, *Oliver Twist* (monthly, Feb. 1837–April 1839).
1841	Clare walks out of High Beach in July, walking home to Northborough; in December, he is admitted to the Northampton General Lunatic Asylum.
1850	Wordsworth dies, and *The Prelude* is published; Elizabeth Barrett Browning, *Sonnets from the Portuguese*; Tennyson, *In Memoriam*; Dickens, *David Copperfield*.
1864	Clare dies on 20 May in Northampton and is buried five days later in Helpston.

ABBREVIATIONS

Unless otherwise stated, all quotations from Clare's poetry in these essays will be taken from the following edition, with volume and page numbers given in the text. The edition presents a 'primitive' text and gives detailed information regarding textual variants and the publication history of each poem. Volumes will be abbreviated as follows:

EP *The Early Poems of John Clare 1804–22*, ed. Eric Robinson, David Powell, and Margaret Grainger, 2 vols. (Oxford: Clarendon Press, 1989)
MP *John Clare: Poems of the Middle Period 1822–37*, ed. Eric Robinson, David Powell, and P. M. S. Dawson, 5 vols. (Oxford: Clarendon Press, 1996–2003)
LP *The Later Poems of John Clare 1837–1864*, ed. Eric Robinson, David Powell, and Margaret Grainger, 2 vols. (Oxford: Clarendon Press, 1984)

Other standard abbreviations used in this volume are as follows:

Critical Heritage *John Clare: The Critical Heritage*, ed. Mark Storey (London: Routledge & Kegan Paul, 1973)
JCBH *John Clare by Himself*, ed. Eric Robinson and David Powell (Ashington: MidNAG; Manchester: Carcanet, 1996)
Letters *The Letters of John Clare*, ed. Mark Storey (Oxford: Clarendon Press, 1985)
Natural History *The Natural History Prose Writings of John Clare*, ed. Margaret Grainger (Oxford: Clarendon Press, 1983)
Prose *The Prose of John Clare*, ed. J. W. and Anne Tibble (London: Routledge & Kegan Paul, 1951)

SARAH HOUGHTON-WALKER

Introduction

Opening Clare's first published volume in 1820, the poet's earliest readers encountered a title, *Poems Descriptive of Rural Life and Scenery*, underpinned first by the classificatory declaration, 'By John Clare: A Northamptonshire Peasant', and then by a quotation from Shakespeare's Sonnet 94: 'The Summer's Flower is to the Summer sweet, / Though to itself it only live and die.' On a cursory reading, it might seem that the book is straightforwardly connecting peasant poet and summer flower as equally insignificant, over-lookable-if-beautiful, natural objects. But there is a knot of contradiction here, relating to the persona that Clare and his publishers constructed. Since the seventeenth century, Shakespeare had been hailed as England's answer to the stellar classical tradition which previously had held literary pre-eminence. Instead of the regulated, formal perfection of Greece and Rome, England had her own national poet. In Milton's words, 'sweetest Shakespeare fancy's child' had 'Warble[d] his native wood-notes wild':[1] as 'native' manages to imply both an inherent personal genius and an affiliation to nation, Milton's Shakespeare becomes a child genius of the English countryside; a kind of national unlettered rustic. Putting Clare's identity next to Shakespeare on the page like this forcefully draws the parallel, in a moment of disingenuous humility. But of course, to know about Shakespeare is precisely *not* to be unlettered: not to be an isolated genius, but to be part of a literary community. Moreover, anyone familiar with the following two lines from Shakespeare's sonnet would know that they contain a rather more radical sentiment: 'But if that flower with base infection meet / The basest weed outbraves his dignity'.[2] These lines suggest that it is what you do that determines worth, not who you are. In this context, Clare's being a peasant, which we've just been told about on the title page, becomes irrelevant to the quality of his verse. As the last line of the sonnet puts it, 'Lilies that fester smell far worse than weeds': Shakespeare's lines speak of the possibility for the lowest of the low to outshine the most highly prized; perhaps even for a Northamptonshire peasant sometimes to surpass a Shakespeare.

Clare knew that people do judge books by their covers and was well aware that the phenomenon of a 'peasant poet' would interest readers as much as his poetry in the first instance. Asserting this persona, Clare participated in a tradition of peasant poetry composed of those whose originality and poetic brilliance supposedly derived from instinct and life experience rather than from book-learning. Beyond his title page, Clare repeatedly aligned himself with this tradition in the early days of his career. An 1818 manuscript containing many of Clare's early poems, for instance, insists that,

> As the ensuing Trifles are nothing but the simple productions of an Unlettered Rustic their faults & Imperfections will undoubtedly be nothing more than what might be expected – as correct composition & Gramatical accuracy can never be lookd for from one whose mental faculties (such as they were) being continually overburthend & depressd by hard labour which fate ordained to be his constant employment – It is hoped the unnoticd Imitation should any occur (being unknown to the author) will not be deem'd as Plagiarisms as the humble station of life in which providence has placed him has ever debarred him from Reaping that advantage of extending his knowledge by reading of Books the small catalogue he has seen might easily be enumerated a Thompson & and a Milton when a school boy was the constant companions of his leisure hours[3]

Here, Clare identifies, justifies, and markets himself as a peasant poet. Here are his claims to being qualified for that job: not being well read; not having had an education beyond a few carefully named 'school boy' hours, and yet producing poetry so good it might be mistaken as having been copied from real, really good poets like Milton. But he is juggling at least two personae here, as all published, self-taught poets must: Clare knows that once he makes the leap to being a published poet, he will by definition no longer be an unlettered rustic, because he will have become part of the metropolitan literary scene. Moreover, peasant poets had to produce poetry which was paradoxically both artful and (supposedly) artless. If verse wasn't good enough, no one would read it; if it was too good, it might lose its selling point as the creation of a genuine peasant. This is latent in the extract above, in the clumsy confusion of tenses, as Clare declares that grammatical accuracy 'can' never be looked for from one whose faculties 'were' overburdened: he can't seem to decide whether he *is* the 'Unlettered Rustic' who has limited mental faculties and therefore doesn't know what a comma is for, or the poet participating in the literary community who is lettered and is looking back to how he *used* to be.

The awkward self-styling demonstrated here, and the reiteration of the idea of unletteredness, continued as publication became a reality. As essays in this volume make clear, Clare's agency in his self-representation depended on the plans of others and on the market, but in his early work, Clare characteristically uses the word 'little' to describe his learning, the range of books available to him, the physical properties of the books he has access to, and the poems he writes. In 'The Author's Address to his Book', Clare addresses his book as '*little* bookey' and tells his volume:

> Tis thine to meet the learned now
> Wi' scraping boot & bending bow
> & tho in manners little read
> Simple, shanny, lowly bred
> Yet never mind push forward book
> Worth will excuse thy clownish look
> (EP 1 424–31, ll. 151–6)

The book becomes a euphemism, representing and also excusing Clare. Yet despite the cultivation of this identity, and whilst his education was largely informal, Clare was always greedy for reading material and knowledge, and resourceful when it came to obtaining it; by the time Clare turned to his second collection, *The Village Minstrel* (1821), he was already trying to move away from the persona he had collaborated in creating, of a little-read poet writing little poems in little books. One problematic corollary of the peasant-poet image, and its associations with instinctive genius rather than learned artistry, is the idea that Clare 'found the poems in the fields, / And only wrote them down' ('Sighing for Retirement', LP 1 19–20, ll. 15–16). Taken literally, this is a severe misrepresentation of the extent of the literary and other knowledge which is manifest throughout Clare's writings. What Clare really means is that nature herself is the best artist: that there is no basis on which to believe that a poet might 'improve' on nature. Persistently in Clare's writing (in descriptions of contemporary landscape gardeners, or ignorant farmers, or greedy landowners, or ill-informed poets), human interference with nature is spoiling and damaging. Rather, Clare claims, the best poetry represents the experience of the poet in the presence of nature, as accurately as possible. In this sense, Clare's early, submissive recourse to smallness is rerouted into a vital attention to minute and specific detail.

Widely recognized as the finest nature poet of the nineteenth century, Clare's verse prioritizes sharpness of attention and accuracy of description, including the visual, auditory, and emotional experience of being in a specific place at a specific moment. This quality has been central to recent critical interest in place, specificity, and identity, but criticism of Clare's poetry has always been concerned with the implications of his status as a nature poet. His superb knowledge of the pettichap's nest, not only of how the nest is built, but even of the history of the materials used in its construction ('withered leaves make up its outward walls / That from the snub-oak dotterel yearly falls / & in the old hedge bottom rot away', MP III 517–19, ll. 17–18), is exemplary of the breadth of his exhaustive attention to intimate detail. His status amongst naturalists is high, and recent scholarship has awarded him laurels according to a set of concerns including conservation, attention, and an awareness of responsibility to the natural world. At times, the idea of Clare's writing as a 'purely' descriptive (which it certainly isn't) has contributed to the sense of him as an unsuccessful Romantic. In his 1757 *Philosophical Enquiry into the Origin of Our Ideas of the Sublime and Beautiful*, Edmund Burke had condemned 'naked description', because he felt it in no way represented any 'strong and lively feeling' in the observer.[4] This attitude gained increasing traction with an emergent nineteenth-century Romanticism. But Clare's capacity for meticulous description, rendered into astonishing verse, doesn't eliminate all else: feeling remains vital. Essays in this volume note Clare's attachment to the declaration 'I love', and he has his own defence against the accusation that attention to specifics might be secondary to other, more conventionally Romantic ideals:

> Trifles may illustrate great mysterys without derogating any thing from their grandeur – thus the oak need not be ashamed of the acorn as it is its parent – the lion of the little Jackall as it is his provider ... & trifles also explain great things the fall of a apple led Newton to the discovery of gravity – the shape of a simple leaf to an order in architecture & the shadow from a lamp on the wall to design and perspective ... little things lead to great discoverys[5]

***

The 'Introduction' to *Poems Descriptive* penned by Clare's publisher and various puff-pieces associated with the book's publication represent the earliest formal responses to Clare's work. Collectively, they intended to celebrate and to excuse any 'provincialisms' or unorthodoxy Clare's first readers might have encountered. They seem to have worked; writing to his publisher in September 1821, Clare remarked: 'I am sought after very much agen ... surely the vanity woud have kill'd me 4 years ago if I had known then how I shoud have been hunted up – & extolled by personal flattery' (*Letters*, p. 215). Then, pessimistically, he adds, '– but let me wait another year or two & t[he] peep show will be over'. To a great extent, it was. *Poems Descriptive* had gone through four editions in its first year, but Clare was disappointed when *The Village Minstrel* did not meet with similar sales figures. *The Shepherd's Calendar* was in progress by 1824 but only crawled into print in 1827, and by 1829 just 400 copies had been sold. The last book of Clare's verse published in his lifetime, *The Rural Muse* (1835), met with a strong critical reception, but sales remained slow. Despite occasional appearances in journals or magazines, Clare's commercial success was over.

And yet Clare has always had his champions, many of them poets themselves. Even in his relative neglect in the later nineteenth and early twentieth centuries, he was always read and celebrated, particularly by poet-editors, including Edmund Blunden, Arthur Symons, and Geoffrey Grigson. Clare's is also an important historical voice, commenting in prose on politics, religion, and aesthetics as well as writing luminous poetry; critics in turn have followed these leads. Modern interest in Clare has risen with the critical fields within which Clare sits so well, including ecocriticism, discourses interested in various forms of dispossession and mental health, and the recovery of the marginalized. Whilst it is not true to say that he ever completely dropped from view, in the last fifty years the significance of Clare's verse has increasingly been recognized.

Most recent criticism has refused to limit itself to the material published (with, we should continue to recognize, Clare's consent) during Clare's lifetime. Clare wrote a vast quantity of poetry he never saw in print, in which he experimented with form and expression. He also invested energy in generically various prose writing. Much of this work does not fit easily into the narrative of the gentle, nature-loving peasant. Already in the early 1820s, for example, Clare had begun his vitriolic 2,200-line satire, *The Parish*, whose tenor differs radically from that of the works Clare managed to publish in the same decade. The tender Clare who emerges from many of his lyrical pieces took delight in brutal Regency boxing tournaments. He drank, and his writing sometimes lashes out at women: aspects of his asylum poem *Don Juan* (LP I 89–102) are disturbing in this regard. Even the folk rituals Clare celebrates in verse have a darker side which prompts his bleak acknowledgement of the vicious tendencies in both men and nature: the sequence of sonnets culminating in the kicking and tearing of a badger (see MP V 360–2) is profoundly representative of the clash of his desire to record and preserve traditional community structures with an abhorrence of the violent inequality of such contests. Some of the best known of Clare's work dates from his time in lunatic asylums, rather than from his printed collections. Whilst certain preoccupations and stylistic habits remain in evidence in this later verse, there are marked discontinuities between it and the earlier material; in particular, interest in the specificity of place is vastly reduced. On the other hand, the seeds of those characteristics commonly identified in the later period are certainly discernible in early work: the 'visionary' poems of the asylum period rework a quality of attention and a kind of intensity which is already strikingly present in the sublime suspension of 'Noon' (EP I 404–7); the 1841 biblical paraphrases build on a tradition of biblical knowledge evident both in paraphrase and allusion throughout Clare's writing; the emphasis of many later poems on questions of identity and being only expands on a preoccupation clearly pressing (if sometimes unoriginally rendered) in his earliest work.

Some of Clare's writing is specifically and directly political, often angrily so. *The Parish* draws its vigour from Clare's disgust at a social system based in class and wealth, rather than taste, intelligence, and honour. He also drew more metaphorical inspiration from the political structures whose reflections he found in the natural world. 'The Ants' (EP II 56) is a good example of Clare's combining political allegory with precise, natural-historical observation. Often, the parallels are even more implicit. Critics who have been attentive to Clare's political attitudes, then, necessarily have drawn on works from across the spectrum of his poetry, and Clare's writing has lent a perspective on political history which is often overlooked. Clare's political stance is not consistent, or always easy to ascertain: his opinions change across time and according to audience. However, regardless of this difficulty in pinning Clare down, the way in which his political ideas find their out-working in verse has consistently rewarded critical attention.

In the personal as in the political, Clare's recorded attitudes fluctuate significantly. For example, his prose autobiographical fragments support the idea of a man who liked looking at, being near, and the physical intimacy of his relationships with, the opposite sex. He paid the price for this pleasure in terms of physical disease and mental anguish, and he could be caustic about women. Yet he reveals profound sympathy with many women in his writing, and a vast collection of love poems, directed at specific figures and none, also exists; these are tonally and structurally various. At the core of the collection of songs, sonnets, lyrical celebrations, and vitriolic denunciations addressed to or about women runs the thread of Clare's first love, Mary Joyce. Mary, or rather the *idea* of Mary, consistently haunts Clare's poetry. Despite his long marriage to Patty Turner, Mary's figure is woven through the fabric of Clare's verse along with his deep and persistent preoccupation with the idea of a more perfect past.

This latter idea is not a simple nostalgia; it takes many forms, some directly or indirectly biblical, some inflected by other literature, and some more mundane. Relatedly, Clare often reflects on childhood as a more perfect state, and this in turn is connected to his attitude towards the historical reality of enclosure (the process by which formerly common land is appropriated and becomes private property). The effects of the 1809 Act of Parliament for the enclosure of Helpston upon the environs of Clare's native village, and their impact on what John Barrell describes as Clare's 'open field sense of space',⁶ deeply mark Clare's work. As Tim Fulford's essay in this volume demonstrates, Clare's feeling with and for the land is articulated in a range of voices and takes a range of forms, from explicit invective in 'The Mores' (MP II 347–50), to the abdication of the possibility of expression to the landscape itself in 'The Lament of Swordy Well' (MP v 105–14) and 'The Lamentations of Round-Oak Waters' (EP I 228–34) (Chapter 14).

In 1832, with financial support provided by local landowner the Earl Fitzwilliam, Clare moved with his family to a cottage in Northborough, a short distance from his native home in Helpston, near Peterborough. Clare had travelled before, on visits to London and in pursuit of employment. However, a long critical tradition has argued that the 1832 move affected Clare more profoundly; from this point, his work expresses a homesickness and, increasingly, a more general sense of desolation: 'There is a cruelty in all', he claims, in the first line of one of the powerful sonnets he wrote in Northborough (MP v 62). It is important to resist the temptations of cod-psychology: Clare was ill before this relocation was ever contemplated. Nonetheless, his mental health deteriorated, and in 1837 he entered High Beach Asylum in Essex as a voluntary patient.

In 1841, Clare produced a large quantity of verse testifying to his interest at this point in specifically religious ideas. In the same year, he composed *Child Harold* and *Don Juan*, though whether Clare's assertion that he was Byron (or any of the other personae he claimed to be) was the product of a genuine delusion, or simply a posture, can only be conjectured. In July that year, Clare walked away from High Beach and continued, hungry, footsore, and unsheltered, until he reached home, eighty miles away. In December, he was admitted to Northampton General Lunatic Asylum, where he remained until his death in 1864. Throughout this time, Clare continued to write, though if his writing was always inconsistent (in quality, subject matter, and form alike), it is even more demonstrably so once he had been removed to these institutions. Derivative, formulaic 'songs' are commonplace. Many poems address specific women (Clare may have been writing some of these to order for hopeful suitors); some adopt the Scottish voice which was part of Clare's heritage. Other works witness Clare's becoming increasingly confident in his use and adaptation of standard poetic forms, and the middle of the nineteenth century saw the production of some of his most brilliant and powerful verse, including 'I Am' (LP I 396–7), and 'The Gipsy Camp' (LP I 29). This latter poem returns to a subject Clare had visited many times before, but whilst its focus is on isolation rather than the wandering community explored in similar, earlier pieces, the sonnet reveals a poet utterly and dazzlingly in command of his form and his craft.

The temptations of biography have always proved irresistible for critics of Clare's work. Identities abound: the boy born into poverty who got into print despite the odds; the thwarted lover, longing for Mary Joyce to the end of his days; the ecological poet born before his time; the disorientated, homesick figure so much of his 'place' that he was unable to settle just a few miles away from his birthplace; the madman who escaped from one institution only to spend the final portion of his life in another asylum. These snapshots have provided a framework which has supported much critical work even when it hasn't drawn its focus. All of them depend upon representations (sometimes self-representations) of Clare which are sometimes partial or false, yet their prevalence behind the critical corpus means that they continue to demand attention. The representation of Clare has caused editorial controversy, too: some of the early attention to the desirability or otherwise of retaining Clare's 'provincialisms' in published works (a term which we might understand to incorporate both particular language uses and the employment of a wider range of cultural artefacts: stories; myths; names; values) has extended into modern editorial praxis. Debate regarding the difference between an idiosyncratic use of language which best represents what Clare wanted to say, and simple error which he might have hoped to see corrected, has led to legal wrangling.[7] As Mark Storey's essay in this volume points out (Chapter 10), Clare like most poets expected and often welcomed editorial intervention, though like most poets, he was at times frustrated by it. Many of Clare's outbursts against grammatical pedantry manifest a sense of frustration at his own limits, as much as being the political statements they have sometimes been held to be. Nonetheless, there are those who argue that Clare's writing should be presented as far as possible without any editorial intervention, as so-called primitive texts. Others advocate a 'light touch' edition. Still others favour the presentation of Clare in a way more in line with standard practice, suggesting that preserving Clare's earliest attempts unfairly privileges clumsy or awkward moments above polished, later versions. Whichever we believe to be appropriate, this peculiarity of presentation means that encountering Clare is often a different type of experience to reading his contemporaries and can lend a particular (arguably contestable) sense of 'Clare'. More troubling still is the possibility that the largely unpunctuated 'primitive' text might deter prospective readers. Yet even in the 'primitive' texts, Clare's own versification and momentum tend to render his work remarkably accessible.

Despite the fascinations of his biography and publishing history, attention to the originality and brilliance of Clare's poetry offers the most valuable rewards to critics. To demonstrate this, I want to turn now to Clare's 'Walcott Hall and Surrounding Scenery', a poem dating from the early

Introduction

1820s. Like many of Clare's poems, 'Walcott Hall' participates in various literary traditions. It is highly aware of the conventions of eighteenth-century loco-descriptive poetry; it begins with a standard, personal poetic address; its iambic couplets cleave to a familiar form, and its phraseology of romance, ruins, and reflection on the past place it squarely within the picturesque tradition:

> I love thee in thy mouldering trance
> Old Walcott like a wild romance
> Thy memory meets the strangers gaze
> Ruins that speak of better days
> ...
> I love thy scenes too wild & free
> For scenes more wild there cannot be
> I love to climb till out of breath
> The uneven surface of thy heath
> In rabbit tracks that streak wi brown
> Steep hill & hollow hurrying down
> Or sidling round the hedges free
> Of pleasant sloping cavity
>
> (MP 11 35–40, ll. 1–4; ll. 7–14)

Amongst the customary picturesque vocabulary here is the word 'wild', which (it turns out) is repeated several times across the 168 lines of the poem. Wildness is associated in line 2 with the specifically literary idea of 'romance'. However, by line 7, Clare is already separating it from that literariness and reclaiming it for the natural scene, a use reasserted in a further repetition of the word in line 8. These superlatively wild scenes are described from within a tradition of 'prospect' poetry, in which the poet conventionally climbs upwards to gain a commanding height. Yet Clare abandons the controlling dignity usually conferred by the privileged, lofty position thus achieved: he is breathless, at risk in an almost Marvellian way of stumbling on rough ground, and awkwardly 'sidling round the hedges' (which sonically recalls that they are liminal *edges*). The lines also contain an idiosyncratic confusion, an enriching rather than a problematic effect, regarding which adjectives, verbs, and nouns belong together. 'Hurrying' is a good example: it attaches semantically to the rabbit tracks, the hilly terrain becoming rabbit-like itself (in its streaking, hurrying movements, its colouring, and the physical and rhymic suggestion of a burrow, in 'hollow'). Yet surely it is Clare who is hurrying? Either way, the reader's eye is dizzyingly dragged up a hill, and then down it again, before moving laterally around whatever it is the hedges encircle. The sense of order usually conferred by the

9

commanding eye of the prospect poet is displaced, as we cannot be certain about the poem's subject, or the direction or focus of our own gaze. The wildness Clare reiterates seems to be mirrored in the apparently unstructured way in which the landscape is encountered.

Yet the poem redeems this wildness. As it runs on, Clare pulls away from convention. Most significantly, nature, not the poet, is responsible for the scene's visual splendour: *nature* 'sprinkles oer them passing bye / Her witching tints of varied dye' (ll. 71–2). This couplet is part of a longer section in which Clare describes the processes of nature's artistry. The poem persistently declares its self-conscious play with aesthetic categories as it flirts with images of natural creativity and recasts Clare's conviction that the true picturesque is an assertion of nature's *own* order and skill. In his attitude towards wildness, Clare decisively departs from eighteenth-century literary traditions in which the 'dressing' of nature is paralleled with the capacities of language to be 'the dress of thought'.[8] Clare critiques such 'dressing up' explicitly, in a letter to the landscape painter Peter De Wint:

> many Painters look upon nature as a Beau on his person & fancies her nothing unless in full dress – now nature to me is very different & appears best in her every day disabille   in fact she is a Lady that never needed sunday or holiday cloaths tho most painters & poets also have & still do consider that she does need little touches of their fancies & vagaries to make her beautiful which I consider deformities   (*Letters*, p. 488)

Here, the best artist is the one who can best record natural scenes, not the one who can most imaginatively 'dress' and transform them. In the picturesque literary tradition, greatness is conventionally measured by the ability of the artist to interfere: as William Gilpin, one of its most influential theorists, put it, 'I am so attached to my picturesque rules, that if nature gets wrong, I cannot help putting her right'.[9] Yet it is *nature's* adornment, these 'tints of varied dye', which Clare finds 'witching': the poet-observer is bewitched – overcome – by nature's artistry. Such a sense of being overwhelmed by the scene that nature has presented is the very opposite of the heartless, selective coldness of the picturesque attitude: as Clare is bewitched, analysis is abandoned; the artistry of nature induces the renunciation of selfhood, and Clare's picturesque tips towards the sublime.

According to Clare, the ability to be counted as a poet resides in a capacity for noticing, for observation, as much as creation. In this sense, Clare is not straightforwardly 'Romantic'. But his verse consistently returns us to a sense of emotional response (most acutely experienced as sublimity). Far from being 'merely' or 'purely' descriptive, Clare's writing is always simultaneously an intimate expression of personal reaction (three of the first nine

Introduction

lines of 'Walcott Hall' begin 'I love'). Such personal response demands an adaptive appropriation of standard forms and lexicons. Typically, Clare exploits conventions only enough to allow his modulation of them into something appropriate to his own perception, as 'Walcott Hall' exemplifies. This is true of form as well as content here: for instance, he writes in iambic couplets but resists the pentameter an eighteenth-century reader might have expected:

> Such barnack heath thy wilderd sight
> Gives taste a picturesque delight
> Though industrys mad meddling toils
> Thy wild seclusions yearly spoils
> Yet there are nooks still left behind
> As wild as taste coud wish to find
> That toil has tryd & tryd in vain
> & left neglect its own again
> Which nature turns at freedoms will
> More sweet more wild & varied still   (ll. 49–58)

In the specific vocabulary of these lines, we find Clare departing from convention and forging his own distinctive stance, as he again exploits the wildness which proved vitally important, but also desperately problematic, to theorists of the picturesque. 'Wild' was not in the 1820s a straightforward adjective, meaning uncultivated. It simply wasn't possible to use that word without invoking political and moral ideas of wildness, as well as an aesthetic property which might be more or less desirable, depending on where one stood along the political spectrum. Wildness might be an attractive property in a woodland hedge, but it was, inevitably, a dangerously radical one at the same time, and a dubious moral one unless one could (paradoxically) impose some sort of limits upon it.[10] Here, wildness belongs to the heath.

But Barnack Heath isn't just wild; it is 'wilderd'. 'Wilderd' is a term apparently specific to Clare (other, similar words exist in the *Oxford English Dictionary*, but Clare's version of it seems to be unique). With the introduction of his own word, which is probably a dialect term, Clare makes a claim to share in the wildness of the heath, because it has become a very specific wildness, as local to Clare's place as his dialect is. This is the particular kind of wildness that we find *here*; to know it is to know this place. Simultaneously, through dialect, Clare draws attention to his diction as similarly ostensibly uncultivated, full of unpolished, unconventional words like 'wilderd'. Yet by the very action of including it in his poem, he registers his self-conscious construction of a personal, poetic voice and simultaneously lays claim to the significance of that unpolishedness: just as wildness is an attractive property in the heath, so it can be an attractive property in poetry. By claiming value in the dialect term, Clare claims value for himself, and for his couplets: it is his term; he shares this wilderdness which originates in the heath and is aesthetically desirable. He is making himself *part of* the same environment, not superior to it, but just another aspect of it. In the very act of self-consciously appropriating this token of the picturesque (the 'wildness' at its aesthetic core), Clare fundamentally alters the standard, modifying the convention within which he is writing so that it is fitting for his experience, rather than making his verse fit convention.

The next line of the extract arguably overplays tokens of the picturesque. 'Taste', 'picturesque', 'delight': Clare could hardly, within the confines of the tetrameter, have included more words belonging to the discourse. However, he quickly moves away from convention, describing the attempts of 'industrys mad meddling toils' to eradicate natural features of the heath. Clare's verse is not usually critical of agriculture, recognizing its vital place within the rural economy. What he does consistently criticize is human activity taking place where (as he sees it) it shouldn't be, whether that be in the enclosure of common land, or simply the expansion of cultivation to areas previously the province of wild nature. The 'meddling' going on here is quite specifically a human thing: it is the 'mad'-ness (that is, the inappropriate illogicality) which he is angry about. It isn't the workers Clare castigates, or even the work; it's the lack of sense behind their activity: the 'mad meddling' renders 'industry' and 'toil' problematic.

These lines contain a clear political charge, both in the discourse of freedom, suppression, and resistance which haunts them, but also more straightforwardly in the criticism of the actions of a class above Clare's in the social hierarchy. That political aspect extends here in the fact that nature's wildness will not be crushed: wildness overpowers the meddling, as 'nooks' are left behind. Clare often uses a nook as a frame for natural description. In this sense, the wildness remaining is literally a picture, even as Clare's poem drops right out of the conventional prospect tradition. Clare has already told us he has 'climb[ed] till out of breath'; we know he is (perfectly conventionally) up a hill. But despite the claims of his opening lines, he isn't looking at and commanding a view now. Somehow, from his position up on the hill, he is looking into little nooks: the two perspectives can't quite be reconciled. And although these nooks which are left behind are conventionally picturesque (they are 'as wild as taste could wish to find'), they are also distinctly not *conventionally* picturesque: Clare celebrates the nooks *because* they are untouched, and specifically neglected; precisely because they are not *made* picturesque by any designing artist: it is their being ignored which makes them valuable. Untouched nature in 'Walcott Hall' is adorned 'at freedoms will', and 'freedom' is characterized as 'More

Introduction

sweet, more wild & varied': three key characteristics of picturesque convention (sweetness, wildness, and variety) are superlatively present in the *untouched* landscape.

In the course of these few lines, Clare repeats the word 'wild' three times and uses it again in 'wildered'. If Clare prizes variety in the natural world, so poetry typically prizes variety in vocabulary, and direct repetition of particular words has generally been understood as a weakness: Clare's editor, Taylor, deliberately minimized such repetitions in Clare's *Shepherd's Calendar*, for example. But Clare is deeply attentive to the possibilities of repetition. In many of his works, repetitions in the form of rhyming words and clusters of sounds play an important role in the structuring of his poems. In 'Walcott Hall', the repetition of the word 'wild' is particularly important because Clare chooses to repeat the very word which might seem to resist ideas of order. There is a powerful tension in the idea of something being wild and yet tethered to a single, reiterated monosyllable. Clare takes the wildness which had been co-opted by this point in literary history by theorists of the picturesque and shaped into something paradoxically tame, and fake, and he returns it adamantly to itself.

There's an obvious irony in the fact that 'Walcott Hall' advocates attention to natural splendour over the artifice associated with the picturesque, whilst it simultaneously reveals Clare adopting and mastering picturesque conventions. That he does so only to subvert them, is entirely typical of Clare's ability to write in a powerfully original manner. The way in which wildness is rehabilitated and put to rich work in this poem exemplifies Clare's writing, which is a storehouse of its own particular brilliances, fully alert to its contexts and traditions. This collection of specially commissioned essays returns us primarily to Clare's poetic craft, before moving on to explore his work from a wide range of perspectives, highlighting the capacity of Clare's writing both to reflect and to enable reflection upon wider Romantic-period issues and debates. Collectively, they show how the complexities of Clare's writing allow critical light shone at a different angle to illuminate multiple aspects of the same thing. For example, one aspect of what Markus Poetzsch calls Clare's 'complicated history' – Clare's habit of taking and collecting artefacts from nature, despite his frequent criticism of despoliation – is raised in discussions by Poetzsch (Chapter 8), James Castell (Chapter 5), Fiona Stafford (Chapter 6), and Robert Heyes (Chapter 7), performing different interpretative work in each case. Situating the poet in received critical traditions, the critics represented here extend and add to those traditions in vibrant and original ways. In this sense, these essays are true to Clare himself, who was fully able to write within convention, and also to forge his own poetic paths; whose work retained an eye on the past and tradition, whilst it moved forward with originality and grace.

Notes

1. 'L'Allegro', in *John Milton: Complete Shorter Poems*, ed. John Carey, 2nd ed. (London: Routledge, 2007), pp. 134–44 (ll. 133–4).
2. William Shakespeare, 'Sonnet 94', in *Shakespeare's Sonnets*, ed. Katherine Duncan-Jones, rev. ed. (London: Methuen, 2010), p. 299.
3. Reprinted in *Critical Heritage*, p. 29.
4. Edmund Burke, *A Philosophical Enquiry into the Origin of our Ideas of the Sublime and Beautiful*, ed. Adam Phillips (Oxford: Oxford University Press, 1990), p. 160.
5. Quoted in Margaret Grainger, *John Clare Collector of Ballads* (Peterborough: The Peterborough Museum Society, 1964), p. 1.
6. See John Barrell, *The Idea of Landscape and the Sense of Place: An Approach to the Poetry of John Clare* (Cambridge: Cambridge University Press, 1972), p. 103.
7. See for example John Goodridge, 'Poor Clare', *The Guardian*, 22 July 2000, www.theguardian.com/books/2000/jul/22/poetry.books.
8. The phrase is Samuel Johnson's (see 'Cowley', in 'Prefaces, Biographical and Critical, to the Works of the English Poets', repr. in *Samuel Johnson: A Critical Edition of the Major Works*, ed. Donald Greene (Oxford: Oxford University Press, 1984), pp. 677–97 (p. 694)), but it was a common trope throughout the long eighteenth century.
9. William Gilpin to W. Mason, 12 February 1784, transcribed in Carl Paul Barbier, *William Gilpin: His Drawings, Teaching, and Theory of the Picturesque* (Oxford: Clarendon Press, 1963), p. 72.
10. On the political, moral, and aesthetic complexities of picturesque discourse, see Peter Garside and Stephen Copley, eds., *The Politics of the Picturesque: Literature, Landscape and Aesthetics since 1770* (Cambridge: Cambridge University Press, 1994).

PART I

Clare the Poet

I

STEPHANIE KUDUK WEINER

On Clare and Lyric Song

John Clare had the good fortune to be born into a period of tremendous excitement and experimentation in poetry. When he came of age in the 1810s, he could – and eagerly did – read contemporaries such as William Wordsworth, Lord Byron, and John Keats as well as great poets from the past, whose works were being reissued in cheaper editions and reinterpreted in light of present-day contests about what poetry was and might be. Those contests were generating tectonic shifts in the cultural geography of the UK, which elevated the meditative lyric to the pinnacle of literary prestige, created new points of contact between poetry and music, and secured footholds for verse and song within a rapidly expanding print market. Ideas about poetry were unsettled, and practices of reading and writing poetry were changing, too. Everywhere one looked, there were new freedoms and opportunities.

To be sure, it could also be a tough time to be an author. A publishing boom in poetry that began in the late eighteenth century was beginning to wane, and by the 1830s living poets were being squeezed out of the market by reprints of older works and increasing competition, including from novelists. In addition, critics could be merciless in their condemnation of new books, and they were often motivated by the cultural implications of partisan politics, or 'party rage' as Clare calls it in *Child Harold* (1841), rather than by a disinterested desire to assess a fellow writer's latest production (LP 1 40–88, l. 5).[1] Clare's first two volumes, *Poems Descriptive of Rural Life and Scenery* (1820) and *The Village Minstrel* (1821), met with commercial and critical success, but after that he found it difficult to get poetry collections into print, and he grew disillusioned with the literary public sphere.

Yet Clare seems never to have become disillusioned with poetry itself. Nor does he seem to have lost faith in the music of nature, the living tradition of popular song, or the poetry he read in books and other publications. He drew inspiration throughout his life from all these types of 'poesy'. They shaped his distinctive contribution to the literature of his moment.

STEPHANIE KUDUK WEINER

Ideas of Poetry in the Romantic Period

Then as now, in the early nineteenth century common-sense conceptions of poetry centred on a distinction between verse and prose. Poetry came in lines, or verses, whereas prose did not. Beyond that definition, however, poetry went by many names and took many forms. In addition to *poetry*, there were *poesy*, *minstrelsy*, *musings*, *ballads*, *hymns*, *odes*, *elegies*, *stanzas*, and so on. Each of these terms carried its own connotations and meanings, as well as conventions regarding what kind of subject matter and language were appropriate to it. Traditionally, those conventions had been organized hierarchically, with epic at the top and ballads and other popular modes at the bottom. But Romantic writers were reordering that hierarchy by raising the prestige of shorter, more personal poems, and they were loosening it by mixing and matching elements from very different types of poems to create new literary hybrids. In his ode-like poem 'Frost at Midnight' (1798), for instance, Samuel Taylor Coleridge roots his metaphysical speculations in his life as a young father. When the poem begins, he is up late in his cottage on a winter night, listening to the gentle breathing of his sleeping child. The poem is at once philosophical and personal, its language is both lofty and colloquial, and it replaces the traditionally public occasion of an ode with a private moment. Wordsworth's 'Lines Composed a Few Miles above Tintern Abbey' (1798) and Keats's 'Ode to a Nightingale' (1819) are strikingly similar in these respects. They, too, 'trace ... the primary laws of our nature' by describing 'incidents of common life' in 'the very language of men', as Wordsworth writes in his Preface to *Lyrical Ballads* (1800).[2]

Everyday experience of the most basic kind, simply being a person, was becoming a worthy subject for ambitious poetry. This seismic realignment can be hard for us to appreciate today because the activities of being alive in the world – both the epistemologically rich events of observing, thinking, and feeling and the humdrum ones of working, having a family, and hanging out with friends – remain fitting, even obvious topics for poetry. That poetry should fuse colloquial and elevated language by revealing the richness of ordinary speech or writing is something we take for granted. Yet it is important to try to feel the earth moving beneath Clare's feet, because his writing relies on this realignment as well as participating in it.

The majority of Clare's poems adopt the modes that were gaining importance within Romanticism. His pen was drawn not to the national epic but to sonnets, meditative and descriptive lyrics, occasional poems prompted by private moments, explorations of consciousness and feeling, and songs and ballads. Moreover, he took part in theorizing the reach and ambition of these poetic modes. He did so directly in manifesto-like poems about poetry such as 'The Progress of Rhyme' (1824–32), 'The Autumn Robin' (1830), 'Songs Eternity' (1832), and 'The Peasant Poet' (1842–64). In these works, Clare identifies poetry with quotidian yet profound thoughts and feelings, as in 'The Peasant Poet':

> He loved the brook's soft sound
> The swallow swimming by
> He loved the daisy covered ground
> The cloud bedappled sky
> ...
> A silent man in lifes affairs
> A thinker from a Boy
> A Peasant in his daily cares –
> The Poet in his joy   (LP II 845)

Everyday sights and sounds give rise to habits of meditation and to spontaneous emotions of love and joy, and these in turn give rise to poetry. Again and again, across his whole career as an author, he associates 'love' and 'joy' with the best subject matter of poetry and with the characteristic temperament of the poet. Scores of poems justify their portraits of the world with the simple phrase 'I love'. For Clare, poetry is an expression of the many types of insight that arise from ordinary experiences in his world, the agrarian countryside of eastern England.

He also praises poems that mimic the music of nature. In 'The Autumn Robin', he writes:

> could my notes win aught from thine
> My words but imitate thy lay
> ...
> So would they share the happy prime
> Of thy eternal song   (MP III 294–5)

The whole project of composing poems modelled on the music of nature is framed as a mere possibility, a yearning, that begins with imitating the robin and ends with taking part in her song. Earlier in the poem, Clare explains that the robin is a 'sweet domestic' bird that is 'met with every where' (MP III 291). Imitating this unremarkable, common creature is, accordingly, another way of grounding poetry in ordinary experiences. What's more, the robin's song grants access, both for listeners and the poet, to the miraculously 'eternal song' of nature. In 'Songs Eternity', Clare explains how nature's music connects humans to the eternal and even the divine:

> Melodys of earth & sky
> Here they be
> Songs once sung to adams ears
> Can it be
> – Ballads of six thousand years
>
> Thrive thrive
> Songs awakened with the spheres
> Alive
> ...
> Every season [has] her own
> Bird & be[e]
> Sing creations music on
> Natures glee
> Is in every mood & tone
> Eternity   (MP v 3–5)

'*Here* they *be*', he says of these melodies (my emphasis). They exist in an ongoing present moment, and they surround us, right here. By calling the chirping and buzzing of birds and bees 'songs' and 'ballads', Clare links them to the words and tunes that humans sing, all of which are 'alive' by virtue of belonging to the 'earth'. Plebeian genres are presented as the ideal vehicles for linking thought, feeling, and wisdom, as well as for fusing colloquial and philosophical language, simple words and the grandest abstract concepts.

Later in his career, Clare's theorizations of verse often took the form of meditations on the themes of language, communication, and the 'silent voice' of writing (LP II 677). Some of his best-known later works, for instance 'First Love' (1842–64) and 'A Vision' (1844), portray poetry in ways that convey its strangeness, suddenness, and overwhelming force:

> Words from my eyes did start
> They spoke as chords do from the string
> And blood burnt round my heart   (LP II 677)
>
> I snatch'd the sun's eternal ray, –
> And wrote 'till earth was but a name   (LP I 297)

There's something natural and instinctive about these moments of creating poetry. Words 'start' from his eyes like tears, and he crafts a pen out of a sunbeam. At the same time, though, there is something supernatural in these moments, too. Are these 'words' even words at all, or only metaphors for tears or for an intense, communicative gaze? What would it mean for 'earth' to become 'but a name'? Is 'earth' still the place where human beings actually live, or is Clare explaining how poetic language can create its own world? His later poems are full of these sorts of riddles, evocative moments when poetry and language appear and disappear in a single breath.

Throughout his career, Clare also theorized poetry indirectly. For example, in his many poems on the subject of bird nests, the nests serve as models for the ways a poem can weave together bits and pieces of nature and of language. Consider 'The Pettichaps Nest' (?1825–6), in which he describes the 'snugly made' nest in detail:

> Brown as the road way side – small bits of hay
> Pluckt from the old propt-haystacks pleachy brow
> & withered leaves make up its outward walls
> That from the snub-oak dotterel yearly falls [i.e., fall]
> & in the old hedge bottom rot away
> Built like a oven with a little hole
> Hard to discover – that snug entrance wins
> Scarcely admitting e'en two fingers in
> & lined with feathers warm as silken stole
> & soft as seats of down . . .   (MP III 518)

The pettichap builds her nest from scraps of 'old' hay and half-rotten leaves from a 'dotterel' tree, one with new pollards, or branches, growing from its stump. Both the hay and the leaves are leftovers from the previous autumn, 'homely stuff' like the 'Dead grass & mosses green' the hedge sparrow uses in 'Birds Nests' (?1832) (MP IV 348). But as the birds 'weave' them together, they transform them into a 'shelter rightly made / & beautiful' (MP IV 348). Clare marvels at this transformation in 'The Thrushes Nest' (1831–2):

> I watched her secret toils from day to day
> How true she warped the moss to form her nest
> & modelled it within with wood & clay   (MP IV 187)

His verbs convey the variety of the birds' tasks and their high degree of skill – 'made', 'pluckt', 'built', 'lined', 'weave', 'warped', 'modelled' – and they apply readily to the work of the poet who takes his own 'homely stuff' and shapes it into something 'beautiful'.

This conception of nest-like poetry has sometimes been seen as especially appropriate for Clare as a labouring-class poet and natural historian. He too has a 'russet coat' like the robin's and an intimate knowledge of local rural and 'rude waste landscapes' like the sand martin's (MP III 287, MP IV 309). Yet it also resonates more generally within Romantic ideas about poetry, explaining the many ways in which verses crafted out of the stuff of everyday life can yield pleasure, discovery, and insight. Indeed, these passages put such ideas into action formally and linguistically as well. The images are precise and appeal to our senses of sight, touch, smell, and hearing. Line by line, details are gathered into shape. The dialect, regional, and agricultural words are like 'small bits ... pluckt' from a field, even as similes such as 'warm as silken stole' and patterns of rhythm and rhyme highlight the rich meanings and resonance of the language.

The Self and the World

Clare's poems about nests are among his best-loved works, and with good reason. They exemplify his unique ability to draw us into his way of being in the world, to let us share in his tender, wise attention to every facet of the places he lived. He zeroes in on the birds and their creations, of course, but in the process he notices so much else: insects, plants, animals, and people, all going about their business; features of the environment and the agricultural setting such as brooks and bridges; and dynamics of change over days, seasons, and a lifetime. His poems offer us a marvellous sense of entering his world and observing it, reacting to it, and understanding it with him. Both that world and his presence in it seem real and immediate. The nest poems also offer helpful suggestions about how he achieves these remarkable effects of accuracy and immersive inclusiveness as well as about how these effects connect him to Romanticism.

Clare offers a kind of instructional manual for his readers in three nest poems that appeared in his last book, *The Rural Muse* (1835): 'The Nightingales Nest', 'The Yellowhammers Nest', and 'The Pettichaps Nest'. In these poems, he addresses us directly and includes us explicitly in his adventure of discovery. The conceit of these poems is that we are taking a stroll with him and come upon the nests and their inhabitants in real time:

> – Hark there she is as usual lets be hush[!]   (MP III 458)
>
> Aye as I live her secret nest is here[!]   (MP III 459)
>
> Stop heres the bird[!]   (MP III 519)

As these exclamations thrust us into the scene and its rapidly unfolding action, we participate imaginatively by obeying his instructions to 'hark', 'be hush', and 'stop', and by directing our creative attention to the sight he is describing – exactly as we do whenever we read Clare's writing. Even in poems that do not directly address us as readers, he invites us to imagine everything he notices and to align our perspective with his own. Indeed, in such poems the distance between him and us shrinks. Once we are no longer next to him, our point of view entirely fuses with his, and we observe exactly what he observes or recalls having observed in the past, perceiving with and through him in the *here and now* of the poem.

In 'The Nightingales Nest', he leads us expertly along a forest path, a 'ride'; through a gate; and under a flowering vine with the evocative name 'old man[']s beard', which is so thick and tangled it 'stops the way' for most people:

> Up this green wood land ride lets softly rove
> & list the nightingale – she dwelleth here
> Hush let the wood gate softly clap – for fear
> The noise might drive her from her home of love
> For here Ive heard her many a merry year
> At morn & eve nay all the live long day
> As though she lived on song – this very spot
> Just where that old mans beard all wildly trails
> Rude arbours oer the rode & stops the way (MP III 456)

The action happens 'here' – he uses the word twice in these first nine lines – and in the present tense, and elements are introduced with the particularizing pronouns 'this' or 'that', or with the definite article 'the', suggesting they are already known to us as well as nearby. These linguistic features are hallmarks of Clare's approach. By means of these tiny choices, he draws us close to him to participate in his experience of the scene and to benefit from his expertise, both as someone who has listened to the nightingale 'many a merry year' and as a poet, a craftsman of language and literary form. These poems, in which Clare treats us like a friend who belongs to his world, make especially palpable the companionable intimacy that characterizes his writing.

There is a vital, reciprocal relationship between the 'here' of the opening lines of 'The Nightingales Nest' and the 'I', the personalized lyric subject of the poem, whom we are invited to identify with Clare himself. We trust in the accuracy of his depiction of the world, for instance the way the old man's beard grows into a wild arbour or the danger that a loud clap of the gate would frighten the nightingale, because we have faith in him as an observer and interpreter. The inverse is also true, which is to say that our faith in Clare is built up from our experience of his credible representations of the world. Even if we have never seen this vine or heard a nightingale sing, we take these elements of the poem as faithful details, and we add to our picture of Clare as the person who notices, understands, and depicts them. Our trust is a specifically literary one. It involves not only the empirical verifiability of his facts, but also his ability to bring the world vividly to life, to interpret its meanings wisely, and to react in ways that are worth honouring, and often emulating.

This reciprocal relationship between the self and the world is the lifeblood of Romantic meditative and descriptive lyrics. The relationship takes various forms in the hands of different poets, and indeed in different poems by the same writer, and it generates both explorations of inner consciousness and depictions of the external world of nature and social life, including the realities of war and poverty. Behind these variations lies an abiding fascination with the dynamic interchange between the self and the world, both of which are assumed to be complex and significant. Thus, expressions of the inner life are often prompted by stimuli from the world, even as descriptions are presented as products of acts of observation and reflection. Romantic lyrics attend minutely to subjective processes of making sense of the world as well as to moments of discovering truths that are out there, ready for anyone to find. As a result, the meanings that emerge in Romantic poems tend to owe something both to human capacities and to external realities, and they tend to apply to both as well. In other words, Romantic poets show us that what the world means is related, in many different ways, to what it actually feels like to be in it. Their philosophy of knowledge is sophisticated and informed by Enlightenment thinkers, whose preoccupations with sense experience, language, and cognition shaped the poets' worldview. One reason Romantic poets are so interested in everyday experience is that they believe it can reveal truths both about the world and about selfhood.

The interchange between interior and exterior is most noticeable in poems like 'The Nightingales Nest', 'Frost at Midnight', and 'Tintern Abbey' that begin by placing the poet in a specific place. Wordsworth, for instance, gives us detailed information in the first stanza of 'Tintern Abbey' about how and where he is positioned: reclining 'under this dark sycamore', within earshot of the river, and with a perfect view of the abbey and its surroundings on the valley floor.[3] Having located himself physically within the scene, he records a process of observing, feeling, thinking, remembering, and otherwise responding to the environment. That record, with all its twists and turns, becomes the poem and lends it its shape. Clare, too, often places himself within a scene, as in the first lines of 'Pewits Nest' (?1825–6): 'Accross the fallow clods at early morn /I took a random track where ... ' (MP III 472). The time, place, and Clare's embodied and active presence within it are all established together.

But poets also approached the reciprocal interchange between the self and the world from the other direction, as it were, by creating a coherent, personalized lyric subject who is present in the *here and now* of the poem itself rather than in any single place and time depicted within it. Clare wrote many poems of this kind, a good example of which is this sonnet:

> The fire tail tells the boys when nests are nigh
> & tweets & flyes from every passer bye
> The yellow hammer never makes a noise

> But flyes in silence from the noisey boys
> The boys will come & take them every day
> & still she lays as [if] none were taen away
> The nightingale keeps tweeting churring round
> But leaves in silence when the nest is found
> The pewet hollos chewsit as she flyes
> & flops about the shepherd where he lies
> But when her nest is found she stops her song
> & cocks [her] coppled crown & runs along
> Wrens cock their tails & chitter loud & play
> & robins hollow tut & flye away.   (MP v 247)

Although the word 'I' never appears in this poem, Clare's repeated past experiences of noticing these phenomena are everywhere implied. He knows what the cry of each bird sounds like, from the nightingale's 'tweeting churring' to the robin's 'tut', and he has witnessed the yellowhammer being startled enough times to say that it 'never makes a noise' when that happens. He is also the one who has recognized that these discrete events cohere together into a pattern, or many patterns: threats, reactions, noises and silence, movements and signals, coming close and moving away, and so on. The vivid accuracy of these snapshots testifies to his expertise as a naturalist and to his skill as a poet. In poems like this one, the self is an organizing consciousness that experiences, discovers, makes meaning, and synthesizes discrete moments into works of literary art.

Forms and Fragments

This poem, 'The fire tail tells the boys when nests are nigh' (1832–7), bears a striking structural resemblance to the nests its birds are protecting. Like a nest, it makes a single whole out of separate pieces, in this case seven rhyming couplets about six different birds: the firetail, the yellowhammer, the nightingale, the pewit, the wren, and the robin. Clare underscores the formal unity of this poem by choosing a highly recognizable poetic genre, the sonnet; focusing on a single topic; and repeating his syntactic format for presenting each bird's sounds and motions. At the same time, though, he strictly keeps each piece of the poem distinct from the others, calling attention to the uniqueness of each bird's response to danger and, as a result, highlighting his method of constructing a poem out of fragments.

This simultaneous embrace of formal unity and fragmentariness is characteristic of Romantic approaches to poetic structure. For Clare and his contemporaries, both the ideal of form and the aesthetic of the fragment were appealing, on their own and in productive tension with one another. Both had been the subject of lively debate in the eighteenth century, particularly within neoclassicism, antiquarianism, and the picturesque movement. Among other things, form promised unity and craft, while the fragment conveyed openness and spontaneity. Received forms enabled writers to connect with earlier poets, while the fragment aligned their writing with old songs and ballads, which often survived in snippets and scraps, and with picturesque ruins. At the same time, fragments had their own formal properties, such as unboundedness, abrupt beginnings and endings, or the roughness, asymmetry, and irregularity associated with picturesque objects. And theories of form grappled with the relation between parts and wholes, a task that necessitated taking parts seriously in and of themselves. In a series of lectures given between 1811 and 1819, Coleridge differentiates between 'mechanic' and 'organic' form, preferring the latter because its organization is that of a 'living body' in which 'the connection of parts to a whole [is such] that each part is at once end and means'. Organic form, he writes, 'is innate; it shapes as it develops itself from within, and the fullness of its development is one and the same with the perfection of its outward form. Such is the life, such the form.'[4]

Romantic ideas about form were also bound up with the ambition to represent the mutual exchange between the self and the world. Formal features of poems were understood to be able in and of themselves to imitate both the experience of the world and the world itself. For example, each stanza of 'Tintern Abbey' and 'Frost at Midnight' focuses on a specific moment in the present, past, or future, while the transitions between them mark shifts in thinking and feeling sparked by interruptions, associations, and changing stimuli in the scenes. The ebb and flow of consciousness is portrayed by this way of dividing the poem into stanzas.

Clare wrote poems of this kind, in which the arrangement of lines and stanzas portrays an unfolding process of observing and reacting to the world. He also used patterns in the world as organizational principles. Time and space are the most fundamental of such patterns and the ones he turns to most often. His titles frequently announce a focus on a particular place or time, or both: 'Emmonsails Heath in Winter' (1819–32), 'Summer Evening' (1830), 'Winter Fields' (?1832), and so on. Many poems begin and end with the assertion of a spatial or temporal boundary such as the first or furthest thing in Clare's field of vision or the imminent arrival of the next time of day or year. These poems capture the boundedness of our experience of the world, the ways we are embedded in space and time and take things in from a single vantage point and at a particular moment. They also celebrate the abundance of things there are to appreciate even within such limits. Poems such as 'The fire tail tells the boys when nests are nigh', which take the form of variations on a theme, model themselves on other sorts of patterns. They can lift themselves out of specific moments and places in order to get a wider view.

Clare's remarkable ability to immerse us in a vivid, vital world is thus a function not only of his precise words and images but also of his inventive approach to form. In different poems and by various means, he manages to capture both the embeddedness of our experience of the world and its larger patterns, both the particularity of each moment and our awareness of the fact that time and space radiate out far beyond our ken. Taken as a whole body of work, Clare's writing offers us an experience akin to the one he praised in a laudatory comment about Peter De Wint's paintings:

> There is no harsh stoppage no bounds to space or any outline further th[a]n there is in nature – if we could possibly walk into the picture we fancy we might pursue the landscape beyond those mysterys (not bounds) assigned it so as we can in the fields (*Prose*, p. 211)

His poems do come to an end, just as De Wint's paintings have edges, but they do so in ways that give us a sense of the larger reality of the landscape just around the corner – the place where the robins are now, just after the last words of 'The fire tail tells the boys when nests are nigh', in which they 'flye away'.

Reading, Speaking, and Singing

From ruined abbeys to De Wint's paintings, art and architecture were inspiring to poets. Similarly, as in the moment in 'First Love' when Clare's 'words ... spoke as chords do from the string', Romantic experiments in poetry drew energy from the interaction between writing, speech, and music (LP II 677). Many of the exciting hybrid forms that Clare and his contemporaries were creating brought them together, from Wordsworth and Coleridge's *Lyrical Ballads* (1798, 1800) and the latter's 'conversation poems' to Byron's embedding of lyric interludes in narrative poems such as *The Corsair* (1814) and *Childe Harold's Pilgrimage* (1812–18). All these hybrids create new relationships between the printed page and the live voice and between written and oral cultures. Clare's composite forms include his imitations of Byron, *Child Harold* and *Don Juan a Poem* (1841), which like their models interweave songs and ballads that evoke singing and speaking with Spenserian stanzas that seem more written by virtue of their syntactic complexity and origins in sixteenth-century poetry. The very title of Clare's book *The Village Minstrel* combines the oral tradition of minstrelsy with the practices of writing, and the collection contains many modes such as dialogues, ballads, and sonnets. Similarly, in his drafts for *The Shepherd's Calendar* (1827), his third book, he juxtaposed 'Village Stories' that present themselves as transcripts of oral storytelling with poems for each month, which were detailed catalogues in the print formats of natural history, pastoral, and descriptive poetry.

Songs offered an especially productive interface between writing and oral cultures.[5] Songbooks such as Thomas Moore's *Irish Melodies* (10 vols., 1808–34) and *The Scots Musical Museum* (6 vols., 1787–1803), which featured dozens of songs collected and written by Robert Burns, were runaway bestsellers. Here was a new print commodity that connected antiquarian collectors, authors, and composers to amateurs who were eager to sing and play their songs. In the process, those amateurs were also connected to the musical repertoires of their own and distant places and to living traditions of music-making in which they might not otherwise have participated. Throughout his career, Clare, too, worked in this vein. He transcribed, reworked, and imitated vernacular music, including sea shanties, work songs, lover's laments, and commercial music that had entered the folk repertoire. A skilled fiddler who was 'stil'd a first rate scraper among my rustic companions', Clare could notate tunes – or 'prick them down', as he put it – and he collected more than 260 melodies in his own hand-ruled music books (*Letters*, p. 138; p. 153).[6] He possessed a broad knowledge of popular music, and he was interested in the distinctive features of songs as literary and musical compositions, such as their use of patterned repetition, verse-and-chorus structures, and familiar situations and stories.

At the same time, poems such as William Blake's 'Introduction' to *Songs of Innocence* (1789) and Walter Scott's *Lay of the Last Minstrel* (1805) tell stories about how songs change when they are written down and published. For Blake's piper and Scott's minstrel, a larger audience and the freedom to circulate their works in distant places come at a high price: they lose the immediate presence of their listeners and their own reflexive immersion in the landscapes they sing about. Yet even literary poems designed to be read could harness aspects of oral song. Whether the audience of written texts was reading them aloud or silently, 'hearing' the words only with the ears of the mind, they could appreciate sound patterns and imagine the situations and embodied experiences of singing and listening. Clare worked in this vein as well. He wrote hundreds of poems in song metres and rhyme schemes, many of which he titled simply 'Song', and these works are comfortably at home within the worlds of print and reading. Some, such as 'A Vision' and 'First Love' take writing as their theme, as we have seen.

Ultimately, Clare was drawn to Moore's and Burns's ability to mingle the experiences of reading, singing, and hearing their words and tunes. Their songs managed to combine ties to ongoing practices of music-making, a nostalgic connection to particular places and to the popular culture of days gone by, and sensuous appeals to the musicality and meaning-making power of poetic language. They were ideal for singing aloud and for memorizing, but they also repaid close attention and rereading. Taken as a whole, Clare's songs seek to achieve precisely this fusion. They strive to share local song traditions; achieve musical dynamism and literary depth; and live on, both on the page and in the voices of their audience. Like the 'melodys of earth & sky', these songs and ballads, too, 'thrive thrive'.

Notes

1. On the early nineteenth-century print marketplace, see Richard Cronin, *Paper Pellets: British Literary Culture after Waterloo* (Oxford: Oxford University Press, 2010); Lee Erickson, *The Economy of Literary Form: English Literature and the Industrialization of Publishing, 1800–1850* (Baltimore: Johns Hopkins University Press, 1996); and William St Clair, *The Reading Nation in the Romantic Period* (Cambridge: Cambridge University Press, 2004).
2. William Wordsworth, 'Preface', in *Wordsworth's Poetry and Prose*, ed. Nicholas Halmi (New York: W. W. Norton, 2014), pp. 78–81.
3. Wordsworth, 'Lines Composed a Few Miles above Tintern Abbey', in *Wordsworth's Poetry and Prose*, p. 66.
4. Samuel Taylor Coleridge, *Coleridge's Shakespearean Criticism*, ed. Thomas Middleton Raysor (Cambridge, MA: Harvard University Press, 1930), pp. 223–4.
5. On Romantic song, see Elizabeth Helsinger, 'Poem into Song', *New Literary History*, 46 (2015), 669–90 and Kirsteen McCue, 'The Culture of Song', in David Duff, ed., *The Oxford Handbook of British Romanticism* (Oxford: Oxford University Press, 2018), pp. 643–57.
6. For a description of the notebooks, see George Deacon, *John Clare and the Folk Tradition* (London: S. Browne, 1983), p. 300.

2

ANDREW HODGSON

Clare's Forms

There are a lot of them. Clare wrote almost 4,000 poems, among which you can find examples of any form or genre you like: epigrams, songs, sonnets, satires, ballads, elegies, parodies, blank verse, couplets, and stanzas in combinations of rhyme and metre both traditional and unique. One difficulty, then, is how to get a handle on the bundle when – as in the world the poems describe – proliferating abundance defies organization. A second is the peculiarity of Clare's approach to form. The range can shade into facility. As Hugh Haughton says: 'Clare moves easily, all too easily perhaps, between the available forms of poetry ... but he might not seem to modern eyes to have confronted the *problem* of form itself at all.'[1] The variety is not the result of a poet setting himself technical challenges in the manner of, say, Herbert or Hardy; nor, for all he valorizes the 'natural', does Clare strive for 'organic' form in the Coleridgean sense of a poem which 'shapes and develops itself from within' towards an integrated whole.[2] The poems arise in response to the profusion of the natural world, limited only by the constraints of time and readerly patience. 'My wild field catalogue of flowers / Grows in my ryhmes as thick as showers / Tedious & long as they may be / To some they never weary me' Clare wrote amid one of his enthusiastic forays ('May', *The Shepherd's Calendar*, MP 1 58–74, ll. 193–6) – though the double syntax created by the enjambment ('as they may be / To some') hints at a slyer artistry than Clare is immediately willing to let on.

Then there is the apparent formlessness of Clare's phrasing. The proper consequences of Clare's suspicion of grammar for his printed voice are a matter of debate but, encountered 'raw', Clare's poems can seem to be shaped from an amorphous substance. Consider the sonnet 'Ere I had known the world', an early meditation on the costs of maturity:

> Ere I had known the world & understood
> Those many follys wisdom names its own
> Distinguishing things evil from things good

Clare's Forms

> The dreads of sin & death ere I had known
> Knowledge the root of evil – had I been
> Left in some lone place where the world is wild
> And trace of troubling man was never seen
> Brought up by Nature as her favoured child
> As born for nought but joy were all rejoice
> Emparadised in ignorance of sin
> Where nature trys with never chiding voice
> Like tender nurse nought but our smiles to win
> The future dreamless – beautiful would be
> The present – foretaste of eternity   (MP IV 272)

The poem's nostalgia for untutored innocence plays out through an idiom which eludes editorial organization. How, for instance, would you punctuate the fourth line, in which the phrase 'ere I had known' looks both forward and backwards, as though the sentences 'The dread of sin & death ere I had known' and 'ere I had known / Knowledge the root of evil' had been laid on top of one another? Those phrases form part of a larger opening movement which seemingly trails off into nothing before '– had I been' takes up a new train of thought. To make joined-up sense of the poem we have to recognize that Clare has reversed the sequence of thought, so that its initial movement serves as a subordinate clause of a sentence whose main thrust is something like 'Had I been left in some lone place before I had known all this . . .' – a syntactical effect conversant with the poem's desire to tread backwards and which would hardly suggest itself to a mind composing with the support of conventional grammatical scaffolding. When the poem was published in *The London Magazine* in 1822, the editors' punctuation served only to impede the exuberance of lines such as 'As born for nought but joy, where all rejoice, / Emparadised in ignorance of sin,' and proved helpless in the face of the fragmentary utterances to which Clare is reduced in the final couplet as he glimpses the 'beauty' of a life based on the Edenic upbringing the poem imagines.[3] The very substance of Clare's voice resists the organized 'wisdom' to which more orderly notions of form aspire.

All of which would seem to make 'Clare's Forms' an unpropitious topic for an essay – a coupling of unrelated concepts, like Shelley and mutton, or modern architecture and beauty. The poetry bypasses or disrupts or reverses the organizing impulse that 'form' ordinarily implies. Yet that attitude in itself produces distinctive patterns. An aesthetic and moral design animates Clare's disorderliness. In one of his rare statements about form in art, Clare wrote admiringly of the paintings of Peter de Wint that they exhibit 'no harsh stoppage no bounds to space of any outline further than there is in nature – if we could possibly walk into the picture we fancy we might pursue the landscape beyond those mysteries (not bounds) assigned to it so as we can in the fields' (*Prose*, p. 211). De Wint's paintings, that is, do not impose order on experience but allow experience to shape them. And we might say something similar of Clare's poems: they are a sustained exploration of how to afford through art the pleasures Clare found in nature; and their formal achievement is inseparable from their tempered regard for the significance of form.

Clare's sonnets are a good place to start since the compactness of the sonnet accentuates the potential 'bounds' of art. 'I have made it up in my mind to write one hundred sonnets as a set of pictures on the scenes & objects that appear in the different seasons', Clare wrote to his publisher John Taylor in 1824 with an enthusiasm which you might imagine wasn't entirely reciprocated: '& as I shall do it soly for amusment I shall take up wi gentle & simple as they come whatever in my eye finds any [inter]est these things are resolves not merely in the view for publication but for attempts' (*Letters*, p. 288). The loose-strung idiom suggests the easy spirit in which Clare approached the form. Like most sonneteers, Clare has a sonnet on the sonnet, in which he speaks cheerfully of its constraints: 'I walked with poesy in the sonnets bounds / With little hopes yet many a wild delight' (MP IV 357). In 1820, he had written a buoyantly phrased comparison of Wordsworth and Milton: 'Milton sat down to write to the rul[es of] art in the sonnet just as a architect sets about a building while wordsworth defies all art & in all the lunatic Enthuseism of nature he negligently sets down his thoughts from the tongue of his inspirer' (*Letters*, p. 87). Whatever the truth of that as an account of Wordsworth's practice, it is helpful as a clue to Clare's. Many of the sonnets about birds and animals Clare wrote in the 1820s mimic the behaviour of the creature they describe. In such poems – the best of them would include 'The Blackcap', 'Hedge Sparrow', and 'The Wrynecks Nest' – the familiar outline of the form plays against an idiosyncratic rhyme scheme in a manner befitting an unpredictable encounter with a familiar creature. A sonnet on the whitethroat is characteristically flexible:

> The happy white throat on the sweeing bough
> Swayed by the impulse of the gadding wind
> That ushers in the showers of april – now
> Singeth right joyously & now reclined
> Croucheth and clingeth to her moving seat
> To keep her hold – and till the wind for rest
> Pauses – she mutters inward melodys
> That seem her hearts rich thinkings to repeat
> & when the branch is still – her little breast
> Swells out in raptures gushing symphonys

> & then against her blown wing softly prest
> The wind comes playing an enraptured guest
> This way and that she swees – till gusts arise
> More boisterous in their play – when off she flies (MP IV 249)

Clare allows his verse to be ruffled by experience like the bough 'sweeing' in the wind.[4] Inverted feet ('Swayed by') and dampened fourth stresses ('on the', 'of the') set anapaestic breezes rippling through the iambic metre of the first two lines; modulation of emphasis threatens to unseat the voice from the metre of the line 'Croucheth and clingeth to her moving seat'. The opening sentence bends and flexes as it passes over the line endings – as when a clause starts up unexpectedly at the end of the third line in conjunction with the bird's unanticipated burst of song, or as in the pacing of 'the wind for rest / Pauses'. Clare's formal agility tests the correspondence between poetic art and creaturely impulse. At the heart of the poem sits the bird whose 'mutterings' mirror Clare's creative activities but whose 'heart' cannot be known directly – a sense of art's limited reach being embodied in the unharmonious rhyme of the bird's inward 'melodies' against its broadcast 'symphonys'. That rhyme is part of an *abab / cdec / dedd / ff* pattern that allows perception to meander before settling into steadying couplets. Yet the ending does not afford rest but generates a sense that the brevity of the form is in step with the poet's time-bound, intermittent knowledge. The wind becomes too 'boistrous' for the bird and 'off she flies'. Experience assigns 'mysteries (not bounds)'.

It is a happy poem, but one that knows that happiness involves a commitment to our existence in time. Clare subdues art to nature; form affords no insurance against transience. Later sonnets become more disengaged, less enthusiastically shaped to the world. Those written in the 1830s, following Clare's move to Northborough, often string couplets together in blank apprehension of a scene which refuses to yield to any ordering vision. The form apprehends a world of chance:

> One day accross the fields I chancd to pass
> When chickens chelped & skuttled in the grass
> & as I looked about to find the seat
> A wounded partridge dropped agen my feet
> She fluttered round & calling as she lay
> The chickens chelped & fluttered all away
> I stooped to pick her up when up she drew
> Her wounded wing & cackled as she flew
> I wondered much to hear the chickens lye
> As still as nothing till I wandered bye
> & soon she came agen with much ado
> & swept the grass & called them as she flew

> But still they kept their seat & left no trace
> & old cows snorted when they passed the place (MP v 382)

This is among Clare's most unsettling scenes. Couplets stack up events in jumbled relation. The murder takes place off stage. The chickens 'flutter' from the partridge's wounded 'calling'; the partridge flies 'cackling' from the poet's attempts to help; attention turns back to the chickens, who lie 'still as nothing', in the terms of Clare's bleak, untutored metaphor; the partridge returns, now 'calling' for the chickens, as though in need; but the call is answered only by silence and the 'snorting' of the cows who intrude upon the final line. Violence has fractured nature's harmony. The verbs 'cackling' and 'snorting', which function as both neutral descriptions and seem, to human ears, to channel manic laughter, bring the animals' indifference up against human sensitivity. Yet the poem itself is unlamenting, deadpan. Form refuses consolation for the purposeless cruelty it documents, and Clare's earlier sense of how the sonnet might afford a form of participation in nature gives way to an uneasy feeling of how different the patterns of art are to the arbitrariness of experience.

***

Clare's sonnets succeed because their openness is in tension with the focus inherent to the form. Giving rein to the 'lunatic Enthuseism of nature' is a less viable strategy for longer works; and the surprise one feels at discovering that in the 1820s Clare set about writing a novel and a verse drama is matched only by the predictability of their incompletion.[5] Clare's most compelling attempts at longer poems either work by taking their structure from something that already exists, as in *The Shepherd's Calendar* (1827), which charts the unfolding of the rural year, or *Child Harold* (1841), whose formal chaos embodies the asylum-bound Clare's fractured state of mind. These are not poems you read for their complex organization of a larger vision. Their formal pleasures are often matters of local metrical flair, as when a description of botanical abundance in 'June' causes the pentameter to momentarily break out into song: 'Round field hedge now flowers in full glory twine' (MP I 75–83, l. 7); or as in 'November' when a description of the day's sleepiness finds its natural home in the drained alexandrine at the close of a Spenserian stanza: 'Thus day seems turned to night & tries to wake in vain' (MP I 144–55, l. 18). In *Child Harold*, conversely, individual stanzas provide refuge amid the wider turmoil:

> The lake that held a mirror to the sun
> Now curves with wrinkles in the stillest place
> The autumn wind sounds hollow as a gun
> & water stands in every swampy place
> Yet in these fens peace harmony & grace
> The attributes of nature are alied

> The barge with naked mast in sheltered place
> Beside the brig close to the bank is tied
> While small waves plashes by its bulky side
>
> (LP I 40–88, ll. 835–9)

How felicitously 'waves *plashes*' muddles individual waves into the wider lake. The serenity of movement which composes the 'wrinkles' of experience into the 'harmony' of a quasi-Spenserian stanza (Clare's closing line is a pentameter) stands in mournful contrast to the chaos of the poem at large.

Again, in *The Parish*, Clare's 1820s satire on the cant and self-interest despoiling rural communities, it is not any larger narrative or argumentative intelligence that compels attention, but the wit with which Clare vignettes individual characters:

> Miss Peevish Scornful once the Village toast
> Deemd fair by some & prettyish by most
> Brought up a lady tho her fathers gain
> Depended still on cattle & on grain
>
> (EP II 697–779, ll. 181–4)

The couplets evince keen artistry: particularly where the deliciously judged indifference is underscored by the reversal through 'some', 'prettyish', and 'most' of the sequence of 'M', 'P', and 'S' in the woman's name and in the rhymes which make visible the proximity of 'gain' and 'grain'. The satire is at the expense of someone who has betrayed their roots, and we can perhaps hear shadowing and sharpening the mockery Clare's own anxiety that writing poetry might make him similarly guilty. The subsequent paragraph, describing how the profits of farming fabricate the life of a London socialite, is shaped to a Crabbe-like warning against self-delusion:

> To Gretna green her visions often fled
> & rattling coaches lumberd in her head
> Till hopes grown weary with too long delay
> Caught the green sickness & declined away
> & beauty like a garment worse for wear
> Fled her pale cheek & left it much too fair   (ll. 221–6)

How tartly 'Gretna green' sours into 'green sickness'; how desolatingly 'fairness' turns from desired gentility to exhausted pallor. Wordsworth's Westminster Bridge sonnet and Keats's 'Belle Dame' blend curiously in the image of the woman's worn beauty. And the episode closes with Clare making a fitting descent from literary elegance to knockabout comedy: 'At last grown husband mad away she ran / Not with squire Dandy but the servant man' (ll. 237–8). Clare corrals a balance of scorn and sympathy that elevates the writing above the 'heavy distress', 'embittered feelings', 'anxiety', and 'oppression' out of which he described the poem as being written.

Though Clare is at his most controlled on a local scale, his most distinctive generic discoveries are poems of medium length, in which an energy of curiosity or distress strains formal intricacy: the accounts of birds nesting from the late 1820s and early 1830s ('The Nightingales Nest', 'The Yellowhammers Nest', 'To the Snipe', etc.), or the poems of ecological lamentation at the desecration of his home environment. The latter are often prized by critics who value the poetry more for its political than its aesthetic power. John Lucas describes 'To a Fallen Elm', a poem of the early 1820s in which Clare elegizes the proposed felling of a familiar elm tree, as unmatched in English for its 'rhetorical grandeur' and 'dramatic force'.[6] That force is shaped and restrained by the poem's formal and tonal control. The argument proceeds through a repeated structure of two sonnets followed by an octet – the first in heroic couplets, the second in cross-rhymed pentameters (Clare disguises the divisions by leaving no gaps between stanzas). The first sonnet establishes a calm, intimate voice, not prone to fury: 'Old Elm that murmured in our chimney top / The sweetest anthem autumn ever made' (MP III 440–3, ll. 1–2). In the second sonnet, the urgency heightens – 'thoust seen times changes lower / But change till now did never come to thee' (ll. 15–16) – though the specifics of the 'change' are left unmentioned; and the restraint persists into the first octet, whose focus remains the tree's companionship:

> Friend not inanimate – though stocks & stones
> There are & many cloathed in flesh & bones
> Thou owned a language by which hearts are stirred
> Deeper than by the atribute of words   (ll. 29–32)

As often happens when Clare insists that words are only a vehicle for 'Deeper' significances, his own words take on extra interest: the riddle of the opening couplet is perhaps best resolved as a kick at the stoniness of human hearts. The second half of the poem begins in a mood of visionary intensity, with Clare foreseeing the tree's fall before he has related it: 'I see a picture that thy fate displays' (l. 37). That 'fate' is related through a grim pun at the end of the third sonnet: 'With axe at root he felled thee to the ground / & barked of freedom' (ll. 49–50). The hypocrisy with which the word 'freedom' is wielded as a cloak for destructive self-interest becomes the object of a furious tirade, which sends turmoil through Clare's couplets – 'wrong was right & right was wrong / & freedoms brawl was sanction to the song' (ll. 65–6) – before the final stanza subsides into a mood of sad retrospection: 'Such was thy ruin music making elm' (l. 67). Even so basic a description of the poem's organization as this demonstrates the care Clare takes to match, in his transitions and tone, the 'music' of the tree he laments.

An opposite impact is achieved in 'The Lament of Swordy Well', in which Clare makes good on his trust in the 'language' of nature by putting the poem in the voice of an exploited piece of land. Poet and landscape sing in unison, deploying common metre (alternating four- and three-stress lines, rhymed *abab*) to defend the shared inheritance of local landscape. This is a powerfully ragged exercise, never published in Clare's lifetime, and which in its most sustained draft is riddled with gaps which suggest stoppages and blanks in composition.[7] It shows the accommodation Clare's art makes, in its urgency, with fragmentation. The poem begins by threading a tongue-twisting argument through its back-and-forth rhymes to expose those who show piety only in the hope of obtaining pity. But intricacy soon gives way to urgency as the voice reveals its identity and an account of the desecration kicks in: 'Im swordy well a piece of land' (MP v 105–114, l. 21). The subsequent argument follows little logical sequence and compels through an unchecked intensity at war with formal constraint. Seamus Heaney, admiring the poem's 'integration of common idiom and visionary anger', writes of the 'mechanical thump' of its metre: appeals to 'pity' are shunned for a resounding, assertive anger.[8] Yet in some of the poem's most arresting moments the 'mechanical thump' falters under the intensity of feeling, as when, towards the end of one of the two sustained manuscript drafts, the cry 'Im swordy well' re-echoes in a fractured timbre:

> I am the last
> Of all the field that fell
> My name is nearly all thats left
> Of what was Swordy Well

These lines form a stanza of their own, and whether it arises from incompletion or a more deliberate irregularity, it records a voice coming to the end of its tether. The poetry is choked as much by despair as fury as it contemplates the draining away of identity, a thought that haunts the poem to its close, two stanzas later:

> Of all the fields I am the last
> That my own face can tell
> Yet what with stone pits delving holes
> & strife to buy & sell
> My name will quickly be the whole
> Thats left of swordy well   (ll. 251–6)

The repetition constitutes a verbal and emotional dead end. The rhymes, too, echo the earlier fragmentary stanza: here to 'tell' one's own face is to recognize oneself, but also secondarily to express it; the name 'swordy well' is clung to amid the awareness that it is only a 'name' – it is 'the whole / Thats left', but a 'whole', rhyming with 'hole', that rings hollow. Words cannot atone for reality; poetic craft yields to political urgency.

***

I have been suggesting so far that Clare tends to surrender artistic control to the pressures of experience. But what about the hundreds of 'Songs' and 'Ballads' Clare wrote which channel personal feeling into conventional three- and four-beat lines, finding in regular form a refuge? Here is one from the 1840s:

> Song
>
> A seaboy on the giddy mast
> Sees nought but ocean waves
> & hears the wild inconstant blast
> Where loud the tempest raves
>
> My life is like the ocean wave
> & like the inconstant sea
> In every hope appears a grave
> & leaves no hope for me
>
> My life is like the oceans lot
> Bright gleams the morning gave
> But storms overwhelmed the sunny spot
> Deep in the ocean wave
>
> My life hath been the ocean storm
> A black & troubled sea
> When shall I find my life a calm
> A port & harbour free   (LP 1 327)

Clare wrote countless 'Songs' like this. Early in his career, they praise nature or women; later, as in this case, they lament disappointed hopes. There might seem little to say about their form, the movement is so regular, the phrasing so limpid; and what there is to say might seem to run counter to the arguments I have been nudging along: the patterns are unmoved by the experience they channel. But Clare respects what already exists: in the more descriptive poems, that involves letting nature impress itself on the forms that would contain them; here, the simple quatrains, grounded in a long-standing oral tradition, pre-exist the experience Clare brings to them. The result is a strange blend of the autobiographical and the anonymous, in which personal feeling is rendered in the most impersonal of mediums. The song takes off from Henry IV's speech on sleep, which envies 'the wet sea-boy' on 'the high and giddy mast' who is granted the repose denied to a king (*Henry IV Part 2*, III. iii. 1–31). Clare's poem is in part an answer to that speech, shunning its assumption that ordinary life does not have its tragedy. But it also shares Henry's envy of the sea-boy, although from a different perspective. The boy may see 'nought but ocean waves', but Clare feels himself to be 'like' the waves themselves: he is whelmed in even deeper gulphs. Clare's reiteration of the comparison in the middle two stanzas discovers an elliptical expressiveness amid the simplicity of the phrasing. You know what he means when he says 'In every hope appears a grave / & leaves no hope for me', but the repetition short-circuits logic in a manner that makes felt the hollowing out of hope ('My hopes are all hopeless' begins one of the *Child Harold* songs). The final stanza breaks gently with the established pattern: it is the first without the artlessly recurring rhyme on 'wave' or 'waves', though any sense of liberation is checked by its echoing of the 'sea' rhyme from the second stanza. The voice moves from present to past and then future tense: its tone shifts from immediate despair into retrospective sadness and then forlorn longing. The pathos of the final question is more tender for being purified of self-pity by its impersonal rhythms, more poignant for anticipating no response. Clare reaches an understanding, implicit through the poem's whole attitude to form, of how structure secures freedom.

Songs such as this model the resolution of the individual and the communal. They respect tradition most profoundly when they realize the scope for variation inherent in conventional form. The 'Song' 'Did I know where to meet thee' from *Child Harold* is typical of the haunting musical and emotional patterns Clare orchestrates in that most anguished of poems. His voice weaves through an intricate nine-line stanza, rhymed *abab / cdccd* with alternating feminine and masculine rhymes; a predominantly anapaestic dimeter expands to a tetrameter in the final line:

> Did I know where to meet thee
> Thou dearest in life
> How soon would I greet thee
> My true love & wife
> How soon would I meet thee
> At close of the day
> Though cares would still cheat me
> If Mary would meet me
> Id kiss her sweet beauty & love them away
>
> (LP 1 60, ll. 567–75)

As it moves to its yearning culmination, the stanza wavers beautifully between doubt and hope. The unpredictable rhyme pattern combines with the unpunctuated voice to achieve a spontaneously shifting syntax: feeling pivots on the line 'Though cares would still cheat me', which in one light closes the doubt-shadowed run of sense from lines 5 to 7 and in another inaugurates a sunnier run to the stanza's finish. Promised simplicity evolves into formal and emotional intricacy. Or, again from *Child Harold*, there is the wistful 'Dying gales of sweet even', which deploys a similar two-stress anapaestic line through octets shaped to an *abab / bcbc* rhyme scheme. The poem wonders at the presence of sorrow in a world of beauty:

> Dying gales of sweet even
> How can you sigh so
> Though the sweet day is leaving
> & the sun sinketh low
> How can you sigh so
> For the wild flower is gay
> & her dew gems all glow
> For the absence of day   (LP I 56, ll. 444–51)

The immediate return of the rhyme between the fourth and fifth lines lends unanticipated urgency to the questioning and is crucial to the writing's plangent serenity in the face of transience. Nature, it seems, consoles all suffering. The question is put one last time in the final line of the second stanza before the third concedes an awareness of a world in which sighing at the end of the day would be appropriate but holds such sadness at a distance:

> Dying gales round a prison
> To fancy may sigh
> But day here hath risen
> Over prospects of joy
> Here Mary would toy
> When the sun it got low
> Even gales whisper joy
> & never sigh so   (ll. 460–7)

Details of Clare's biography – his incarceration at High Beach Asylum, the sustaining, haunting figure of Mary – enter the poem obliquely, just as the writing recognizes but never admits grief (beyond the 'sigh' that disturbs the rhyme scheme). The poem becomes a celebration of sadness overcome, and, in its final lines, a kind of lullaby that as it implores nature to bring peace implicitly acknowledges art's own soothing influence: 'Dying gales gently sweep / O'er the hearts ruffled motion / & sing it to sleep' (ll. 474–6).

Clare's Forms

Counter-intuitively, Clare often seems most himself in these conventional song forms; he adopts their idiom without artifice or rhetoric. The form purifies experience of personal idiosyncrasy; variations endow thought and feeling with intricate aesthetic shape. Occasionally, an individualistic vein wins out more completely, and one of the pleasures of reading Clare's work in its entirety is encountering isolated poems which plough lone furrows of lyric expression. Sometimes, they discover an unusual stanza, as in the song 'The daiseys golden eye', a poem from the 1840s in which Clare's descriptive and expressive faculties are happily united. Clare writes in an *aabccb* pattern, five three-stress lines expanding at the last into a pentameter:

> The daiseys golden eye
> On the fallow land doth lie
> Though the spring is just begun
> Pewets watch it all the day
> & the sky larks nest of hay
> Leans agen its group of leaves in the sun (LP 1 328–30, ll. 1–6)

Nothing is hurried. The rhythms pay careful attention to the scene they depict; the expansion in the final line slows the momentum in a fashion that suggests an eye taking the time it needs, not carried onward by the metre. The intensity of perception brings into focus a landscape that is cherished though not necessarily explicable: the daisy has wilted though the year is just beginning; the pewits watch it (out of care?); the skylark's nest either cosies up to the leaves or leans on them for support. In the next stanza, a mouse finds shelter from the hawk underneath the 'pile wort all in gold' (l. 7). The third, which describes the speedwell on the riverbank, is the only one without the elongated final line – a moment of strange (calculated?) irregularity. The writing seems nervous: attentive but vulnerable. Then the final two stanzas return to the initial pattern to take the poem to its close:

> Here the cowslap chill with cold
> On the rushy bed behold
> Looking for [the][9] spring all day
> Where the heavy bee will come
> & find no sweets at home
> Then quakes his weary wings & flyes away
>
> & here are nameless flowers
> Culled from cold & rawky hours
> For Marys happy home
> They grew in murky blea

>   Rush fields & naked lea
>   But suns will shine & pleasing spring will come   (ll. 19–30)

The poem gives the impression both of being loosely composed and of moving towards an inevitable conclusion. The placid drift to this point, as Clare picks out features of the landscape as they occur – 'There's this ... ', 'Here's that ... ' – lends the intensification and contrast in the stanzas above enigmatic force. The penultimate stanza shows a world in which spring does not deal out its gifts equally; joy and dissatisfaction, beauty and desolation coexist. Then with restrained pathos the final stanza gathers itself to a resolution, as if working round to a topic that has been there all along: Clare's love for Mary. Yet the nature of his devotion is mysterious. It is carried in flowers whose namelessness may simply suggest their abundance, but which in a poet ordinarily so precise about his surroundings also hints at dislocation. They have been 'Culled' (not, say, 'gathered') in 'rawky' hours and grew in a 'blea' landscape, yet Clare's dialect terms suggest a happy accommodation with these drab environs. The turn in the final line is affectingly modest and trusting in its sense of what it takes to convert hopelessness to hope.

Such poems are continually open to surprise; they pursue arguments cheerfully free of purpose. Clare is happy to let them find their own shape. An earlier lyric, 'The Woods', follows a similar form to 'The daiseys golden eye': unrhymed six-line stanzas of trimeters expanding out into two pentameters at their close.[10] A conventional Clare opening, 'I love to roam the woods' (MP III 545–6, l. 1), promises a poem of open-ended exploration, though the deepening and slowing of attention at the stanza's close, and the absence of rhyme, invites unanticipated turns. 'I seem to be myself / The only one that treads / The earth at such a time' (ll. 7–9) Clare writes of such moments of solitude, in lines which might speak self-consciously of Clare's lonely experimentalism and whose enjambment isolates a phrase, 'I seem to be myself', which conveys his sense of being most at home when most independent. By the third stanza, he is exploring a state of visionary solitude:

>   No human eye is visible
>   No human sound attracts
>   The ear – but musing solitude
>   One unembodied thought
>   Thinks the heart into stillness as the world
>   Was left behind for somthing green & new
>
>   & lonely –   (ll. 13–19)

Form comes under the strain of vision. The first and third lines stretch into tetrameters; the thought overspills the stanza to suggest a continually

Clare's Forms

unspooling apprehension of experience. As he describes how the peacefulness of the surroundings 'Thinks the heart into stillness', as though the environment actively infiltrated consciousness, Clare displays the ability to forge 'unusual and unprecedented combinations of words' that Taylor admired when introducing *Poems Descriptive of Rural Life and Scenery* (1820).[11] Subsequent stanzas retreat from this Marvellian serenity to a more pragmatic evaluation of the temptations of a rural 'hermitage or hut', turning to rhyme to capture Clare's indecision: 'How sweet t'would be but then again / I've turned to my old home & felt it vain' (ll. 23–4). Instead of resolving the opposed claims of solitude and society, however, the final stanza picks up on a thought about the 'happiness & pleasing fears' of isolation and drifts into a contemplation of the imaginative thrills of reading:

> Fear books can give us
> When we read strange tales
> Of dwellers in the depths
> Of earths untrodden shades
> Where woods surround lone huts impassable
> & nought lives near them but the hope of heaven (ll. 31–6)

The lines intrigue on account of their seemingly unpremeditated extension of the poem's thought, their self-reflexiveness – the poem itself is a 'strange tale' – and for the foretaste they afford of the desolated poetry of Clare's asylum years: the peacefulness of 'earths untrodden shades' is inseparable from its loneliness. The final glimpse of 'heaven' (or at least the 'hope' of it) is likewise unexpected, a closing touch which holds the solaces of belief in delicate balance and which typifies a lyric art whose moods and images are always in a state of unpredictable evolution.

***

For the last twenty-five years or so of his life, Clare was almost exclusively a poet of songlike lyric. The most famous poems ('I Am', 'A Vision', 'An Invite to Eternity') achieve a ferocious mixture of convention and visionary power; some ('Spring', 'Mary', 'The sharp wind shivers') endow Clare's formal experimentations with new sophistication; many sink into doggerel. But I'll land this tour of Clare's forms back on a poem from the 1820s, 'Autumn', which draws together several characteristic traits: a fluid, spontaneously suggestive idiom; concern to subdue artistic to natural shape; readiness to tailor individual expression to existing styles and verse forms; understated experimentalism. The poem is an ode – an elevated lyric address to an entity or phenomenon, in this instance, autumn – and its opening line takes its cadence from Keats's ode to the same season. But where Keats finds 'mists and mellow fruitfulness', Clare's autumn is a 'Syren of sullen moods & fading hues' (MP III 258–68, l. 1), a harbinger of decay. Ordinarily an ode twins its tribute to the phenomenon it addresses with a claim for the poet's own significance. Here, Clare's voice is winningly self-abnegating. The writing wavers between succumbing to a disorganized welter of impressions and radiating attentiveness to the connectedness of an apparently entropic world. Sentences wind through stanzas of alternating unrhymed pentameter and trimeter couplets, adopted from William Collins's 'Ode to Evening'. But Clare blurs Collins's artfulness: syntax continually threatens to unravel; subjects and verbs connect hazily; every time a sentence seems to reach a place of rest it melts into a new thought or image. The poetry accommodates itself to a season whose glories are entwined with its transience and which shows us how to embrace our own losses:

> sublime in grief thy thoughts delight
> To show me visions of most gorgeous dies
> Haply forgetting now
> They but prepare thy shroud
> Thy pencil dashing its excess of shades
> Improvident of waste till every bough
> Burns with thy mellow touch
> Disorderly divine   (ll. 97–104)

Clare rises to a passionate wit. The 'gorgeous dies' of autumn are a signal of its own decay; the 'shades' of its pencil are ghostly; 'waste' is at once abundance and decrepitude; the boughs 'Burn' colourfully but are consumed. The unpunctuated final line is a triumph of suggestiveness: either we read two adjectives descriptive of autumn's 'mellow touch' – 'disorderly, divine' – or we imagine an ingenious compound adjective, a label not just for the spirit of the season but the artistry of the poem that hymns it. Clare's poetry, in its canny evasion of artifice, shows us beauty in disorder and embraces the transience that form would ordinarily resist.

Notes

1. Hugh Haughton, 'Progress and Rhyme: "The Nightingale's Nest" and Romantic Poetry', in Hugh Haughton, Adam Phillips, and Geoffrey Summerfield, eds., *John Clare in Context* (Cambridge: Cambridge University Press, 1994), pp. 51–86 (p. 52).
2. Samuel Taylor Coleridge, *The Collected Works of Samuel Taylor Coleridge: Lectures, 1808–1819*, ed. R. A. Foakes, 16 vols. (Princeton, NJ: Princeton University Press, 1987), v, 495.
3. John Clare, 'Sonnet', *The London Magazine*, 6 (1822), 272.

4. For fuller discussion, see Richard Lessa, 'John Clare's Voice and Two Sonnets', *John Clare Society Journal*, 3 (1984), 26–32, and Francesca MacKenney, *Birdsong, Speech and Poetry: The Art of Composition in the Long Nineteenth Century* (Cambridge: Cambridge University Press, 2022), pp. 126–8.
5. See Jonathan Bate, *John Clare: A Biography* (London: Macmillan, 2003), p. 234, and Sara Lodge, 'Clare's Drama', *John Clare Society Journal*, 23 (2004), 68–84.
6. John Lucas, *John Clare* (London: Northcote House, 1994), p. 35.
7. Drafts of the poem, whose title is a later editorial invention, exist in Peterborough MS A59, Peterborough MS B6, and Northampton MS 7. When referring to manuscript versions of the poem, I have Peterborough MS A59 in mind.
8. Seamus Heaney, 'John Clare: A Bi-centenary Lecture', in Hugh Haughton, Adam Phillips, and Geoffrey Summerfield, eds., *John Clare in Context* (Cambridge: Cambridge University Press, 1994), pp. 130–47 (pp. 140–2).
9. The word is supplied by the Oxford editors to balance out the metre, and the reading is partly supported by an alternative manuscript version of the song which has the line 'Looking for spring all the day'. But there is a case for retaining 'Looking for spring all day' as being in step with the poem's courting of slight metrical unsteadiness.
10. A draft of 'The Woods' appears in a notebook alongside two other poems, 'Fears' and 'Fancys', whose titles pick up on words and concepts which arise unpredictably in the closing stanzas of 'The Woods' (see Peterborough MS A54, R115–110). These two poems follow 'The Woods' in Clare's neat version of the *Midsummer Cushion* (Peterborough MS A54). The organization of the rough draft material suggests a meandering habit of composition that blurs the boundaries of individual poems.
11. John Taylor, 'Introduction' to *Poems Descriptive of Rural Life and Scenery* (London, 1820), pp. i–xiii (p. xiv).

3

CASSANDRA FALKE

On Clare's Translation of Perception to Poetry

It is an open question whether what a poet perceives can be translated to a reader's understanding. Many literary theorists emphasize that reading a work of literature is an event, and like any event, a reading can never be duplicated in just the same way. If readers do not understand the same poem the same way twice, then certainly we never understand it the way the poet did, particularly if the poet's life differs from readers' as much as Clare's did from someone living today. He came of age 200 years before this book's publication. His frequent walks took him through a more biodiverse landscape than most twenty-first-century readers will ever experience. If something translatable across time and differences reaches us, it is not because Clare conveys eternal, still perceivable ideals but rather because he wrote about how perception can respond to the givenness and changeability of a renewing living world. To borrow a phrase from Sara Guyer, Clare's poems partake of the 'eternity ... of weeds'.[1] His writing renews itself through different readers voicing his poems to themselves or to others, with each reading being similar but unique. Reading events, like weeds, proliferate, and as Clare writes: 'Theres many a seeming weed proves sweet' ('To an Insignificant Flower, obscurely blooming in a lonely wild', EP 1 216–18, l. 7). In this chapter, I want to suggest that Clare's ability to translate perception into poetry depends, first, on readers' willingness to accept the specific modes of perception to which his poetry invites us and, second, on the application of these modes of perception to the poems themselves and to whatever life we see proliferating around us, which might be quite different to what Clare perceived. In short, I will emphasize *how* he encourages readers to perceive more than *what*.

The chapter will unfold in three main parts and a conclusion. I begin by discussing humility and other-centredness, both exemplified in 'To an Insignificant Flower', as habits of perception that Clare's poems encourage readers to adopt, especially when perceiving nonhuman nature. Then, I will look to a few of his shorter bird poems to discuss the ways he bids readers yield control over a moment of perception by placing his speakers below or in the midst of what they observe and having them strive to see what is not perceivable in other lives. He presents other living things as directing the speaker's, and therefore the reader's, attention. Examining 'The Fens', the third part discusses Clare's offering multiple perspectives in a single poem, a practice that emphasizes the need to take responsibility for perception as well as action. The conclusion returns to the question of how we might direct the manner of perception Clare exemplifies to the poems themselves and our own surroundings.

Cultivating Generous Perception

Clare's early poem 'To an Insignificant Flower' hints at a mode of perception Clare would celebrate and perfect throughout his writing, one characterized by external provocation, humility, wonder, and close attention. The poem engages the convention of comparing underappreciated rural poets to flowers 'born to blush unseen', as Thomas Gray's 'Elegy Written in a Country Churchyard' famously puts it.[2] In contrast to Gray's unseen and generalized flower, Clare comes upon a particular weed. Upon seeing it, he addresses it:

> And tho thou seemst a weedling wild
> Wild & neglected like to me
> Thou still art dear to natures child
> & I will stoop to notice thee   (ll. 1–4)

Beginning with 'and', the first line suggests a conversation already underway, with the seeming weedling the only interlocuter in sight. The other-directedness begun with the first line persists until the final stanza with the speaker addressing the insignificant flower twenty times throughout the poem. The poem compares the flower and the speaker, who sees himself as 'Wild & neglected' (l. 2 and l. 12), but it is not a case of 'the human's identity overwhelm[ing] and elid[ing] the plant's identity'.[3] Clare approaches the weed as given – the centre of its own unnoticed life prior to and beyond whatever the poet might say about it. It is neither a product of his imagination nor the object of a search. The poem's existence seems to depend on the flower's calling out to Clare's attention.

Many of Clare's poems begin, like this one, as though he is responding to an external prompting: 'One day across the fields I chancd to pass / When chickens chelped & skuttled in the grass' (MP v 382); or 'Just by the wooden brig a bird flew up' ('The Yellowhammers Nest', MP III 515). There is no sense that Clare walked out intending to meet a partridge or a yellowhammer or that the poems originate from 'emotion recollected in tranquillity', as William Wordsworth would have it.[4] Instead, Clare's speaker seems ready to receive what the day gives him, and when something calls his attention, he responds by actively taking notice and responding, not just with sight or thought, but with his whole body. Clare preserves the sense of discovery in the present tense, and when he describes the emotions of these moments, he typically presents them as belonging to the particular situation he describes as much as to himself as a distinct subjectivity. He thereby minimizes the uniqueness of his own perceiving consciousness and presents the situation as one the reader could imagine stepping into.

Even when he writes about things he sees regularly, Clare often presents them in his poem as though they have initiated the poem-worthy meeting:

> In the hedge I pass a little nest
> Green morning after morning
> ...
> The old ones on a distant bough
> With victuals in her bill
> Waits back to see me passing now
> & tweets in fear of ill
> But soon as bye she hurrys in
> They twitter caw & cree
> The laughing brook wont let me win
> A peep to reach & see
>
> Right pleasant brook Im glad ye lie
> Between them & the road
> ...
> I've past the nest so often bye
> They seem my neighbours now
>   ('In the hedge I pass a little nest', MP v 187–8,
>   ll. 1–2, 17–26, 33–4)

Clare presents the 'I' walking as an agent, but so are the mother bird and laughing brook. They seem his neighbours. He does not imply that this speaker is possessed of some remarkable ecocritical hospitality that allows only him to see them as neighbours but instead normalizes the speaker's perspective, as though anyone walking the road would, or at least *could*, perceive birds as neighbours and brooks as merrily competitive. Both here and in 'To an insignificant Flower', the verb 'seem' detaches the perceptive act from the lyric speaker without making neighbourliness or weediness intrinsic properties of the birds or flower he perceives. Clare thereby retains

On Clare's Translation of Perception to Poetry

a focus on perception while implying that this manner of perception is available to anyone.

When Clare was nearing fifty at High Beach Asylum and reflecting on decades of his own poetic practice, he wrote that he 'found the poems in the fields / And only wrote them down' ('Sighing for Retirement', LP 1 19, ll. 15–16). Clare here elides his own craftsmanship. However, many of his poems do read as though the poetic encounter he would translate into verse began outside of himself. His attunement to finding, if not poems, at least living things worthy of poetic address, is a key feature of the sort of perception his poems encourage. Thanks to John Goodridge's first-line index of Clare's poems, we know that over sixty begin with 'I love' or 'I loved'.[5] In 'Sighing for Retirement', where he writes that his poems are found before they are written, he says characteristically 'I love to seek the brakes and fern, / And rabbits up and down' (ll. 21–2). Love may seem a different issue to perception, but not for Clare. He finds fault with 'common eyes' that would view thickets of ferns as 'A desert waste and drear' (ll. 25–6). 'To taste and love', he asserts, 'they always shine, / A garden through the year' (ll. 27–8). It is an eye cultivated to see with 'taste and love' that perceives beauty even when the ferns turn brown in autumn (l. 24). Similarly, Clare implies that perception cultivated in taste and love will begin poetically musing in *response* to what it sees or hears rather than bringing predetermined ideas from literature, biology, or philosophy and imposing those on the living things of the world.

In 'To an Insignificant Flower', Clare contrasts a proud eye with a polished one (ll. 24 and 26), suggesting that this sense of common and cultivated forms of perception stayed with him throughout his poetic career. Still addressing the flower, Clare writes there that:

>   when beautys cloath'd
> In lowly raiment like to thee
> Disdaining pride (by beauty loath'd)
> No beauties there can never see
>
> For like to thee, my Emma blows
> Flowers like to thee I dearly prize
> & like to thee, her humble cloaths
> Hides every charm from prouder eyes
>
> Altho like thee, a lowly flower
> If fancied by a polish'd eye
> It soon would bloom beyond my power
> The finest flower beneath the sky   (ll. 13–24)

Pride, including pride in how perceptive one is, would interfere with the receptiveness Clare tries to cultivate. The goal of cultivated perception is not to view something in a predetermined right way, certainly not in the elitist way that the terms 'polished' or 'cultivated' might at first imply, but rather to view it in the way that lets what one fancies bloom beyond the preconceptions that could limit our reception of what is there, such as the preconception that some flowers are weeds and therefore insignificant. For all this poem's flirtation with convention (country girls and country poets as neglected flora), Clare proposes a philosophically significant insight about perception: that the goal should not be accurate categorization of what one sees or even self-cultivation geared towards increased attentiveness. To perceive with taste and love, we should get out of our own way, focus on the other before us and let it 'bloom beyond' our power of expectation and understanding.

Directed Attention

Many poems from the Romantic period begin from mountaintops, with only the mightiest cataracts or deepest valleys reaching the speaker's perception across a span of distance, but the perceptive acts Clare describes often happen up close. Clare reinforces the epistemological humility of his speakers by positioning them spatially level with or below the living things he describes. He portrays them not only stooping to talk to weeds, but 'wad[ing] right through' clumps of thorns ('The Nightingales Nest', MP III 456–61, l. 50) and 'scrambl[ing] in the highest glee' or 'sluther[ing] down' a tree (MP v 290, l. 7; l. 14). This positioning rejects the privilege and sense of command that comes with height and distance and highlights instead humans' embodied limitations. Even when regarding minute details – eggs the size of fingertips, crimping edges of ferns – Clare narrates attempts to be as precise as possible in his descriptions. In 'The Nightingales Nest', for example, he describes the eggs first as 'deadened green' but then finds this is not quite right; they are 'rather olive brown' (l. 90). His documentation of trying more than once to get it right conveys not just fidelity to what he perceives, but wonder, which 'supersedes thought' rather than merely provoking it.[6] The 'splendid gift that nature gives' ('The Robins Nest', MP III 532–6, l. 9) merits climbing, wading, scrambling, looking, listening, and looking again.

In a particularly elegant eight-line poem, Clare puts his speaker below a crane, literally, and uses this spatial orientation to reinforce a humble and responsive attunement. Clare often interprets the emotions of birds,

On Clare's Translation of Perception to Poetry

extending his human empathy as far as it can go, but here he does not presume to know the crane's feelings.

> High overhead that silent throne
> Of wild and cloud betravelled sky
> That makes ones loneliness more lone
> Sends forth a crank and reedy cry
> I look the crane is sailing oer
> That pathless world without a mate
> The heath looked brown and dull before
> But now tis more then desolate (ll. 1–8)[7]

The would-be lyric 'I' makes its sole appearance only in the second quatrain. The speaker claims no special powers of feeling or perception but suggests that 'one', anyone, already feeling lonely would feel lonelier watching a mateless bird in a pathless sky. The fullest perception, as portrayed here, entails openness to being changed by forces beyond the self. Emphasizing the speaker's subordinate position as observer, Clare credits the crane with freedom and power to sail that he lacks. The long open vowels of lines 3 and 5 contrast strongly with each other. Whereas the 'oh's of line 3 sound mournful and weepy (Poe exploits them similarly in 'The Raven'), the long 'ay's of line 5 feel expansive. The sibilant and liquid sound of 'sailing' seems a command to soar. Apparently mateless like the bird, the speaker seems to have far less power, managing only to register the connection between its cry and the shifting mood of the place. Clare presents, not a speaker's mood colouring the landscape, but the landscape colouring a speaker's mood.

Even when Clare places a speaking 'I' at the spatial centre of a poem, as he does in 'The Robins Nest' (MP III 532–6), he shirks egotism by highlighting that the speaker's perception of the world as radiating from his centre is just that, a matter of perception. At first, the speaker of 'The Robins Nest' seems powerful: 'Come luscious spring', he commands, 'come with thy mossy roots / Thy weed strown banks–young grass–& tender shoots' (ll. 1–2). Perhaps already the lowliness of roots and weeds undermines the sense of command, but the diction of the first few lines is grand; 'opening blooms' offer truer happiness than 'sordid pelf' (l. 3; l. 7). But in line 11, the narrative situation becomes clear. We read that our speaker is sitting by an old oak tree, eye level with 'crimping ferns uncurling now'. His sense of having command over spring was a 'splendid gift' (l. 9) brought by the 'birds' that 'unbid come round' (l. 17) and wildflowers that 'smile & bloom' for him, 'Paying [him] kindness like a throned king' (l. 19; l. 22). He feels himself to be issuing commands for what is already happening due to the kindness of birds and flowers. Being both inside the poem sharing his on-the-ground point of view and outside the poem as a reader, we see that the birds and flowers that smile and greet him are received as royal courtiers because of his generous attention. The language of 'like' and 'as' is too prominent for the similes of royal greeting to overtake the more concrete perception of tiny leave uncurling. Readers do not perceive a king as much as we perceive Clare's act of perception. When he uses the stronger language of metaphor, he is not a king but a child being taught by an elder:

> each ancient tree
> With lickens deckt–times hoary pedigree
> Becomes a monitor to teach & bless
> & rid me of the evils cares possess
> & bids me look above the trivial things
> To which prides me[r]cenary spirit clings
> The pomps the wealth & artificial toys (ll. 32–8)

The trees are honourable instructors, 'The very weeds as patriarchs appear' (l. 63); wealth is a childish toy to be left behind compared to these grander objects of attention.

One other feature of Clare's generous perception should be mentioned. In addition to the qualities discussed previously – receptiveness to external prompting, humble attention to what one finds, and an other-directedness that lets mood and insight originate from the other – Clare's poems also encourage his readers to see potential futures in a moment of perception. This is not the 'life and food / For future years' that Wordsworth senses he will glean from his visit to Tintern Abbey but imagined futures for the place or creature being looked at.[8] Another lonely bird poem, 'On seeing two Swallows late in October' (MP IV 328), illustrates how Clare's attention follows creatures even after they leave his perceptive field. The poem consists of two stanzas of seven couplets each. The first stanza reads:

> Lone occupiers of a naked sky
> When desolate november hovers nigh
> & all your fellow tribes in many crowds
> Have left the village with the autumn clouds
> Carless of old affections for the scene
> That made them happy when the fields were green
> & left them undisturbed to build their nests
> In each old chimney like to welcome guests
> Forsaking all like untamed winds they roam
> & make with summers an unsettled home
> Following her favours to the farthest lands
> Oer untraced oceans & untrodden sands

On Clare's Translation of Perception to Poetry

> Like happy images they haste away
> & leave us lonely till another may (MP IV 328, ll. 1–14)

Here, Clare's perception of the swallows gives way quickly to what he cannot see, the 'fellow tribes' that have flown south 'like untamed winds'. It is a beautiful image, the swallows making 'with summers an unsettled home'. Puzzlingly, the 'us' in the final line seems to credit its creation equally to the two swallows he addresses, to himself, and to the reader. Once initiated by the speaker's upward glance to the 'naked sky', the perceptive act described in the stanza is refracted. From the speaker, it moves to the remaining swallows, for whom the departees are 'fellow tribes' and November desolate. Then, it seems linked to the departing swallows, who, backward looking, remember the old chimneys. Then it joins the forward-looking perspective of the same departed swallows following summer up ahead. The fact that perception itself seems to haste away like the swallows strengthens the sense of loneliness at the end, but there is more here than emotional effect. Clare models trying to imagine the swallows' attachment to home and to one another. Without claiming correctness or exclusive insight, Clare implies that the act of imagining these creatures' past, present, and future is no more than what careful perception demands.

In 'On Seeing Two Swallows', no reference is made to the speaking 'I' at all. He disappears into the 'all' forsaken in line 9. The 'I' appears once in 'High overhead that silent throne'. The 101-line 'Robins Nest' features 'I' three times, but the speaker more often appears as the grammatical object 'me' (two times) or absorbed into a 'we' (two times) of solitude seekers. Of course, there are Clare poems centred on the speaking subject, like his famous late poem 'I Am' or his painful account of displacement, 'The Flitting', but Clare's minimal focus on consciousness and ego distinguishes him from his contemporaries. When 'the great Romantic lyrics', as *Norton Anthology* editor Deidre Lynch puts it, 'remark on an aspect in the natural scene, this attention to the external world serves only as a stimulus to the most characteristic human activity, that of thinking'.[9] That claim does not hold for Clare. His minimization of the lyric 'I' serves most obviously to direct readers' attention beyond him to the other creatures and forces in the world, but it also indicates that Clare's poems invest more in what Jonathan Culler calls 'voicing' than voice. This is a point I will return to later (p. 55). Culler uses this distinction to contrast poems that present an emplaced speaker in a specific mood and situation feeling strong feelings (poems emphasizing voice) with poems that offer themselves as events for the reader to experience (poems inviting voicing). With their sound effects and unstable referentiality, poems, after all, are quite different from regular speech acts.

Read as a 'voicing', a lyric poem makes 'claims about our world', not about a fictional person in a specific situation.[10] Like an incantation, a lyric poem is something for the speaker to take up and use at will. It comes free of its particular situation (in this case the nineteenth-century fenland) in a way a novel could not. The loneliness of a pathless sky that must nevertheless be travelled and travelled 'without a mate' is ours to imagine. The 'I' in 'High overhead' defers to the reader to interpret what such pathless travelling might imply and defers to the crane – or the swallows or the ferns – credit for creating the event that prompts that question. Clare's lyrics open possibilities for readerly perception by leaving the first-person subject at the centre vague or, as I will discuss in relation to 'The Fens', inviting us in to a generalized ('one') or shared ('we') subjectivity (pp. 54–57). And, as mentioned in the introduction (p. 46), reading one is its own event, before and beyond what the poem might teach us, an important point to which I will return in my Conclusion.

Choosing How to Perceive

Clare's exceptional perceptiveness has been noted by his best readers from his time to our own. An anonymous reviewer in 1820 noted his 'unmixed and unadulterated impression of the loveliness of nature', his 'vivid perception and strong feeling'. One hundred years later, John Middleton Murry proclaimed that if looking for 'intensity of perception', one 'may choose at random any page' in *Poems Descriptive of Rural Life and Scenery*. At the end of the twentieth century, Seamus Heaney celebrated the 'painterly thickness' with which Clare portrayed the world, while still noting that any Clare poem is 'as surely made of words as one by Mallarmé'.[11] The sense of 'thickness' arises from Clare's reluctance to select only one or two creatures or elements in a landscape; he often crowds his poem with a plenitude of sights and sounds.

And yet his poems are made of words. That seems an obvious point for Heaney to make, but Clare's sensitivity to the solidity and specific sonority of words leads him to use them in a way that stops a reader short. He might choose a dialect word that readers from beyond the fenland or beyond his century do not understand, or pack lines with consonants and play with staccato rhythms, as he does in the poem that Eric Robinson and David Powell have titled 'The Fens' in *The Major Works*.[12] Written in the early 1830s, 'The Fens' (MP v 27–30) captures well the painterly thickness Clare's poetry strives to convey and the foregrounding of language that reminds readers of the solidity of words themselves and their separateness from the perceptive act they evoke. Clare's sound effects detach themselves from his speakers in a way that realistic speech could not. Furthermore, the poem highlights Clare's tendency to add alternative perceptual positions as a poem goes on. In 'Two Swallows', the perceptive act tentatively followed birds, but in 'The Fens', two human ways of looking are contrasted. This conveys that the sense of present-tense fecundity Clare's speakers so often perceive is not the only way to look. The reader immersed in reading Clare's poems about the fenny landscape around Helpston learns to value Clare's manner of perception, not only on its own merits, but because he contrasts appreciative, attentive looking with looking that sees only a chance of gain.

In 'The Fens':

> Among the tawney tasseled reed
> The ducks & ducklings float & feed
> ...
> Tails topsy turvy in the air
> Then up & quack & down they go
> Heels over head again below   (ll. 35–6; ll. 39–41)

On one level, this is just sonic play, conveying in sound the whimsy it is easy to feel watching ducks tip 'Heels over head', with alliteration dominating the first half of most lines. The preponderance of single-syllable or trochaic words reinforces the emphasis of the iambs, and when the alliteration leaves off in line 40, its absence makes 'up & quack & down' sound sillier than they already would. 'Voicing' this sonic play captures the mood, but also the fun of *trying* to capture mood in mere words. The mood of the poem changes drastically as it progresses, however. The fitness between the sound and rhythm of the words and the scene the words would paint sets the reader up for a jarring displacement. After fifty-eight lines of rustling through sedge (l. 2) with kingfishers (l. 14), snakes (l. 8), and waterfowl (ll. 35–41; ll. 42–55), we read a wish: 'Ah could I see a spinny' (a small wood) or 'A puddock [red kite] sailing in the sky' (ll. 57–8) or could he 'meet a heath of furze in flower' (l. 61). Instead, the speaker sees:

> grounds of oats in curly green
> & crowded growth of wheat & beans
> That with the hope of plenty leans
> & cheers the farmers gazing brow   (ll. 70–3)

The fenlands around Clare's home were beginning to be drained and converted to farmland at this time. It is hard to tell at this stage of the poem how sympathetic the speaker might be to the gazing farmer. Perhaps the speaker shares the farmer's 'hope of plenty' and is cheered, with him, to see the crops thrive.

Then Clare works a clever division of the poem's perspective:

> & muse & marvel where we may
> Gain mars the landscape every day (ll. 83–4)

Co-opting the reader into the speaker's perspective with the use of 'we', Clare separates, here, the community of us and him from the farmer. The farmer belongs to a 'they' that cuts the 'docks & thistles' (l. 101) every year, even though small animals could have sheltered there from the 'quaking winter' (l. 103). In 'spite of all they' (the farmer and those like him) 'eat & kill' (l. 107), in spite of the fact that the bramble edge would have been 'a sort of living grace' (l. 112) to cows that could have sheltered behind it (ll. 113–14) or toads (l. 99) that could have hidden within, the bramble is cut.

> Change cheats the landscape every day
> Nor tree no[r] bough about it grows
> That from the hatchet can repose (ll. 92–4)

Whereas the first half of the poem followed the logic of a wandering gaze, discovering beauties that need not be tamed to be lovingly described, the second half wavers between two perspectives – that of the gazing farmer 'Who lives & triumphs in the plough' (l. 74), who is glad to see 'The meadow grass turned up & copt / The trees to stumpy dotterels lopt' (ll. 85–6) and that of the original speaker who sees the land denuded by these processes.

Nakedness is mentioned twice in the poem. In the first instance, prior to the introduction of the farmer's gaze, we read:

> Some taller things the distance shrouds
> That may be trees or stacks or clouds
> Or may be nothing still they wear
> A zemblance where theres nought to spare (ll. 31–4)

Distance clothes the shapes resembling trees, stacks, or clouds on the horizon, seemingly because the fenny flatland cannot 'spare' even a semblance of attire. When we read, after this, that grasses and trees are being taken anyway, the plunder seems all the more unjust. The second mention of nakedness conveys a hope for renewal that comes with the spring but remains unfulfilled. Situated between narration of the hatchet's clear-cutting (l. 94) and the news that even docks and thistles will not be left to stand (ll. 101–2), mention of the fen's 'nakedness' sounds like the land has been violently stripped:

> & the orison stooping smiles
> Oer treeless fens of many miles
> Spring comes & goes & comes again
> & all is nakedness & fen (ll. 95–8)

On Clare's Translation of Perception to Poetry

In Eric Robinson and David Powell's glossary of Clare's poetic vocabulary, 'orison' is glossed as a variant of 'horizon'.¹³ Clare certainly uses the term this way, such as when he walks to the 'edge of the orison' as a child to find the edge of the world (*JCBH*, 39–40). But the word also means 'a prayer'. The horizon, brought low by the destruction of the few trees that could have stood, still smiles, perhaps with benediction, perhaps with the offer of 'living grace' (l. 112); spring comes, but 'all is nakedness & fen'. Whatever hope spring could have brought seems to have passed over the land.

Clare does not lock readers into a single perspective the way many lyric poets do. Because readers see the 'warmest mirth' that the cut firewood brings to cottages 'on coldest nights' (l. 90), the gain-oriented perspective of the farmer and hatchet wielder does not seem unreasonable. Even if Clare includes the reader in the 'we' that muses and marvels (l. 83), actual readers may choose to see the described landscape otherwise. But we cannot choose that without stepping away from the whimsical wandering perspective of the poem's first half. This was the perspective that compared geese to 'gossips over tea' (l. 46) and created playful rhymes about upside-down ducks. We, who formerly marvelled, are forced to recognize that with the farmer's gain comes a loss, not just of oak trees and the kites that could sail above them, but of a perspective of acceptance and wonder.

Conclusion

Acceptance, wonder, humility, other-directedness, receptivity, active and embodied notice-taking – I am not the first to find these qualities in Clare's perceptive acts. Because he is willing to let the gifts of birds and flowers outshine Enlightenment-derived systems of categorization, Clare has been read as a forerunner of contemporary ecopoetics. According to Jonathan Bate's definition of the term, 'ecopoesis knows that things have a life, but it also has to recognize that it can only communicate that knowledge in the form of propositions by using the divided Cartesian language of subject ("we see") and object ("the life of things")'.¹⁴ However, through his lyric practice of detaching the voiced poem from a defined ego, Clare engages a phenomenology of perception that would overcome that subject/object division. He narrates perceptive acts as though we readers could inhabit them.

Some lyrics invite readers to imagine specific speakers more fully than others, but equally, each reader is free, silently or out loud, to voice a poem as though speaking for themselves. It may be easier to imagine oneself, in the flesh, sitting beside a tree like Clare, than 'Revisiting the Banks of the Wye during a Tour, July 13, 1798' like Wordsworth, but what fan of Romantic-period poetry has not, 'with tranquil restoration', recalled some specific place of their own with 'sensations sweet / Felt in the blood, and felt along the heart' (ll. 31, 28–9)? However much the poem may ground the experience described in a particular speaker's subjectivity, or a particular poet's history, readers can still break it free. But compared to other Romantic-period poets, Clare describes perceptive acts in ways that are more easily inhabitable.

What would it mean to direct towards Clare's poems the humility and receptivity he directs to places and other creatures? First, it would inspire readers to accept Clare's invitation to be part of the 'all' that feels forsaken when swallows leave and the 'we' that marvels at ducks feeding. To emulate those manners of perception is to be receptive of his poetry, in the same way that his speakers are receptive to moods or insignificant beauties. This is not the same as treating his poems didactically, as though they offered a proposition we must decide to accept. Rather, it is a matter of reading his lyrics in one's own 'voicing'. It is to take seriously the idea that a lyric poem might make 'claims about our world' and not just claims about the situation of a poem's speaker. Second, it would mean being willing to read a poem, think about it, and read it again. If nightingale's eggs call for more than one interpretation, surely poems do too. A humble regard for poetry, like a humble regard for anything beautiful one finds, requires patient investigation of the details and trying out different ways to describe one's experience. That includes the physical experience that reading a poem aloud can be. Clare's speakers engage the world with their bodies. Why should we be more self-conscious reading poetry aloud than wading through thorns or climbing trees? Third, simply, we could allow our attention to be directed towards smaller beauties that might otherwise have been passed over and appreciate their irreplaceability. And finally, perceiving Clare's poems as he bids us perceive his beloved places and creatures would mean letting them bloom beyond expectations. Every reading, like every weed, will be different. Prejudice about his class, his rurality, and his temporal distance from today's readers have, over the years, led some scholars to read his life story as a substitute for rather than a complement to attentive formal analysis. But Clare's work rewards close attention and merits reading with 'taste and love' ('Sighing for Retirement', l. 27).

Notes

1. Sarah Guyer, *Reading with John Clare: Biopoetics, Sovereignty, Romanticism* (New York: Fordham University Press, 2015), p. 98.
2. For an analysis of Clare's engagement with Gray's 'Elegy', see Mina Gorji, *John Clare and the Place of Poetry* (Liverpool: Liverpool University Press, 2009), pp. 47–9.

3. David Tagnani, 'Identity, Anthropocentrism, and Ecocentrism in John Clare's "To an Insignificant Flower"', *The Explicator*, 72.1 (2014), 34–7 (p. 36).
4. William Wordsworth, 'Preface to Lyrical Ballads (1802)', in *The Major Works*, ed. Stephen Gill (Oxford: Oxford University Press, 2008), p. 611.
5. John Goodridge, A First-Line Index to the Poetry of John Clare, https://sites.google.com/site/johnclareresourcepage/first-line-index-to-clares-poetry.
6. Erica McAlpine, 'Keeping Nature at Bay: John Clare's Poetry of Wonder', *Studies in Romanticism*, 50.1 (2011), 79–104 (p. 95).
7. *John Clare: Major Works*, ed. Eric Robinson and David Powell (Oxford: Oxford University Press, 1984), p. 241.
8. William Wordsworth, 'Lines Composed a Few Miles above Tintern Abbey, On Revisiting the Banks of the Wye during a Tour, July 13, 1798', in *Major Works*, pp. 131–5 (ll. 66–7).
9. Deidre Shauna Lynch, 'Introduction' to *Norton Anthology of English Literature: The Romantic Period* (New York: Norton, 2018), pp. 3–27 (p. 13).
10. Jonathan Culler, 'Extending the Theory of the Lyric', *Diacritics* 45.4 (2017), 116–29 (p. 10).
11. *Critical Heritage*, p. 55; *Critical Heritage*, p. 335; Seamus Heaney, 'John Clare: A Bi-centenary Lecture', in Hugh Haughton, Adam Phillips, and Geoffrey Summerfield, eds., *John Clare in Context* (Cambridge: Cambridge University Press, 1994), pp. 130–47 (p. 134).
12. *John Clare: Major Works*, pp. 238–40.
13. See Eric Robinson and David Powell, 'Glossary', in *John Clare: Major Works*, pp. 506–16 (p. 512).
14. Jonathan Bate, *The Song of the Earth* (London: Picador, 2000), p. 149.

4

ROSS WILSON

Clare and the Sublime

Clare's early poem 'Helpstone' (1809–19, pub. 1835) is addressed to his native village. At first sight, it hardly suggests that the sublime will be a productive framework through which to consider the distinctive concerns and features of Clare's work:

> Hail humble Helpstone where thy valies spread
> And thy mean village lifts its lowly head
> Unknown to grandeur and unknown to fame
> No minstrel boasting to advance thy name
> Unletterd spot unheard in poets song
> Where bustling labour drives the hours along (EP I 156)

Valleys rather than mountains; a village rather than Troy, Rome, Hell, or any of the other towering urban achievements of human (or superhuman) ingenuity and design; 'bustling labour' merely getting through the day, instead of outstanding acts of heroism causing a breach in time itself; 'Unknown to grandeur and unknown to fame': little wonder no minstrel had thought to announce the name of Helpston to the world. Of course, Clare himself is now that minstrel, though he explicitly eschews the epic mode apparently evoked by that initial 'Hail', preferring instead the lyric mode for the simpler, quieter virtues of his native environment. As Clare puts it at the end of 'Recollections after a Ramble' (1819–20), another early poem:

> Rurality I dearly love thee
> Simple as thy numbers run
> Epics song may soar above thee
> Still thy sweetness yields to none
> Cots to sing and woods and vales
> Tho its all thy reed can do
> These with nature shall prevail
> When epics war harps broke in two (EP II 196)

Britain's involvement in the Napoleonic Wars (it is worth recalling that Clare briefly served, albeit without distinction or incident, in the Eastern Regiment of the Northampton Militia)[1] is doubtless in the background here, but more generally Clare's emphasis on 'Cots' (cottages), 'woods and vales', and on the simplicity and 'sweetness' of the 'numbers' in which 'Rurality' is celebrated, contrasts with the distinctly elevated tone and register of epic ('Epics song may *soar above* thee').

Clare's affinity for the low and level, hospitably expressed in the lyric, contrasts with the elevated and exalted, which seemingly finds its generic home in epic. Four of the five definitions for 'SUBLIME, adj.' given in Samuel Johnson's *A Dictionary of the English Language* (1755), for instance, contain the words 'high', 'exalted', or 'elevated' (the fifth definition is 'haughty; proud'). And, as Herbert F. Tucker has remarked, 'epic's traffic with the sublime is a long story', one that receives significant expression in Edmund Burke's *A Philosophical Enquiry into the Origin of our Ideas of the Sublime and Beautiful* (1757), which was a major contribution to the anglophone theorization of the sublime.[2]

But none of this is to say, Clare's early strictures on epic notwithstanding, that Clare was averse to the sublime. Indeed, the focus of this chapter is on the repeated appearances of the sublime in Clare's verse – not least his repeated deployment of the word itself – and the ambivalent relationship his understanding and practice of the sublime has to eighteenth-century and Romantic aesthetic discourse. Clare certainly often expressed a sceptical, sometimes troubled relationship to what had become the standard images and markers of the sublime by the time he was writing. In addition to the two early poems I quoted above, we can discern this scepticism and ambivalence in Clare's response to the request from his publisher, John Taylor, for commentary on the beautiful and the sublime in a range of contemporary poets. Clare's reaction to Taylor's request is worth quoting at length:

> I so seldom see other peoples judgments who are considered not only men of taste but men of unerring critisism coinciding with mine that I feel I am only an individual indulging in an erroneous fancy   what other people often bring forward as specimens of the sublime appear to me nothing more then a series of bomb bursting images taggd together by big sounding words to represent shadows or creations of the terrible but having no more effect on the mind as terrible then the unmeaning rant of a maniac – & what many consider beautiful is nothing more to me then an affected string of unnatural images cloathed in the pomp of illused words sounding musical to the ear & nothing but empty sound to the sense   (*Letters*, p. 539)[3]

Clare opposes his conception of the sublime (though what that conception *is*, he does not yet say here) to that, as he mordantly puts it, of 'men of unerring critisism'. It is tempting to detect something of the heroic solitude often associated with the sublime itself in Clare's own opposition to the crowd of fashionable critics whose standard view he rejects. But the main point to emphasize here is that Clare is rejecting what he casts as the assumption that the merely loud and large ('bomb bursting images taggd together by big sounding words') will as it were mechanically yield the sublime. Given his own lifelong struggles with mental health, there is, of course, a pathos in Clare's dismissal of attempts to represent 'the terrible' (the central criterion of the sublime according to Burke) that turn out only to have as much 'effect on the mind as terrible then the unmeaning rant of a maniac' – and it might be thought that 'the unmeaning rant of a maniac' could indeed affect the mind as 'terrible' and hence sublime.

This hint in Clare's account that it is not quite so easy to disentangle the sublime from false or inadequate versions of it is, in fact, also registered in his scorn for writings 'taggd together by big sounding words', in his similar comments on the beautiful where he excoriates 'an affected string of unnatural images', and in the draft of a letter to Taylor when Clare remarks that 'I could give this sheet full of specimens of bombastic fancy that critics are daily stringing as pearls of sublimity' (*Letters*, p. 541). In the account of the sublime he presents in his *Critique of Judgement* (1790), Immanuel Kant distinguishes between two versions or sources of the sublime: the dynamic sublime and the mathematical sublime. As the name of the former suggests, the dynamic sublime is brought about by the contemplation of power or might (*dunamis* in Greek) – whether that be the power of nature as manifest in storms, waterfalls, and so forth, or, as long as one is conscious of 'having a disposition that is upright and acceptable to God', of God.[4] The mathematical sublime is instead produced when the mind demands the presentation of 'a progressively numerical series' as a coherent whole – something that it is impossible to do because while we can continue to apprehend more and more individual units in a series ad infinitum, there are limits to our power of comprehension, such that, 'as much, then, is lost at one end [of a series] as is gained at the other, and for comprehension we get a maximum which the imagination cannot exceed' (p. 82). The sublime results, for Kant, not because our mental operations have failed (that would be merely horrible (p. 76)), but because it is our own minds that issue the demand that we should comprehend something immeasurably large in the first place. The point it is worth making here, in connection with Clare's repeated recourse to the figure of a sequence of things that have been (to borrow his terms) tagged or strung together, is that the sublime often seems to involve as one of its conditions the confrontation with, for example, a seemingly endless sequence that the mind struggles to comprehend. Readers of Kant, especially those focusing on his theory of the sublime in the late twentieth century, have often failed to recognize his distinction between the merely horrible feeling arising from the inability to wrestle a series of intuitions into unity, on the one hand, and the feeling of the sublime proper, which arises from the awareness that it is our own mind that is capable of issuing this demand in the first place, on the other. But that failure is nevertheless not a simple error of interpretation: it is often difficult to distinguish the sublime from the simply over-awing, the terrifying, the horrible. As we shall see at the conclusion of this chapter, something akin to the difficulty of this distinction is important to Clare's late, dark sublime.

But it is high time now to give a brief overview of how the sublime came to be understood in the years before Clare wrote. I touched above on the English linguistic record in Samuel Johnson's entry for 'sublime' in his *Dictionary*; and we have briefly examined one aspect of Kant's complex theorization (almost certainly unknown to Clare) of the sublime at the end of the eighteenth century. Yet a slightly more concerted exploration of how the sublime was understood, what was considered essential to its production, and its association, in particular, with poetry will enable us to examine in more detail Clare's own relationship to (and significant departures from) this discourse. The rediscovery and translation of the ancient Greek text *Peri Hypsous*, usually translated as *On the Sublime,* by 'Longinus' (whose name appears in scare quotes because we now know that he was not the author of *Peri Hypsous*) at the end of the seventeenth century instigated a renewed effort throughout the eighteenth to theorize both the achievement of an elevated or lofty style in writing (chiefly poetry) and, increasingly as the century wore on, the experience of the awesome and magnificent in nature. A good insight into the assumptions about humanity that excited interest in the sublime can be gleaned from William Smith's translation of 'Longinus' (1743), when he declares that nature 'implanted in [man's] soul an invincible love of grandeur, and a constant emulation of whatever seems to approach nearer to divinity than himself'.[5] Writing in 1721, Thomas Reresby had anticipated Smith's emphasis on the emulation of the divine, ascribing it explicitly to poetry:

> The sublime then, in my opinion, consists in a complete and lively imitation of nature, or of that which surpasses nature. I suppose, that a bare imitation of nature constitutes the sublime of orators; and the imitation of what is above nature, the sublime of poets. For it will not be disputed, I believe, that there goes into the composition of poetry, something supernatural and divine.[6]

Perhaps the most concerted alliance between poetry and sublimity, however, is to be found in the celebration of John Milton in Burke's widely influential *Philosophical Enquiry* (1757). Milton was, indeed, a foundational influence on Clare, and he went so far as to state that 'the opening and end of "Paradise Lost" I consider sublime and just as the beginning and end of an Epic Poem should be', underlining thereby the affinity between the sublime and epic (*JCBH*, p. 178). In his *Enquiry*, Burke argued that 'terror is in all cases whatsoever, either more openly or latently the ruling principle of the sublime'.[7] And obscurity, in turn, is necessary to making anything seem terrible because, according to Burke, when we can see something clearly, we have the measure of it, and it thus mostly ceases to terrify us. The master of the kind of 'judicious obscurity' necessary to the production of the sublime is Milton, and Burke's account of the sublime is full of references to him: Milton's description of Death in the second book of *Paradise Lost* ('If shape it might be called that shape had none') is 'dark, uncertain, confused, terrible, and sublime to the last degree'; in his description of Satan ('He above the rest / In shape and gesture proudly eminent / Stood like a tower'), the 'mind is hurried out of itself, by a croud of great and confused images; which affect because they are crouded and confused'; and so on (pp. 55; 57).[8]

Many of these features of the eighteenth-century theorization of the sublime – the valorization of obscurity and confusion; the faith that poetry is divine – can be detected in Clare's Romantic forebears and contemporaries. But perhaps most notable in the writing of, for example, Wordsworth, Coleridge, and Shelley is an emphasis on nature in its most powerful and colossal manifestations as either itself inspiring the sublime or betokening a power experienced as sublime. There are of course native examples of the sublime in English Romantic poetry – the famous boat-stealing episode in Wordsworth's *Prelude* would be one – but it is fair to say that for these writers the Alps became something of a touchstone for the sublime. Elsewhere in *The Prelude*, Wordsworth's crossing of the Alps is the occasion for another celebrated experience of the sublime, and his friend Coleridge's poem written in the vale of Chamonix contemplates Mont Blanc as an index of the might of the divine creator. Shelley's 'Mont Blanc' responds to Coleridge's poem written in the same location, though to markedly different effect.[9] In the guestbook of an inn in the Alps, Shelley had signed himself (in Greek) 'atheist, democrat, and lover of humanity', and his experience of Mont Blanc results in the contemplation of an inscrutable but distinctly material power, in contrast to Coleridge's God, that is none the less sublime for that. Although in the three instances of Wordsworth, Coleridge, and Shelley, the so-called Romantic sublime certainly has a great deal in common, not least its affinity for mountain scenery, it cannot ultimately be said that it tends to affirm a commonly held view of the universe or of humanity's place within it. There is a divide as wide as any Alpine crevasse between Coleridge's Christianity (however heterodox it initially was) and Shelley's materialism.

A number of points in this necessarily brisk overview of the theorization of the sublime in Britain, from the reception of the rediscovery of 'Longinus' to Romantic contemplation of the Alps, are worth underlining here. The sublime is produced by magnitude and power; it is associated, especially in poetry, with the human striving towards the superhuman, whether that be a divine or physical force; the obscure, dark, and confused are essential to it. It hardly needs stating here that none of these features seem much in evidence in Clare's verse. Were we to attempt to align Clare's verse in general with one of the categories of eighteenth- and early nineteenth-century aesthetic discourse, then the picturesque might appear more promising. As Ashfield and De Bolla have cogently argued, the discourse of the picturesque arose not only in response to changing attitudes to landscape 'but also to what it perceived as the bankruptcy of a specific form of the analysis of the sublime' – an analysis in which it was claimed that certain features (grandeur, elevation) necessarily produced the feeling of the sublime and which, more important still in the context of thinking about Clare's relationship with the land, 'was indifferent to the needs of both the land and its users, to the productive capacity of the land to yield sustenance or organise social relations: it was content for the land to look like a picture'.[10] Ashfield and De Bolla go on to argue that the picturesque 'enjoyed the friction caused between the real and the imaginary and sought to occupy the terrain between them' and 'softens the focus in its domestication of the landscape'. It is not hard to find affinities with something like the picturesque understood along these lines in Clare's verse. 'The yellowhammer like a tasteful guest', writes Clare in 'Shadows of Taste' (1830), 'Neath picturesque green molehills makes a nest / Where oft the shepherd with unlearned ken / Finds strange eggs scribbled as with ink and pen' (MP III 303–4). Both yellowhammer and mole are domesticating (even if not domesticated) creatures here, the molehill evidence of the mole's underground habitation and the yellowhammer's nest taking harmless advantage of it. Clare is always making molehills out of mountains, and it is notable too that this particular bird could hardly be further from soaring like the sublime eagle, instead building its nest on the ground. The marks on the yellowhammer's eggs and the shepherd's imagination of them as writing are even an instance of the relation 'between the real and the imaginary'.

'Shadows of Taste' clearly does embrace the picturesque, and Clare elsewhere describes 'A picture of picturesque joy & delight / Where beauty & harmony be' ('The Heath' (MP IV 578)) and states that 'Old ponds dim shadowed with a broken tree / These are the picturesque of taste to me' ('Pleasant Places' (MP IV 225)). Yet Ashfield and De Bolla's useful account of the picturesque as an oppositional response to the sublime tends to align it with a social formation to which Clare emphatically did not belong. The position of the picturesque in between the real and the imaginary, along with its softening, domesticating focus on landscape, make it sound like a compromise position of the kind typical of the eighteenth century's rising middle class. The picturesque is opposed both to the heroic ethic of the sublime, but also, in fact, to the more intimately involved and embodied perspective of members of the labouring class, who daily experienced (rather than necessarily 'enjoyed') the 'friction' often resulting from the attempt to get the land to yield sustenance and the organization of social relations. The land, for Clare, is in any case not landscape, even of a picturesque kind, and, as should by now be clear, any attempt to wrestle it into established aesthetic categories is met by him with suspicion.[11] Whatever his attitude to the picturesque ultimately is, he certainly, as one critic has persuasively put it, 'subverts the aesthetic categories of the beautiful and the sublime, the latter by replacing the criteria of terror and grandiosity with the criteria of ordinariness and minutiae, the former by assigning beauty to what are commonly regarded as ugly, invasive, and undesirable things such as weeds, wastelands, and decaying tree stumps'.[12]

What 'subverts' in the last quotation means, however, is open to question. Is it that Clare's work evinces distinctive versions of the sublime and beautiful, albeit operating with different criteria (ordinariness instead of terror, for instance), or is it that he simply dispenses with the categories of the sublime and the beautiful altogether? Indeed, all of the foregoing discussion may seem to suggest that Clare's relation to the sublime – and to the whole of aesthetic discourse as it was constituted at the time he was writing – was one of more or less outright rejection. His emphases on the small, the local, and the flat, on the quotidian, and on the land as the supplier of needs and the medium of labour put him at odds with the prevailing characteristics of the sublime both in eighteenth-century aesthetic discourse and in the work of his near-contemporaries such as Wordsworth, Coleridge, and Shelley. We might even instance the fact that Clare's gaze is barely ever upwards but rather downwards – and then from the low eminence of his own stature[13] – where it is met, not by humans striving towards the divine, but by creatures like the roach ('Here silent from its watery bed, / To hail its coming, leaps the roach' ('Last of March, Written at Lolham Brigs', EP II 473)) or the ubiquitous mole erupting through the surfaces of their own environments.

But before we altogether discount any relation between Clare and the sublime (let alone other aesthetic categories, such as the beautiful and the picturesque), we need to attend to the wide range of evocations of the sublime throughout Clare's career. Indeed, in 'Shadows of Taste', the poem whose first detailed description is of the yellowhammer's nest 'Neath picturesque green molehills' discussed previously, Clare goes on to declare his insistence on the observation of nature in terms of the sublime itself: 'Thus truth to nature as the true sublime / Stands a mount atlas overpeering time' (MP III 306). Expanding on the implication that Clare radically revises, rather than simply rejects, the sublime, Richard M. Ness has emphasized that in these lines Clare 'draws our attention to different kinds of immensity and awe, such as the immeasurable duration of nature and the enormous quantity of its minute particulars'.[14] In fact, we can already see in 'Helpstone', the poem with which I opened this chapter, the first inklings in Clare's work of a version of the sublime attuned not to grandeur in its usual habitations (mountains, ravines) but rather in the world Clare so intimately knew. The poem's second stanza turns, as Clare's verse often does, to birds – but this turn introduces a different note to the poem, one in which striving and elevation are in fact central. Clare is watching the birds search for food and 'better life' (a phrase he puts in scare quotes) in inhospitable conditions:

> First on the ground each fairy dream pursue
> Tho sought in vain – yet bent on higher view
> Still chirp and hope and wipe each glossy bill
> Nor undiscourag'd nor disheartn'd still
> ...
> Till warm'd at once the vain deluded flies
> And twitatwit their visions as they rise
> Visions like mine that vanish as they flye   (EP I 157–8)

Unlike the picturesque ground-nesting yellowhammer, the birds here are 'bent on higher view', striving for something that is not immediately available to them, impelled by 'visions' that fit them to serve as an analogue for the poet, who is likewise one of the 'vain deluded' whose visions 'vanish as they flye'. The stanza continues with a maudlin shrinking of perspective as the poet, like the birds, finds 'Each prospect lessen and each hope decay' (EP I 158). The point to emphasize here is that even in this early poem, which I began this chapter by suggesting was emblematic of those aspects of Clare's poetry that make it difficult to consider in terms of the sublime, there are elements that do come much closer to an interest in elevation, striving, a 'higher view'.

There are many similar instances with an affinity for the established characteristics of the sublime throughout Clare's early poetry. The sonnet 'A Scene' (pub. 1835), for example, ends with an evocation of pleasure in visual profusion that is in excess of language's powers of description (it is worth recalling here the outline of Kant's mathematical sublime above): 'All these with hundreds more far off & near / Approach my sight – & please to such excess / That Language fails the pleasure to express' (EP 1 413). The roughly contemporary 'To a Winter Scene', another sonnet, is even more compulsively drawn to the natural grandeur and violence associated with the sublime, as well as the singular blend of pleasure and pain that Burke, for instance, took to be characteristic of the feeling of sublimity (and called 'delight'):[15]

> Hail scenes of Desolation and despair
> Keen Winters over bearing sport and scorn
> Torn by his Rage in ruins as you are
> To me more pleasing than a summers morn
> Your shatter'd scenes appear – despoild and bare
> Stript of your clothing naked and forlorn
> – Yes Winters havoc wretched as you shine
> Dismal to others as your fate may seem
> Your fate is pleasing to this heart of mine
> Your wildest horrors I the most esteem. –
> The ice-bound floods that still with rigour freeze
> The snow clothd valley and the naked tree
> These sympathising scenes my heart can please
> Distress is theirs – and they resemble me   (EP 1 417)

It is, in fact, a disturbing poem. Though the 'ice-bound floods that still with rigour freeze' may evoke Caspar David Friedrich's famous painting of 'The Sea of Ice', the tone of 'To a Winter Scene' is more violent – aggressive, even – than Friedrich's contemplative, serene depiction. At the beginning of the eighteenth century, John Dennis, apparently summarizing 'Longinus', had notoriously written that the sublime in writing 'commits a pleasing rape upon the very soul of the reader';[16] here, the poet delights in winter's ravishing of the land, which is depicted in unmistakably sexualized terms ('despoild and bare / Stript of your clothing naked and forlorn'). This sense of the sexualized violence of the scene is hardly alleviated by the masochistic insistence that the speaker's esteem for winter's 'wildest horrors' arises from the resemblance between the scenes they produce and his own 'heart'. The poem is relentlessly excessive – in the over-identification of speaker and scene, in the violence of its imagery, even in the threefold rhyme (the only thrice-repeated rhyme in the poem) on 'scorn', 'morn', 'forlorn', itself yet further amplified by the excessive conjunction of 'scorn / Torn' across the second and third lines.

Clare and the Sublime

There are, then, several instances of a version of the sublime that is distinct to Clare's own poetic vision. Clare reflects on his early poetic formation in his 'The Progress of Rhyme' (1824–32), where he casts the sublime as crucial to his desire to write in the first place. The venues of Clare's writing are significant here:

> & each old leaning shielding tree
> Where princely palaces to me
> Where I would sit me down & chime
> My unheard rhapsodies to rhyme
> All I beheld of grand – with time
> Grew up to beautifuls sublime
> The arching groves of ancient Limes
> That into roofs like churches climb
> Grain intertwisting into grain
> That stops the sun & stops the rain
> & spreads a gloom that never smiles
> Like ancient halls & minster aisles
> While all without a beautious screen
> Of summers luscious leaves is seen   (MP III 497–8)

Though it initially seems that the wood groves serve as a kind of umbrella, keeping the elements off Clare so he can write, there is more to Clare's chosen writing venue than that. Expanding on his insistence that obscurity is essential to the propagation of the sublime, Burke remarked that 'despotic governments' (it is perhaps worth noting here 'princely palaces' in the lines above) 'keep their chief hidden as much as may be from the public eye', going on to observe that 'the druids performed all their ceremonies in the bosom of the darkest woods, and in the shade of the oldest and most spreading oaks'.[17] It might be far-fetched to suggest that Clare is seeking continuity with Britain's ancient pre-Christian culture by taking to groves not, here, of oaks, but of 'ancient Limes'. But the conduciveness of the 'arching groves' to his composition of 'song sublime' is impossible to miss and is, indeed, reinforced by the implicit contrast of the 'gloom that never smiles' within the grove, on the one hand, with the 'beautious screen / Of summers luscious leaves' without, on the other. It is immediately after his evocation of druidic ceremonial practices that Burke goes on to hymn Milton's powers as a poet of 'gloomy pomp',[18] and we can see in Clare's description of the haunts of his early verse-writing a strong affinity with just this Miltonic quality.

The Miltonic affinity for darkness to which Clare gives expression in his account of his own poetic formation has an important resonance for his later poetry. In an influential essay, Timothy Morton has responded to the celebration of Clare as a nature poet by elaborating instead what he has called his 'dark ecology' – an ecological perspective attuned to the destruction of nature and to the frequent experience of the world as inhospitable to humanity.[19] In turning, in conclusion, to Clare's later poetry, we might analogously speak of a dark sublime emerging in Clare's work. Sarah Houghton has revealingly excavated a sublime mode in Clare's work that is 'wholly without the terror of Burke's account' and that appears as 'a welcome exhilaration'.[20] But in Clare's late work, we begin to witness the return, if not of terror, then of a sublime characterized by the shrinking of prospects and hopes, by the extinction, rather than the excessiveness, of natural phenomena. In a poem of early 1845, for instance, Clare wrote of 'Old times forgetfull memories of the past', which 'the eternal blast / Oblivion leaves the earth in which they rot / Darkness in which the very lights forgot' (LP I 211). Perhaps Clare's most characteristic expression of the sublime of oblivion, however, is his sonnet with the Burkean title 'Obscurity' (?1832), in which Clare imagines the condemnation to oblivion of an old tree (the titular word 'obscurity', incidentally, nowhere appears in the poem itself, though 'oblivion' occurs twice). The tree's 'history' is, 'to a thinking mind', 'Blank and recordless' (MP IV 256). A fly or a sheep, the poem concludes, 'can know with time / Almost as much of thy blank past as I / Thus blank oblivion reigns as earth's sublime'.[21] We have come a long way here from the eulogy to 'meads and brooks and forests [which] asking lie / Lasting as truth and the eternal sky / Thus truth to nature as the true sublime / Stands a mount atlas overpeering time' in 'Shadows of Taste' (MP III 306) – though perhaps the fact that meads and brooks and forests 'lie', one of the favourite puns of the poets, already intimates that all is not well under the eternal sky.[22]

In 'Obscurity', Clare draws an equivalence between a 'thinking mind' and the minds of ewe and fly, which, in what initially seems an unusually anthropocentric move for him, do not think, or which are not even minds at all. The apparent anthropocentrism is of course tempered by the fact that neither thinking mind, nor ewe, nor fly can have any knowledge of the old tree's history. Kant had argued at the end of the eighteenth century that the feeling of the sublime is not so much a response to natural objects but rather a kind of implicit recognition of the supersensible powers of the human mind. 'Obscurity' reduces the capacities of the human mind to those of a ewe or a fly. Thus 'blank oblivion' becomes not only 'earth's sublime' but also, in a parodic inversion of Kant's sublime and its valorization of the powers of the human mind, the characteristic of human thought and memory too.

Given the apparent turn to oblivion of both earth and mind in this late poem, and hence something like the inversion of the sublime's assumption (at least in its Kantian version) of the power and endurance of the mind, it seems fitting, in conclusion, to turn to the apparently contrasting vision of the sublime advanced in Clare's late poems, 'I Am' and 'Sonnet: "I am"' (1846). If the sublime arises with the mind's recognition of its own powers to overcome threats to it, then we might suggest that the context of the asylum, in which Clare was confined when he wrote these poems, is significant to their affirmation of selfhood and attendant evocation of the sublime. Likewise, Michael Nicholson has persuasively read a significant class dimension in the lines 'I was a being created in the race / Of men disdaining bounds of place and time: – / A spirit that could travel o'er the space / Of earth and heaven, – like a thought sublime' (LP 1 398), commenting that, 'in defiance against the idea that he – as a working-class man – can be settled in a specific place ... Clare's poetic voice asserts a working-class "sublime" that is occasioned by free "thought" rather than expensive excursions to imposing landscapes.'[23] Though Nicholson does not remark it, Clare's insistence on the freedom of his mind to determine its own place was anticipated by another figure who rejected the place assigned him in a repressive hierarchy, namely, Milton's Satan: 'The mind is its own place, and in itself / Can make a heaven of hell, a hell of heaven. / What matter where, if I be still the same ...?' (*Paradise Lost*, 1. 255–6). This is a motif that recurs, in fact, at a number of places in Clare's late poetry, such as 'Written in a Thunderstorm July 15th 1841', his long discursive poem that treats the world as delusory and life as a dream, and in which he asserts 'But hell is heaven, could I cease to mourn' (LP 1 50). The first of the three six-line stanzas that comprise the lyric 'I Am' opens in terms familiar from 'Obscurity' and Clare's other poems of oblivion yet ends with a reassertion of the existence of the 'I', which in turn gives way to a resurgent statement of the nothingness of the speaker's life: 'And yet I am, and live – like vapours tost / Into the nothingness of scorn and noise' (LP 1 396). Both the long dash (the fifth of eight in this short poem) and the stanza break enact the radical qualification of what initially appears to be an affirmation of existence and life: I am, and live – but, like vapours, in nothingness, which is to say, not at all. In a virtuoso reading of this poem, Sara Guyer has argued that its apparent resolution in the final stanza's vision of 'scenes, where man hath never trod' where the speaker can rest 'Untroubling, and untroubled where I lie, / The grass below – above the vaulted sky' (LP 1 397) is fraught with interpretative difficulty.[24] The poem's 'I' does not stand upright, fronting the world, but is instead prone and sleeping, a state figured in the very appearance on the page of the poem's final long dash – the 'I' not only fallen over, as Guyer wittily remarks, but also rendered non-verbal, a merely graphic mark. The conclusion of the poem, 'for all its thematic and textual resolution, nevertheless repeats the chaos and disturbance of the poem's first two stanzas. In this sense', Guyer notes, 'what appears to be the overcoming of pain through the imagination (i.e., in an act of mind) turns out rather to repeat and reveal the failure to recognize the self.'[25] We have seen throughout this chapter Clare challenge the accepted version of the sublime, attesting to, as it were, the elevation and exaltation of the low and the local over the standard images of sublimity. Here, in one of Clare's most celebrated and apparently affirmative poems, his sublime emerges as one in which even the upright human self is cast as troubled, ultimately enjoying no peace wrested from adversity but instead reposing in an ambivalent position where the mind is condemned to continue its struggle to make a heaven of hell.

Notes

1. See Jonathan Bate, *John Clare: A Biography* (London: Picador, 2003), pp. 77–9 for details.
2. Herbert F. Tucker, *Epic: Britain's Heroic Muse 1790–1910* (Oxford: Oxford University Press, 2008), p. 42.
3. For further commentary on this important passage, see Mark Storey, 'Clare and the Critics', in John Goodridge and Simon Kövesi, eds., *John Clare: New Approaches* (Helpston: John Clare Society, 1994), pp. 28–50 (p. 33); Sarah Houghton, '"Enkindling ecstacy": The Sublime Vision of John Clare', *Romanticism*, 9 (2003), 176–95 (pp. 178–9); and Richard M. Ness, 'Song of Experience: John Clare's Empirical Taste', *John Clare Society Journal*, 38 (2019), 13–31 (p. 18).
4. Immanuel Kant, *Critique of Judgement*, trans. James Creed Meredith, rev. Nicholas Walker (Oxford: Oxford University Press, 2007), p. 94.
5. William Smith, *Dionysus Longinus on the Sublime* (1743), in Andrew Ashfield and Peter de Bolla, eds., *The Sublime: A Reader in British Eighteenth-Century Aesthetic Theory* (Cambridge: Cambridge University Press, 1996), pp. 22–9 (p. 28).
6. Thomas Reresby, *A Miscellany of Ingenious Thoughts and Reflections* (1721), in *The Sublime*, pp. 43–4.
7. Edmund Burke, *A Philosophical Enquiry into the Origin of Our Ideas of the Sublime and Beautiful*, ed. Adam Phillips (Oxford University Press, 1998), p. 54.
8. *Paradise Lost* quoted by book- and line-number from the second ed. by Alastair Fowler (Harlow: Longman, 1997).
9. See Wordsworth, *The Prelude: The Four Texts (1798, 1799, 1805, 1850)*, ed. Jonathan Wordsworth (London: Penguin, 1995), 1805 text, Book I, ll. 371–427 (boat-stealing) and Book VI, ll. 398–548 (crossing the Alps); Coleridge, 'Hymn Before Sun-rise, In the Vale of Chamouni' (1802), in *The Complete Poems*, ed. William Keach (London: Penguin, 1997; repr. 2004), pp. 323–5; Shelley, 'Mont Blanc' (1816), in *Shelley's Poetry and Prose*, ed. Donald H. Reiman and Neil Fraistat (New York: Norton, 2002), pp. 96–101.
10. Ashfield and De Bolla, 'Introduction' to *The Sublime*, p. 15.

11. This is the argument of John Barrell's seminal *The Idea of Landscape and the Sense of Place, 1730–1840: An Approach to the Poetry of John Clare* (Cambridge: Cambridge University Press, 1972). On Clare and the picturesque, see, for instance, Mark Storey, *The Poetry of John Clare: A Critical Introduction* (London: Macmillan, 1974), p. 11.
12. Ness, 'Song of Experience', pp. 13–14.
13. Bate, *John Clare: A Biography*, p. 3.
14. Ness, 'Song of Experience', p. 19.
15. Burke, Philosophical Enquiry, pp. 122–3.
16. Dennis, *The Grounds of Criticism in Poetry* (1704), in *The Sublime*, p. 37.
17. Burke, Philosophical Enquiry, pp. 54–5.
18. Burke, Philosophical Enquiry, p. 55.
19. Timothy Morton, 'John Clare's Dark Ecology', *Studies in Romanticism*, 47 (2008), 179–93.
20. Houghton, 'Enkindling ecstacy', pp. 179, 194n10.
21. For a somewhat alternative reading of this poem, see Ross Wilson, 'Clare's Indistinct Array', *Romanticism*, 17 (2011), 148–59.
22. I am drawing here on Christopher Ricks, 'Lies', in *The Force of Poetry* (Oxford: Oxford University Press, 1984; repr. 2002), pp. 369–91.
23. Michael Nicholson, 'The Itinerant "I": John Clare's Lyric Defiance', *English Literary History*, 82 (2015), 637–69 (p. 653).
24. Sara Guyer, *Reading with John Clare: Biopolitics, Sovereignty, Romanticism* (New York: Fordham University Press, 2015), pp. 53–5.
25. Guyer, *Reading with John Clare*, p. 55.

PART II

Clare the Naturalist

5

JAMES CASTELL

Clare and Animals

In the nineteenth century, contemporary reviewers of John Clare's poetry recognized his capacity to observe the 'habits' of 'plants, insects and animals with the eye of a naturalist' as well as a poet (*Critical Heritage*, p. 69; p. 98). In the early twentieth century, as part of a revival in critical interest, John Middleton Murry wrote that Clare was 'a true nature-poet' with an 'intimate and self-forgetful knowledge of the ways of birds and beasts and flowers' which 'rises like the scent of a hay-field from every page' (*Critical Heritage*, p. 330). Before the formation of animal studies as a distinct sub-discipline, readers did not always distinguish between Clare's eye for nature more broadly and the specific role of animals in his poetry. Recent work, however, often has a more singular focus on nonhuman creatures. In our own century, for example, Onno Oerlemans claims that no 'poet of the romantic period paid more attention to animals' and that Clare 'is the first great animal poet – a poet for whom animals, animality, and the diversity of species were central themes'.[1] Two of the most widely available selected editions of Clare's poetry in recent years include sections dedicated to birds specifically and to animals in general.[2] Over the past three decades, Clare's writing has become central to a broader critical interest in the role of animals in literature, as well as to the related emergence of ecocriticism as a dominant force both in the humanities generally and in Romantic studies in particular. From his earliest published pieces in *Poems Descriptive of Rural Life and Scenery* (1820) to the final poems transcribed from manuscripts in Northampton Asylum, Clare's poetry is packed with animal life.

In the middle of this biographical span, two sonnets are beautifully representative of the range of animals in Clare's poetry, as well as some of his preoccupations with nonhuman creatures. The first sonnet, written in 1830, is titled 'Summer Evening':

> The frog half fearful jumps accross the path
> & little mouse that leaves its hole at eve

> Nimbles with timid dread beneath the swath
> My rustling steps awhile their joys decieve
> Till past – & then the cricket sings more strong
> & grasshoppers in merry moods still wear
> The short night weary with its fretting song
> Up from behind the molehill jumps the hare
> Cheat of its chosen bed – & from the bank
> The yellowhammer flutters in short fears
> From off its nest hid in the grasses rank
> & drops again when no more noise it hears
> Thus natures human link & endless thrall
> Proud man still seems the enemy of all   (MP IV 147)

At the beginning of the poem, Clare describes a scene of quiet disturbance as a 'frog half fearful jumps accross the path' and a 'little mouse ... / Nimbles with timid dread beneath the swath'. Clare is unusually precise in charting animal behaviour through movement, and the verb 'nimble' is one of Clare's favourite words for describing the movement of small creatures: it also appears in a much more celebrated and whimsical animal poem, 'Little Trotty Wagtail' (LP II 705). In 'Summer Evening', both animals are troubled into motion by the 'rustling steps' of a human figure, the first-person speaker who is barely present in the poem and implied only by a single possessive adjective ('my') which is attached to the disruptive sound. As the speaker passes on, the poem's animals return to a less disturbed state: the songs of the cricket and the grasshoppers become noisier, the hare emerges from behind a molehill, and the yellowhammer, having fluttered off its nest, 'drops again when no more noise it hears'.

In 'Summer Evening' and more broadly across his work, Clare's attention ranges impressively across taxonomies of animal life. In this short poem, he writes about the behaviour of an amphibian, two insects, a bird, a small rodent, another larger mammal, and, implicitly, a further subterranean mammal. These creatures are dynamic, vigorous, and highly responsive to phenomena. Such animal openness to external influence is characteristic of Clare's broader engagement with nonhuman creatures in his work: Clare is remarkably sensitive to the sensitivity of the animal world. Many other writers of the Romantic period record encounters with animals, but few do so with such consistency and commitment to detail. Where the most celebrated examples of the greater Romantic lyric often focus on interchanges between the human mind and the natural world, this sonnet's primary interest does not centre on an exploration of the speaker's psyche. For the first twelve lines of the poem, mankind is reduced to nothing more than an unsettling bipedalism suggested by the sound of contact with dry vegetation.

Instead, and even though the speaker's steps have a defining impact, the focus of 'Summer Evening' is firmly on the nonhuman animals and their consequent actions.

Are these animals simply overreacting to a human figure who turns out not to be threatening? Such a presumption is undercut by three noteworthy features of the poem. First, because the poem focuses on the animals more closely than on the human subject, they are consequently more nuanced beings in their representation: the frog is 'half fearful'; the mouse's 'dread' is 'timid'; the grasshopper is in a 'merry mood' even though the effect of its song on the night is 'fretting'; the hare resists a natural impulse to sleep as it cheats its bed; and the yellowhammer inadvertently reveals its nest through 'short fear'. Secondly, the continuation of their creaturely activities once the human has passed suggests resilience and independence as well as oversensitivity. In fact, the continuity of movement between both the disturbed and undisturbed creatures troubles any absolute sense of the power of human malevolence. Thirdly, the final couplet of the poem, which attempts to draw a more general conclusion on the relationship between human and nonhuman animals, is less easy to interpret than is often recognized, not least because of the disproportionate relationship between the human agency in the poem and the expansive moral of the conclusion.

Stephanie Kuduk Weiner recognizes that the whole couplet feels 'tacked on', which may reflect a compositional history where an earlier version ended at line 12.[3] But critics have most often focused, like James McKusick, on the apparently straightforward statement that 'Proud man still seems the enemy of all'.[4] Even in that last line, however, there is a sense of qualification. The word 'seems' weakens its assertion by introducing a state of exception: the animals are fearful because they are accustomed to 'proud man' seeming the enemy of all, but the implication in this case is that the speaker is no such enemy. Furthermore, the compression of the first line of the closing couplet – 'Thus natures human link & endless thrall' – introduces an important ethical ambiguity. The primary sense of the line is clearly that nature's connection to humanity is one of 'endless thrall', a condition of being permanently overpowered and perhaps even held in captivity. But the proximity of the word 'human' to the 'endless thrall' in the syntax and the misrecognition of human malfeasance by the animals in this poem reveals a coincident situation which places the human figure into a state of bondage. Against his will and regardless of his intention, the speaker is inevitably alienated from the surrounding creatures. The couplet expresses, in other words, a condition of power possessed by mankind, but it also imprisons the ineluctability of human disturbance in a dejected state of corresponding weakness. The 'all' with which the poem ends might signify, therefore, not only nonhuman victims but also man's enmity to himself. In addition to demonstrating the dynamism of Clare's animals, this reasonably well-known but much less frequently discussed poem is resultantly a good example of the significant philosophical ambiguities in Clare's writing about nonhuman creatures. Clare's engagements with nonhuman life are undoubtedly full of carefully observed details, but they are also characterized by hesitations and obscurities that can be easy to overlook.

However the complexities of its final couplet are interpreted, 'Summer Evening' is primarily interested in wild creatures and the incursion of a human figure into a habitat dominated by nonhuman animals. This is a recurrent scenario of animal encounter in Clare's verse, and there are numerous other celebrated examples. But it is by no means the only mode of interaction. A complementary sonnet from around 1832, 'Winter Evening', presents a different set of animals in a different setting and with a different set of consequences:

> The crib stocks fothered – horses suppered up
> & cows in sheds all littered down in straw
> The threshers gone the owls are left to whoop
> The ducks go waddling with distended craw
> Through little hole made in the henroost door
> & geese with idle gabble never oer
> Bate careless hog untill he tumbles down
> Insult provoking spite to noise the more
> While fowl high perched blink with contemptous frown
> On all the noise & bother heard below
> Over the stable ridge in crowds the crow
> With jackdaws intermixed known by their noise
> To the warm woods behind the village go
> & whistling home for bed go weary boys   (MP IV 343–4)

Where 'Summer Evening' focuses on wild animals, 'Winter Evening' is dominated by domesticated creatures, a significant but more critically neglected category in Clare's poetry which includes, for example, a series of elegies written early in his career for 'Dead Dobbin' (EP I 84–90, EP II 407, and EP II 630–6). Those poems awkwardly blend genuine pathos, brutal tragedy, and affectionate mock-heroic, but the atmosphere in 'Winter Evening' is more straightforward. It presents a scene of satisfied completion as evening draws in: the 'crib stocks' and horses are foddered, the cows are tucked away in sheds, and the ducks are characterized by a 'distended craw', having eaten their fill during the day. Although the day's work is over, the sonnet is nevertheless crowded with continued activity. The owls are whooping, the ducks are 'waddling' into the henhouse, the geese's never-ending 'gabble' is annoying the hog, the chickens are blinking in judgement over the scene, and the crows and jackdaws are making a racket above them all. Perhaps because the humans have either left or are leaving the scene, there is little sense of fear in this poem. Instead, the animals are ebullient and vocal. It is appropriate, therefore, that the word 'noise' appears no fewer than three times in its brief fourteen lines, and the poem's language also rings with its own sonic elements, including most noticeably a preponderance of hard consonants.

Unlike 'Summer Evening', there is no first-person speaker in 'Winter Evening', which suits the time of day when rural workers are withdrawing and also lends the language of the poem itself a sense of agency in foregrounding the nonhuman relationships to which the barely individualized 'threshers' and 'weary boys' seem largely oblivious. Without the mediating figure of a speaker, the poem more directly represents a nonhuman dynamism which exists beyond everyday human attention and constructions of time. Where the earlier sonnet 'Summer Evening' focuses on a singular encounter between a human figure and various animals, 'Winter Evening' threads together varied interactions between creatures. This is a poem marked by liveliness, intersecting plurality, and carefully delineated difference. The animals are crossing or have crossed thresholds between interior and exterior spaces. Their activities interact in nuanced ways with each other and create consequent emotions of comfort, satisfaction, mischief, annoyance, contempt, and indifference. As a result, the closing lines about the crows and jackdaws are a fitting conclusion and culmination to the sonnet. They represent an interspecies community: a 'crowd' of two types of closely related animals that are 'intermixed', but which remain nevertheless distinguishable from each other. In this respect, the coexistence of these corvids (and their sharing the same space with numerous domestic animals) in 'Winter Evening' is a good example of how the category of 'animal' in Clare's verse often draws multiple creatures together without deleting the differences between them. Such a situation reflects Clare's engagement with the natural world more broadly. His poetry carefully observes and records natural diversity, pulling it into the same physical and literary spaces and often without a clear sense of hierarchy between different orders of life: the lack of a concluding couplet in this sonnet contributes to this latter effect. Nevertheless, with its commitment to precision and particularity, Clare's poetry also mostly refuses to flatten other modes of being or the relationships between them into broader totalizations. As Joseph Albernaz writes, Clare's work resists 'a facile holism of the everything is connected, everything is everything, everything is whole and one variety'. Instead, he argues (with more than half an eye on contemporary environmental concerns) that 'Clare and his work challenge us to think a thought that we desperately need to think today: interconnectedness and interdependence without totality'.[5]

Nonhuman animals are central to thinking such 'interdependence without totality' in Clare's writing. Crucially, however, humans are potentially as much a part of an interspecies community in this sonnet as they are alienated from it in 'Summer Evening'. As well as in many other parts of Clare's work, there is a greater sense of possible connection between human and nonhuman in 'Winter Evening' where, in the final lines, the sounds of crows and jackdaws heading to 'the warm woods behind the village' are joined by the whistling of 'weary boys' heading 'home for bed'. Even without a first-person speaker, human vocalizations are present in the differentiated soundscape of this poem. Furthermore, because of their prominent positioning at the end of the poem but without being isolated off in their own couplet, they play an important role in the precise distribution of difference across physical and formal space and time. The poem records not only the changing positions of various human and nonhuman animals but also the crossing of numerous thresholds, both spatial and temporal. In this sense, 'Winter Evening' occupies a dynamic versified space between diachronic narrative and synchronic description. Like many of Clare's poems, it balances an attachment to the unique particularities of singular incidents with a powerful sense of the continuousness of temporal progression at both the diurnal and seasonal level. American poet John Ashbery captures the richness of this doubleness beautifully in 'For John Clare' where 'There is so much to be seen everywhere that it's like not getting used to it, only there is so much it never feels new, never any different.'[6] Through its commitment to attending to multiple particulars in their similarities and their distinctness, Clare's verse holds together a variety of different spaces and timescales, as well as the human and nonhuman animals that inhabit them.

I have read these relatively undiscussed sonnets in such detail because, taken together, they provide excellent examples in a compressed form of the extent to which Clare's animals exceed singular statements that might be made about them. From just two of Clare's many short poems on animal life, we have seen that Clare writes about domestic and wild creatures. He writes poems about animal victims and animal agents. He is not only aware of the large and small differences between different species of creature, but his poetry also repeatedly registers an interest in the fact that even the same animals might behave differently in different situations and provoked by different stimuli. Already, we have explored one poem concerned with flight and evasion and another that evokes comfortable shelter. We have seen a relationship of fear-inducing trespass between man and animal, but also an example of human coexistence with a more expansive nonhuman community. Examples of animals range widely across Clare's work, but it is also important to recognize that they range widely in what they do in his poetry. Our juxtaposition of 'Summer Evening' and 'Winter Evening' also highlights a paradox which is at the heart of Clare's broader engagement with animals: on the one hand, he feels a deep attraction to and identification with nonhuman living things, but, on the other, animals can also inspire a profound awareness of human alienation from the natural world.

The paradox is perhaps most tragically expressed in some of the poems written in Northampton Asylum and transcribed from manuscripts by William Knight. For example, in the devastatingly titled 'Written in Prison', the poet proclaims how 'I envy e'en the fly its gleams of joy' and its 'settling in the sun / On the green leaf' (LP II 1023). Numerous poems in this period yearn for an animal's physical proximity to a lost love, as in the opening lines of 'I wish I was a little bird / To sing in my loves ear' (LP II 1017). These are poems of frustrated desire and absent joy, which powerfully emphasize the gap between animal freedom and human captivity. However, in another Knight transcription, the speaker still finds a sense of escape through a skylark's song:

> Although I am in prison
>   Thy song is uprisen
> And singing away to the cloud
>   In the blueness of morn
>   Over fields of green corn
> With a song sweet rural and loud   (LP I 315–16)

In contrast to the other two asylum transcriptions, this poem's creature offers imaginative transport to the confined poet. The song, which is not only 'sweet' and 'loud' but also 'rural', rises into the sky and across the fields, giving the poet the opportunity to recall familiar flowers and even 'Old friends with old faces'. The animal's capacity through song to move the poet in this way induces an additional sense of identification. The skylark is apostrophized as both 'the bard of the spring' and finally as a 'feathered poet':

>   And thou feathered poet
>   I see thee, and know it
> Thou'rt one of the minstrels that cheered me last spring
>   With nature thou'rt blest
>   And green grass round thy nest
> Will keep thee still happy to mount up and sing   (LP I 315–16)

Like James Thomson's *The Seasons* (one of Clare's favourite works), Clare's poetry often uses animals to register the rhythms of rural life across the course of a day, a season, a year, or even longer timescales.⁷ This is especially true in a long poem such as *The Shepherd's Calendar* which, as well as numerous descriptions of animal behaviours, has a clear interest in cyclical patterns of repetition and change.⁸ But this skylark poem transposes such concerns into a more personal and lyric mode through an animal encounter of doubled recognition.

First, the speaker identifies an individual among the 'minstrels that cheered me last spring'. This is not any old skylark or the mere idea of a skylark ('Blithe spirit! / Bird thou never wert', as Percy Bysshe Shelley's more famous skylark puts it to very different purposes).⁹ It is a particular skylark from a group of skylarks that have had a specific affective impact on the poet in the past. Secondly, the fact that this first act of recognition occurs through song leads the speaker to a further insight: a redoubled identification between bird and poet. Comparisons between songbirds and poets are, of course, one of the most common tropes of Romantic lyric. Clare himself writes several skylark poems throughout his life with similar preoccupations. Nevertheless, there is a distinctiveness to his approach in this poem. Despite the analogy, the avian poet remains stubbornly 'feathered' and does not lose its bird-ness through figurative hybridization. The lyric speaker finds a connection with the bird in this relatively late skylark poem to express a shared blessedness in nature which inspires the song. The poem's final image for such blessedness is highly characteristic of Clare's interest in animals: a nest surrounded by a verdant ring of grass.

Clare's interest in bird nests is perhaps one of the most critically well-trodden domains within his work. His last poem, scribbled shakily on a sheet and published immediately after his death in 1864 in the *Stamford Mercury* and *Gentleman's Magazine*, was entitled 'Birds Nests' and describes a chaffinch that carries 'moss in his mouth' to 'filbert hedges' while charming 'the poet with his beautifull song' (LP II 1106). Thirty years earlier, Clare wrote another poem with the same title.

> How fresh the air the birds how busy now
> In every walk if I but peep I find
> Nests newly made or finished all & lined
> With hair & thistle down & in the bough
> Of little awthorn huddled up in green
> The leaves still thickening as the spring gets age
> The Pinks quite round & snug & closely laid
> & linnets of materials loose & rough
> & still hedge sparrow moping in the shade
> Near the hedge bottom weaves of homely stuff
> Dead grass & mosses green an hermitage

> For secresy & shelter rightly made
> & beautiful it is to walk beside
> The lanes & hedges where their homes abide   (MP IV 348)

Nests are representative, here, of that broader sense of differentiated natural abundance and multiplicity that we have seen elsewhere in Clare's treatment of animals. The sonnet achieves this both by emphasizing profusion ('how fresh the air'; 'how busy now'; 'if I but peep I find') and by particularizing difference within that profusion. Some of the nests are 'newly made'. Some are 'finished all'. Those made by pinks (or chaffinches) are 'round & snug & closely laid', while those made by linnets are 'loose & rough' and those belonging to hedge sparrows are tucked away 'in the shade' at the bottom of hedgerows.

I will briefly return to the sense of 'secresy & shelter' in the final lines of this poem. For now, it is worth underlining that Clare writes numerous celebrated short poems on the nesting habits of various types of bird, which have been widely discussed and which further demonstrate his poetry's commitment to precise delineation of nonhuman particularity within broader multiplicities.[10] Such diversity is also apparent in 'Birds Nesting', a more extended poem which explores in a singular literary space the characteristics of various avian nests and nesting behaviours, describing how pleasant it is 'To mark the nests of many sorts / & which in building most excells / The number of their eggs to note / & curious colour of the shells' (MP II 163–84).[11] Clare's commitment to careful observation of the natural world has often led to critics ascribing to him a disciplinary double vision: as an unsigned *Quarterly Review* puts it in 1820, Clare looks 'abroad with the eye of a poet, and with the minuteness of a naturalist' (*Critical Heritage*, p. 98). Such attentiveness is also undoubtedly central to his ambition to write a 'Natural History of Helpstone' in prose, a work which he hoped would be eventually titled '"Biographys of Birds and Flowers" with an Appendix on Animals and Insects' (*JCBH*, p. 217). In journal drafting for that work, Clare pays such remarkably close attention to nonhuman creatures that he goes so far as to measure time and distance so that he can calculate the precise speed of a snail (*JCBH*, p. 237).

In earlier moments of critical history, recognition of Clare's propensity for natural historical observation can feel as much a denigration of Clare's poetry as a championing of it. Even before publication, M. M. Mahood observes that John Taylor reduced 'November' from *The Shepherd's Calendar* to half its original length 'by driving out successively its ass, cows, cat, turkey cock, hogs, steer, geese, carthorse, bull, mastiffs, geese, goat, guinea fowl and colt'.[12] John Middleton Murry, whom I cited at the beginning of this chapter, writes that Clare 'was an observer whose consuming delight was to watch – to watch a grasshopper or a snail, a thistle or a yellow-hammer'. But such observation can seem to be accompanied by a creative limitation. For Murry, Clare's 'poetry is a mirror of things rather than a window of the imagination'. Where Wordsworth and Shelley use the animals that they see or hear to 'open the door ... to still more wonderful things', Murry's estimation is that, to Clare, 'the skylark was most wonderful as a thing seen and noticed: it was the end, not the beginning of wonders' (*Critical Heritage*, pp. 340–1). As a result, when confronted with 'the hare, the whitenosed and the grand-father bee', Murry finds that Clare 'hardly humanized them; he seems rather to have lived on the same level of existence as they, and to have known them as they know each other' (*Critical Heritage*, p. 331). There is considerable truth to Murry's position here, which is sensitive to aspects of Clare's work that have been much more prized by recent criticism: Clare's modesty in the face of the natural world, his tendency to avoid violent anthropomorphism of animals, and, more often than not, his inclination to turn away from co-opting animals to broader human purposes. Alan Vardy, for example, argues that a sonnet from the Northborough period on a vixen and her young presents a 'stunning final image' that shows the 'final incomprehensibility of their behaviour' and 'insists on the intrinsic value of the foxes'.[13] James McKusick has also suggested that Clare 'does not base his arguments on economic utility or aesthetic pleasure' but instead attributes 'intrinsic value to all the flora and fauna that constitute the local ecosystem'.[14] Nevertheless, there is also a risk in Murry's position which perhaps moves dangerously close to reducing Clare's aesthetic achievement as much as it praises his poetic insight. Although for different (and more ecologically minded) reasons, it is arguable that McKusick inadvertently performs a similar reduction when he states that Clare simply 'regards himself as a normal participant in the living world around him, just another inquisitive mammal going about its daily activities'.[15]

Murry and McKusick are just two examples of a broader critical tendency to align Clare with the animals about which he writes. In the late nineteenth century, Maurice Hewlett draws a firm and, to modern ears, uncomfortable analogy between the rareness of labouring-class poets and some of Clare's avian subjects: 'The peasant is a shy bird', he writes, 'by nature wild, by habit as secret as a creature of the night' (*Critical Heritage*, p. 357). John Barrell, in his justly celebrated study of Clare's poetry, argues that Clare's sand martin sonnet (MP IV 309), 'in which he describes the bird as a hermit', is also making another comparison: 'we are entitled, I think, to read the poem as one in which Clare to some extent at least is identifying himself with the bird'.[16]

McKusick takes Barrell's insight further, arguing for 'a deep sense of identity between the speaker, himself a loner who feels excluded from the haunts of men, and the bird, which likewise partakes of a hermit-like seclusion'.[17] Anne Barton is even more exuberant in expressing a relation between another animal and the poet. 'The humble mole was, for Clare, a highly significant animal', she writes: 'Obscure, like himself, it tunnelled along vigorously in ignorance of the great world above it and, when it tried to emerge, was likely to be trapped, or hit over the head.'[18] Once again, there is truth to these observations. As Barrell makes clear and as I have also explored, there is a clear sense of self-identification in several examples of Clare's engagement with nonhuman animals. Nevertheless, it is important to acknowledge that there are also potentially problematic ethical consequences to the comparison, especially for a writer who has been both successfully marketed as and, indeed, limited by the label 'peasant poet'.

Onno Oerlemans recognizes the class implications of this explicitly: it is impossible, he writes, 'to read through even a sampling of the poetry of John Clare without being struck by how his concern for the rural poor (figured very often by the poet himself) parallels his concern for animal life. Both are classes of beings whose welfare is ignored by the oppressive classes that own and increasingly occupy the land they live on.'[19] Nevertheless, Oerlemans, like David Perkins in an extended reading of Clare's sonnets about badger baiting (MP V 360–2), also recognizes a contradiction between this observation and 'the continuous harassment' of animals by the 'same working poor'.[20] A similar paradox lies at the heart of Clare's fascination with nests. In some poems, they offer the sort of 'secresy and shelter' which is to be found at the end of the sonnet 'Birds Nests', with its doubled sense of home in the final line: 'beautiful it is to walk beside / The lanes & hedges where their homes abide'. But, in other poems, nests expose birds to unwanted attention and even to danger. In 'The Yellow Hammer's Nest', for example, Clare recognizes the vulnerability of a nest to both a human boy and to snakes, writing that even 'in the sweetest places cometh ill' (MP III 515–17). He also writes in autobiographical fragments about his own childhood spent 'poking about the hedges in spring to hunt pootys & I was no less fond of robbing the poor birds nests' (*Prose*, p. 16). Nests have, in other words, another form of exemplarity in Clare's various engagements with animals. They embody both ingenuity and vulnerability. They represent both shelter and a need for shelter.[21] Even here, however, there is further complexity to be found. After recalling another boyhood activity of 'poking sticks into the rabbit holes & carefully observing when I took it out if there was down on the end which was a sign of a nest with young', Clare points out the potential for nature to bite back:

> then in went the arm up to the shoulder ; & then fear came upon us that a snake might be concealed in the hole our bloods ran cold within us & started us off to other sports ... we usd to get boughs from the trees, to beat a wasps nest till some of us were stung & then we ran away to other amusements
>
> (*Prose*, p. 16)

Animals can be victims in Clare's verse, but they can also be pests and predators. Humans frequently persecute nonhuman animals, but that position of dominance can flip quickly, and nonhuman life can gain the upper hand.

I have repeatedly stressed the multiplicities of Clare's engagement with animals. As a result, this chapter can only be a partial interaction with almost overwhelming variety. There are numerous other examples of animals in Clare's poetry. Michael Nicholson and Mina Gorji have brilliantly demonstrated, for example, that Clare is one of the greatest poets of insects, writing beautiful poems on ants, butterflies, ladybirds, and glow-worms, among many others.[22] Unsurprisingly, Clare's striking openness to animals meaning different things in different circumstances remains even when discussing these smallest of creatures. In 'Wild Bees', for example, the 'childern of the sun which summer brings' are described as 'pastoral minstrels' that 'Pipe rustic ballads upon busy wings' and 'sweet poets of the summer field' who delight the human poet as he strolls along 'Catching their windings of their wandering song' (MP III 453–4). But, in 'To An Angry Bee', he addresses a more 'Malicious insect' as a 'little vengeful bee / Wi venon sting thourt wiring round & round / A harmless head that neer meant wrong to thee' (EP II 364). The variousness of creatures and their behaviour in Clare's verse is reflected in the variousness of his responses and the styles that he employs to write about them. As we have seen, he writes both descriptively and lyrically, as well as with considerable flexibility in poetic form. He is capable of great natural historical precision, but he also experiments with poems which are very different in their approach. Although far less frequently read than his 'nest poems', the fabular 'The Eagle and the Crow' (EP I 132–5) or the didactic anthropomorphism of 'Adventures of a Grasshopper' (MP III 119–32) are as much a part of Clare's poetic works as his more celebrated studies of animal life. Clare's reverence for the natural world is not limited to nonhuman animals. Nevertheless, they remain a special presence in his poetry and are often a dynamic starting point for the extension of his poetic interest to plants and even the land itself. The liveliness of nonhuman animals as individual creatures and as a category means that they escape the bounds of singular statements that we might make about them. Instead, and following his example, Clare's animals beg to be read closely in all their glorious multiplicity and difference.

Notes

1. Onno Oerlemans, *Poetry and Animals: Blurring the Boundaries with the Human* (New York: Columbia University Press, 2018), p. 100; p. 105.
2. John Clare, *Selected Poems*, ed. Geoffrey Summerfield (London: Penguin, 1990), pp. 98–122; John Clare, *Major Works*, ed. Eric Robinson and David Powell (Oxford: Oxford University Press, 2004), pp. 205–49.
3. Stephanie Kuduk Weiner, *Clare's Lyric: John Clare and Three Modern Poets* (Oxford: Oxford University Press, 2014), pp. 79–80.
4. James C. McKusick, *Green Writing: Romanticism and Ecology* (Basingstoke: Macmillan, 2000), p. 85.
5. Joseph Albernaz, 'John Clare's World', *European Romantic Review*, 27 (2016), 189–205 (p. 196).
6. John Ashbery, 'For John Clare', *Poetry*, 114 (1969), 5–6 (p. 5).
7. For Clare discussing the importance of Thomson, Milton, and others, see *JCBH*, p. 56.
8. For more on this, see Sarah Houghton-Walker, 'John Clare's *The Shepherd's Calendar* and Forms of Repetition', in Simon Kövesi and Erin Lafford, eds., *Palgrave Advances in John Clare Studies* (Cham: Palgrave Macmillan, 2020), pp. 137–56.
9. Percy Bysshe Shelley, *Shelley's Poetry and Prose*, ed. Donald H. Reiman and Neil Freistat, 2nd ed. (New York: Norton, 2002), pp. 304–7.
10. For a good selection of these poems, it is worth starting with the 'Bird Poems' section in *John Clare: Major Works*, ed. Eric Robinson and David Powell (Oxford: Oxford University Press, 2004), pp. 205–43. For examples of critical work explicitly focused on Clare's nest poems, see John Goodridge, *John Clare and Community* (Cambridge: Cambridge University Press, 2013), pp. 134–48 and Cassandra Falke, 'Thinking with Birds: John Clare and the Phenomenology of Perception', *Romanticism*, 26.2 (2020), 180–90.
11. See Katey Castellano, 'Multispecies Work in John Clare's "Birds Nesting" Poems', in Simon Kövesi and Erin Lafford, eds., *Palgrave Advances in John Clare Studies* (Cham: Palgrave Macmillan, 2020), pp. 179–97.
12. M. M. Mahood, 'John Clare: The Poet as Raptor', *Essays in Criticism*, 48 (1998), 201–23 (pp. 219–20).
13. Alan D. Vardy, *John Clare, Politics and Poetry* (Basingstoke: Palgrave Macmillan, 2003), p. 21.
14. McKusick, *Green Writing*, p. 85.
15. Ibid., p. 81.
16. John Barrell, *The Idea of Landscape and the Sense of Place, 1730–1840: An Approach to the Poetry of John Clare* (Cambridge: Cambridge University Press, 1972), p. 123.
17. McKusick, *Green Writing*, p. 93.
18. Anne Barton, 'Clare's Animals: The Wild and the Tame', *John Clare Society Journal*, 18 (1999), 5–21 (p. 19). For more on Clare's moles, see Katey Castellano, 'Moles, Molehills, and Common Right in John Clare's Poetry', *Studies in Romanticism*, 56 (2017), 157–76.
19. Onno Oerlemans, *Romanticism and the Materiality of Nature* (Toronto: University of Toronto Press, 2002), p. 79.

20. David Perkins, *Romanticism and Animal Rights* (Cambridge: Cambridge University Press, 2003), pp. 89–103.
21. For influential work on nests, shelter and Clare, see Jonathan Bate, *The Song of the Earth* (London: Picador, 2000), pp. 153–75.
22. Michael Nicholson, 'Unheard Swarms: John Clare and Romantic Entomology', *The Wordsworth Circle*, 51 (2020), 338–59; Mina Gorji, *John Clare and the Place of Poetry* (Liverpool: University of Liverpool Press, 2009), p. 123.

6

FIONA STAFFORD

John Clare's Plants

Throughout his life, John Clare relied on plants. For income and inspiration, for subjects and sustenance, plants proved an endlessly renewable resource. From his earliest poems to his latest, Clare expressed a deep affinity with natural vegetation. 'Noon', written in 1809–10 when he was in his mid teens, describes seeking refuge from extreme summer heat on a shady bank and lying down 'Where the grass in bunshes rank / Lifts its Down on spindles high' (EP 1 406). Some forty years later, in 'Written in Prison', a late sonnet from the Northampton Asylum, he admitted to envying the fly 'in the green woods' and the 'hare her grassy bed' (LP 11 1023). On his long, solitary walk from High Beach asylum in Epping Forest to his childhood home in Helpston in July 1841, Clare slept in dykes and porches and appeased his hunger 'by eating the grass by the roadside which seemed to taste something like bread'.[1] When he wrote down these fragmentary memories in 'Journey out of Essex', he recalled eating 'heartily till I was satisfied and in fact the meal seemed to do me good'.[2] What for many poets might have merited no more than a passing reference in a pastoral, or at best an emblematic image, assumed the character of a cherished comforter in the writings of John Clare. As far as he was concerned, grass was never to be taken for granted, plants never to be regarded as mere material. They were living companions and lifelong friends.

The poet who shared his pleasure in the spring with literature's friendliest address to an April daisy – 'Welcome Old Maytey!' (1819, EP 1 135) – was already showing an unusual sympathy with plants in his earliest compositions. 'Noon' begins with the stillness of a summer idyll but almost immediately introduces a sense of unease, as conventional praise of the season is replaced by bees that 'cease to hum', 'panting sheep', and birds 'overpower'd and dumb' (EP 1 405). The extreme temperature provokes special concern for the flowers:

> How It grieves me when I look
> Ragged robins once so pink

> Now are turnd as black a[s] ink
> And the leaves being scorch'd so much
> Even crumble at the touch
> Drowking lies the Meadow sweet
> Flopping down beneath ones feet
> While to all the flowers that blow
> If in open air they grow
> The injurious deed alike is done
> By the hot relentless sun   (EP I 406)

Flowers that in other hands might be included as shorthand for summer, or perhaps for elegiac strewing, are lamented here for their own sake – this catalogue of summer casualties reflects not on human misfortune but rather on the disastrous physical effects of direct heat on flowering plants. The accuracy of Clare's observation is striking in its botanical specificity and the details through which the distress of plants is conveyed. This is more than vivid documentary. The speaker's perception charges the passage with unexpected feeling: it is difficult to avoid a growing sense of dismay and even indignation at the 'relentless' sun's 'injurious deed'. For Clare, familiarity with the local flora meant both the reassuring stability of perennial cycles and dramatically shifting emotional experience.

His poems about plants are often passionate. Whether it is a general declaration of his love of trees in 'Reccolections after a Ramble' ('The wood is sweet – I love it well', 1819–20, EP II 187), or more specific praise of particular species such as the violet ('Sweet tiney flower of darkley hue / Lone dweller in the pathles shade / How much I love thy pensive blue', 'To the Violet', EP II 10) or the hawthorn ('I have met thy bower / & thou hast gaind my love', 'To a Bower', 1819–20, EP II 231), Clare's response to vegetation is unusually powerful. 'The Wild Flower Nosgay', written in 1820, paints a picture of a childhood spent among fields, woods and streams, with hours of intense happiness arising from gathering numerous flowers:

> Crimp frilled daisey bright bronze butter cup,
> Freckt cows lip peeps gilt wins of mornings dew
> & hooded aron early sprouting up
> Ere the white thorn bud half unfolds to view
> Wi' eager joy each filld my playfull hand
> & wan hued Lady smocks that love to spring
> 'Side the swamp margin of some plashy pond
> With all the blooms that early aprils bring   (EP II 410)

In a stanza bursting with life and colour, a combination of compound adjectives, alliteration, assonance, and rhythmic variety conveys the sudden profusion of wildflowers and the palpable pleasure of the spring. Although each flower is carefully distinguished, the acoustic chimes of 'daisey' and 'dew', 'dew' and 'hooded', 'frilled' and 'freckt', 'frilled', 'gilt', and 'fill'd', 'wins' and 'white thorn', 'bright bronze butter cup', 'bud', 'blooms', and 'bring', as well as the visual patterns of 'bronze' and 'gilt', 'white thorn' and 'wan-hued', create a growing sensation of life and unity. The arum 'sprouting up' matches the 'Lady smocks that love to spring' – parallel actions that stand for the individual plant, the species and the broader seasonal awakening. '[E]ager joy' seems the natural human reaction in the midst of this heady, shared experience.

The joyful evocation of natural energy takes a slower pace in the next stanza, however, as the fresh blooms are observed pushing through the rotting vegetation of the previous year:

> The jaundice'd tincturd primrose sickly sere
> Mid its broad curdl'd leaves of mellow green
> Hemm'd in with relics of the parted year
> The mournfull wrecks of summers that has been
> Dead leaves of ash & oak & hazel tree
> The constant covering of all woody land
> With tiney vi'lets, creeping plentiously,
> That one by one enticd my patient hand   (EP II 410)

Dead leaves are as much part of the spring as early wildflowers, while the primrose, vividly described, carries a reminder of the fragility of life even amidst the burgeoning freshness. Neither 'Jaundice'd tincturd' petals, though true to the flower's natural colour, nor 'curdl'd leaves' augur well for the plant's survival. '[S]ickly sere' looks back to last year's withering and forward to a similar disappearance all too soon. Unlike the ivy, envied in John Milton's *Lycidas* for being 'never sere', the primrose carries old associations of appearing early and dying 'forsaken'.[3] Clare's vivid evocation of childhood cannot avoid being coloured by the adult poet's mature reading and reflection, imbuing 'The Wild Flower Nosgay' with strains of Wordsworthian yearning even as it celebrates an early delight in natural beauty. Though an unlikely jailer, the pale primrose introduces shades of the prison house that become more prominent by the closing stanzas. What initially seems a straightforward recollection of favourite flowers unfolds with subtle shifts in tone and texture, mood and metaphor. Carefully chosen vocabulary offers opposing possibilities – the 'constant covering' of dried leaves might suggest warm protection or the grave of infancy; the 'tiney' woodland violets, vulnerability or potential growth. So too, the boy's instinctive desire to pluck wildflowers becomes charged with troubling implications.

Clare's skill in conveying both the varied delights of his rural childhood and the mixed feelings of adulthood is evident in the poem's progress through the cycle of spring and summer vegetation into late autumn. Amidst the falling leaves, the younger self is depicted leaving home 'far behind' to venture into the wilderness in search of the 'last lingering of the flowery kind / Blue heathbells', which lie trembling beneath the 'sheltering furze' (EP II 412). Pursuit of the last flower is at once an accurate representation of the natural blooming season, a metaphor for the boy's steady growth away from childhood, and of the adult's urgent desire to recover the imaginative energy of youth. The poem ends with the mature voice looking back on 'childish scenes' as if waking from a vision and wishing 'to sleep and dream it o'er again' (EP II 412). Caliban or Coleridge? Clare's intense feelings for plants prompted the creation of poems that might recapture visionary experience while recognizing its loss.

'The Wild Flower Nosgay' is both a personal Immortality Ode and a brief Biographia Botanica. Clare's portrait of the artist as a young botanist was developed at greater length in his more ambitious narrative poem of 1819–21, 'The Village Minstrel'. Although he avoided the first person in his longer exploration of the poet's formative years, the depiction of Lubin includes similar emphasis on the passion for spring flowers:

> O who can speak his joys when springs young morn
> From wood & pasture opend on his view
> When tender green buds blush upon the thorn
> & the first primrose dips its leaves in dew
> Each varied charm how joyd woud he pursue   (EP II 129)

Like the boy in 'The Wild Flower Nosgay', Lubin, at times an isolated child, finds his own delights in fresh woods and pastures new. An aesthetic sense nurtured by the beauties of the natural world was an essential element of Clare's self-presentation. If Taylor introduced him to the world as a 'Northamptonshire peasant', Clare's poems presented a natural poet – sensitive, observant, sympathetic, and deeply knowledgeable. The countryside around Helpston offered not just temporary retreats from agricultural labour or playground politics, but also a natural education which enabled him to flourish. What he delighted in was available for anyone to enjoy, but his poems reveal a strong awareness of his own special powers of perception. Clare knew very well that few people saw quite as he did.

In her groundbreaking study of *The Poet as Botanist*, Molly Mahood identified Clare's relationship with plants as a key aspect of his self-fashioning. Her fine chapter on his work is entitled 'John Clare: Bard of the Wildflowers', an epithet taken from the verses 'By Clare – to be Placed at the Back of his Portrate' (LP II 696–7), which he composed late in life, as a patient in the Northampton asylum.[4] As in the 1820s, when Clare first found success as a published poet and sat for his portrait, he continued to cultivate the identity of the 'bard of the wildflowers'. Not only was he an author of poems on botanical subjects, but one whose own growth depended on flowers and who could be understood as a voice for plants.

The corollary of Clare's strong, deeply rooted and long-lasting botanical attachments, however, was profound and recurrent distress over the destruction of plants. While many of his poems include declarations of vegetable love, many others are lamentations for love lost. 'Helpston Green', for example, recalls 'Long waving rows of willows grey / And clumps of awthorn shade' only to emphasize their shocking disappearance: 'But now alas your awthorn bowers / All desolate we see' (EP II 11–12). 'To a Favourite Tree' similarly expresses a sharp sense of grief over the felling of an old tree, 'dragd a captive' in full summer foliage from the wood where it had always stood (1808–19, EP I 240). The poem's mournful farewell, 'Adieu old friends ye trees & bushes dear', is the obverse of the cheerful spring greetings offered in 'To an April Daisey' and 'The Primrose'.

Eight years after the appearance of *The Poet as Botanist*, Mahood published *A John Clare Flora*, listing more than 400 plants mentioned by Clare, together with the relevant references to his poems, letters, and journals, and illustrated by colour photographs of some of the key species in their natural habitats. It is an essential point of reference for readers with serious interests in Clare's records and representations of British flora and an invaluable resource for those more confident in their capacity to interpret poetry than identify plants. As Richard Mabey comments in a foreword, *A John Clare Flora* is 'magisterial and intimate' in its even-handed attention to both rare botanical species and weeds – at once comprehensive and particular.[5] Especially helpful for readers of Clare's poetry are Mahood's illuminating explanations: a term such as 'bottle' is a 'country word for the individual floret in a head of clover', while 'bottle brush' can refer to the Marsh Horsetail, *Equisetum palustre*.[6] Understanding Clare's vocabulary depends on context, just as the plants which he gathered depended on their environment.

A John Clare Flora grew from years of cumulative research into Clare's botanical interests. Mahood acknowledges particular debts to *Flora Britannica*, Mabey's encyclopaedic collection of native plants and their cultural associations, and to Margaret Grainger's edition of Clare's *Natural History Prose Writings*, which includes his 'Natural History

Letters', Journal, Plant and Bird Lists, short essays, notes, and memoranda. Although Robert Heyes has produced an important corrective to Grainger's account of the 'Natural History Letters', pointing to the absence of consistent dates or correspondents and questioning whether Clare was really fulfilling a commission from Hessey and Taylor for a Helpston equivalent of Gilbert White's *Natural History of Selborne*, her edition still provides an invaluable compendium of Clare's nature writings.[7] Whoever Clare might have had in mind as a correspondent when drafting the 'Natural History Letters', readers find themselves in the role of recipient, hearing the voice of an ardent, expert, and abundantly curious observer and urgent recorder of the natural world:

> I took a walk to day to botanize & found that the spring had taken up her dwelling in good earnest she covered the woods with the white anemonie which the children call Lady smocks & the hare bells are just venturing to unfold their blue drooping bells the green is covered with daiseys & the little Celandine the hedge bottoms are crowded with the green leaves of arum
>
> (25 March 1825, *Natural History*, p. 59)

The meticulous lists of plants and birds transcribed from Clare's manuscripts, included in *The Natural History Prose Writings*, also help to counter any idea of carelessness that might arise from the appearance of his unpunctuated writings. The 'Orchid list' jotted down in the cover of Isaac Emmerton's *A Plain and Practical Treatise on the Culture and Management of the Auricula, Polyanthus, Carnation, Pink, and the Ranunculus* is organized and orderly, more indicative of a plant scientist than an impressionist painter (*Natural History*, p. 300). Clare's observation of the 'Male and Female Flowers of the Oak' (*Natural History*, p. 108) and his note 'On the Notions of Male & Female Spieces in Trees & Flowers' (*Natural History*, pp. 101–2) show his engagement with the concerns of contemporary scientists and plant breeders about the sexual parts of plants. 'I know not what to say about this opinion of sexes in trees & plants' is not the voice of ignorant prejudice, but of intellectual curiosity (*Natural History*, p. 101).

Clare was a trained gardener and well-informed botanist, bent on identifying and understanding plants. His note on English Orchises reveal his interest in how and where different plants live, from the *Orchis pyramidalis* and *Orchis arinifera* (pyramid and spider orchids) at Swordy Well to the *Orchis viridis* (frog orchid), abundant 'at the west end of Herrings Park' to the *Orchis latifolia* (early marsh orchid), 'in a low part of Mr Clarks Close at Royce wood end & by a brook side in a close near Brigges's Barn' (*Natural History*, p. 301). Clare was conscious of the relative success of certain plants in different conditions and the way changes in the landscape could pose a serious threat to the life forms it supported. Marsh orchids had been 'very plentiful before Enclosure on a Spot called Parkers Moor near Peasfieldhedge & on Deadmoor near Sneef green & Rotten moor by Moorclose but these places now are under plough' (*Natural History*, p. 301).

As John Barrell emphasized in his foundational study, *The Idea of Landscape and the Sense of Place, 1730–1840*, much of Clare's work registers the impact of the widespread changes to the local countryside brought about by the Enclosure Acts. From around 1809, when Clare was fourteen, Helpston began to undergo the changes in land ownership that were transforming the face of Britain during the long eighteenth century. His reactions to the process inform many of his poems, including 'The Village Minstrel', but are perhaps aired most explicitly in 'The Mores', 'The Fallen Elm', or 'Enclosure', where familiar open stretches of spring blossom and forest flowers have been replaced by 'little parcels' of fenced land ('The Mores', 1823, MP II 347). The phrase 'under plough', included in his note on Marsh Orchids, often tolls the death knell for wildflowers, whose ancient habitats were being casually destroyed in the name of productivity.[8]

Clare not only recognized that the survival of plants depended on their surroundings, but also that plants provided vital habitats for other life forms. The 'Natural History Letters' record the diet of goldfinches ('groundsel seed & the broad leafd plantain', *Natural History*, p. 44), the hiding places of nightingales ('hazel') and cuckoos ('oaken foliage', *Natural History*, p. 38), and the nesting materials of thrushes ('blades of dead grass moss & cowdung lined with warmer materials of wool & a finer sort of grass', *Natural History*, p. 47). These first-hand observations come alive in his marvellous bird poems, where breeding and survival are as important as songs and flight. The characteristic behaviour of different birds is embodied in poems as well built as their nests, but while the titles direct attention to the birds, avian and plant life are shown to be inseparable. A pair of kingfishers are spotted on the grey branch of a 'leaning willow' ('Birds Nesting', MP II 170), whereas a redcap (goldfinch) favours a lilac tree and larks take cover in a field of wheat. Woodpeckers and wrynecks seek insects in the rotten wood of an 'old oak dotterel' ('Birds Nesting', MP II 176–7), the snipe thrusts its long beak into the 'gelid mass' of a muddy swamp ('To the Snipe', 1832, MP IV 574), while blackcaps (great tit) seek out 'silk-cased insects' hidden among twigs during the spring and then rely on 'gleaning what the orchard spares' ('The Blackcap', 1832, MP IV 346–7).[9] The chiffchaff's oven-like nest is made from 'small bits of hay ... & withered leaves' ('The Pettichaps Nest', 1825–6, MP III 518), the yellowhammer's from 'bleached stubbles and ... horses sable hair' ('The Yellow Hammer's Nest', 1825–6, MP III 515) while the nightingale's, 'an hermits mossy cell' ('The Nightingales Nest', 1832, MP III 461) is built from dead oak leaves, moss, scraps of grass, down, and hair.

A rare ability to see how plants sustain birds, insects, animals, and invertebrates made Clare value them not only for aesthetic or utilitarian reasons, but also in relation to other beings. As a result, his sympathies extended to plants which most gardeners and farmworkers would be inclined to root out. A plant such as a thistle, normally regarded as an undesirable, invasive weed, emerges in Clare's poem on the subject as an 'Armed warrior', defending many species, including clover, lapwings, yellowhammers, partridge, larks, and bees ('Where the broad sheep walk', 1832–7, MP v 203). Plants provide safe hiding places from predators, as well as shelter, food, and nesting materials: without them birds and insects would not survive. By implication, neither would human beings. Clare's many poems about woodmen, tree-felling, farmyards, arable fields, grazing sheep, egg collecting, nutting, cress gathering, orchards, markets, and agricultural produce offer multifaceted parallels to the bird poems, cumulatively highlighting human dependence on plants.

Clare's deep understanding of the complexities of natural habitats and the interdependence of life forms meant that his objections to the transformation of his home were not so much private nostalgia as collective outrage. The bard of the wildflowers could see the damage caused by contemporary changes of land use, the agricultural 'improvements' and increasing extraction of raw materials, facilitated by and demanding enclosures. His poems have often been read as protests on behalf of the common man in the face of powerful landowners and legislation driven by vested interests. But his poems were also speaking out for other silent witnesses and victims – for the wildflowers and trees destroyed as a result of local enclosures, the birds, animals, and insects that depended on the disappearing vegetation. In his poem on Swordy Well, Clare gave voice and personality to 'a piece of land' robbed of 'trees banks & bushes', and therefore bereft of butterflies, bees, beetles, mice, and rabbits ('Petitioners are full of prayers', 1832–7, MP v 107). Long before Charles Darwin explained the web of life to Victorian readers, Clare was conveying the essential connections between species through his imaginative capacity to adopt a nonhuman perspective.

Clare's lifelong attention to the local flora and fauna gave him special insights into their mutual and multiple relationships. Although he collected seeds and plants, along with snail shells, birds' eggs and other specimens, his occasional objection to the kind of natural history that demanded 'collections of dryd specimens' and 'carcasses in cases' in preference to observing living phenomena reflects a certain unease over the removal of species from their habitats (*Natural History*, p. 38). While this may have been intensified by personal anxieties over displacement from home, it can be seen to anticipate by two centuries a modern understanding of ecosystems. What Clare also possessed was a highly imaginative outlook and capacity to sympathize with and ventriloquize the perspectives of local flora and fauna. His poems embody a unique perception of natural interdependency, which has had a strong appeal to influential ecocritics in recent years. At the start of the twenty-first century, both Jonathan Bate and James McKusick made Clare a central figure for any ecological reading of Romanticism, a position reinforced by the subsequent diffusion and intensification of environmental concerns.[10] Though Clare's language is different from that of the twenty-first-century environmentalist, his understanding of the interconnectedness of living things was similarly evidence-based.

Clare was already being valued for his ecological vision before the environment began to dominate critical studies. In 1995, a Special Issue of *The John Clare Society Journal* was devoted to 'Clare and Ecology', in which distinguished contributors including Eric Robinson, Ronald Blythe, Jonathan Bate, and Tim Fulford explored the ecological dimensions of Clare's work. In his guest editorial, Richard Mabey commented that 'Clare is remarkable in exploring *his* role in the network of natural interdependency, and unique in seeing his poetic voice as part of that interdependency.'[11] The poet's place in a natural ecosystem has proved a complicated issue for ecocriticism, not least because language is often singled out as a peculiarly human attribute. Scott Hess's more recent approach to Clare draws on posthumanism in its concern with the poetry's inclusion of multiple subjects and rapid shifts between perspectives that are often non- or 'other-than' human. He also emphasizes, however, that rather than separating humanity from other species, language is part of a multi-relational living world: 'Our language and representations do not divide us from other-than-human beings, but instead emerge out of and depend on our relations with them.'[12] Clare's poetry, accordingly, is part of the natural world, the production of one species among many. But his poetry is also a celebration of human creativity – and such a wonderful achievement offers its own affirmation of language and art, and the vital connections between individuals and fellow generations, contemporary, past, and future.

While the inclusion of human activity in a multi-relational living universe can offer a positive way of restoring poetry to ecological discourse, Clare was acutely aware of the peculiar capacities of human beings, including himself, to affect other life forms – often adversely. Many of his writings register the destruction of woods, trees, and wildlife by contemporary workforces, of which he was sometimes part, while his modest hybridization experiments involved radical alterations to plant species. Much of the rural landscape, even pre-enclosure, had been created by human activity. The farm animals central to *The Shepherd's Calendar* had taken shape through years of selective breeding. Clare understood the practical benefits of improving crops and livestock for better yields of corn, meat, and wool, conscious of the needs of his family, community, and nation. As Simon Kövesi has pointed out, Clare was himself part of the process of enclosure: 'he was poor and the money for fencing and planting hedges was pretty good'.[13] Instead of reconstructing Clare as a 'sin-free, green messiah', Kövesi emphasizes his complexity and the importance of seeing him in his own historical context.

Although the idea of Clare setting hedges and fences and burning lime may seem at odds with the poetic voice of 'Enclosure' and 'Swordy Well', it is not perhaps so very contradictory. Participation in a process of land management does not necessarily diminish feelings of loss over the transformation of a familiar landscape. Instead, Clare's work made him acutely aware of the changes in his surroundings. As a thoughtful agricultural worker, Clare knew only too well that the countryside was not an eternal pastoral retreat, but a constantly changing site of often violent, unpredictable events. This made the idea of enclosure especially painful, while also enhancing the significance of more enduring physical features. Old trees and common arboreal species animated his pen, while the consciousness that their days were inevitably numbered intensified his portraiture.

Clare turned to trees again and again throughout his writing career, often devoting entire poems to them. The definite article in 'The Maple Tree', 'The Surrey Tree', 'The Sycamore', or 'The Crab Tree' can be read as a species or as an individual tree – these poems celebrate distinct arboreal kinds but draw on examples known and observed by the poet. 'The Maple Tree with its tassell flowers of green / That turns to red a stag horn shaped seed' (1850s?, LP II 1025) is an accurate description of the species *Acer campestre*, but the sonnet's concern with the surroundings of 'blotched leaved orchis and the blue bell flowers' also suggests a clear memory of a particular field maple in a familiar spot. 'The Crab Tree', on the other hand, is less concerned with minute physical characteristics than with the blossom's capacity to reawaken childhood feelings. The perennial habits of crab-apple trees mean that the blossom seen in adulthood is exactly like that encountered as a child: 'crab blossoms blush among the may / As wont in years gone bye' (1819–32, MP IV 189).

The most memorable sonnets are, however, devoted to the most memorable trees. 'The Old Willow', 'The Hollow Tree', 'Burthorpe Oak', 'Langley Bush', and 'The Shepherds Tree' all focus on local trees whose characters have grown through years of personal familiarity and, often, communal significance. 'The Old Willow' is both the poet's 'old hut' for sheltering from the rain and a magnificent local landmark 'That's kept its ancient place for many a year' (1819–32, MP IV 267–8). The 'Hugh Elm' known as 'The Shepherds Tree' was a favourite refuge where the poet might 'hear the laugh of summer leaves above' or 'reflect / On times & deeds & darings that have been' (1830, MP IV 154). Ancient trees had special private meaning, strengthening Clare's inner sense of continuity with his own past, while at the same time reminding him of the centuries through which they had stood as living witnesses to forgotten generations. 'The Shepherds Tree' is 'notched & scarred / Like to a warriors destiny' and yet still 'towering' in its 'strength of heart' (MP IV 154), while the 'Old Hugh ash dotterel' featured in 'The Hollow Tree' retains a 'vigorous head' in defiance of its overall wasting (1832?, MP IV 298). 'The Burthorp Oak' is 'Age rent & shattered to a stump – Yet new / Leaves come upon each rift & broken limb / With every spring' (1832?, MP IV 254). Indeed, it still survives beside a farmhouse in south Lincolnshire, sprouting fresh foliage each year. These grand old trees are heroic and inspirational, subjects of awe and respect as well as deep affection.

When Richard Mabey was defending his own work against what seemed a gratuitous attack on 'new nature writing', he commented that most nature writers prefer to think of themselves 'just as writers who simply wish to embrace a rather larger than usual cast of characters – the other beings and landscapes with which we share the planet; and to respect them as subjects in narratives, not simply as objects'.[14] No wonder then that Clare, whose cast of characters include flowers, trees, weeds, birds, animals, streams, and pieces of land, is the poet to whom Mabey turns and returns, as an unfailing model for the twenty-first-century writer. Clare's plants are characters in their own right, not so much objects of observation as subjects and sources of inspiration. His botanical characterizations are at once anthropomorphic and deeply attentive to their distinctive habits, which is why they can become muses. Trees, especially, live longer, different lives from humankind and so offer us new ways of thinking about existence. Their generosity is endless – and incidental. Clare's lifelong love and knowledge of plants allowed for the development of new kinds of writing, though just as important in his literary growth was his love and knowledge of poetry.

Clare's journal reveals a man who took pleasure from both an autumn walk and an afternoon spent reading. These were activities enjoyed in tandem not in conflict:

> Set some box edging round a border which I have made for my collection of ferns – read some passages of Blairs grave ... who has not markd the following aged companions to many such spots of general decay

'A row of reverend elms
'Long lashd by the rude winds. Some rift half down'
(2 November 1824, *Natural History*, p. 198)

Plants reminded Clare of poetry as well as prompting his own: as he reflected in his third Natural History Letter, 'who sees the taller buttercup carpeting the closes in golden fringe without a remembrance of Chattertons beautiful mention of it' (*Natural History*, p. 41). This is one of a dense thicket of literary allusions illustrating the essential interdependency of poems and plants: 'to look on nature with a poetic eye magnifys the pleasure she herself being the very essence & soul of Poesy' (*Natural History*, p. 41). The original shared identity of 'poesy' and 'posy' came naturally enough to Clare. When he wrote poems depicting a boy collecting wildflowers, he was also recalling the poems he had gathered from various places. A 'Midsummer Cushion' was a traditional summer decoration made by children in Helpston by setting flowers into a piece of turf. It was also a perfect name for a collection of Clare's poems – though in the event, Clare's ideas (not unusually) had to be adapted to the literary markets of the 1830s, and so his new volume was published under a more conventionally literary title: *The Rural Muse*.

The crossing of Clare's botanical and literary knowledge is evident in every plant-focused sonnet he wrote, but their literariness is not just a matter of form. The presence of earlier writings and traditions is often less obvious than the botanical observation but nevertheless enriches his plant poems and helps to ensure their long-term survival. 'The Spindle Tree', for example, includes not just accurate observation of a native species, but also confident engagement with literary tradition. The poem celebrates a tree that comes into its own in the autumn, 'when leaves save weeds are else but scant & few' (1819–32, MP IV 330). The spindle, *Euonymus europeaus*, is a relatively small native tree, not especially noticeable during the summer in an old hedge or along the edge of mixed woodland but distinguished later in the year by the eye-catching pink and orange berries that cover its slim, green-barked branches. Clare's admiration for a tree that defies autumn with its springlike colours, remaining resplendent while other species stand denuded or succumb to vigorous parasites and frost, animates the second half of his sonnet:

> Yet one gay bush is beautifully seen
> As full of berries as its twigs can be
> Glittering & pink as blossoms washed in dew
> Gleams the gay burthen of the spindle tree
> The old mans beard the saplings grains pursues
> Like feathers hung with rime – but autumns showers
> Makes their rich berries shine like summer flowers   (MP IV 330)

The spindle is a natural paradox, turning autumn to spring, winter to summer, unbowed by its 'gay burthen'. While young saplings are covered in the pale grey of Old Man's Beard (*Clematic vitalba*), a wild plant more obviously in keeping with the season with its frostlike, feathery fruit, the spindle brings warm, bright colour to winter woods and hedges.

In defiance of the 'rime', Clare is inspired to rhyme. His poem is lit by literary as well as natural inspiration. The image of the wild clematis seed heads as 'feathers hung with rime' is vivid and visual but also suggests an idea of quill pens filled with poetry. Old man's beard may belong to the hedgerow or to the bards of earlier ages. Though pre-empting the traditional volta after the octave with a change of direction at the start of line 8, 'The Spindle Tree' follows a regular Shakespearean rhyme scheme. Clare's choice has the effect of recalling and then unsettling the Shakespearean model, which is just what his subject does. His celebration of the spindle tree's defiance of autumn's depredations quietly recalls Shakespeare's own response to winter, especially in 'Sonnet 73':

> That time of year thou mayst in me behold,
> When yellow leaves, or none, or few, do hang
> Upon those boughs which shake against the cold,
> Bare ruined choirs where late the sweet birds sang[15]

Clare may have been responding primarily to the spindle trees he saw on winter walks around Helpston, but his admiration for his subject is enhanced by memories of familiar winter sonnets and the old associations between the onset of winter, old age, and failing strength. Clare's poem delights in 'things simple yet new', wittily setting his portrayal of the spindle tree against established autumnal tradition. While other plants are smothered in old man's beard and weighed down with rime, the spindle has a self-refreshing vibrancy.

Clare looked and read and wrote, but what he created was never a straightforward copy of natural or literary sources. His botanical vocabulary often included more than one name for a single species, his poetic language included puns and allusions. His work has been enjoyed and sometimes dismissed for its simplicity or directness, but Clare's poetry often demonstrates deep knowledge and knowingness. A poem such as 'The Lamentations of Round-Oak Waters' (1818, EP I 228) works clearly on its own terms, but once the multiple allusions to Robert Burns are apparent, its rippling protest deepens. The injured brook of Round-Oak Waters is as naked as Burns's Bruar Water, but while the little Scottish river running through the Duke of Atholl's Perthshire estate makes a plea for decent replanting, the willows surrounding the fenland brook have been cut down leaving no hope of recovery.[16] 'The Lamentations of Round-Oak Waters' begins with a loud echo of Burns's 'Despondency: An Ode' and ends with cold comfort more akin to 'Man was Made to Mourn' than the playful 'Humble Petition of Bruar Water'.[17]

Knowledge of plants and poetry was complementary and gave Clare's own art a perennial freshness. At the same time, the fragility of flowers and the vulnerability of trees imbued his poetry with a lasting urgency. The opening line of his sonnet, 'Obscurity', runs 'Old tree oblivion doth thy life condemn' (1832?, MP IV 256), while in 'Nothingness of Life' he admitted:

> I never pass a venerable tree
> Pining away to nothin[g]ness & dust
> Ruins vain shades of power I never see
> Once dedicated to times cheating trust
> But warm reflection warms her saddest thought
> & views lifes vanity in cheerless light   (1822, MP IV 278)

He knew only too well that even the strongest, most long-lived trees could be brought down in a matter of hours or simply rot slowly until they were forgotten. Though unable to stop the axemen and even occasionally joining forces with the agents of destruction, he also felt compelled to record what was disappearing. Many of the plants in his poetry were already dead before he started to write, and yet they live on in his lines. His powers of observation and recollection, intensified by a dual passion for poems and plants, animated his poetry and so immortalized his natural subjects. Two centuries later, we can still see the flowers and trees of Helpston in the mind's eye, which may in turn prompt a desire to see them at first hand. Clare's writings help us to see what is around us, as well as what has gone – and what might still be recovered. The loss of biodiversity in twenty-first-century Britain surpasses anything witnessed by Clare, but still his bright, celebratory, and challenging poetry has the power to send sympathetic readers out to do whatever they can in order to preserve and replenish the natural heritage.

Notes

1. *JCBH*, p. 263.
2. *JCBH*, p. 263.
3. *Lycidas*, in John Milton, *Complete Shorter Poems*, ed. John Carey (London: Longman, 1971), pp. 237–56 (l. 2). For primrose meanings and traditions, see Fiona Stafford, *The Brief Life of Flowers* (London: John Murray, 2018), pp. 24–38; Richard Mabey, *Flora Britannica* (London: Sinclair-Stevenson, 1996), pp. 164–8.

4. M. M. Mahood, *The Poet as Botanist* (Cambridge: Cambridge University Press, 2008), pp. 112–46.
5. 'Foreword', M. M. Mahood, *A John Clare Flora* (Nottingham: Trent Editions, 2016), p. xv.
6. Mahood, *A John Clare Flora*, p. 50; p. 21.
7. Robert Heyes, 'John Clare's Natural History', in Simon Kövesi and Scott McEathron, eds., *New Essays on John Clare: Poetry, Culture and Community* (Cambridge: Cambridge University Press, 2015), pp. 169–88.
8. Bill Phillips has highlighted Clare's ambivalence about ploughing in 'When Ploughs destroy'd the green', *John Clare Society Journal*, 21 (2002), 53–62.
9. On the identification of the 'redcap', see Richard Mabey, *Birds Britannica* (London: Chatto and Windus, 2005), pp. 448–9; for the 'blackcap', *The Prose of John Clare*, ed. J. W. Tibble and Anne Tibble (London: Routledge & Kegan Paul, 1951), II 239.
10. Jonathan Bate, *The Song of the Earth* (London: Picador, 2000); James McKusick, *Green Writing: Romanticism and Ecology* (New York: St Martin's Press, 2000).
11. 'Guest editorial', *John Clare Society Journal*, 14 (1995), 5–6 (p. 6).
12. Scott Hess, 'Biosemiosis and Posthumanism in John Clare's Multi-centred Environments', in Simon Kövesi and Erin Lafford, eds., *Palgrave Advances in John Clare Studies* (Cham: Palgrave Macmillan, 2020), pp. 199–220 (p. 212).
13. Simon Kövesi, *John Clare, Nature, Criticism and History* (London: Palgrave Macmillan, 2017), p. 16.
14. Richard Mabey, *Turning the Boat for Home* (London: Chatto and Windus, 2019) pp. 220–1.
15. *The Arden Shakespeare: Shakespeare's Sonnets*, ed. Katherine Duncan Jones (London: Thomas Nelson, 1997), p. 257. Duncan Jones points out that the reversed order of line 2 'ensures that we focus on several stages of the process of seasonal decay, which includes both the leafless trees of midwinter and the partly stripped trees of mid-autumn, rather than simply on the period when the stripping of vegetation is complete' (p. 256).
16. 'The Humble Petition of Bruar Water to the Noble Duke of Athole', in *The Poems and Songs of Robert Burns*, ed. James Kinsley, 3 vols. (Oxford: Clarendon Press, 1968), I, 355–7.
17. *Poems and Songs of Robert Burns*, I, 232; 116.

7

ROBERT HEYES

John Clare and the Community of Naturalists

Sometime around 1830, John Clare was contemplating an essay 'On Lying', a subject on which, as a man addicted to the truth, he had strong views. His notes on the subject contain excerpts from two books whose veracity he evidently doubted; one was *Five years residence in the Canadas including a tour through part of the United States of America, in the year 1823*, by Edward Allen Talbot; the other was *Narrative of a pedestrian journey through Russia and Siberian Tartary, from the frontiers of China to the frozen sea and Kamtchatka*, by Captain John Dundas Cochrane, RN.[1] Both books first appeared in the mid 1820s and are substantial two-volume works, and Clare had evidently read them very carefully. Paul Smethurst has suggested that 'travel writing was the most widespread and popular literary genre of the period'.[2] Clare shared this taste and had several books of this type in his library, notably *The Three Voyages of Captain Cook Round the World*, as well as reading other books of travel and exploration borrowed from friends.

Such books usually contained much natural history,[3] and I mention this aspect of Clare's reading because he has often been described as someone who wrote about what he knew. So he did, but there is often a corollary, sometimes explicit, at other times implied, that this was *all* Clare knew. In fact, he was well informed about other parts of the world, including their natural history. Apart from his wide reading, there was his experience as a gardener, both in the gardens at Burghley and working for a nurseryman at Newark-on-Trent, and his friendships with other gardeners. During this period, flowers, shrubs, and trees were arriving in Britain in large quantities from many parts of the world, and the successful nurturing of exotic species required an understanding of the conditions in the countries where they originated. In addition, there was Clare's acquaintance with travellers, for example Robert Gouger, one of the founders of South Australia. We must also consider the shows he saw on his visits to London, such as Bullock's Museum,[4] and the travelling shows he may have seen in Stamford. When considering Clare's activities as a naturalist, this wider context should always be borne in mind. He wrote about his locality, but he was very aware of what lay beyond the woods and fields of Helpston.

The main source of Clare's knowledge and skill as a naturalist seems to have come from his friendships with other naturalists. The period immediately before and after the publication of his first book in 1820 was a period of rapid intellectual growth for Clare. That first book was called *Poems, Descriptive of Rural Life and Scenery*, and yet what strikes us now is how little of either there is in the book. There is certainly little about the natural world, and there is plenty of evidence that Clare's knowledge of that world was limited, and that he knew little about the activities of naturalists. For example, in February 1822, when working on a poem on April for the *London Magazine*, he had to ask John Taylor whether he was right in thinking that the swallow arrived in that month and the cuckoo sang (*Letters*, p. 233). This, one would think, would be fairly basic information for a country dweller.

In one of his *Autobiographical Fragments*, Clare wrote:

> I also was fond of gather[ing] fossil stones   tho I never knew these was the subject of books yet I was pleasd to find and collect them which I did many years tho my mother threw them out of doors when they was in her way   a Dr Dupere of Crowland collected such things and my friend John Turnill got some for him   this gave me the taste for fossil hunting   my friend Artis had what was left when I became acquainted with him   (*JCBH*, p. 62)

At this date, before the professionalization of science, natural historians were largely amateurs, mainly gentlemen and ladies, landowners, clergy, and gardeners; Clare had friends and acquaintances in all these classes. Among naturalists in the early nineteenth century, there was always a strong representation of doctors, reflecting the close relationship between medicine and botany which had existed for centuries, and doctors were still trained in botany since many medicines had their origin in plants. One such was Fenwick Skrimshire of Peterborough, Clare's doctor, who Clare described as 'a curious man & collects the eggs of English birds' (*Natural History*, p. 34). Fenwick Skrimshire came from a family of naturalists including his brothers William, a surgeon living in Wisbech, Cambridgeshire, and Thomas, a Norfolk clergyman. He received his medical training in Edinburgh, qualifying in 1798. His time there led to his first mention in the scientific literature; in the first of the three volumes of Sir James Edward Smith's *Flora Britannica*, Skrimshire is credited with finding a species of campanula, the Creeping Bell-flower, at Blair, in Kinross.[5]

Fenwick Skrimshire is mainly remembered for the part which he and his brother played in establishing that the Large Copper butterfly was native to Britain:

> Adrian Haworth seems to have learnt of the Large Copper from his friends William and Fenwick Skrimshire, who were travelling to Ely in a gig when they chanced to notice a number of unusual 'Copper' butterflies by the roadside. On the return journey they stopped to examine them and confirm their earlier impression that they were an unknown species. There is little doubt that Fenwick Skrimshire would have recognized these butterflies if they had been already known. He was a distinguished naturalist, being President of the Natural History Society of Edinburgh; he was also the author in 1805 of *A Series of Essays Introductory to the Study of Natural History*.[6]

The discovery of this spectacular butterfly was mentioned by Haworth in 1802, in his *Prodromus Lepidopterorum Britannicorum*, which remained the principal checklist of British butterflies for a decade and a half.

One must always beware of mistaking absence of evidence for evidence of absence, and I have no doubt that there were gardeners and other naturalists whom Clare knew but who have left no trace in the historical record. But among the naturalists it is Edmund Artis and Joseph Henderson about whom we know most. Edmund Artis was the house steward to Earl Fitzwilliam, and Joseph Henderson was the head gardener at Milton Hall; this was the Fitzwilliam family's winter residence, a few miles from Clare's home in Helpston. There is little doubt that these two men were John Clare's most important teachers; both were all-round naturalists, but both had their areas of expertise.

Clare had first visited Milton in early February 1820, shortly after the publication of his first volume, but, although he dined in the servants' hall, he does not seem to have struck up any close friendships there at that time. There is no indication of any contact with Artis or Henderson earlier than Clare's letter to John Taylor of 24 January 1822 in which he says: 'I have been to Milton & spent 3 days with Mr Artis the Antiquary very pleasantly' (*Letters*, p. 224). He went on to describe some of Artis's archaeological discoveries, concluding: 'he seems to me quite a clever man & every thing but a poet' (*Letters*, p. 225). Clare's correspondence with Artis and Henderson began shortly afterwards. It is probable that Clare's first meeting with the two men is to be found described in a letter he wrote to John Taylor on 24 April 1821:

> visitors comes on me every other day or nearly & I had a sensible Gent: yesterday no doubt you know him 'Dr Noehden British Museum' he talked civily & unasuming & I felt the loss of his company after he left me – he has

given me an Invitation when in London to visit him & see the Museum which he thinks will please me – he odd enough said 'he had seen my *pretty poems* & that curosity had urged him to seize the first oppertunity of seeing the author' he was accompined with 2 other gents who did not leave their names

(*Letters*, pp. 184–5)

Georg Heinrich Nöhden, who anglicized his name to George Henry Noehden on leaving his native Germany for England, was a man of many interests and accomplishments, and at this time was curator in the Archaeological Department of the British Museum. In this capacity, he travelled the country, and he took a close interest in Artis's archaeological and palaeontological work. If he was in the vicinity, it would have been to spend a day or two at Milton to bring himself up to date with Artis's research; it is no coincidence that *Drakard's Stamford News* of 20 April 1821 had announced:

> Mr. Artis, house steward to Earl Fitzwilliam, in searching last week for fossils, discovered in front of the manor house at Castor, near Peterborough, a beautiful tesselated Roman pavement of an oblong shape, being twenty one feet long and twelve broad. It has a splendid Mosaic centre, six feet ten inches long and four feet six inches wide; the colours are quite fresh, and the design is elegant

It must have been the news of this discovery which brought Georg Noehden to Northamptonshire. We can reasonably assume, therefore, that the '2 other gents' who accompanied Dr Noehden on his visit to John Clare were Edmund Artis and Joseph Henderson. What happened next is unknown, but sometime between April and the end of 1821 that initial acquaintance developed into a friendship. This was not Dr Noehden's only visit to Milton; he went there on at least one other occasion because he spent the Christmas of 1822 there. Joseph Henderson would also have been a congenial companion for him, because botany and horticulture were among Noehden's interests; he contributed a number of articles to the recently founded *Transactions of the Horticultural Society*.

Edmund Artis was a palaeontologist and antiquarian. Much of the Fitzwilliam family's wealth came from the coal mines they owned near their summer residence at Wentworth Woodhouse in the West Riding of Yorkshire. Artis collected fossil plants which are found in the coal measures and in 1825 published a book on them under the title of *Antediluvian Phytology*. The books and journals he named in this work make it plain that he was abreast of the latest research in this area not just in this country but on the Continent. Among those he names as having helped him in his researches were William Buckland, perhaps the most eminent geologist in what is often regarded as the golden age of geology, Robert Brown, the equally distinguished botanist, and, inevitably, Dr Noehden. Baron Cuvier, the founder of the science of comparative anatomy and one of the most famous men in Europe, and Jean-François Champollion, who earned undying fame by deciphering Egyptian hieroglyphics for the first time, were among those credited with assisting his researches while he was in Paris.

In the early 1820s, Artis, while searching for fossils in the Nene valley near Milton, found Roman remains in and around the village of Castor and began exploring them; at this time, there was still a close relationship between antiquarianism and natural history. Again, his research resulted in a book, a series of sixty plates, many of them hand-coloured, illustrating his discoveries and published over several years under the title of *The Durobrivae of Antoninus*. In both palaeontology and archaeology, Artis was a pioneer, adopting what was, for the time, an unusually scientific attitude in these pursuits. Artis was also a subscriber to Curtis's *British Entomology* and had an interest in ornithology; Clare mentions his collection of stuffed birds (*Natural History*, p. 38).

Artis travelled around with the Fitzwilliam family, to Wentworth and their London residence in Grosvenor Square, and was only at Milton for part of the year. Joseph Henderson, as head gardener, was there all the time and was therefore more of an influence on John Clare. Henderson was one of the many Scottish gardeners who were to be found in Georgian and Victorian England.[7] He grew up at Blair Adam in Kinross, where his grandfather and father were successively the head gardeners. This was an important garden, having a close relationship with the Edinburgh Botanic Garden, with a constant exchange of seeds and plants between the two; indeed, it has been claimed that 'the Blair Adam collection of trees and shrubs did not differ greatly from what was growing in the Edinburgh Botanic Garden'.[8] It was a horticulturally and scientifically sophisticated environment in which the young Joseph grew up.

As well as having a full-time, and demanding, job, Henderson contributed to many areas of the rapidly developing natural sciences. He knew a lot about birds, and Clare tells us that he had a collection of stuffed birds; he also collected nests and eggs (*Natural History*, p. 115). Henderson is mentioned several times by Lord Lilford in his two-volume work, *Notes on the Birds of Northamptonshire and Neighbourhood*, published in 1895. Lord Lilford lived at Lilford Hall, near Oundle, about ten miles from Milton Hall, and was the pre-eminent ornithologist of late Victorian England. He was one of the founders of the British Ornithologists' Union in 1858 and its President from 1867 until his death in 1896; he was also the first president of the Northamptonshire Natural History Society. He didn't know Henderson, being only a child when Henderson left Milton for Wentworth, but he knew Lady Mary Thompson, who was a Fitzwilliam; she was able to relay to Lord Lilford the contents of conversations she had had many years previously with Joseph Henderson on the birds to be found around Milton. Thus, we find in Lilford's book, when discussing the Golden Oriole:

> The earliest notice I have is in a list of birds observed in and about Milton, kindly sent by Lady Mary Thompson, who tells me that about the end of May or early in June 1836 she saw one of these birds in the garden at Milton, evidently, from the description given, a male in full plumage. Lady Mary tells me also that, on speaking on the subject to a Mr. Henderson, then gardener at Milton, who was a good observer and a collector of birds, he told her that he had seen the bird several times, and made several unsuccessful attempts to secure it alive or dead.[9]

In his section on the Osprey, Lilford writes: 'A specimen was obtained at Milton, near Peterborough, in 1823.'[10] Sure enough, when we look at the entry for the Osprey in the extensive Bird List which John Clare drew up in the mid 1820s we find: 'one shot by Henderson in Milton Park' (*Natural History*, p. 123).

Joseph Henderson was also a noted botanist, publishing several papers on various aspects of the subject, one of which was read before the Linnean Society and led to him being appointed an associate of the Linnean Society, a rank rarely conferred on gardeners. His particular interest was in cryptogams, the non-flowering plants. He was a pioneer of fern culture, and one of the forerunners of what became the Victorian fern craze, establishing a fine collection of ferns; it is, perhaps, no coincidence that there had been a notable collection of ferns at Blair Adam.[11]

Another area of Clare's naturalizing where Henderson was influential was conchology: Clare had long been fascinated by snail shells and had been a collector of them since boyhood; he mentions, in one of his recollections of childhood, that: 'Searching of Snail shells we call "Pooties" was a Favou[r]ite Amusement' (*JCBH*, p. 33). Under Henderson's influence his interest became more sophisticated; in his Journal entry for 15 November 1824, he wrote:

> Went out to gather pootys on the roman bank for a collection found a scarce sort of which I only saw two in my life one pickd up under a hedge at peakirk town end & another in bainton meadow its color is a fine sunny yellow larger then the common sort & round the rim of the base is a black edging which extends no further then the rim it is not in the collection at the British Museum (*Natural History*, pp. 202–3)

This is a rather astonishing statement, but he had, by this time, obviously studied the collections in the British Museum in great detail, presumably taking advantage of the invitation extended to him by Dr Noehden as the museum was not then readily accessible to members of the public. The shells Clare collected probably found their way into Henderson's collection; Clare recorded in his journal on 7 May 1825: 'Sent some Pootys & Ferns to Henderson yesterday' (*Natural History*, p. 238).

Another way in which Henderson helped Clare to expand his knowledge and understanding of the natural world was by acting as a source of information, and by helping in the identification of plants, animals, birds, and insects which Clare was not sure about. Thus, on 14 August 1825, after staying overnight at Milton, Clare noted in his Journal:

> Returned from Milton brought home some flower seeds & roots – saw two very large catterpillars which a man found among the Potatoes in his garden one was about 3 Inches long & the other 4 the smaller one was green with triangular marks of black, light blue, and yellow, the other was yellow with triangular marks of the same colors as the other save that were the other was yellow this was white (*Natural History*, p. 253)

Clare wrote to Henderson about this discovery, and the latter replied on 18 August telling Clare what he wanted to know. Thus, the next time Clare encountered one of the caterpillars, he was able to note in his journal, on 23 August, without any doubt or ambiguity: 'Found a beautiful Deaths head Moth catterpillar in Billings Potatoes' (*Natural History*, p. 254).

One of the most significant botanists known to Henderson was the Rev. Miles Berkeley, a young curate at nearby Thornhaugh; he had been appointed in 1826 after graduating from Cambridge where he, like Charles Darwin at much the same time, had studied botany under Professor Henslow. Berkeley shared with Henderson a particular interest in the cryptogams and became a world authority on fungi, describing over 6,000 species; he was one of the great botanists of Victorian England and became a Fellow of the Royal Society among his many honours. Henderson's friendship with Berkeley was of great use to him because Berkeley gave him a connection with the wider world of botanical science and horticulture and seems to have provided Henderson with opportunities for developing his knowledge in these fields as well as communicating his discoveries to the scientific world; it was he who read Henderson's paper before the Linnean Society.

Henderson first achieved notice as a cultivator of orchids, a group of plants which grew rapidly in popularity in the early Victorian period with the increasing importation and cultivation of exotic species. The earliest reference I have discovered to Joseph Henderson in the botanical or horticultural

John Clare and the Community of Naturalists

literature is in *Edwards's Botanical Register* in 1832, in a description of an orchid, *Herminium cordatum*, the Heart-leaved Herminium. This is accompanied, as always, by a hand-coloured plate showing the flower, and Professor Lindley, the editor, begins his account of the plant thus:

> A native of the north-west of Africa and south-west of Europe; Link and Brotero have found it in Portugal; we have specimens from shady hills near Tangier, collected by Salzmann; and the Rev. Mr. Lowe found it on walls and rocks in Madeira. For the specimen from which our drawing was taken, we are obliged to the Rev. Mr. Berkeley, at whose request it was forwarded to us from the rich collection of Lord Milton, by Mr. Joseph Henderson. To the latter excellent cultivator we are indebted for the following note upon its habits:–
> 'The plant grows very well in the Greenhouse; but it requires a little more heat at this season, which seems to be its flowering season (November), than the Greenhouse affords; and I find that it flowers best in the coolest part of the stove.'

Lord Milton was an early enthusiast for the growing of orchids, and his gardeners, at both Milton and Wentworth Woodhouse, acquired great expertise in overcoming what had, hitherto, been regarded as intractable problems in successfully cultivating exotic species. The enthusiasm which Lord Milton and Joseph Henderson showed for the collecting and cultivating of orchids was rapidly communicated to John Clare; on the front paste-down of his copy of Isaac Emmerton's *The Culture & Management of the Auricula, Polyanthus, Carnation, Pink, and the Ranunculus* (1819) is a list of twenty-two orchids, containing twelve different species, which is headed 'Orchis's counted from Privet hedge'. Margaret Grainger prints a table summarizing Clare's orchids from this list and other sources (*Natural History*, pp. 298–9); she was, however, unaware of Henderson's letters to Clare on the subject.

In the early nineteenth century, there was no easy way for naturalists to make contact with others who had similar interests; many naturalists worked in isolation. It was only when John Claudius Loudon began publishing his *Magazine of Natural History* in 1829 that channels of communication began to develop. Before then, to discover people in other parts of the country who shared one's enthusiasms was very largely a matter of happenstance; this is what happened to Joseph Henderson, leading to an unexpected link with one of the artisan botanists of Lancashire. In the late eighteenth and early nineteenth centuries, there were many botanical societies in the manufacturing districts of south Lancashire, such as the Tyldesley Botanical Society, the Boothstown Botanical Society, the Middleton Botanical Society, the Hulme Field Naturalists Society, and the Lower Mosley Street Natural History Society amongst others. I would emphasize that these were not just people with a hobby; these were expert naturalists. Foremost among them was Edward Hobson, a Manchester warehouseman, who had devoted his leisure to the study of botany; he specialized in the study of mosses and was acknowledged as one of the country's leading experts on this group of plants.

Henderson's involvement with Edward Hobson came about purely by chance; Thomas Rogers, who was head gardener to Edward Jenkins of Thorpe Hall, a neighbouring property to Milton Hall, moved to Manchester. Rogers made the acquaintance of Edward Hobson, and, having been friendly with Joseph Henderson and sharing his interests, he suggested to Hobson that he might profitably contact Henderson. Hobson therefore wrote to Henderson on 3 April 1826, outlining his interests in insects and plants, particularly mosses, and suggesting that there was scope for an exchange of specimens between the two men. Henderson replied, three days later, agreeing enthusiastically to the suggestion and including a list of some of his local insects, from which Hobson might like to choose some which he would like to have. He also explained that he had never had the opportunity of making a collection of mosses, so there he could not offer much in exchange.[12]

This is a classic example of how an exchange of specimens and information began, with offers to add to each other's collections. When Henderson sent a list of the species of butterflies and moths he could offer, Hobson was clearly rather overwhelmed by the length of the list because, as he said, this was far greater than the number of species to be found around Manchester. However, he explained that entomology was a relatively new departure for him and his friends; they had mostly devoted their time and attention to botany. Hobson felt that he had little more to learn about botany, and particularly about mosses, so he had branched out into a new area of natural history. Since he could not hope to match Henderson in the lepidoptera, and since Henderson said he had never had the opportunity to form a collection of mosses, Hobson offered him upwards of 260 species of moss in return. He was as good as his word and soon sent to Henderson the first volume of his great work, *Musci Britannici*. In this volume, Hobson used preserved specimens of mosses, each stuck down to a page of the book and correctly labelled, to illustrate the variety of British mosses. Given the nature of the work, it is believed that only about two dozen copies were ever produced, and it is, of course, a rare and precious item nowadays.[13]

With his book of mosses, Hobson included some insects, explaining that since he was a novice in this area he would value Henderson's advice on the setting and storing of insects. One of the many interesting features of this correspondence is that, because Hobson lacked experience as an entomologist, Henderson had to explain, sometimes quite elementary, things to him, and thereby gives us an insight into contemporary techniques, the reference works he used, and his personal knowledge and ideas. His response to Hobson's box of insects was typical; he said that many of the insects had been spoiled because Hobson had used unsuitable cork to pin the insects, and consequently some had worked loose, damaging other specimens.

Another topic of the correspondence is the sparse and unsatisfactory literature of the subject, and the difficulties this posed in identifying specimens. Writing to Hobson in November 1826, Henderson revealed that he was in communication with John Curtis who had recently begun the publication of his great work, *British Entomology*, which eventually ran to 16 volumes, 193 parts, with 770 hand-coloured plates. It is one of the great natural history works of the Romantic period, and Curtis became the country's leading expert on insects. Since Curtis would necessarily see a huge range of British insects in producing his work, he would, Henderson hoped, be able to assist in the identification of specimens. Henderson contributed information to Curtis and is mentioned in the *British Entomology*; John Clare records seeing the work at Milton (*Natural History*, p. 210).

By this time, Hobson had sent Henderson the second volume of *Musci Britannici*. Henderson thanked Hobson for his wonderful gift, saying how much his botanical friends admired the work. We may be sure that John Clare would have been one of the friends to whom Henderson showed the two volumes of mosses. The correspondence between Edward Hobson and Joseph Henderson continued until 1829 when Edward Hobson was taken ill; he died the following year, of consumption.

In one of his last letters to Hobson, Henderson revealed that he had received a call from John Curtis and James Dale. Dale was Curtis's collaborator on his *British Entomology*; he was Lord of the Manor of Glanville's Wootton in Dorset, and a skilled and enthusiastic entomologist. Many of the insects illustrated in *British Entomology* are labelled as 'figured from a specimen in Mr. Dale's cabinet'. The fact that Henderson was visited by two such distinguished entomologists gives us some idea of the position he held in this area of science. The Oxford Museum of Natural History has Dale's extensive archive, which includes letters from Henderson to Dale, and these reveal that one of the entomologists whom Henderson cooperated with was Fenwick Skrimshire of Peterborough. Henderson and Dale exchanged specimens and information over many years.

One butterfly which Henderson seems to have been able to capture in large quantities for other collectors was the Swallowtail, the largest and most spectacular of the English butterflies. This is now a very rare insect, found only on the Norfolk Broads, but two centuries ago it was much more widespread and was particularly plentiful in Whittlesea Mere, a few miles to the south-east of Milton. Whittlesea Mere was the largest lake in lowland England and was well known for its rare plants and animals; collectors travelled from far and wide to explore its riches, and its proximity was important to Henderson, and to Clare. Another spectacular butterfly, now extinct in the British Isles, which Henderson found there was the Large Copper, first identified by Fenwick and William Skrimshire and eagerly sought by Edward Hobson and other collectors. When Curtis first published his information on the Large Copper in *British Entomology*, nobody knew what the caterpillar looked like, or what its food plant was. It was Henderson who provided Curtis with this information, enabling him to include it when the relevant part of his work was reissued. We have an attractive vignette of Henderson from this period:

> In Mr. Henderson's garden, there was a spring so arranged as to supply a small pond, round which he cultivated roots of the Bullrush: and, bringing home from the Fens larvæ of the large Copper Butterfly, he placed them among the plants so that they might there effect their final change, and sometimes there would be several of the perfect insects flying round the pond at once.[14]

A recurring theme of Henderson's letters is his fear for the unique habitat of Whittlesea Mere, partly because of over-collecting of specimens, but mainly because he foresaw that the whole area would be drained and turned into farmland, as indeed happened, with the loss of many precious species of plants and insects, the Large Copper among them.

What is very noticeable when one looks at Clare's naturalizing is that Henderson led the way and Clare followed. Thus, I've said that Henderson was a pioneer in the cultivation of ferns. Clare tells us in his journal for 19 November 1824:

> Had a visit from my friend Henderson & I felt revivd as I was very dull before: he had pleasing News to deliver me having discoverd a new species of Fern a few days back growing among the bogs on Whittlesea Mere & our talk was of Ferns for the day   (*Natural History*, p. 204)

The effect on Clare was instantaneous, because next day he recorded in his journal: 'Went out to hunt the harts tongue species of fern' (*Natural History*, p. 204). His journal over the next few months contains several references to walks, searching for ferns and planting them in his garden just as Henderson was doing. Writing to Charles Abraham Elton in Bristol at this time, Clare said: 'I am now amusing myself when I am able at hunting the woods for the Diferrent sorts of Ferns of which I am making a collection for I love wild things almost to foolishness' (*Letters*, p. 310).

John Clare and the Community of Naturalists

When we look at insects, we find, again, that Clare was following, and enthusiastically helping, his friend. In November 1827, Henderson ended a letter by saying that he would return Clare's insect bottle as soon as he had disposed of the carcasses within it, and he thanked Clare for the eggs and shells he had sent. One of the many myths about John Clare is that he eschewed collecting flowers, insects, birds' eggs, and so on, but there is plentiful evidence to contradict this; he was always eager to collect things for his friends. An entomologist known to Clare, and to Henderson, was George Marsh, the younger son of the Bishop of Peterborough. On 19 October 1829, Clare told Mrs Marsh, in a postscript to a letter: 'I have ventured to send two or three Specimens of Moths for Mr G Marsh they are badly set up but thinking there might be one among them which he had not I preserved them as well as I could & waited the first oppertunity to send' (*Letters*, p. 469). That was clearly not the end of Clare's help for George Marsh; in a letter the following year, Mrs Marsh wrote thanking Clare for the butterflies which he had sent for George, and returning his cork. So, it is clear that Clare not only killed butterflies and moths for his friends, but he had learned how to set them by pinning them out on sheets of cork.

Finally, the mosses. We have seen that Joseph Henderson told Edward Hobson, in April 1826, that he had never had the opportunity of making a collection of these. That changed as soon as Hobson sent Henderson the two volumes of his book of mosses. In 1828, Henderson told Clare that he had completed his book on the mosses and that it contained 100 species, all collected within a few miles of Milton. Again, we find John Clare following his friend's lead. Marianne Marsh, the bishop's wife, who was German, sent Clare a gift of a magnifying glass suitable for studying insects and mosses which she had brought with her from Germany. This I suppose to have been the 'Pocket Microscope used by John Clare in his studies of Natural History' which is listed in the catalogue of the exhibition held in Peterborough in 1893 to mark the centenary of Clare's birth.

To conclude, Clare's friends included some very accomplished, and well-connected, naturalists who, between them, covered most areas of the subject. Clare could, and did, learn a great deal from them. How does this feed into his poetry? Sometimes the connections are obvious. For instance, Clare wrote many poems about birds and birds' nests. He was an expert observer, and skilled at finding nests, but much of the information for those poems must have come from studying collections of birds' nests and stuffed birds such as those owned by Henderson and Artis. In those days, many naturalists collected eggs, but others collected nests with the complete clutch of eggs inside. It may well be that at least some of the inspiration for the long poem

Clare wrote under the title of 'Birds Nesting' came from studying such a collection.[15]

It was not only the subject matter of Clare's poems which altered but the style too. Much of his earlier poetry has a rather lifeless and static quality, but from the mid 1820s onwards, there is a more dynamic quality to his verse. Timothy Brownlow has described how Clare utilized the 'kinetic elements inherent in the picturesque vision' to avoid 'the obvious pitfalls of descriptive poetry', and he argues that 'Clare not only admits more detail into his work than most of his predecessors, he is also aware that those details are in constant mutation'.[16] Clare seems to have outgrown the models which had been initially enabling, but finally restrictive. His work becomes more specific and detailed, and at the same time much less conventional; his intense involvement with contemporary natural history, combined with his wide reading, contributed to a more modern outlook and introduced a new dimension into his work. As Jerome Bump has suggested, it is in his poems inspired by the natural world that he first achieved 'that balance between accurate mimesis and Romantic self-consciousness which characterizes Clare's best poetry'.[17]

Notes

1. These notes are in manuscript MISC 0198 in The Carl H. Pforzheimer Collection of Shelley and His Circle, New York Public Library, Astor, Lenox, and Tilden Foundations.
2. Paul Smethurst, *Travel Writing and the Natural World, 1768–1840* (Basingstoke: Palgrave Macmillan, 2012), p. 5.
3. Anne Troelstra, *A Bibliography of Natural History Travel Narratives* (Zeist: KNNV Publishing, 2016).
4. Richard D. Altick, *The Shows of London* (Cambridge, MA: Belknap Press, 1978), chapter 18.
5. James Edward Smith, *Flora Britannica*, 3 vols. (London: J. White, 1800–4), I, 238.
6. Michael A. Salmon, *The Aurelian Legacy: British Butterflies and Their Collectors* (Colchester: Harley Books, 2000), pp. 280–81.
7. Alice M. Coats, 'When Scottish Gardeners Came South', *Country Life*, 12 March 1964, pp. 572–3.
8. Forbes W. Robertson, 'John Adam's Eighteenth-Century Walled Garden at Blair, Kinross', *Garden History*, 31.1 (Spring 2003), 48–66 (p. 49).
9. Lord Lilford, *Notes on the Birds of Northamptonshire and Neighbourhood*, 2 vols. (London: R. H. Porter, 1895), I, 84.
10. Lord Lilford, *Notes on the Birds of Northamptonshire*, I, 7.
11. Robertson, 'John Adam's Eighteenth-Century Walled Garden at Blair, Kinross', p. 55.

12. Henderson's letters to Hobson, and the drafts of Hobson's replies, are preserved among Edward Hobson's botanical correspondence in the Botany Department of Manchester Museum.
13. An illustration of a copy can be found on the internet among '101 Treasures of Chetham's', https://library.chethams.com/collections/101-treasures-of-chethams/hobsons-musci-britannici/.
14. Alfred Newton, 'Memoir of the Late John Scales', *Transactions of the Norfolk and Norwich Naturalists' Society*, 4.1 (1885), 81–119 (p. 89).
15. MP II 163–84.
16. Timothy Brownlow, *John Clare and Picturesque Landscape* (Oxford: Clarendon Press, 1983), p. 116.
17. Jerome Bump, Review of W. J. Keith, *The Rural Tradition*, James Sambrook, *William Cobbett*, and Mark Storey, *The Poetry of John Clare*, *Victorian Studies*, 20 (1976–7), 96–8 (p. 98).

8

MARKUS POETZSCH

Clare and Ecocriticism

John Clare and ecocriticism have come of age together in academic circles. Indeed, the proliferation of scholarly work on Clare over the last thirty years, unrivalled by any period since his death, coincides with what Lawrence Buell has characterized as ecocriticism's 'two-stage affair since its inception as a self-conscious movement in the early 1990s'.[1] One could in fact suggest that these contiguous bodies of research – one a subject and the other a network of methodologies – have had a mutually inspiring effect upon one another, which is in itself significant given that Clare's work roots itself in a very specific cultural, regional, and temporal domain (British Romanticism) while ecocriticism tends to be defined by its transgressiveness, its crossing of borders, habitats, disciplines, languages, ideologies, timescales, subjectivities, species, even worlds. In fact, so diverse (one might say, indiscriminate) has the practice of ecocriticism become as a mode of literary inquiry that questions have been raised about its definitional parameters. To put it simply, scholars have faced considerable difficulty in resolving what exactly ecocriticism is (or has become) as part of their effort to harness its potential as a form of cultural analysis and environmental activism. Nirmal Selvamony summarizes the issue in the following terms: 'ecocritics are not agreed on what constitutes the basic principle in ecocriticism, whether it is *bios*, or nature or environment or place or earth or land. Since there is no consensus, there is no common definition of the term. But without an acceptable definition it is hard to deal with a subject collectively, especially in an academy.'[2]

The typical response to this problem – which is at once a lexical, theoretical, and practical conundrum – has been to establish the terms and principles of ecocriticism (the latter often embedded in the former) as broadly as possible. Cheryll Glotfelty's enduringly popular definition from 1996 is a useful example: 'ecocriticism is the study of the relationship between literature and the physical environment'.[3] The scholarly territory covered by this summation is vast, admitting everything from the seemingly peripheral and obscure, like book production histories, contextualist narratologies, and design dramaturgy, to the pointedly political and activist, such as manifestos on radical conservation or sci-fi novels on mass extinction events. With the ecocritical net cast so wide, 'it is possible to argue', according to Claire Colebrook, 'that all literary criticism is ecocriticism' and that all texts are inherently ecological in the sense that they are both systems of their own and 'ongoing proliferation[s] of relations'.[4] While such analogical arguments are compelling in the abstract, they tend to overlook one other key element of ecocritical discourses: their ideological orientation. Ecocriticism is not value-neutral; it is not satisfied with the mere discovery, description, and codification of ecological relations, whether in art or in the physical world. On the contrary, as Timothy Clark has reminded readers, the ecocritical enterprise has from the outset cultivated 'deep ties to the liberatory politics of the progressive left' and continues to function in academic circles as 'a kind of worthwhile activism' with an associated set of values oriented to interrogating 'the nature and causes of environmental crises, the ways they are represented in language and culture, or contested or interpreted in literature, in art or daily discourse'.[5]

First- and Second-Wave Ecocriticism

For a writer like Clare, the implication of ecocriticism's political dimension is that his work has been made serviceable in our own environmental causes – slotted neatly, that is, into a progressivist narrative that, in the words of Anahid Nersessian, 'treat[s] texts as resources to be pumped … for prophecy'.[6] Such extractive and at times anachronistic reading practices through which Clare has been established not only in Romantic circles but in environmental literature more broadly as the quintessential poet of nature were a particular feature of what is often described as first-wave ecocriticism, a period of scholarship extending roughly from 1990 to the early years of the twenty-first century. Buell associates this first wave with nation- and genre-focused approaches that prioritized Anglo-American contexts, the work of male writers, and a somewhat idealistic rendering of both nature and ecology. Other scholars, most notably Timothy Morton, have also pointed out that the analytical practice of first-wave critics tended to diminish, if not entirely elide, the structuring conditions of language itself, relying instead on a superficial version of ecomimesis to suggest the immediacy – the illusory 'here and now' – of writing.[7] As a result, certain representational modes or mediations of nature loosely characterized as 'realistic' or 'authentic' gained a privileged position in the early ecocritical canon: first-person travel narratives, loco-descriptive poetry, natural philosophy, local and regional histories, nature journals, and so on.

Not surprisingly, Clare has featured prominently in the work of first-wave critics. Jeremy Davies, commenting on the foundational figures of Romantic ecocriticism, lists Clare along with Gilbert White and Dorothy Wordsworth as 'the authors who have long seemed to be the special province of green reading'.[8] What these three writers have in common – and what thus reveals itself as the overriding focus of early 'green reading' – is a perspective rooted in the experience of dwelling in a particular place and committed to a celebratory elaboration of the natural life, infinitely varied and complex, by which that place is constituted, all of it rendered in a language that carefully sets limits on the ordering powers of human agency. Yet what Clare offers additionally that White and Wordsworth do not is a distinct voice of environmental protest that many contemporary readers have found indicative of a common and to some extent continuous history of literary activism. Greg Garrard, for example, highlights the 'rage' evident in poems such as 'The Mores', 'Helpstone', and 'To a Fallen Elm' (prominent examples of Clare's so-called enclosure elegies) and argues, in alignment with scholars such as Jonathan Bate and James McKusick, that 'Clare decidedly thought further ahead of his fellow Romantics'.[9] Clare, in other words, was more modern, at least in his environmental concerns. Bridget Keegan, while drawing upon a different sample of texts, namely Clare's varied reflections on fens and other wetland habitats, makes a similar claim for his contemporary relevance, suggesting that the levelling effect of his work 'anticipates ecocentric [as opposed to anthropocentric] ethics'.[10] Certain of Clare's poems, most notably 'The Lament of Swordy Well' (c. 1832–7) and 'The Lamentations of Round-Oak Waters' (1818), even manage to conjoin the voice of outrage with an ecocentric worldview, making them touchstone texts for first-wave ecocriticism. Commenting on 'Swordy Well', a text unpublished in Clare's lifetime possibly because of its combative politics, Clark lingers on the poet's decision to make the land (an ancient Roman quarry enclosed by 1820) the speaker of the poem and concludes that such 'linguistic and conceptual inventiveness [is] often required to give voice to environmental outrage'.[11] The image that thus emerges of Clare is of a radical environmentalist, unafraid to ruffle the feathers of established power, and arguably even more relevant in our age of eco-degradation than he was in his own.

The temptation to foreshorten history in this manner, to bring the voices of the past directly into the exigencies of the present and thereby to generate momentum for meaningful environmental change, is reflective of the activist project of ecocriticism, particularly (though not exclusively) in its first wave of development. Commenting on the academic pressure to make our literary past responsive to our current climatological reality, Simon Kövesi acknowledges an ongoing 'systemic urgency in the humanities generally that green thinking has to make itself explicitly relevant to contemporary problems; that it has to try to be scientifically engaged in a present, material environment, the way the natural sciences might more directly be'. Green thinking, in other words, has to become indivisible from green doing. Clare's status not merely as an eco-prophet but as an eco-warrior depends on that conflation. As Kövesi observes, in extreme cases of agenda-driven literary analysis, Clare has been deployed 'as a sort of proto-ecological weapon' against the forces of global capitalism – a weapon seemingly wiped clean of any traces of its own complicated history.[12] That history includes Clare's direct participation in the business of enclosure, most notably as a day labourer building fences and planting hedges to divide what was once common land from common people. The revelation of such inconvenient autobiographical details, which Kövesi mobilizes in order to inflect the self-assured political agenda of modern eco-conscious readers with the messy historical realities of class struggle, signals a decisive shift away from the reading practices, historiographies, and dominant environmental narratives of first-wave critics.

Second-wave ecocriticism is defined by such revisionism, which entails a willingness to re-examine historical records, to excavate the past more thoroughly and dispassionately, while also admitting the intersections (and occasional interjections) of other disciplines, perspectives, and epistemologies. The scholarship of second-wave critics is oriented, one might say, to a recognition of uncomfortable diversity in environmental theorizations rather than the establishment of convenient consensus. The impetus for this greater plurality of perspectives can be attributed in part to the pioneering work of eco-feminists, who, as Clark points out, 'trac[ed] environmentally destructive behaviour to patriarchal norms of entitlement and ownership, and to fantasies of mastery both over nature and each other, in denial of human bodily finitude'.[13] Such exploitative practices, however, are not the exclusive province of patriarchy. They are also evident in other forms of social and cultural organization and, moreover, in other relational spheres where power between human communities – or indeed between human and nonhuman communities – is unequally distributed or liable to misappropriation. Hence the growing focus in second-wave ecocriticism on the plight of the socially marginalized and impoverished, including Indigenous peoples, post-colonial subjects, climate refugees, political migrants, and exploited labourers in industrial and post-industrial economies. While much of this work is driven by environmental justice initiatives, second-wave ecocriticism is also defined by a renewed interest in humans' obligation to other living creatures, animals in particular, and not only endangered or displaced species but livestock and even household pets. Critical animal studies were of course already a dominant feature of first-wave scholarship, yet more recent forays in this field are notable for interrogating the conceptual boundaries between human and animal being, with a particular focus on notions of transcorporeality, which Buell defines as 'a construal of being in the world that is simultaneously animal, technological, and environmental'.[14]

Such an interest in hybridity is evident not only in the ontological questions raised by second-wave ecocriticism but also in its dealing with place. Whereas earlier scholarship tended to privilege British and North American settings, particularly rural or wilderness spaces, more recent studies have vastly expanded the territory of ecocritical inquiry, taking in global contexts, speculative geographies, and of course a growing diversity of urban and suburban landscapes that definitively collapse the long-contested binaries of nature and culture, country and city. Along with this dilation and differentiation of space, there is also a concomitant movement towards concentration in second-wave ecocriticism. Bodies are increasingly theorized as environments – bodies as effects, as sites or repositories of natural despoliation, bodies of flesh and bone, plastics and chemicals; but also bodies as becomings, as ongoing networks of relation, nodes in a mesh, points in the constellations of ecology, bodies as possibilities. Davies subsumes this burgeoning field of scholarship under the heading of 'new materialism' and suggests that an investment in material reality – not only flora and fauna but the objects through which humans relate to them – may be particularly productive for Romantic ecocriticism as it seeks ways to reinvigorate its 'well-established historicizing impulses'.[15] An investment in materiality as part of environmental discourse may also have to consider the expanding role of digital environments in our relation to texts and to the world we inhabit. Although ecocriticism has typically been wary of digital technologies and their capacity to draw us away, even estrange us, from the physical world and the reality of environmental crisis, Stephanie Posthumus and Stéfan Sinclair argue that certain ecological activities, such as the practice of reading, can be transformed through technological interventions to foster more creative and collaborative explorations of spatial information in texts. The digital, as such, may play an important role in 'materialising and making visible some of the processes of interpreting and reading', which are essential to ecocriticism.[16]

The work of John Clare, as I have suggested, was central to first-wave scholarship and continues to generate considerable interest from second-wave revisionist critics who have complicated but also thereby enriched our understanding of the poet's environmental legacy. Even before Kövesi traced the class fault lines beneath the green gloss of Clare's ecological advocacy, scholars such as Robert Heyes had exposed uncomfortable discontinuities between modern conceptions of natural history and Clare's actual practice of it in the nineteenth century. Drawing on Clare's descriptions of his occasionally invasive and appropriative engagements with the natural world – his tendency to kill snakes, to keep birds in captivity, to plunder and disassemble their nests, to uproot ferns and relocate orchids and other wild flowers (to say nothing of his childhood recollections of eating the flesh of badgers and hedgehogs) – Heyes juxtaposes the received image of Clare as 'the finest naturalist of all Britain's major poets' with a characterization that few readers had encountered before: Clare as 'a one-man ecological disaster'.[17] Essentially, Heyes's work confirms Clare's own conclusions in poems such as 'Shadows of Taste' (1830) about the need for 'dark employs' in the study of nature; the 'man of science', as he notes, 'strangles beetles all to make us wise' (MP III 303–10). The lesson for modern readers is that environmentalism is not always a gentle or benign affair – a reflection, one might add, of the fact that second-wave scholarship also increasingly frames environments (and the ecological relations within and between them) in less than ideal or harmonious terms. Clare's reference to 'dark employs' anticipates a relatively recent interest in 'dark ecology', which Morton associates with a pervasive or 'existential quality of doubt' about the physical world and our place within it; dark ecology, moreover, makes space in nature for confusion and ugliness, predation and horror – for 'things ceasing to be what [we] expect' or indeed want.[18] Underpinning this turn away from idealist or pastoral conceptions of nature is a growing conversance among ecocritics with scientific research and modelling that call into question our long-standing assumptions about the stability, cohesion, and tendency towards homeostasis in complex natural systems. As Mackenzie Wark argues, nature is also at times 'recalcitrant, enervating, unpredictable'.[19] At the very least, our notion of harmony or unity must admit the interpenetrations of chaos, especially in short-lived species and non-linear natural systems. According to the logic of dark ecology, harmony and chaos are not mutually exclusive states – a conclusion that perhaps also allows us to come more fully to grips with the complexity of Clare as an environmental actor.

The revisionist lens offers of course only one perspective through which to gauge Clare's ongoing role in and relevance to second-wave scholarship. Ecocriticism's evolution as a global academic discipline that now includes the literatures of Australia, East Asia, continental Europe, Latin America, and the Middle East raises important questions about which writers and regions, narratives and worldviews, languages and vocabularies, are to be regarded as paradigmatic – or, alternately, reorienting – to the field as a whole. Scholarly interest has not suddenly shifted away from Anglo-American texts and contexts, but their centrality, their taken-for-grantedness in the ecocritical canon has undeniably been called into question. As Ursula Heise points out, the literary perspectives of the global north that were celebrated by first-wave ecocriticism emerged from centres of industrial wealth and political power that had little in common with life in the global south, 'where human populations and natural systems disproportionately suffer[ed] the consequences of economic exploitation, toxification, and climate change'.[20] Whether the writing of Clare – given its cultural heritage (to say nothing of its dialect, provincialisms, and slang) – can reach across that divide or contribute meaningfully to the environmental perspectives of non-English readers is unclear. To date, there are only scattered scholarly translations of his work, the most notable being Renichi Suzuki's 2004 Japanese version of the Everyman Edition of Clare's poems and his 2021 *John Clare Poems*, as well as isolated online translations of select poems in Spanish, German, Hindi, and Urdu. Clare's international profile, in other words, is far from established.

The other question that looms large in the internationalization of second-wave ecocriticism is whether local perspectives such as Clare's have any relatable connection to, or means of addressing, global issues. Is locality at all compatible with globality, or are these spatial designations, these geographic spheres of experience, these habits of consciousness the very basis upon which ecocritical discourses tend to divide themselves? Heise suggests that locality – typically read as a marker of distinctiveness or difference that underpins notions of alterity in human and nonhuman populations – is still the predominant focus of second-wave critics, especially through the influence of post-colonial theory. Even the global context of a warming planet can be reduced to a series of unique climatological manifestations across different geographies. Indeed, the human perception of environment may be so radically individuated or idiosyncratic, so intractably local, that any sense of common ground or shared experience – any resonant globality – becomes elusive, chimeric. However, as Clark reminds readers, local environments and ecosystems also fluctuate and change over centuries and are thus part of dynamic, long-term processes that a single fixed perspective in history cannot comprehend. Even Clare's lifelong reflections on Helpston, so particularizing and unwaveringly devoted, are but freeze-frame glimpses of a region subject to the perturbations of 'deep time'.[21]

Any effort, therefore, to reconcile the local with the global in ecocritical discourse, to bring these dynamic spheres into meaningful relation, must account for temporal as well as spatial scale. To date, relatively few studies of Clare's work have addressed the issue of scale. Paul Chirico has examined the way that land for Clare, in the process of disgorging antiquarian relics, is revealed to be 'physically constituted by the past', while Richard Irvine and Mina Gorji characterize the poet's reflections on the 'different temporalities' of a given landscape as a provocation for modern readers to consider their role as geological actors in the Anthropocene.[22] Yet less clear is Clare's scalar sense of space. As Joseph Albernaz argues, the varied references to 'worlds' in Clare's autobiographical prose and poetry appear to deny a totalizing or holistic construct of globality – a single, shared world. What Clare foregrounds instead are 'the scattered fragments of an infinite play and plurality of *worlds* – worlds which simultaneously are given and must be made, or formed. Worlds that bump up and push against each other, and overlap at times (and places).'[23] In part, Clare's tendency to pluralize (or localize) the global may be attributable to the fact that he was not spatially mobile in the way that other writers of his day were. By virtue of his class, he could not travel for leisure and expand his geographic horizons as Wordsworth or Byron, for example, did. Nevertheless, Albernaz's reference to an 'infinite' plurality of worlds is at least suggestive of the possibility that even a constrained existence such as Clare's may yet contribute to a consciousness of spatial proliferation, of worlds upon worlds – and with that proliferation also a sense of interconnection, even interdependence, such as the contemporary discourse of an ecological mesh tends to promote.

There are, however, limits to a scalar argument by which Clare is (again) modernized. The 'world' of the Romantic imaginary was not our world in the sense that it was less precisely surveyed, mapped, theorized, studied, and known. Moreover, the reality of a shared global crisis that we now face was not yet evident in Clare's day, even though that crisis has its roots in the onslaught of eighteenth- and nineteenth-century industrialization. As Davies suggests, the very construct of 'nature' that writers like Clare and the scientific discourses of his day were addressing was in many ways not like our own; it was understood to be changing, 'constantly metamorphosing ... [but] not diminishing'. What all of this suggests, in other words, is that the issue of scale, touching both locality and globality, each as it were interpenetrated by the other, is itself conditioned by historical context. Clare's work cannot simply be made to anticipate, prefigure, or directly address our environmental realities because those were not his realities. However, this is not to suggest that his writing is no longer relevant to modern audiences or no longer capable of illuminating for us anything about our own environmental agency and responsibilities; on the contrary, the very *dis*continuities between Clare's historical perspective and our own may be key to the enduring relevance of his work. As Davies so astutely concludes from his sweeping assessment of Romantic-era environmental literature, 'in order for the Romantic period to teach us something about the present, it must be different from the present'.[24]

Clare's Attentive and Self-Circumscribing Mode

As an illustration of such difference, I would like to consider two recurring features or modes of relation in Clare's work – one might think of them as governing predispositions to natural otherness – that may be particularly instructive to modern readers because they challenge us to confront and reorient our own habits of green thinking and doing. The focus here on 'doing' is reflective of what Buell characterizes as an accelerating shift in second-wave criticism 'from ecocriticism as textual practice to environmental criticism as cultural practice'.[25] Textual practice is by no means to be abandoned or relegated to a position of mere scholarly delectation, but at the same time it cannot function as the sole purpose or culmination of ecocritical enquiry – not while ecocriticism continues its cross-pollination with non-literary disciplines such as climatology, social ecology, biopolitics, environmental psychology, urban planning, sustainable design, and so on. Moreover, our global context of multiple, interfused, escalating environmental crises invites us to consider whether textual practice in academic settings and primarily for academic audiences constitutes a sufficient response. At its core, the analysis of literature in its historical, cultural, and material contexts is a form of knowledge production, and that knowledge may yield insights to addressing our shared environmental predicament, a process that typically begins by addressing ourselves as ecological actors.

For the careful reader of Clare's work, the insights guiding that process of self-address tend to transmit themselves in subtle and beguiling ways. For while there is evident 'rage' in some of the aforementioned protest poems and often a reflux of withering despair, of arguably greater significance than these extremities of tone is the way that his texts stage or frame the encounter between human speaker (or interlocutor) and the natural world. From the quality of Clare's descriptive process – so often particularizing and paratactic, sometimes building up layers of materiality and relation, sometimes paring them away to reveal a single object of aesthetic interest – certain deductions can be made about his perceptual process and, more broadly, about how to position oneself so as to get at or into the thickness of the world. Of particular note is Clare's careful adjudication between spheres of action and passivity in the rendering of natural encounters – the initial expense of energy in seeking or drawing near and a subsequent stillness or willingness to be wrought upon, whereby the centre of narrative action shifts from human observer to natural object. The active mode is typically supplanted by or subordinated to the passive, yet the passive – or what I will designate as the *attentive* and *self-circumscribing* – is itself charged with a dynamic multi-sensory receptivity to what is other. Clare's work sensitizes the reader to the ecological value of attentiveness, the way it alternately reveals, renews, and enlivens our connection to the world around us. At the same time, this attentiveness circumscribes the egoic subject, by which I mean not simply restraining or delimiting its agency but rather defining that agency through its immediate points of contact, its proximate nodes of relation, which is to say the pressing reality of coexistence. Attention and self-circumscription are in Clare's oeuvre two sides of the same coin.

If the quality of attentiveness that Clare models in his poetry and prose was distinctive and unusual even by the standards of nineteenth-century naturalism, its relation to what we today designate by the same word can be captured by the apposition of the verbs 'listening' and 'hearing'. Unlike the latter, the former signals a preparatory phase of anticipation (listening *for*), a readiness to hear before the processing of auditory stimuli, a focused suspension of other activity, a finely poised stillness. In both scope and degree, Clare's attentiveness to nature was remarkable; he was at once indiscriminate, giving himself up to all manner and manifestation of ordinariness (e.g., the murmuring wind, wheat ripening, a quagmire of black mud, the stench of fens, hedgerow shadows, a raven's rough song), and meticulously disciplined in directing his scrutiny to isolated objects of interest. Attentiveness was for Clare not a style or an aesthetic programme, a way of strategically summoning energy and channelling it into poetic production or natural history; rather, it was a lived and long-nurtured habit of being – and being interested – in the world. For that reason, it also offers itself as a potent source of inspiration for modern readers. Attentiveness is a process to be learned in small steps, an ongoing mode of discovery and relation that begins at our sensory extremities, our perceptual borders, at the very margins of subjectivity, and leans out from there into the world of our surroundings.

'The Nightingales Nest': A Case Study

Perhaps no work of Clare's so compellingly dramatizes the attentive and self-circumscribing mode as 'The Nightingales Nest' (MP III 456–61). Published in 1832, shortly after Clare's disorienting relocation to Northborough, the poem recalls an earlier time and more familiar topography, likely Royce Wood south of Helpston village where he had frequently heard the nightingale and sought its nest. The poem is thus both temporally and spatially reintegrating, yet its connective tissue extends even further. The opening lines – 'Up this green wood land ride lets softly rove / & list the nightingale' – offer themselves as a gesture of sociality that may hearken back to Clare's companionate walks with fellow naturalists such as Joseph Henderson or perhaps with his own children, who also serve as an inspiring presence in his nest poems. There is of course another possibility suggested by Clare's use of present tense, and that is the reader, who figures here not only as a vicarious pursuer of the nightingale but also as an observer of the poetic speaker, an attentive witness of his watching. Clare's openness to such scrutiny suggests that the poem itself is driven by the need for a secure and socially integrated sense of being in the world. Yet while human company satisfies the poet's need to a degree, it is the elusive nightingale that rouses him to 'rove', its song, as Clare relates, having long ago drawn him into relationship: 'For here Ive heard her many a merry year / At morn & eve nay all the live long day'. This is a foretaste of Clare's attentiveness, couched in a colloquialism indicating a tedious duration ('all the live long day'), but suggestive here of that rapt quality of listening (both for and to) by which the subject is waylaid and his agency (i.e., the entire action of a day) suspended.

As Clare makes clear, however, audition is but one form of engagement with avian otherness. A disembodied sound or note can at times disorient and conduct one away from a meaningful encounter – that is to say, from the felt reality of coexistence. Poems such as 'The Land Rail' (1832) (MP III 553–4), for example, narrativize the confusion that attends a sound that cannot be traced to a source, with the bird itself becoming an empty signified, 'A sort of living doubt', as Clare styles it. In 'The Nightingales Nest', however, the bird's song is for the speaker an inducement to further inquiry which reveals itself, line by line and layer by layer, not so much as a pursuit but rather as a partaking, a physical accommodation of the self to the habitat and existence – the raw ontology – of the other:

> I hunted like a very boy
> Creeping on hands & knees through matted thorns
> To find her nest & see her feed her young
> & vainly did I many hours employ
> All seemed as hidden as a thought unborn
> & where these crimping fern leaves ramp among
> The hazels under boughs – Ive nestled down
> & watched her while she sung – & her renown
> Hath made me marvel that so famed a bird
> Should have no better dress then russet brown
> Her wings would tremble in her extacy
> & feathers stand on end as 't'were with joy
> & mouth wide open to release her heart
> Of its out sobbing songs – the happiest part
> Of summers fame she shared – for so to me

> Did happy fancies shapen her employ
> But if I touched a bush or scarcely stirred
> All in a moment stopt – I watched in vain
> The timid bird had left the hazel bush
> & at a distance hid to sing again
> Lost in a wilderness of listening leaves

This astonishing passage enacts in the opening declension from 'hunted' to 'creeping' a kind of surrender, a self-deposition of almost penitential intensity as the speaker describes his arduous progress across 'matted thorns' to the uncertain nest. And all of this physical mortification is but a prelude to attentiveness. As Clare points out, merely to put oneself in a position to see and hear and partake of the existence of another is an investment, sometimes vain, of many hours. More than that, the accommodation of the speaker to the occluded habitat of the nightingale demands a further physical prostration, a movement down and in and around, a circumscription that gathers together: 'under boughs – Ive nestled down / & watched her while she sung'. In many ways, this is the centre or culmination of the encounter, this coexistent nestling, poet-bird and bird-poet, the lines between them seemingly effaced.

Yet lest the image of this unlikely propinquity suggest a levelling of spheres of relation, Clare is quick to refocus the reader's attention on the true subject of 'renown'. Whatever his own lines of verse may accomplish as a dedication to the bird, hatched as they are from within his man-made nest, the nightingale's 'sobbing songs' have an incomparable animating force that gathers within its trembling body and issues out to 'a wilderness of listening leaves' and from there to 'every flower / That blossoms near thy home' until the nightingale's entire 'world is wide' with music. This ecology of interconnection, notably, is not assumed beforehand or somehow intuited; it is revealed by the poet's rigorously attentive and self-circumscribing focus on one small creature attired inconspicuously in 'russet brown'. The epiphany of coexistence, in other words, is a product of the experience of coexistence, and that experience is arrived at with considerable difficulty – on hands and knees, with bowed back, and a will likewise chastened by hours of waiting. And if that were not enough, Clare also reminds us throughout the poem of the precariousness of such encounters. A sudden movement, an over-eagerness to touch, a brief interlude of self-absorption, and 'All in a moment stopt'. Even when the speaker seems assured of success ('Aye as I live her secret nest is here'), the next line has him searching again 'For hours in vain'. Meaningful connections in the natural world are not in Clare's experience cheaply won.

The lessons for the modern reader are legion, but it may be enough to suggest, as a general conclusion, that our current focus on ecological thinking needs a prior grounding in environmental praxis. I take this term 'ecological thinking' from Morton, who claims in his influential book *The Ecological Thought* that our response to environmental crisis demands first of all a cognitive reorientation. Rather than persisting with a nomenclature that designates something over there as 'nature' and something over here as 'humanity', thus effectively sundering the two, Morton argues for integrated thinking or, as he calls it, 'the thinking of interconnectedness'. Such thinking, he suggests, will perforce usher us into the radical intimacy of coexistence by 'reframing our world, our problems, and ourselves'.[26] While he acknowledges the need for a practical outworking of such cognitive retooling, he accepts the Aristotelian verdict that contemplation is the acme of all praxis. It is a sentiment that appears to suit not only academic audiences, at least those satisfied with the parameters of 'textual practice', but also that growing cohort of techno-solutionists for whom activism begins (and often ends) with an algorithm. The work of Clare, however, sets itself firmly against an environmentalism of ideas. However coexistence may be conceived, it is the experience thereof that meaningfully attunes us to the other. And that experience calls us out into the world, works us down to our hands and knees, tutors the mind through the inlets of the sensorium. Clare's insistence on active and attentive encounters of coexistence, not on a mere existential enmeshment with other living things, is arguably his most enduring contribution to the environmental movement.

Notes

1. Lawrence Buell, 'Ecocriticism: Some Emerging Trends', *Qui Parle*, 19.2 (2011), 87–115 (p. 88).
2. Nirmal Selvamony, 'Introduction', in Nirmal Selvamony, Nirmaldasan, and Rayson K. Alex, eds., *Essays in Ecocriticism* (Chennai: OSLE-India, 2007), pp. xi–xxxi (p. xix).
3. Cheryll Glotfelty, 'Introduction', in Cheryll Glotfelty and Harold Fromm, eds., *The Ecocriticism Reader: Landmarks in Literary Ecology* (Athens: University of Georgia Press, 1996), pp. xv–xxxvii (p. xviii).
4. Claire Colebrook, 'Ecocriticism', in Jeffrey Di Leo, ed., *The Bloomsbury Handbook of Literary and Cultural Theory* (London: Bloomsbury, 2019), pp. 173–85 (p. 173; p. 177).
5. Timothy Clark, *The Value of Ecocriticism* (Cambridge: Cambridge University Press, 2019), pp. 3–5.
6. Anahid Nersessian, 'Romantic Ecocriticism Lately', *Literature Compass*, 15.1 (2018), 1–16 (p. 5).

7. Timothy Morton, *Ecology without Nature* (Cambridge, MA: Harvard University Press, 2007), p. 32.
8. Jeremy Davies, 'Romantic Ecocriticism: History and Prospects', *Literature Compass*, 15.9 (2018), 1–15 (p. 11).
9. Greg Garrard, *Ecocriticism*, 2nd ed. (London: Routledge, 2012), pp. 51–2.
10. Bridget Keegan, *British Labouring-Class Nature Poetry, 1730–1837* (New York: Palgrave Macmillan, 2008), p. 149.
11. Clark, *Value of Ecocriticism*, p. 7.
12. Simon Kövesi, *John Clare: Nature, Criticism and History* (London: Palgrave Macmillan, 2017), pp. 13–15.
13. Clark, *Value of Ecocriticism*, pp. 3–4.
14. Buell, 'Ecocriticism', p. 106.
15. Davies, 'Romantic Ecocriticism', p. 12.
16. Stephanie Posthumus and Stéfan Sinclair, 'Reading Environment(s): Digital Humanities Meets Ecocriticism', *Green Letters: Studies in Ecocriticism*, 18.3 (2014), 254–73 (p. 270).
17. Clare's various accounts of predation and habitat disruption are drawn from 'The Autobiography: 1793–1824', 'Natural History Letters', and 'Nature Notes' (*Prose*, p. 181; pp. 203–4; pp. 198–9; p. 119; p. 37); James Fisher, 'The Birds of John Clare', in *The First Fifty Years: A History of the Kettering and District Naturalists' Society and Field Club* (Kettering: n.p., 1956), p. 26, and Robert Heyes, 'John Clare's Natural History', presented at 'John Clare in Space: Poetry, Nature, and Contemporary Culture', Oxford Brookes University, 30–1 May 2014.
18. Timothy Morton, 'John Clare's Dark Ecology', *Studies in Romanticism*, 47.2 (2008), 179–93 (p. 192).
19. Mackenzie Wark, *Molecular Red: Theory for the Anthropocene* (London: Verso, 2015), p. 82.
20. Ursula Heise, 'Globality, Difference, and the International Turn in Ecocriticism', *PMLA*, 128.3 (2013), 636–43(p. 639).
21. Clark, *Value of Ecocriticism*, p. 43.
22. Paul Chirico, *John Clare and the Imagination of the Reader* (London: Palgrave Macmillan, 2007), p. 95; Richard D. G. Irvine and Mina Gorji, 'John Clare in the Anthropocene', *Cambridge Anthropology*, 31.1 (2013), 119–32 (p. 121).
23. Joseph Albernaz, 'John Clare's World', *European Romantic Review*, 27.2 (2016), 189–205 (p. 192).
24. Davies, 'Romantic Ecocriticism', pp. 11, 6.
25. Buell, 'Ecocriticism', p. 104.
26. Timothy Morton, *The Ecological Thought* (Cambridge, MA: Harvard University Press, 2010), pp. 7–9.

PART III
Clare's Image

9

TIM CHILCOTT

Self-Identity in a World of Influence

Some things, perhaps, are best defined by what they are not; and the physical and material world into which John Clare was born in July 1793 could scarcely be more different from our own, in any number of respects. Totally absent from that world, it is worth remembering, were gas, electricity, and running water; railways, cars, and planes; radio, television, computers, phones; machines and factories; shops and supermarkets; anaesthetics and hospitals. In 1793, almost none of these things, as well as numerous others that have become so domesticated and embedded in our twenty-first-century lives, had even been dreamed of, yet alone realized. In their place was something far more basic, even elemental: a powerful sense of direct, unmediated physicality – a raw, unsanitized sensuousness that is, in our contemporary world, almost unknowable. In 1793, in rural Helpston, time is largely told by the sun and by how light or dark it is; space is the distance you can walk or run or ride a horse; heat measured by how much you're sweating or shivering; sustenance by how much your belly is rumbling or quiet. Your body and its five senses centre your lived experience, and that body has to work tenaciously in order to survive. On average, it will give up the struggle well before you are forty.[1]

The effects of this physicality upon Clare's boyhood and adolescence show themselves in two contrasting ways: his early responses to the material world he finds about him, and those hints of a latent, internalized world that has yet to find a voice. Indoors, that material world is affirmative and supportive. The family cottage in Helpston is rudimentary but accommodating, his mother and father are caring parents and actively encourage his development, his teachers in the local schoolhouse similarly foster his sense of inquiry and interest in learning. Outdoors, even more, he begins to find in the fields and paths and landscapes around Helpston a source of growing fascination and delight that is to last his entire life. The fascination takes distinctive forms: it is almost always of the specific, closely observed details of the natural world, rather than its spacious, wide-angle panoramas; it very often looks downwards, towards what is nearby at ground level, and only occasionally upwards, to the clouds and the tall, immense skies of the fenland around; it is attracted by fragility, evanescence, secretiveness, more than by the tough, unsparing endurance of natural things. And these personal responses to the natural world are underpinned by a village society and culture that continue to confirm a rural identity, even as that identity is being threatened by the enclosure of lands and by the ever-noisier machines of nineteenth-century industrial life. Shared dates in the yearly calendar, celebrating love or sowing or harvest, meeting places for worship or drink, talk and gossip with neighbours – these are some of the rural traditions and customs that confer a sense of mutual, communal life. By no means is that life idyllic, and its privations are numerous, but it is at least there, as a common physical reality to be lived.

In parallel, though, there emerge hints of more fracturing events that begin to internalize his experience. The intertwining themes of time and loss, which are to so haunt his later poetry especially, are sounded early, when his twin sister, Bessy, dies within weeks of their joint birth. His closest boyhood friend, Richard Turnill, similarly dies prematurely, catching typhus at the age of seventeen. Yet the internalizing is more affirmative, too: the first stirrings of affection for the village girls, and especially for one Mary Joyce, who not only attracts his adolescent imagination, but who captures it so entirely as to become the centre of his emotional life. He courts and weds another woman, Martha ('Patty') Turner, and their married life is kindly but unexceptional. But it is Mary who becomes the lodestar image from which he can never take his eyes.

And underpinning both these external and internal worlds is the growing awareness of language, of words as a powerful and instinctive means, not simply of communication, but also of creativity. At first, and naturally so, the awareness is primarily receptive rather than active: the reading of words rather than the writing of them. But at the age of thirteen, he is given a battered copy of James Thomson's poem *The Seasons*, originally published in the 1720s; and at a stroke, language for him seems to undergo an almost Damascene conversion, becoming vivifying, vibrant, galvanizing an adolescent imagination. He never forgets the sensation of reading the first few lines of 'Spring':

> Come, gentle Spring, ethereal mildness, come;
> And from the bosom of yon dropping cloud,
> While music wakes around, veil'd in a shower
> Of shadowing roses, on our plains descend.

Self-Identity in a World of Influence

He feels a 'twitter of joy' in the heart, and so strong is the impact of this evocation of the natural world that he commits to paper the first poem he ever writes down, 'The Morning Walk', soon followed by a companion piece, 'The Evening Walk' (see *JCBH*, p. 11). This first act of writing down words that have poetic resonance and shape may at first seem trifling; but it is in fact of considerable significance. Up until now, Clare's awareness of language has been largely of its orality. It is the sound of words – their pitch and timbre, rhythm and pulse – that have so powerfully informed the ballads and songs he has heard spoken and sung at home and in Helpston. In later years, the continuing power of that orality shows itself in several ways: in the recourse to dialect forms derived from the spoken rather than the written language; in the continuing use of lyrical, song-like forms; in the aural precision that can discriminate between, say, the 'wherrying' of ducks, the 'whewing' of starlings, the 'whirl' of peewits, and the 'wizzing' of stock doves. But to this influence of language as sound, there is now added a further dimension: language as sight, as an agency that is seen and read, as well as heard and listened to. The implications of the addition are considerable.

They introduce the young Clare, first, to the world of literary tradition and history, a world transmitted through the power and influence of print, rather than the spoken words and voices heard around Helpston. As well as the revelation of Thomson's poem, he begins to read in the poetry of Milton, Goldsmith, Cowper, and Bloomfield, as well as in the prose of Walton, Bunyan, and Defoe. And this growing, youthful awareness of literary precursors, of a historical community of writers, begins to validate his own slowly emerging sense of what poetry is, and of what it might be to be a poet. Like almost all apprentices, he begins by copying; and a good deal of his earliest verse shows how substantially he is at first influenced by his eighteenth-century predecessors. Even when a first poem like 'Helpstone' is grounded in the palpable, physical reality of enclosure, for example, it still studiedly positions itself within the framework of rhetorical address and sentimental apostrophizing that can mark a good deal of eighteenth-century loco-descriptive pastoral poetry ('Hail humble Helpstone where thy valies spread / & thy mean Village lifts its lowly head', EP 1 156). But the words of another very early poem, 'The Gipsies Evening Blaze', probably written in his mid teens, give the first hints of a new direction:

> To me how wildly pleasing is that scene
> Which does present in evenings dusky hour
> A Group of Gipsies center'd on the green
> In some warm nook where Boreas has no power
> Where sudden starts the quivering blaze behind

> Short shrubby bushes nibbl'd by the sheep
> That alway on these shortsward pastures keep
> Now lost now shines now bending with the wind
> And now the swarthy sybil [k]neels reclin'd
> With proggling stick she still renews the blaze
> Forcing bright sparks to twinkle from the flaze
> When this I view the all attentive mind
> Will oft exclaim (so strong the scene pervades)
> 'Grant me this life, thou spirit of the shades!'   (EP 1 33)

The fading, neoclassical furniture here is everywhere apparent, from the syntactic inversions of 'to me how wildly pleasing' and 'when this I view', through the classical references to 'Boreas' and a 'swarthy sybil', to the grandiloquent appeal of the last line. But there are two moments – they are no more than this – when a different voice is sounded: the old woman kindles the 'flaze' with her 'proggling' stick. The sounds of a vernacular dialect dart into the conventional diction that prevails in the rest of the poem, creating a momentary stylistic edge, a slight unresolved angle in its predominant verbal register.

During Clare's late adolescence and on into his twenties, this sense of edge and angle in his developing poetic language becomes emblematic of much larger changes and tensions in his life and experience. The sounds of intimate, local speech, the words of Helpston, move more and more into a public space, not only that of the printed word but also that of booksellers and publishers, patrons and reading public, trade and commerce. His experience, once born and nurtured in localization, indeed almost defined by it, is now drawn into the larger arena of a world that is urban, accelerated, commercial, crowded, plural, in its concerns and demands. Nothing, perhaps, defines that new world better than a journey he makes in the early months of 1820. He is just twenty-six, and he comes to London for the first time, to celebrate the publication of his first book of poetry, *Poems Descriptive of Rural Life and Scenery*.

The 100-mile journey that Clare takes by stagecoach down to London takes well over twelve hours, and looking out at the different workers now engaged in his old occupations of ploughing and ditching creates a sudden sense of displacement, 'such strange feelings that I coud almost fancy that my identity as well as my occupations had changd that I was not the same John Clare but that some stranger soul had jumped into my skin' (*JCBH*, p. 134). The displacement is only temporary, but the very notion of an identity changing, an idea he has never previously articulated, sounds a prophetic note. As the coach nears London, there is a further disturbance: he mistakes some lamps lining the road for the city itself, which is still several miles away, and is laughed at for his ignorance. The moments recall an earlier experience when, as a boy, he had excitedly wandered into unknown countryside until 'I got out of my knowledge when the very wild flowers & birds seemd to forget me & I imagind they were the inhabitants of new countrys the very sun seemd to be a new one & shining in a different quarter of the sky' (*JCBH*, pp. 40–1). In all these instances, space, and place, rather than validating an assured knowledge, temporarily disturb it, rendering it insecure, indeterminate, problematic.

Given the impact of first impressions, Clare might well at first have responded to London in two very different ways: either bewilderment at its seemingly mindless freneticism, in contrast to the slower pulses of Helpston life, or enchantment at its sheer metropolitan energy, in contrast to the quietly dulling rhythms of rural experience. In fact, his response is considerably more nuanced than either. In his accounts of London life, he places relatively little emphasis upon the city's physicality – its sights and sounds and smells, its architecture and interior spaces – and much more upon the human and literary society he finds there. Acute, verbal portraits of individual figures such as Lamb, Hazlitt, De Quincey, Reynolds, Cary, and not least his publishers Taylor and Hessey, show how readily and how charitably he is drawn into that sense, experienced for the first time in his life, of writers as a community, and of writing as a public, shared, communal act. There are meetings and conversations and invitations and dinners; and at all of them he is welcomed as a fellow and an equal. It is scarcely surprising that, leaving this society behind on a later occasion, he should write: 'my heart achd as I lost sight of London at the thought of being forc'd away perhaps for ever from the merriest set of fellows I ever met with – ' (*Letters*, p. 243).

However, this sense of personal social affirmation and delight is counterpointed by the increasing prominence of more neutral, sharper-eyed issues: editorial debates about literary content, the moral and political influence of patrons, the impact of contemporary reviews, the power of advertising and of market forces such as pricing and sales. Writing about the process of poetic composition, Clare is later to declare, 'I found the poems in the fields and only wrote them down' (LP I 19). Yet whether these words are interpreted as a rather guileless account of poetic creativity, or as a profounder statement about the relationship between language and the phenomenal world, the transparency they evoke is now problematized by these broader social issues. Put baldly, when poems found in fields become books, things can get muddled. And there is no better example of that muddle than the preparations for his third volume, *The Shepherd's Calendar, with Village Stories, and other Poems*.

Finally published in 1827, *The Shepherd's Calendar* is nearly four years in preparation and is beset with the pressures and questions that this wider world applies.[2] What is – what should be – the professional and personal relationship between poet and publisher, Clare and Taylor? What powers does, or should, either party wield as the book is made ready for publication? How far should the demands of 'standardized' English prevail over the strength and authenticity of dialect variants? How resilient can any publication be against the social and cultural context that confronts it? This last question has particular relevance to the eventual fate of the book. By 1827, the national mood is changing. The previous year has seen a serious economic slump, resulting in the bankruptcy of several well-established publishing houses. More widely, public interest is shifting away from poetry and imaginative literature towards the more urgent concerns of political reform, of industrial and scientific advance, of the dawning of the Victorian machine age. As one of its most astute commentators remarks, 'every time has its genius ... the genius of *this* time is wholly anti-poetic'.[3] Against such pressures, it is scarcely surprising that the reception *The Shepherd's Calendar* receives is fitful, even desultory. Clare's first book had sold over 4,000 copies within a year. Now, more than two years after publication, *The Shepherd's Calendar* has sold only 425. In a telling self-analysis of his public, literary life since his first success, he compares himself to Sisyphus:

> Like the poor purgatorial convict of the grecian mythology I have for these nine years been rolling hopes to that mountain of promises pointed out to me in the beginning by friendly inte[r]ferences & often I have seemed as if I had accomplis[h]ed to the very top when down went hopes & all together to the bottom again – in the shape of broken promises stinging impositions & other trouble unaccounted for and unknown till they made their appearance – I am but as an alien in a strange land (*JCBH*, p. 161)

A simple list of the haunted terms in this summary is enough to highlight the brokenness they express: poor, purgatorial, convict, inte[r]ferences, down, bottom, broken, stinging, trouble, unaccounted, unknown, alien, strange. But personal disappointment has no place in the new national mood, whose concerns are aptly summarized in the *Westminster Review*, the mouthpiece of Jeremy Bentham's philosophical radicalism:

> we have risen to the station which we occupy, not by literature, not by the knowledge of extinct languages, but by the science of politics, of law, of public economy, of commerce, of mathematics ... Literature is a seducer; we had almost said a harlot. She may do to trifle with; but woe be to the state whose statesmen write verses, and whose lawyers read more in Tom Moore than Bracton.[4]

Self-Identity in a World of Influence

Against such powerfully entrenched philistinism, Clare's attempts to revivify interest in his work by trying himself to sell his books around Helpston are almost destined to fail. From London, his publisher John Taylor writes to him bleakly, 'I am no publisher of poetry now.'[5] The years that both are to remember as a golden age (Clare characterizes them as 'the happiest period of my life' (*Letters*, p. 513)) are now conclusively ended.

Yet it is not a national mood or a temper of the times that is now to shape Clare's life, but a domestic event. In 1832, he moves from Helpston to Northborough, a neighbouring village not three miles away and comfortably reached within an hour's walk. Unlike Helpston, though, Northborough is in the deep fenland, where the tall skies are even higher and where he never ultimately feels at home. He has lived in Helpston for nearly forty years, coming to know almost every blade of grass in the village and the countryside around, and his reaction of alienation and dispossession is immediate. Less than two months after moving, he writes 'The Flitting' (MP III 479) and two closely related works, 'Decay: a Ballad' and 'Remembrances' (MP IV 251; MP III 130).

As ever, it is the detailed textures of Clare's language that reveal the sudden erosion of known things. In contrast to any number of earlier poems, his diction now is narrower, tighter, more concentrated, as vital words like love, heart, time, to be, to feel, are repeated like a swelling ground bass of loss and obsession. Particularizing, dialect forms still appear, but they now are embedded in memory and in the lost landscapes of Helpston:

> [I] hear bird music here & there
> From awthorn hedge & orchard come
> I hear but all is strange & new
> – I sat on my old bench in June
> The sailing puddocks shrill 'peelew'
> Oer royce wood seemed a sweeter tune   (MP III 479)

Significantly, in the Royce Wood close to Helpston, 'puddocks' shrilly call 'peelew'. In Northborough, 'bird[s]' simply make a generic 'music'. But most of all, perhaps, it is the syntax of these and similar poems that marks a decisive change. In so many poems before 1832, Clare's syntax evokes a sense of connectedness and continuum, of known things in an observed and observable world. Take those countless first lines that begin with the definite article – *the* field, *the* crow, *the* hedgerow, *the* morning, *the* ploughman – where the article anchors items of reference that are known and securely familiar. Take those opening words where different parts of speech (pronoun / verb, adverb / adjective) seem to elide almost effortlessly into each other – '*I love to* . . . hear / see / wander', '*How sweet* . . . is the whisper / the winds / to sit', '*Come* ... early morning / lovely Jenny / rural muse', '*Now* ... glaring daylight / swarthy summer / the cowslips in the grass'. Take, too, those frequent paratactic constructions that draw the objects of observation into a foreground of almost simultaneous reference by the repetition of the word 'and' ('& shining pansys ... & tall tuft larkheels ... & woodbines climbing ... & London tufts', MP 1 81). All of these stylistic features begin now to change. The authority of the definite article is explicitly challenged by the greater uncertainties of the indefinite (in 'Decay', '*the* stream' becomes '*a* naked stream'; '*the* sky' hangs over '*a* broken dream'; '*the* brambles' are 'nothing but *a* bramble', my italics).⁶ Parataxis is displaced by main verb forms that take on an increasing energy and urgency. The emotional elisions implied by 'I love to ... ' or 'How sweet ... ' now become emotional collisions, 'I ve left ... I miss ... I feel the loss ... I hardly know ... I cannot find ... I never thought ... I never dreamed'. Two lines from 'The Flitting' capture the change from a world of physical assurance to an ambiguous, alien realm where nothing is secure:

> Strange scenes mere shadows are to me
> Vague unpersonifying things   (ll. 89–90)

In these ten words, the Helpston world of assured predication all but disappears, its known details more and more blurred into amorphous, unindividualized 'things'. The particularizations of place have become the indeterminacies of space.

Clare is to remain in Northborough for five years, living through periods of increasing emotional and mental volatility – hallucinations, burning sensations, sleeplessness, physical numbness, heightened sensitivity to sound – and by 1837, his condition has worsened sufficiently for him to be committed to a mental hospital, the humane asylum High Beach in Epping Forest. Few documents now survive from the first three years of his stay there, but one – a brief letter written to his wife, Patty – is telling in its suggestion of how his sense of selfhood is changing:

> I write to tell you I am getting better   I cant write a long letter but wish to know how you all are   the place here is beautiful & I meet with great kindness   the country is the finest I have seen   write & tell me how you all are   I cant write a long letter but I shall do better   (*Letters*, p. 642)

Stylistically, this account could scarcely be more lucid: the expression is simple, direct, and entirely intelligible. Yet, as Geoffrey Grigson first noted, it is marked by a curious structuring of response.⁷ Clare makes four statements (that he is better, that he cannot write much, that he wishes to know how his family is, that the place is beautiful), followed by a pivotal declaration that he has met with great kindness, after which the opening four statements are repeated, with some change of writing, in reverse order.

Such plays of language may at first sight seem insignificant, but they later take on larger and more emphatic forms: in lines and stanzas where every single word is capitalized, in letters and poems where every vowel is omitted, in coded scraps of writing, or in Bosch-like delusions that his head had been cut off and all the letters of the alphabet pulled out through his ears. In all these examples, the earlier transitive power of his language to *refer*, to evoke a sense of whole, complete meanings where word and world seem almost one, is undermined by a sense of fractured intransitiveness, where language is increasingly self-reflexive, playing with its own codes, its own fictiveness. Yet the changes in Clare's perception of both external and internal worlds, as well as the continuities, are perhaps best shown by placing together four brief passages, which will for the moment deliberately be left unidentified:

> it is now very pleasant to take walks in the morning & in fact at any time of the day though the mornings are misty and 'the foggy dew' lies long on the grass – here is a drove leads us on its level sward right into the flaggy fens shaded on each side with white thorn hedges covered with awes of different shades of red   some may be almost called red-black others brick red & others nearly scarlet like the coats of the fox hunters

> This twilight seems a veil of gause & mist
> Trees seem dark hills between the earth & sky
> Winds sob awake & then a gusty hist
> Fanns through the wheat like serpents gliding bye
> I love to stretch my length 'tween earth & sky
> & see the inky foliage oer me wave
> Though shades are still my prison where I lie

> I really can t tell what this poem will be
> About – nor yet what trade I am to follow
> I thought to buy old wigs – but that will kill me
> With cold starvation – as they're beaten hollow
> Long speeches in a famine will not fill me
> & madhouse traps still take me by the collar
> So old wig bargains now must be forgotten
> The oil that dressed them fine has made them rotten

> Thy glory encircled the face of the sky
> & the earth it was full of thy praise from on high
> Thy brightness was glory the essence of light
> & thy hands held the horns of thy power in my sight
> Before thee pale famine & pestilence came

> & coals at thy feet burnt & kindled to flame
> He measured the earth in loud pealings of thunder
> He beheld & the nations were driven asunder

Even a cursory reading of these four extracts will highlight their difference from each other. The first presents localized, familiar natural details drawn into a foreground of imaginative attention. Discriminations of colour are effortlessly communicated, without uncertainty or ambiguity. The second, though, is more wavering and tentative. Natural objects are no longer in focus but have become blurred and indeterminate ('This *twilight seems a veil* of *gause* and *mist* / Trees *seem dark* hills *between* the earth & sky' (my italics)). The third dramatically wrenches such tentativeness into a loud, self-dramatizing, subversive thrust against public authority. Noticeably, the 'I' in the extract is now fractured, shifting, manipulating, improvising constantly – with itself, with language, with reality, with the very act of writing the lines themselves. The fourth, a rendering of the prayer of the Old Testament prophet Habakkuk, is voiced into what seems an almost primordial universe of fierce religious truths, a world of terrifying, cosmic shock, at the very beginning of time. Even were they to derive from different periods of Clare's career, these passages would be notable for their imaginative compass. Yet, far from deriving from different decades, or even from different years within the same decade, all four extracts are composed during just one year, 1841, and – the period can be narrowed even more – almost certainly within the four months between June and September.[8]

The year 1841 is extraordinarily prolific for Clare, even by his own standards. During it, he writes over 3,000 lines of poetry, as well as a substantial body of prose, including his harrowing account of his escape in July out of Essex, walking back the eighty-odd miles to Northborough. But the writing of this year is also significant because it foreshadows the two fundamental strains that are to be heard in almost everything he subsequently writes, during the long asylum years until his death in 1864. In their different ways, both these strains explore what is now a fully emerged concern with the question of self, and selfhood, and the meaning of personal identity. In a short prose piece, he explicitly addresses the concern:

> A very good common place counsel is *Self Identity* to bid our own hearts not to forget our own selves & always to keep self in the first place lest all the world who always keeps us behind it should forget us all together – forget not thyself & the world will not forget thee – forget thyself & the world will willingly forget thee till thou art nothing but a living-dead man dwelling among shadows & falshood ...

Self-Identity in a World of Influence

> Self Identity is one of the first principles in everybodys life & fills up the outline of honest truth in the decision of character – a person who denies himself must either be a mad man or a coward ... surely every man has the liberty to know himself
>
> (*JCBH*, p. 271)

Yet what *is* self-identity? Who *is* the self that calls itself 'I'? Does it, can it ever, exist as an invulnerable and inviolable essence, a transcendence of phenomenality, or is it always dependent, wholly or in part, upon the predications of the world? Two of Clare's most celebrated poems starkly confront these questions:

> I feel I am; – I only know I am,
> And plod upon the earth, as dull and void:
> Earth's prison chilled my body with its d[r]am
> Of dullness, and my soaring thoughts destroyed,
> I fled to solitudes from passions dream,
> But strife persued – I only know, I am ...   (LP 1 397)

> I am – yet what I am, none cares or knows;
> My friends forsake me like a memory lost: –
> I am the self-consumer of my woes; –
> They rise and vanish in oblivion's host,
> Like shadows in love's frenzied stifled throes: –
> And yet I am, and live – like vapours tost
> Into the nothingness of scorn and noise, –
> Into the living sea of waking dreams,
> Where there is neither sense of life or joys,
> But the vast shipwreck of my lifes esteems ...   (LP 1 396–7)

Far from being a triumphant and inviolable assertion of selfhood, the 'I' in these lines is a numbed, almost depersonalized, figure, unconfirmed by anything outside of itself, living the nightmare of solipsism. In other poems from these years, it is worth noting, Clare takes the primal verb of existence, 'to be', and tortuously wrenches it into discordant antiphonies, as if in an attempt to force it into a fixed significance: 'At once to be, & not to be / That was & is not –' ; 'nothing is nought / & there is nothing less – but something is'; 'To be & not to be & still to know it'. But here, the 'I am' seems drained of energy and will, able to project itself only into shadows, and oblivion, and nothingness. It is without protection.

This is a selfhood severed from its own history, from its own place in time, where nothing corroborates it – not physical objects, not natural world, not the human memory of things past, not even language itself. For even when Clare attempts to claim a new self by projecting his identity onto contemporary figures such as Byron, or Napoleon, or Nelson, or the Duke of

Wellington, the result is just that – a projection, a deluded verbal fiction that is bound eventually to collapse.

This purgatorial emotional landscape, though, is counterpointed in the asylum years by a second pervasive strain. In a contrast that could scarcely be greater, it can take ecstatic form, as is found in poems like 'Song Last Day' or 'A Vision', where the self, the 'I', achieves a kind of transcendent neutrality, finally freed from all data and referents in a vision of eternity:

> I lost earths joys, but felt the glow,
> Of heaven's flame abound in me:
> 'Till loveliness, and I did grow
> The bard of immortality.   (LP I 297)

Equally, it can be found in those literally hundreds of poems that address the twin themes of love and nature, often invoking that lodestar image of Mary, and often voiced with an almost crystalline lucidity and lyricism:

> O' come to my arms i' the cool o' the day
> When the veil o' the evening falls dewy and grey
> O' come to me under the awthorn green
> When eventide falls i' the bushes serene
>
> O come to me under the awthorn tree
> When the lark's on his nest and gone bed is the bee
> When the veil of the evening falls dark on the scene
> And we'll kiss love and court i' the bushes so green   (LP II 840)

These eight lines must stand for countless others, where human love and natural life are seen as an effortless mirroring of each other, and where the self merges into both with ease and lightness. The 'me' in these lines is doubtless far less dramatic, and far more domestic, in its celebration than the apocalypses of 'Song Last Day' or 'A Vision'. Yet it no less evokes a kind of timelessness, the ancient rhythms and images of folk song and ballad first heard some fifty years previously, in the family cottage in Helpston.

How far this world continues to exert its pull, if only in memory, can be seen in two quiet and undemonstrative documents. In the first, a letter written to his son Charles in 1849, Clare remembers, and specifically cites, the names of numerous families, who had lived in the village when he was a boy:

> William & John Close ... John Cobbler ... John & Mary Brown & their Daughter Lucy & John Woodward & his Wife & Daughter – William Bradford & his Wife – Sally Frisby & James Bain & old Otter the Fiddler & Charles Otter & John & Jim Crowson   (*Letters*, p. 663)

Self-Identity in a World of Influence

The list continues with a further thirty names, all remembered without any indication of lapse or hesitancy, conveying a knowledge that is communal and secure. In the second document, a sonnet dated with unusual exactness 10 February 1860, Clare writes of what was almost certainly an event of his boyhood, remembered now in his sixty-seventh year:

> Well honest John how fare you now at home
> The spring is come and birds are building nests
> The old cock robin to the stye is come
> With live feathers and its ruddy breast
> And the old cock with wattles and red comb
> Struts with the hens and seems to like some best
> Then crows and looks about for little crumbs
> Swept out bye little folks an hour ago
> The pigs sleep in the sty the bookman comes
> The little boys lets home close nesting go
> & pockets tops and tawes where daiseys bloom
> To look at the new number just laid down
> With lots of pictures and good stories too
> & Jack the jiant killers high renown   (LP II 1102–3)

There could be few greater contrasts with the tortured apostrophes to the self of the mid 1840s than this sonnet, entitled by Clare himself 'To John Clare'. If there is any conscious irony in his wry self-characterization as 'honest', or in the reference to 'home' when he has lived in two asylums for over twenty years, it is an irony that is unrhetorical and lightly borne. Indeed, in the sudden, child-like speech of 'With lots of pictures and good stories too / & Jack the jiant killer', it may seem, in a momentary and moving enactment, as if adulthood and madness had never really happened, Eden never really been lost. All of maturity had been a nightmare from which he would eventually awake.

***

Many years ago, in a search for a fitting title to a book I had written on Clare, I happened upon two lines from *The Shepherd's Calendar* – the resonant conclusion to 'January' – that suggested some kind of synthesis, some crystallization, of his life and work:

> Those truths are fled & left behind
> A real world & doubting mind   (MP I 25)

Within the two words, 'real world', are embraced all the clarities of Clare's physical and material environment evoked at the beginning of this essay – a realm where the self and everything external to it exist in a known and coherent relationship – and throughout his work, Clare powerfully advances the claims of this 'real world' to imaginative authority and authenticity. But the other two words, 'doubting mind', point to something that is never far away, threatening the validated self with an anxiety and rootlessness that seem almost prophetic in their anticipation of the modern world. In these four words, though, I continue to find that telling crystallization of years ago. It would be fruitless to speculate which of the two pressures prevail, when both are experienced during a long life, sometimes literally within days of each other, as the work of 1841 shows. What can be said, though, is that, between that confirming, almost primitive sensitivity to place and to natural things first recorded by the young Clare, and the despair and baffled dispossession voiced during his asylum years, there is a quite massive change of perception and understanding. Few poets in the language, perhaps, have ever explored so broad an imaginative and mental space.

Notes

1. The average life expectancy of someone born between 1790 and 1795 in the United Kingdom was 37.65 years (Statista.com, accessed July 2022).
2. I explore the many issues raised in the introduction to my edition of the poem, John Clare, *The Shepherd's Calendar: Manuscript and Published Version* (Manchester: Carcanet Press, 2006).
3. Bulwer Lytton, *England and the English* (Paris and Berlin: Baudry, Ascher, 1834), p. 322.
4. 'Present System of Education', *Westminster Review* 4 (July 1825), 147–76 (p. 151; p. 166).
5. British Museum, Egerton MS 2248, fol. 208, 6 January 1830. The remark is cited in my *A Publisher and His Circle: The Life and Work of John Taylor, Keats's Publisher* (London: Routledge & Kegan Paul, 1972), p. 190.
6. I give a fuller account of Clare's use of definite and indefinite articles in 'An Article on Articles', *John Clare Society Journal*, 9 (1990), 31–43.
7. *Poems of John Clare's Madness* (London: Routledge & Kegan Paul, 1949), p. 6.
8. My edition of Clare's work of 1841, *The Living Year 1841* (Nottingham: Trent Editions, 1999) clearly demonstrates the extraordinary variety and productivity of that year. The four passages quoted, which are taken from '[Autumn]', *Child Harold*, *Don Juan*, and the [*Biblical Paraphrases*] respectively, appear on p. 159, p. 52, p. 39, and p. 25 of the edition.

10

MARK STOREY

'Leading Strings'
Editing and Revision in Clare's Poetry

> O TAKE me from the busy crowd,
> I cannot bear the noise!
> For Nature's voice is never loud;
> I seek for quiet joys.
> . . .
> I never feared the critic's pen,
> To live by my renown;
> I found the poems in the fields,
> And only wrote them down.
> ('Sighing for Retirement', May 1841, LP I 19–20,
> ll. 1–4; ll. 13–16)

As so often with Clare, what he says here is, with its modesty and quiet self-confidence, both instructive and only half-true. He cherished his solitude (provided it didn't become isolation), to the extent that he was often writing without any audience in mind. As he declares in 'The Progress of Ryhme',

> I whispered poesys spells till they
> Gleamed round me like a summers day
> (MP III 492–503, ll. 165–6)

Shelley speaks of the poet as a 'nightingale, who sits in darkness and sings to cheer its own solitude with sweet sounds', and Keats talks of 'whispering his results to his neighbour'.[1] Clare's awareness of poetic aloneness is matched by that of some of his contemporaries. But he knew that, when it came to publication, he depended on others, especially his publisher and editor John Taylor, to strike the right note for any degree of public acceptance; although remarkably and determinedly independent in many ways, he relied on Taylor's pen to save him from himself.[2] Furthermore, the notion that he 'found the poems in the fields, / And only wrote them down' is really pretence. He had said something similar, it is true, in his autobiographical writings:

> when I fancyd I had hit upon a good image or natural description I usd to steal into a corner of the garden and clap it down ... I always felt anx[i]ous to conscealm my scribbling and woud as leave have confessd to be a robber as a ryhmer ... I usd to drop down behind a hedge bush or dyke and write down my things upon the crown of my hat ... thus I went on writing my thoughts down and correcting them at leisure (*JCBH*, pp. 77–8)

Even here he is acknowledging the fact that correction was part of the process. He makes a similar point elsewhere, whilst admitting to the general speed with which he writes:

> I always wrote my poems in great haste and generaly finishd them at once wether long or short for if I did not they generaly were left unfinishd what corrections I made I always made them while writing the poem and never coud do any thing with them after wards (*JCBH*, p. 101)

The manuscripts show, clearly enough, the speed with which he could write, leading Taylor, more than once, to urge patience: 'Your best Pieces are those which you were the longest Time over, & to succeed in others you must not hurry' (*Critical Heritage*, p. 34). Edward Drury, the Stamford bookseller who could claim to have 'discovered' Clare, told his cousin Taylor that Clare appeared almost crazed when he was writing, reflecting how Clare himself felt: 'I am all madness for writing but how long its to last I dont know' (*Letters*, p. 228). The fact that the Muse was 'a fickle Hussey' made it all the more important to get the words down on paper (*Letters*, p. 230).

Taylor's role was, it seemed, to keep Clare in check: 'your taste is preferable to any I have witnessd & on that I rely – mines not worth twopence'; 'the rod of critiscism in your hand has as much power over your poor sinful ryhmer as the rod of Aaron in the Land of Egypt'; 'I cannot feel satisfied without leading strings yet tho I think I want them less then before' (*Letters*, pp. 162–3; p. 64; p. 132). He might, in frustration, curse Taylor's interventions (or lack of them): 'you rogue you', 'you neglecting idle rogue you'; but ('vain as I am of my abilities I must own your loppings off have bravely amended them') he usually succumbed to Taylor's often reasonable blandishments (*Letters*, p. 204; p. 207; p. 204). It should be said that, equally, Taylor was ready to acknowledge his own uncertainties as to the value of his own corrections. Theirs was a genuine correspondence, a conversation conducted, for the most part, on amicable terms: 'do as you have done for you cant do better we must as you justly observe have it as free from faults as possible' (*Letters*, p. 152). They both went to extraordinary lengths to get things right; this went far beyond the correction of spelling, occasionally of grammar, and the insertion of punctuation into a text that had gone its own sweet way in all such matters.

Poet and publisher, with occasional help from other interested parties, were anxious to present to the public poems that were not only full of the incidental but crucial details of a unique vision, but which had, also, a structure that gave that vision an aesthetic wholeness. Clare needed those 'leading strings', as they helped him towards the fullness of vision he could not, at least initially, reach. To this end Drury, Taylor and his partner James Hessey, Mrs Eliza Emmerson, and other supporters picked their way very carefully through a mass of material, much of it seemingly repetitious, circling round his absorption in and by the natural world, the world of work, and his place in it. It is a wonder that they managed to find order within such variety and diversity, especially when Clare simply responded, 'do as you please' (*Letters*, p. 124). But it is important to register that, long before he knew any of these people, he was already making changes to his verse, altering as he copied, sometimes making two different versions of the same poem.

An early example of these efforts can be seen in two brief poems about spring (there are many such poems on the same theme: as he noted in his Journal on 20 March 1825, 'Spring is a wonderful mother for ryhmes' (*JCBH*, p. 219)); they both appear on the same page, neither of them published in his lifetime. The first version begins:

> Welcome gentle breathing Spring
> Now the birds are heard to sing
> And the budding tree is seen
> Putting forth her tender green   (EP 1 83)

This is echoed in the alternative version, except that in the second line he writes, more actively, 'Now the birds begin to sing', whilst the third line becomes, 'Now the Swelling shade is seen' (EP 1 83). This is strikingly unusual, showing Clare's ability, at this early moment in his writing life, to reach beyond the obvious to something both more idiosyncratic and more literary. As the quotation at the start of the later *Midsummer Cushion* demonstrates ('How can such sweet & lovely hours / Be reckoned but with herbs & flowers'), Marvell lurks behind much of Clare's thinking and writing (he even passes off one of his own pieces as by Marvell for William Hone's *Every-day Book*: see *Letters*, p. 335). Here Marvell's 'green shade', with Clare picking up 'tender green', becomes the 'swelling shade'; very few poets could imagine that conjunction. At this point in the second version Clare adds two lines ('While the Suns extended way / Sweetly shows the lengthend day' (EP 1 83)) whose compression and intimacy ('sweet' and 'sweetly' are such personal words for Clare) owe much to the metaphysical tone. The first version concludes:

> O delightful season hail
> May my footsteps never fail
> When time permits to visit thee
> And view thy new born scenery   (EP 1 83)

Clare's second version keeps the first two lines but then branches out into something more personal, less conventional: 'When I've time to trample where / All thy beauties reappear' (EP 1 83). In the process, a short eight-line poem has become a ten-line poem of considerable force and poignancy. And he has done this without any help from anybody.

A more extended example of such reworkings can be found in 'Summer Morning' (EP 1 550–4), a shorter trial run for which, 'The crowing coks the morns for told' (EP 1 242–4), can be found in the notebook which included so many of his early poems. The longer version, with a couple of stanzas omitted, was included in *Poems Descriptive*; in the process a poem of 48 lines has become one of 136 lines, with several lines of the first version incorporated, in a different order. The other main difference is that in the first version there is greater rhythmic variety: the octosyllabic first and third line are answered by lines of two fewer syllables:

> Now Slow the hazy mist retires
> A Wider Circle's seen
> Thin Scatterd Huts & Neighbouring Spires
> Augment the Bounded Scene   (EP 1 242–4, ll. 25–8)

Furthermore, in the second version, after line 48, Clare resorts to a seven-syllable line:

> Roaming where the dewey field
> Neath its morning burthen leans
> While its crops my searches shield
> Sweet I scent the blossomd beans   (EP 1 550–4, ll. 49–52)

Very early in his writing life, Clare is experimenting with different line lengths, different rhythms – something he does throughout his career. Once again, we need to note how determined he is, at this early stage, to work over material, trying to build a larger, more complex structure out of an initial foray.

There are already structural issues here, as well as line-by-line detail. As he moves towards lengthier formats, Clare begins an accretive process, whereby apparently different poems find their way into longer, sometimes more leisurely, verse. Although two later poems on spring (again) might be written

'Leading Strings'

five years apart, it could be argued (*pace* Robinson *et al.*), that the first version is a dry run for the second. They do, after all, begin with almost exactly the same eight lines:

> How beautiful the spring resumes its reign
> Breathing her visions oer the earth again
> The veriest clown that hath a pulse to move
> Looks on her smiling face & falls in love
> He plucks the wild flowers scattered from her hand
> & feels warm rapture round his heart expand
> Joys of the soul which nature prompts to seek
> The all of poesy but its power to speak
> (MP III 48–68, ll. 1–8; compare MP III 25–47, ll. 1–8)

Whilst there are echoes in this second version of other poems, such as 'Jealousy', 'A Spring Day', 'A Spring Morning', and 'Sunday Evening' (MP I 276–90; MP II 316–17; MP IV 165–6; MP IV 151), Clare also grapples with different possible openings, before deleting them, for the first version. There are similar hiccoughs in 'Pleasures of Spring' (MP III 48–68): before the final version of the couplet, '& daylight even stays the whole night long / To list the nightingales unsleeping song' (ll. 390–1), he has two attempts, surprisingly in different metres:

> As in the summers prime
> Tis music will prevail
> To keep the day behind the sun at night
> To list the nightingale   (see notes to MP III 64)

and:

> In summer night can find no room
> With darkness to assail
> For day stays all the night
> To list the nightingale   (see notes to MP III 64)

In this instance, the poem's second version is a hundred lines shorter, and more compact, than the first.

Once there was the possibility of publication, Clare had to confront the conflicting demands of his various supporters. Questions of taste and politics could not be avoided, and wealthy influential patrons such as Mrs Emmerson and her friend Lord Radstock sometimes made demands. It is no longer merely a matter of cutting for the sake of brevity, or altering words and phrases. There were several poems in the neatly copied manuscripts that played on the tradition of country tales, folklore, and ballads, some of them embracing the coarseness of that tradition. Taylor was brave enough to include some of them in *Poems Descriptive*, but this caused endless trouble. 'Dolly's Mistake' and 'My Mary' were two such poems, and Lord Radstock wanted both of them 'excised' from later editions; and, sure enough, in spite of Clare's, even Taylor's, protestations, they were omitted from the third edition.

'My Mary' (EP 1 78–82) is an interesting early example of Clare's readiness to challenge any pastoral idealization of country folk; behind this poem lies Cowper's melancholic address, with the same title, to a more poignant dying Mary. There was one moment in Clare's poem that caused particular distress to delicate sensibilities:

> For theres none apter I believe
> At 'creeping up a Mistress' sleve'
> Then this low kindred stump of Eve
>   My Mary
> Who when the baby's all besh-t
> To please its mamma kisses it?
> And vows no Rose on earths so sweet
>   My Mary   (ll. 33–40)

Although Clare dug his heels in (as Drury told Taylor, 'the dirty verse he *prizes*!' (*Critical Heritage*, p. 60)), he had to accept 'unfit' in the second edition. No one got the chance to question his alternative version of line 43, which gives, instead of '& pinches it', 'gripes its ar-e'. Nor did any readers or critics know about two poems built on very similar lines, 'My Matey' (EP 11 302–4), and, this time addressed to his dog, 'My Rover' (EP 1 107–10).

Two of the poems in *Poems Descriptive* were of a more far-reaching personal bent, in that Clare's desire for a more truthful portrayal of country life naturally led to political sentiments unlikely to find favour with Lord Radstock and his ilk. 'Dawning of Genius' (EP 1 451–2) is unashamedly about his own struggle to rise above the conditions that might cramp his ambition. Radstock insisted that a couplet about the evils of wealth be removed from the fourth edition: 'Those nessascery tools of wealth & pride / While moild & sweating by some pasture side' (ll. 17–18). He was even more angered by a passage in 'Helpstone' (EP 1 156–63), the poem that, placed first in the volume, was Clare's most personal early declaration of his identity and ambition as a poet, both working out his own almost impossible and intractable plight whilst also writing, at least in part, within a tradition marked by Goldsmith's 'Deserted Village', as the final line of the version in *Poems Descriptive* insists: 'Find one hope true to die at home at last'. Clare's attack on 'Accursed wealth' (l. 127) called forth Lord Radstock's fury. Although apparently supported by both Taylor and Hessey, Clare gave in: against the powerful figures in London, he felt he had no defence.

'Leading Strings'

Increasingly, he had to learn how to cope with such pressures, when to assert himself, and when to accept that Taylor and Hessey might just be right.

Before Clare's second volume, *The Village Minstrel*, was published in 1821, there was a lot of quite detailed correspondence between him and his publishers, not only about which poems should be included, but also about suggested alterations and omissions. At the same time, Clare was busily writing further poems, long and short, whilst ruminating over the possibility of an extended poem that would become *The Shepherd's Calendar*, published after complicated and frustrating delays in 1827. An understandable worry was the likelihood of repetition: surely if Clare was writing about the seasons, in whatever form, he must end up reworking the same material?

One of the poems Clare was writing and rewriting was 'Winter', of which there are two versions (EP II 682–91; EP II 692–6). The second version ('Winter (a)') is almost three times as long, and in his favoured octosyllabics. But he also says he prefers the 'all-ten measure', and although the first version ('Winter (b)') starts with two stanzas in octosyllabics, corresponding to the first and third stanza of the second version, he then continues in the 'all-ten measure'. In comparing the two versions, we can see how, even as his second version is that much longer, its octosyllabics allow, paradoxically, a compression of the first. In addition, he resorts to words and phrases that he has used in other poems of that period, and which will crop up later in *The Shepherd's Calendar*. Increasingly, it is as though Clare is facing backwards and forwards: anything he writes might echo or pre-echo his own words.

A simple example occurs with the word 'shroud': in 'Winter (b)', he has '& field & forest leaves the dazzld view / One blea cold picture neath her stretching shroud'; in the sonnet 'Winter', he writes of Winter that 'from day to day / Unmelted still he spreads his hoary shroud' (EP II 492–3). An earlier short poem, 'Winter Rainbow', has the line 'As the shy sun beams shrinketh from its shroud' (EP II 307–8). In another instance, in 'Winter' he uses the word 'beetle' (i.e. a heavy mallet): '& as the swain with ponderous beetle breaks / Yon ponds thick ice for waiting stock to drink' ('Winter (b)', ll. 73–4) becomes 'Save when some clown with beatle breaks / The ponds thick ice for stock to drink' ('Winter (a)', ll. 97–8). In 'January' in *The Shepherd's Calendar* (MP I 3–12), he writes:

> The soodling boy ...
> Wi heavy beetle splinters round
> The glossy ice wi jarring sound
> While huddling geese as half asleep
> Doth round the imprisond water creep   (ll. 75–90)

What Clare effects in this instance is a kind of studied, allusive repetition, whereby each particular version asserts its own individuality and independence.

There are two other anticipations of *The Shepherd's Calendar*, which show how Clare can rework his own efforts to startling effect. In 'Winter (a)', we have 'each idle plough / Froze in the snow hid furrow lyes' (ll. 127–8), which becomes in 'January', 'While in the fields the lonly plough / Enjoys its frozen sabbath now' (ll. 55–6). This brilliant reworking is matched by what Clare does with a few lines earlier in 'Winter (a)':

> The heron brawls its lonley cry
> Who interscepts the dazzld light
> & looks a cloud speck in the skye   (EP II 686, ll. 118–20)

He works on these lines: he originally wrote 'drawls' but changed it to 'brawls' because the next stanza begins 'The herdboys drawling noise is oer'. Another manuscript (Pforzheimer MS 198) has, for this line, 'The herons urge their fainting crye'. (The same manuscript has 'brawling' for 'drawling'.) 'St Martins Eve' (written in 1823 or thereabouts), has:

> No song is heard save one that wails aloud
> From the all lone & melancholly crane
> Who like a traveller lost the right road seeks in vain
>   (MP III 269–78, ll. 16–18)

In 'March', Clare devotes four wonderful lines to this image:

> While far above the solitary crane
> Swings lonly to unfrozen dykes again
> Cranking a jarring mellancholy cry
> Thro the wild journey of the cheerless sky
>   (MP I 36–50, ll. 113–16)

'Swings' was originally 'cranks', which had to be altered because of 'cranking' in the next line; 'unfrozen' dykes were originally 'his marshy' dykes, the 'wild' journey was originally 'cold', 'cheerless' originally 'changing' or 'stormy'. Clare has, with several different attempts at this image, arrived at the best. Each version has its own merits in the context of that particular poem, but *The Shepherd's Calendar* shows how compact and disturbing his vision can be; against the promptings of Taylor and Hessey, expansion and length did not necessarily rule out a surprising degree of concentration.

Even before publication of *Poems Descriptive*, Clare had started work on, and written a large part of, a long poem with the provisional title of *The Peasant Boy*. Because Drury, not always a reliable critic, had scrawled at the top of the manuscript, 'Let it pass in Oblivion', Taylor had ignored it. But when, at Clare's prompting, he looked at it, Tayor declared it the 'greatest Ornament of the new Work. There are a few Stanzas which require to be omitted & a few Corrections here & there necessary, but on the whole it is an excellent Poem' (*Letters*, pp. 134–5). It would, with the title 'The Village Minstrel', be placed at the front of the new volume. Clare went over the poem again, deciding it contained 'some of the best rural descriptions I have yet written [...] I think it will take when your Pencil has just gone over it here & there as its printing.' Taylor thought some of the apparent diversions ('Lubins Song', 'Lubin's sigh', and 'Woodcroft Castle') 'less poetical' and omitted them (*Letters*, p. 136; p. 144). As so often, he had to cope with Clare's prolixity, his tendency to go off in different directions, to forget that, at some point, a poem has to have some structure; in the process of editing, the poem becomes tauter and more coherent.

In addition to such aesthetic considerations was the inevitable political nature of the poem, and of course Lord Radstock's sensibilities were occasionally affronted. Against one stanza of 'The Village Minstrel', Radstock had written 'This is radical Slang.' When Clare was told of this he leapt to his own defence: 'what he dont like he must lump as the dog did his dumpling   I woud not have "There once were lanes" &c left out for all the Lord Rs in Europe' (*Letters*, p. 135; p. 139). Taylor was happy to agree, and this was a battle Clare could now win.

If *The Village Minstrel* had been, in places, something of a collaborative effort, *The Shepherd's Calendar* was much more so. The original plan, of a division of the year into each month (there were many literary forebears from Spenser onwards), becomes more complex the more Clare writes. Everyone seems eager to pitch in with plans and bright ideas. His publishers expressed their doubts about the enterprise: Hessey declared of the poems, 'they have evidently been written in too much haste and without the fear of the Public before your eyes ... they abound too much in mere description & are deficient in Sentiment and Feeling and human Interest' (*Critical Heritage*, p. 194); Taylor was no less discouraging, describing it as 'a descriptive Catalogue in Rhyming Prose of all the occupations of the Village People, scarcely one Feature of which has not been better pictured before by you' (*Critical Heritage*, p. 197). Undeterred, Clare forged ahead with the 'Cottage Tales' which, in some ways, and perhaps surprisingly, he preferred; he recognized in these the narrative voice he had been discovering in his satire, *The Parish* (never published in his lifetime, as Mrs Emmerson's comments forewarned: in spite of their mutual liking of it, it was '*not* for *present* publication' (*Critical Heritage*, p. 192), though interestingly, it is one of the most copied, recopied, and deleted poems in the two volumes of *Early Poems*).

The published volume reflected a compromise. Taylor had been infuriated by Clare's lengthy version of 'July'; Clare obliged (seemingly with little reluctance) with a much shorter version, which has the virtues of his more compact, compressed vision. Even the dozen lines in 'July' that Taylor deemed real poetry (and the only part of the poem worthy of that accolade) do not survive unscathed: 'The restless heat swims twittering bye' becomes 'The restless heat seems twittering bye' (MP 1 115; 302). Taylor made the alteration in a letter to Clare of 28 January 1826 (*Letters*, pp. 357–8). Although 'swims' would seem to be *le mot juste* here, Clare (rather fond of things 'seeming' to be this or that) accepts 'seems'. Taylor cut passages from each month, whilst including a few of the narrative tales at the end of the volume (the original plan had been to relate each of these much more closely to the relevant seasonal section). A glance at Tim Chilcott's detailed chart of the different manuscript versions of 'October' and the printed 1827 version shows the dizzying task confronting Clare's editors past and present.[3] As Chilcott observes, there can never be a definitive, conclusive text of this poem; by implication that is true of most of Clare's longer works. Added to this are the numerous changes within each manuscript, as Clare copies and recopies, adding and deleting as he goes along.

After publication of *The Shepherd's Calendar*, the relationship between poet and publisher lost its intensity: Taylor withdrew from publishing, and Clare, when he needed help, turned to Mrs Emmerson, and later, for *The Rural Muse*, to the publisher Jeremiah How.[4] Taylor still hovered in the background, but his influence was more generalized. Of 'Summer Images', a poem Clare was working on in 1830, Mrs Emmerson wrote:

> What a train of lovely visions she [your Muse] hath brought unto me – 'Summer Images' yea, in all their glowing beauty, in all their native freshness, and simplicity of attire: – truly, this muse of thine, is a most *bewitching* sort of *modeller* – she makes dame Nature and her progeny (tho' always the same) ever varying, *ever new* – she robes them with such peculiar grace.
> (*Critical Heritage*, p. 212)

Taylor was much more cautious in his praise:

> I cannot altogether approve the Poem of 'Summer Images', in many Parts it is as good as anything you ever wrote, but it is too long, too little select – you have gathered into it many Images which you have given before in Language sometimes more happy, – & it rambles too much. (*Critical Heritage*, p. 212)

Whilst it is no surprise to find Mrs Emmerson and Taylor at odds about their likes and dislikes, this particular disagreement reflects something of a shift in Clare's writing. He has arrived at a degree of self-confidence that allows him to

'Leading Strings'

explore a different literary world. Having done most of what he wanted to do in larger formats, he would now concentrate on the possibilities of the sonnet (there would be over 200 of them in *The Midsummer Cushion* (never published in his lifetime)), and of more complex, ode-like poems. His model for 'Summer Images' and 'Autumn' was the eighteenth-century poet William Collins, whose elaborate odes Clare had known since his youth. In both these poems, Clare adopts the stanzaic structure of Collins's 'Ode to Evening', except that in 'Autumn' he joins two stanzas together to form an eight-line unit and makes no recourse to rhyme (in itself an unusual move for Clare). The manuscripts show Clare working over drafts of both poems, almost, at times, as though they are parts of the same poem (which has now become a regular feature of his poetic praxis). It is fascinating to observe how much he is discovering, as he goes along, what is possible in this, for him, unfamiliar form.

The first version of 'Summer Images' (MP III 143–6) is shorter (sixty-five lines), and begins with lines that, altered, only appear in the finished poem at line 127:

> The south west wind I love the sudden sound
> & then to feel it gush upon my cheek
> & then with weary pause
> Await the creeping storm   (ll. 1–4)

The second poem's version of this is different in tone, and not necessarily any better:

> I love the south west wind or low or loud
> & not the less when sudden drops of rain
> Moistens my palid cheek from ebon cloud
> Threatening soft showers again
>   (MP III 147–62, ll. 127–30)

Two other openings deserve a mention:

> The southwest wind I love the sound
> How beautiful it gushes round
>   (see notes to MP III 155)

and

> The south west wind breaths in his face by stealth
> & without purchased phisic leaves him health
>   (see notes to MP III 155)

This second version is wisely rejected; it is interesting that the first alternative resorts to the octosyllabics he finds so appealing. The alert reader, with the sonnet 'Summer Moods' (MP IV 146) in mind, might hear an echo of that poem in the following lines from 'Summer Images':

> & in the juicey corn to list the quail
> Cry 'wet my foot' & hid as thoughts unborn
> The Land rail piping on
> Her craiking fairy song   (MP III 144, ll. 33–6)

The sonnet reads:

> While in the juicey corn the hidden quail
> Cries 'wet my foot' & hid as thoughts unborn
> The fairy like & seldom-seen land rail
> Utters 'craik craik' like voices underground   (MP IV 146, ll. 9–13)

'Autumn' (MP III 258), with its lack of rhyme and its more varied rhythmical structure, is a much more elaborate poem, more successfully in the line of Collins. This is perhaps another instance of his editors' instincts getting the better of Clare's more loose-limbed intentions: two stanzas were omitted from the version that appeared in *The Rural Muse*, stanzas over which Clare laboured in more than one manuscript, and which he deleted in some of them, as though, after having tried different versions, he decided to cut his losses. If Clare had not made fair copies of the poems he thought worth publishing (and Taylor and his employees also made copies), it is hard to imagine how any editor could have made sense of the several drafts that occupied so many different notebooks, sheets of paper, scraps here and there.

When, in 1832, Clare moves from Helpston to Northborough (a mere three miles, but for Clare a devastating distance), he contends with a host of contradictions, ranging from apprehension to something like acceptance. The poems he writes in that spring reflect his confusion, but also his determination to embrace what amounts to a new life: we can chart the passage from despair in 'Remembrances' to the hard-won stoicism of 'The Flitting'. Even here, where Clare is facing an unprecedented upheaval, physical and emotional, he works at his poems, not knowing whether these poems will be published ('Remembrances' would have been in *The Midsummer Cushion* but was not selected for *The Rural Muse*).

The first stanza of 'Remembrances' is striking in its confrontation of the hopeless loss of the vibrant past against the deadened present:

> Summer pleasures they are gone like to visions every one
> & the cloudy days of autumn & of winter cometh on
> I tried to call them back but unbidden they are gone
> Far away from heart & eye & for ever far away
> Dear heart & can it be that such raptures meet decay

'Leading Strings'

> I thought them all eternal when by Langley bush I lay
> I thought them joys eternal when I used to shout & play
> On its bank at 'clink & bandy' 'chock' & 'taw' & ducking stone
> Where silence sitteth now on the wild heath as her own
> Like a ruin of the past all alone   (MP IV 130–4, ll. 1–10)

In early versions of this poem, we can see Clare opting for 'we' rather than 'I', but he needs to emphasize that this experience is his, and his alone. Just as importantly, the poem begins life with only eight lines for each stanza; in this opening stanza, for example, line 8 originally reads 'On cowper green at "taw" & "ducking stone"'. In the next stanza, he writes 'O I never dreamed that trouble had a sting', which becomes 'O I never dreamed of parting or that trouble had a sting' (l. 18), and then adds, 'Or that pleasures like a flock of birds would ever take to wing / Leaving nothing but a little naked spring' (ll. 19–20). We can see how he establishes the poignant shift of rhythm in the final two lines of each stanza, as he works through the poem, turning the eight-line stanza into a much more plangent ten-line stanza. The poem's final couplet provides its own grim conclusion:

> But love never heeded to treasure up the may
> So it went the common road with decay   (ll. 79–80)

Even here, Clare frets over that final preposition: initially he writes 'to decay' in three different manuscripts, before settling for the unsettling 'with'.

'Decay A Ballad' (MP IV 114–18) grows naturally out of that final word of 'Remembrances', whilst anticipating 'The Flitting':

> O poesy is on the wane
> For fancys visions all unfitting
> I hardly know her face again
> Nature herself seems on the flitting   (ll. 1–4)

He has two attempts at this opening (printed in the notes to MP IV 114), instances of his scrupulous desire to get things just right:

> O poesy is on the wane
> I hardly know her face again
> The wind that blows the grass that springs
> Are each & all but common things
> I walk their presence knows me not
> Or I their beautys have forgot
> Where are the scenes that used to shine
> When

and

> O poesy is on the wain
> For fairey visions all unfitting
> I hardly know her face again
> Nature herself seems on the flitting
> [& strangers hath her dwelling taen]
> [The grass a springing winds a blowing]
> The fields own new & common things
>
> The grass the sky the winds a blowing
> & spots were still a beauty clings
> Are sighing oer their beauty going
> O poesy is on the wane
> I hardly know her face again
>   'going all a going'

The way Clare works at this poem is reflected in 'The Flitting' (MP III 479–89), a longer and more complex poem, similar in form to 'Decay', but striving towards some kind of resolution, thanks to the lasting power of poetry itself. The first eight stanzas, which Clare sent to Mrs Emmerson in June 1832, were included in *The Rural Muse* (1835), as an accompaniment to the engraving of Clare's cottage; there are in fact a further eighteen stanzas in the manuscript intended for *The Midsummer Cushion*. He had initially drawn a rule under line 64, and, with a new title – 'Pastoral Affections' – continued the poem at stanza 12, 'Strange scenes mere shadows are to me / Vague unpersonifying things'. He added three stanzas in the margin, to connect, as it were, these two shorter poems into one longer, more complex whole.

Within two years of the publication in 1835 of *The Rural Muse*, Clare enters the enlightened asylum of Dr Matthew Allen in Epping Forest, where he stays until a dramatic and heart-rending escape in the summer of 1841. Even when confined, first in Epping Forest and then in the asylum in Northampton, Clare plays on the hope of publication, whilst exploring his own solitude, his sense of himself as a poet of privacy. In 1841, before he escapes from Allen's establishment, High Beach, whilst walking the long trek back to Northborough, and after he is back there and before his removal a few months later to Northampton Asylum, he writes, astonishingly, two of his most remarkable poems, *Child Harold* and *Don Juan*. In these poems, in which he wears his Byronic hat, he pursues the notion of poetic accretion that he had developed throughout his writing life. He now has no Taylor to help lend structure and coherence to his work; he does not finish the fair copy of *Child Harold* before he is removed to the asylum, so we are left with another unfinished, teasing stump of a poem. Even here, though, in these small

'Leading Strings'

notebooks which he carries with him on his journey home, even in the margins of newspapers, he alters and corrects as he copies. Although he is in effect writing for himself, with no prospect of publication (even as he pretends to himself that there is), he is still writing poetry. He cannot imagine a life without writing. *Child Harold* becomes another cumulative poem, to which he attaches the title, 'Prison Amusements'.[5]

As one stanza in *Child Harold* has it, 'I am a poet & a lover still'. (He would go on, a few years later, to declare, 'I am – yet what I am, none cares or knows' (LP 1 396–7).) But when he copied this out, into MS 6, he made an important alteration: 'I sigh a poet & a lover still' (LP 1 40–88, ll. 443). Just as he had sighed throughout his life, and then in retirement, in that poem of May 1841, so here he sighs, both to himself and, very quietly, to anyone who might, one day, read what he has, so carefully, written, and rewritten. At this most harrowing time of his life, he knows that he can do without leading strings.

Notes

1. See Peter Kitson, ed., *Romantic Criticism* (London: Batsford, 1989), p. 139, and *The Letters of John Keats*, ed. H. E. Rollins, 2 vols. (Cambridge, MA: Harvard University Press, 1958), 1, 232.
2. See Tim Chilcott, *A Publisher and His Circle* (London: Routledge and Kegan Paul, 1972), and Zachary Leader, *Revision and Romantic Authorship* (Oxford: Clarendon Press, 1996).
3. See *John Clare: The Shepherd's Calendar*, ed. Tim Chilcott (Manchester: Carcanet Press, 2006). Chilcott's 'Introduction' to the text (pp. vii–xxviii) explores some of the challenges facing any editor of this work.
4. See *The Midsummer Cushion*, ed. R. K. R. Thornton and Anne Tibble (Ashington: Mid Northumberland Arts Group and Carcanet, 1979), and *The Rural Muse*, ed. R. K. R. Thornton (Ashington: Mid Northumberland Arts Group and Carcanet, 1982).
5. See *John Clare. The Living Year: 1841*, ed. Tim Chilcott (Nottingham: Trent Editions, 1999).

11

SCOTT MCEATHRON

Constructed Image
Portraits of Clare

It is hard to think of a literary figure for whom the issue of public image is more central, more foundational, and more multilayered, than for John Clare. Appearing first to the public in 1820 within a narrative framework that had been carefully constructed by his publisher John Taylor, Clare's entire career and still-evolving legacy in literary history can be understood as the stressful interplay between well-intentioned forms of packaging (commercial, artistic, scholarly) and the ideal of an essential, authentic Clarean self. If the desire to fully capture a biographical subject is necessarily doomed to failure, the quest has nonetheless maintained a particular urgency in the case of Clare: from the perspective of his early sponsors, there was an image, even a commodity to be codified if Clare was going to succeed; from the perspective of his later literary supporters and recoverers, there was, and continues to be, an unusual degree of moralistic advocacy concerning the liberation of the 'real' or unfettered Clare; and from the perspective of Clare himself, the question of identity – the expression of who he was, as a person and poet – was a recurring concern even before the psychological issues and dissociations that dominated the final decades of his life.

This essay examines a particular set of Clare images: paintings and visual depictions of the poet made during his lifetime. There are only about a dozen such surviving objects. The skill levels of the associated artists vary widely – several of the items are the work of amateurs – and they exist in a range of media, including oil paintings, sketches and line drawings, watercolours, and a bust. Nonetheless, the assemblage as a whole can be divided into two main groups: those that depict Clare as nervous, uncertain, uncomfortable in literary culture, and those that render him as strong and stolid, with a big head and obvious mental capacity. A choice is implied: some of the artists have deemed that Clare is best portrayed as a sensitive soul whose quivering intensity should tug at the heartstrings, while others have seen this same intensity and made it suggest latent power – strength, rather than weakness.

Constructed Image

Both of these types, it should be noted, are readily assimilable to prevailing notions of the visionary poet.

To some degree, these two categories break along chronological lines: Clare did gain weight as he aged, and the later images tend to reflect this. But the issue is more complicated than this. A visitor who saw Clare in the High Beach Asylum in 1841 – a moment in time near the centre of Clare's lifespan and one which also coincided with the most extreme crisis in his mental health – 'was surprised to see how much the poet was changed in personal appearance, having gained flesh and being no longer, as he was formerly, attenuated and pale of complexion. We found a little man, of muscular frame and firmly set, his complexion fresh and forehead high, a nose somewhat aquiline, and long full chin.'[1] The sense that these two versions of Clare came and went is writ large in many of the biographical accounts. In pursuing this point, I will begin with the most familiar two images of Clare, the 1820 oil painting by William Hilton that hangs in London's National Portrait Gallery (Figure 11.1), and the 1828 bust by Henry Behnes that is displayed in the Northampton Central Library (Figure 11.2). Though produced in fairly close proximity to one another, these two objects can usefully be taken as the endpoints in the tension between weak and strong Clare.

Figure 11.1 John Clare, by William Hilton, portrait in oils, 1820. © National Portrait Gallery, London.

167

Figure 11.2 Henry Behnes [later Burlowe], plaster bust, painted, of John Clare, 1828. Photograph reproduced with the kind permission of Northamptonshire Libraries.

William Hilton's 1820 oil is the most accomplished portrait of Clare and also the most historically significant, even given its formality and aura of artificiality. Commissioned by John Taylor the same year that he and James Hessey were publishing *Poems Descriptive of Rural Life and Scenery*, it has achieved canonical status not only because of Hilton's redoubtable talent and the institutional endorsement of the National Portrait Gallery, but also because it was quickly engraved and then printed as the frontispiece to Clare's second volume of poems in 1821. This engraving, by Edward Scriven, became the most widely circulated image of Clare in his lifetime. There has been a tendency to read Clare's entire interior life as laid bare in the Hilton portrait: in such a reading, the painting is said to show the volatile mixture of aspiration, concentration, and fragility which was destined to erupt in Clare. Though there may be some small element of truth in this, it is important to first step back and see the material circumstances out of which the painting arose.

The commissioning of the Clare portrait represented a melding of John Taylor's personal and business interests and should be understood as equal parts promotion of Clare and patronage of Hilton. Indeed, after the portrait was completed 'the publishers placed [it] on exhibition in their shop together with the poet's MSS'. Taylor had known Hilton since they were boys in grammar school in Lincoln in the 1790s. The close friendship had been maintained such that when Taylor was running Taylor and Hessey and, subsequently, the *London Magazine*, he directed a series of commissions Hilton's way spanning a period from at least as early as 1806 until as late as 1821, when an etching of a Hilton allegorical picture appeared as the first illustration in the *London*.[2] And we know that for a short time at least, Taylor lived at Hilton's London residence. The closeness of the men's friendship – and Hilton's reliance on Taylor's understanding of his career and business interests – is suggested by a rare surviving Hilton letter, provisionally dated 7 March 1820, probably the same week he began the Clare portrait. Here, Hilton urgently seeks Taylor's advice 'upon some arrangements I am about to make with a young man – whether to become my Pupil – he is to call on me in the morning and I should like to give him a definitive answer. Therefore if you dare brave the frost and are not better engaged, do let me see you today'.[3]

The scope of Hilton's professional indebtedness to Taylor emerges even more clearly when we look at the shape of his career and body of surviving work. Literary historians might reasonably assume that Hilton was a widely accomplished portrait artist, but in fact he forcefully resisted the lucrative financial opportunities portraiture offered, committing himself instead to history painting; this choice was widely seen by his peers as contributing to his professional frustration and privation.[4] Looking at the examples of Hilton portraiture that do survive, we find that beyond a handful of scattered, apparently unconnected pictures,[5] the bulk of the work falls into two categories: (1) portraits of family members (by far the most numerous); and (2) portraits associated with Taylor and his partner James Augustus Hessey. This latter group consists of the Clare portrait; a portrait of Keats, c. 1822 (probably not commissioned by Taylor, but later owned by him); and companion portraits of Taylor and Hessey (c. 1817). These last two commissions, which were arranged by Taylor, were probably vital for Hilton's sustenance. Readers of Clare have tended to think about the sitting through his eyes, focusing on his later confession to Hessey that, prior to meeting Hilton, 'my foolish opinion of these Celebrated London Writers & Painters was that they was som[e] thing different to other men', and describing his surprise when Hilton turned out to be 'most unlike a Londoner … like a neighbour of the Country' (*Letters*, p. 43). But if we step away from Clare's point of view, we can see that there was a complex intertwining of commerce, art, and beneficence that lay behind the portrait's production, with Taylor hoping that all three men would be served, materially, by a successful project.

Hilton depicts Clare as physically slight, and narrow of face, with his rapidly thinning hair only partially covering his forehead. He has a slightly upward gaze, as if looking towards the distance, or even the future. This upward-directed gaze was accentuated by George Scharf, director of the National Portrait Gallery, in the notebook sketch he made of the portrait, and indeed, Clare's eyes appear not to be focused in precisely the same direction, with the left more upraised. In Scriven's engraving, the eyes are slightly evened out, and the expression is blanker.

Comments have often focused on Clare's appearance in the portrait as delicate, intense, and pinched, with the expression ethereal, almost translucent, but also uncomfortable. Scharf saw the work as 'finely & clearly painted with careful drawing' while also noting in Clare 'An unhealthy expression'.[6] More sensationally, an *Illustrated London News* piece from 1951 asserted 'there is a look in those eyes which any doctor at first glance would tell you threatened insanity'.[7] Writing in 1962, the journalist and naturalist Brian Vesey-Fitzgerald, whose interests in the countryside, Gypsies, even boxing strangely paralleled Clare's, observed:

> Looking at that portrait ... and not knowing who it is, most people, I believe, would say 'that man was a poet'. It is an innocent, unworldly, face: a weak face. But it is the eyes that hold the viewer. There is a strange intensity about them, and yet they are remote, looking inwards as it were, but still far-seeing eyes that missed very little, one would say. The portrait does not lie. John Clare was a poet of the eye.[8]

These comments typify a certain extreme biographical reading of Clare – that he was always, palpably, destined for madness – and the Hilton has become a reference point for such perspectives. I would argue, though, the portrait does not readily convey nervousness or anxiety (and certainly not insanity) as much it suggests the wilful desire to sit quietly and get it over with. One can read a certain resignation in Clare's expression: he is doing his duty, knowing that it was important to Taylor, and to Hilton, and was probably also for his own good.

Produced less than a decade after the Hilton portrait, Henry Behnes's bust of Clare is believed, like the Hilton, to have been commissioned by John Taylor. Though the object projects strength and confidence, all three of the principals involved with its creation were struggling in one way or another.

Taylor, no longer in partnership with Hessey, had published Clare's third volume *The Shepherd's Calendar* the previous year after what Clare felt was an exceedingly long delay, and it was apparent that Taylor's firm was getting out of the poetry business. Clare's early popular success had collapsed, his money woes were increasing, and signs of increasing mental distress, even beyond depressive episodes, were appearing. Meanwhile, the talented portrait sculptor Behnes (c. 1802–37) was operating in what Tom Bates, in the fullest critical discussion of the artist, describes as a period of 'apparent inaction.'[9] With professional difficulties on all sides, Taylor characteristically attempted a kind of reprise of the doubly directed Hilton commission, here seeking to help Clare and Behnes simultaneously. This gesture was also typical of Taylor insofar as it was generous to Clare in one sense while pushing aside the two men's more problematic, unresolved financial arrangements, specifically the request for a full accounting of payments and liabilities that Clare had been seeking from Taylor for some years.[10]

Behnes's depiction of Clare is a radical departure from Hilton's and gives us the other side of visionary Clare: the head and brow are big and forceful, the bones of the skull blunt rather than fine, and the gaze stoical if grim. In a celebratory poem that is otherwise anodyne, Clare's patron Eliza Emmerson noted 'Th' expansive forehead – the soul-speaking eye – / The lip that struggles 'tween a smile and sigh!'[11] E. V. Rippingille, an artist and mutual friend of sitter and sculptor, described the bust as 'bold' and without 'any taint of mannerism or conventional imitation', and Bates has similarly argued that is less sentimental than the Hilton and more 'credible', reflecting trends in portrait sculpture that were placing a greater value on realism. (We would be able to say more about Behnes's style and tendencies if he had lived longer, but he died of cholera in the Rome epidemic of 1837, choosing to remain in the city to work on a backlog of commissions.)[12]

For the sitting with Hilton, Clare had moved from suspicion to relief when realizing that the painter was more like a countryman than a Londoner. In this case, Clare had developed a strong friendship with Behnes before the bust was ever envisaged, Behnes having visited him at home in July 1827 and being struck with the power of 'This Extraordinary Being', and then promptly setting to work crafting toys for Clare's children. So while critical opinion may have consolidated around the idea that Behnes is more accurate than Hilton, it is also clear that when Behnes came to do the portrait sculpture, he understood himself to be depicting a figure he viewed as a 'real Genius in every sense of the word'.[13] Clare had used similar language upon meeting Behnes ('the proudest feelings I posses[s] in becoming known to the world arise from the lucky accidents that introduce me to men of genius'); a few months later, he was confiding to Behnes the extent of his psychological stress: 'I am very unwell & what ails me I know not but my head is horribly afflicted with a stupid vacancy & numbness that is worse th[a]n hell itself' (*Letters*, p. 393; p. 411). By the time the bust was taken, then, there was some level of common understanding and intimacy between sitter and artist, and that included the notion that Clare was an unusual subject with a profoundly felt, difficult, mental life.[14]

For the remaining depictions of Clare discussed here, we move out of the London orbit and to Northampton and the work of provincial and amateur artists. Thomas Grimshaw (1817–75) was born in Northampton and lived there for most of his life, and his local connections presumably enabled his access to Clare and perhaps even fostered some level of trust between himself and his subject. Northampton newspapers make repeated references to Grimshaw's artistic activities, including various commissions, especially in the 1840s. He also found work in Leeds and other locales, and so while we may be tempted to view his Clare portrait as the product of a talented amateur, it is clear that painting and portraiture were Grimshaw's life work. He focused on portraits and family groupings but also produced landscapes and some equine scenes.[15]

Grimshaw's half-length portrait, measuring 28 3/4" × 23 7/8", is extremely important for the documentary record (Figure 11.3). Painted in 1844 when Clare was fifty-one, it is located in time between the 1820 Hilton

Figure 11.3 Portrait of John Clare, by Thomas Grimshaw, portrait in oils, 1844. Photograph reproduced with the kind permission of Northamptonshire Libraries.

Constructed Image

and two important late images also reproduced here, the sole surviving photograph of Clare by W. W. Law (1862) (Figure 11.5) and the line drawing by G. D. Berry (c. 1863) (Figure 11.6). Grimshaw allows us to perceive the transition between youth and age as it played out in Clare's lifespan. Further, we see both sides of the tension between his quivering, pinched fervidity and his later, more stolid projection of intellectual force. Clare is portly and well-dressed, situated against a conventional natural backdrop that alludes vaguely to his poetry. The portrait's key features are Clare's forehead and eyes, elements of his appearance that were mentioned numerous times by observers over the years, perhaps most memorably by Samuel Carter Hall: 'he had a look and manner so dreamy, as to have appeared sullen – but for a peculiarly winning smile; and his forehead was so broad and high, as to have bordered on deformity.'[16] The extent to which Grimshaw accentuates these features is striking, and we also see a variation on Hilton's upward gaze, rendered here as powerful yet ambiguous, balancing pleasure and suspicion. (In an 1885 review of a fund-raising exhibition for a permanent Art Gallery in Northampton, the *Northampton Mercury* referred to the painting as revealing Clare's 'determination of features'.[17])

In looking at the work, one wonders to what extent Grimshaw was influenced by, and extrapolating from, the fact that Clare was in the asylum. This is perhaps the most important point: even if Grimshaw's regional roots made for some level of sympathy between himself and Clare, it also meant that he knew Clare's story – the reasons he had been confined, and perhaps rumours of his more extreme behaviours. Even if he did not witness any of these behaviours himself, it must have been difficult for Grimshaw to banish the notion that his subject was a kind of archetype, the 'mad poet'. This is a very different lens than Hilton had brought to bear and would also represent a step beyond Behnes's sense that he was depicting a depressed genius.

Grimshaw visited Clare in the asylum again nearly twenty years later, in the period shortly before Clare's death, and this visit may have given rise to Grimshaw's production of a lithograph of the original portrait 'on stone' referenced in a newspaper report of 1863 but now lost.[18] On the occasion of this visit, Grimshaw is supposed to have told Clare that he was exuding 'quite his young look again'.[19] This was probably the most innocent of remarks, nothing more than a friendly compliment, but it is another small bit of evidence suggesting that there was, in fact, some sort of ongoing fluctuation in Clare's appearance. In this regard, it would be extremely useful to know if Clare really was the sitter in an 1855 watercolour by George Clarke of Scaldwell that was printed as the frontispiece to the first volume of the Oxford edition of Clare's *Later Poems* (1984). That painting (unavailable for reproduction here) is strongly reminiscent of the Hilton portrait of thirty-five years earlier – indeed, its similarity to the Hilton is closer than that of any other rendering of Clare from any period of Clare's life. The volume's editor, Eric Robinson, says 'there can be no doubt of the identification of the sitter', and there seems to be some justification for this conclusion even though the matter is not settled.

George Maine's watercolour portrait of a seated Clare looks at first glance to be little more than an earnest piece of folk art (Figure 11.4). Produced four years after the Grimshaw, it depicts Clare at age fifty-five, seated in the colonnaded niche at All Saints' Church, Northampton that was, by all accounts, his regular station. For many years, Clare was given the freedom to leave the Northampton asylum, and the church was only about a mile

Figure 11.4 John Clare, portrait by George Maine, watercolour, 1848. Photograph reproduced with the kind permission of Northampton Museums and Art Gallery.

Constructed Image

Figure 11.5 John Clare, photograph by W. W. Law, 1862. © National Portrait Gallery, London.

away. Various witnesses suggest that Clare frequently engaged in some light composition while thus ensconced, fuelled by the steady intake of tobacco.

The fact that George Maine produced several versions of this portrait but otherwise left little biographical trace would seem to confirm that he was at best a minor artist, and that the painting is little more than a historical curiosity. Yet the painting seems to improve the more closely one examines it. The rendering of Clare's face is far from bland, even though the painting's muted overall design and colouration fools the viewer into thinking it so. In fact, close inspection of Clare's face reveals that Maine has deftly captured many of the details – of gaze, forehead, eyes, long-but-thinning hair – that earlier artists had also featured. There is also a fair amount of detail in the renderings of Clare's clothing and the architecture of the portico: in each case, Maine has given special attention to lines, folds, and shadows.

Indeed, at his death two years later Maine was described by a local paper as an artist by profession: 'Mr. George Maine, artist, of St. Giles's Street,

Figure 11.6 G. D. Berry, pen and ink drawing, c. 1863. Image reproduced with the kind permission of Sotheby's.

Northampton, aged 49 years. Deceased was the only surviving son of Mr. George Maine, gardener, of the above place, and expired rather suddenly after a very short illness.'[20] Still, Maine did not have the sort of prominence that Grimshaw did locally; we have many examples of surviving works by Grimshaw, and a good number of mentions in Northampton newspapers, while in the case of Maine we have neither.

For his part, Clare seems to have felt warmly towards Maine. He signed the portrait at the time of its production and at some point over the next three years made Maine the subject of an acrostic, a verse form in which the opening letters of each line are made to spell out an individual's name. Note that Clare's habitual use of the ampersand is here employed as a stand-in for the 'a' in Maine's surname, which he renders as 'Mayne':

> Good & substantial painter merits raise
> Encouragement from censure into praise
> On the plain canvass in poetic strife
> Rich pictures rise from nothingness to life
> Great in semplicity the pencil vies
> Endearing nature with her simple dyes
> Making the portraits look from out the frames
> & almost speak in answer to their names

Constructed Image

> Yea Landscapes too & many a pleasant scene
> Naked in winter grow to evergreen
> Enjoy thy labours & relapse between (LP 1 246)

The poem at once echoes characteristic Clarean themes and speaks directly to Maine as an artist. Those themes, especially pronounced in Clare's asylum period, involve familiar contrasts between 'strife' and peace; presence and 'nothingness'; barren winter and 'evergreen' spring; 'censure' and 'praise'; and finally labour and rest. As with many of Clare's sonnets and sonnet-like shorter poems, the final note of rest also suggests Clare's felt exhaustion after the work of the poem. Clare praises Maine for creating, from nothingness, embodiments of his sitters that border on the wondrous: 'Making the portraits look from out the frames / & almost speak in answer to their names'. Of course, this is also what the acrostic itself aims to do, but Clare keeps the focus on Maine, first hinting at his modest reputation, and then defending him: Maine's 'semplicity' of approach is akin to nature's, or is at least worthy of her, 'Endearing nature with her simple dyes'. Do the last lines of the poem suggest that Maine also produced landscapes? Probably not: Clare's reference is to natural landscapes that create life from barrenness, analogous to the creative conjuring act of the visual artist.

Of the major Romantic poets, Clare is the only one for whom we have a photograph (Figure 11.5). An account by John Taylor of Northampton (1831–1901) – a printer and Northampton book collector, not to be confused with Clare's publisher, who died in 1864 – describes something of the circumstances. The photograph, he says, 'was taken by Mr. Law, of Gold-Street, I having special permission from the Doctor at the Asylum for Clare to visit Mr. Law's for the purpose. His fine head and exceedingly fine long eyelashes are well represented in the photograph. At the same time he signed his name on a dozen slips of paper to be placed under the portrait.'[21]

From this account, it appears that Taylor, not Law, was the driving force behind the production of this photograph, and the arrangement of this session can be seen as part of his broader interest in preserving Clare's legacy. The most consequential element of that programme was Taylor's purchasing of many of Clare's manuscripts and books from his widow Patty upon Clare's death in 1864, a process in which he was aided by the editor of the *Northampton Mercury*, G. J. De Wilde. Importantly, though, this purchase did not include the copyright to Clare's work, which was obtained separately by Joseph Whitaker, and thus began the convoluted, still-contested history of the Clare copyright. As Taylor then described it, 'The curious part of the purchase by Mr Whitaker of the Clare MS.S. and the sole right to publish anything already printed or unpublished was that I had secured most of the valuable items in his library without the right of publishing. Mr Whitaker held the right of publishing without the materials.'[22] Whitaker did, in fact, possess a good number of Clare manuscripts himself, but Taylor's point about the situation's legal complexities and possible pitfalls holds nonetheless.

The photograph itself is striking for the power and ambiguity of Clare's gaze. As with the other depictions, Clare is looking fixedly outward, but does not appear entirely at his ease. The eyebrows, as Taylor noted, are long, though less suggestive of 'fineness' than of the deep retreat into self that characterized the very end of Clare's life. In capturing Clare's latent power, the photograph is consistent with remarks on Clare offered by William Jerom, another patient at the asylum: 'He was like the King of the Forest, there was a prowess in his limbs and a majesty in his fiery eye that showed the vigour and energy of a mind whose greatness even in ruins reminded one forcibly of what is said in Scripture of the Leviathan: "None dare stir him up, nor make him afraid."'[23] The photograph would seem to be less encumbered by artistic preconceptions and expectations than the other Clare images. Nonetheless, the simple fact of its execution suggests to us the presence of many people with an interest in Clare who were hovering just off-camera, as it were. Taylor had enough status and persuasive ability to arrange for the sitting; we don't know what Clare's feelings were. The photographer William Wilby Law headed an established local business that specialized in 'Album Portraits and every other variety Executed in the first style'.[24] His brother, Edmund Francis Law (1810–82), had briefly been mayor of Northampton and was an important architect with an interest in cultural preservation; he also was the owner of the Grimshaw portrait. De Wilde, the newspaper editor, would later help found the Northampton Museum, which would become the repository for many of the items Taylor acquired. All of this suggests that there was a small community of concerned individuals that was already forming around the Clare legacy – not a cottage industry, to be sure, but a community with interests in history, literature, and cultural preservation.

George Duval Berry was a fellow inmate of Clare's at the Northampton asylum and depicted him several times. The Peterborough Museum and Art Gallery holds two pencil sketches and two watercolours of Clare that Berry made immediately after his death, but the one reproduced here (Figure 11.6), measuring about 7" × 9.5", is believed to have been produced in 1863 while Clare was still alive. This level of repeat production indicates that Berry had a seriousness of purpose and a particular interest in Clare as a subject. We are extraordinarily lucky to have the drawing at all. Joe Goddard, its former owner, describes finding it in a group of portfolios that had lain in his family's 'damp stable building' for many decades; he believes it 'was almost certainly acquired by my great-great-grandfather, Henry Goddard, an architect whose day-books show he did a lot of work around Stamford'. Goddard sees the image as showing an 'utterly vulnerable, defenceless face', and, in language reminiscent of Behnes's early account, describes Clare as 'the genius surrounded by every possible obstacle'.[25]

Berry's marvellous drawing can legitimately be viewed as, if not an apotheosis, a culmination of the trends I have identified. Elements that the other representations tend to focus on – Clare's forehead, his faraway look, and the upward turn of his eyes – are all notable here. Yet, perhaps more than any other image, Berry's drawing reconciles and harmonizes those aspects of Clare's features which conditioned the weak-or-strong dichotomy in earlier portraits: the forehead is still large, but the lips especially are delicate. Similarly, the thickness of the body is implied but not allowed to dominate. One could also argue that there is a greater sense of repose here than in earlier renderings, though that is a subjective judgement, and one might just as easily read fatalism. Most striking, of course, is Clare's dramatically long hair, which Berry depicts in such a way as to make it blend with the other cross-hatched elements of clothing and background. These lines make Clare into a kind of inverse sun god, radiant but unable to beat back the darkness. The overall effect is of a messy, dark swirl out of which shines a centrepiece of battered but dignified calm. This skilful work is both daring and honest, a fitting last look at Clare as he approached the end of his life.

Notes

1. Cyrus Redding, 'Clare, The Poet', *English Journal*, 15 May 1841, repr. in *Critical Heritage*, pp. 247–56 (p. 248).
2. Edmund Blunden, *Keats's Publisher: A Memoir of John Taylor* (London: Jonathan Cape, 1936), p. 106; p. 26; pp. 125–6.
3. William Hilton to John Taylor, 7 March 1820. Carl H. Pforzheimer Collection of Shelley and His Circle, New York Public Library, Astor, Lenox, and Tilden Foundations. Evidence of Taylor living with Hilton a few years earlier is found in a letter of 1813, when Taylor writes to a friend, 'There is a spare Bed at all times for you at Hilton's, 10 Percy Street, where I now lodge' (qtd in Blunden, *Keats's Publisher*, p. 244).
4. Scott McEathron, 'John Clare, William Hilton, and the National Portrait Gallery', *John Clare Society Journal*, 32 (2013), 5–25.
5. The Usher Gallery in Lincoln holds Hilton portraits of an 'unknown man' and of a 'Reverend La Tour', identified by Sam Ward as the Rev. Peniston La Tour (1769–1851), rector of St Andrew's Church, Boothby Graffoe, Lincolnshire. Surviving examples of Hilton's history paintings are most easily seen on the ArtUK website.

6. George Scharf, *Trustees Sketchbook* vol. 9, p. 32. Heinz Archive, National Portrait Gallery.
7. E. D. O'Brien, 'The Northamptonshire Peasant Poet', *Illustrated London News*, 9 June 1951, p. 936.
8. 'Poor John Clare', *The Sphere*, 28 July 1962, p. 22.
9. Tom Bates, 'On the Portrait of John Clare by Henry Behnes', *John Clare Society Journal*, 27 (2008), 45–58 (p. 50).
10. The accounting that Clare was seeking eventually came in August 1829; Clare's letters of 1828 often recur to his financial worries.
11. 'Lines on Receiving the Bust of the Northamptonshire Poet, Executed by Henry Behnes, Esq', *Morning Post*, 14 April 1829, p. 3 (ll. 9–10). She adds near the end of the poem: 'The Poet Clare stands all confess'd to me, / In mental character, in feature shewn' (ll. 17–18).
12. 'Personal Recollections of Artists by the Late E. V. Rippingille, no. 3: Burlowe the Sculptor', *Art Journal*, 21 (1859), 201–2; Bates, 'On the Portrait', p. 46.
13. Behnes, 19 July 1827, John Rylands Research Institute and Library, qtd in Jonathan Bate, *John Clare: A Biography* (London: Farrar, Straus and Giroux, 2003), p. 326.
14. Both the Hilton portrait and the Behnes bust were purchased at auction by Clare's first biographer, Frederick Martin, in 1865, immediately before the publication of his *Life of John Clare*.
15. See, for example, 'Mr. T. Grimshawe', *Northampton Mercury*, 16 February 1867, p. 5.
16. S. C. Hall, *Gems of the Modern Poets: With Biographical Notices* (Philadelphia: Carey and Hart, 1842), p. 224.
17. 'The Art Exhibition', *Northampton Mercury*, 9 May 1885, p. 9.
18. 'St. Sepulchre's Bazaar', *Northampton Mercury*, 5 December 1863, p. 5.
19. Peterborough Manuscript G2, quoted in Bate, *John Clare: A Biography*, p. 525.
20. 'Deaths', *Banbury Guardian*, 31 January 1850, p. 3.
21. 'The Clare Exhibition', *Peterborough Standard*, 9 September 1893, p. 6.
22. Ibid.
23. Qtd in June Wilson, *Green Shadows: The Life of John Clare* (London: Hodder & Stoughton, 1951), p. 254. Jerom's manuscript, titled 'Reminiscences of Clare. The Northamptonshire Peasant Poet. By a Fellow Patient', is item G5 in the Peterborough Museum Collection.
24. *Northampton Mercury*, 1 August 1863, p. 4.
25. Joe Goddard, 'A Formative Influence of John Clare', *John Clare Society Journal*, 3 (1984), 49–52 (p. 51; p. 52). Goddard's belief that the drawing was originally acquired by his ancestor Henry Goddard is confirmed by an 1867 newspaper article, 'Archeological Meetings and Excursions', *Bedfordshire Times and Independent*, 11 June 1867, p. 5.

PART IV
Influences and Traditions

12

EMMA MASON

Clare and Religion

Clare's religious beliefs are often downplayed by both critics in the field of Romanticism and those interested in nineteenth-century Christianity. His most read and commented-on nature poems overshadow his biblical paraphrases and inquiries into the church, such as *The Parish*, and while his writing is sometimes visionary and cosmic, it is more likely to be cited as a restorative alternative to the transcendental spiritualism sometimes associated with Wordsworth or Blake. Moreover, the critical focus on his intimate relationship with landscape and nature tends to obscure Clare's interest in religion, as if the two are mutually exclusive. It is not that critics directly dismiss the religious in his work, but rather that they deflect from it to secularize his reflections on creation. Janet Todd, John Barrell, and Paul Chirico all admit the importance of Eden imagery in their studies of Clare, for example, but spend little time with its biblical, religious, or metaphysical significance for the poet.[1] Erica McAlpine even suggests that Clare anxiously stands outside of the abundance of creation and registers the world as a catalogue of things – individual birds, trees, fields, plants, places – rather than an interdependent incarnation of God.[2] Yet Clare's writing about religion also reveals a less anxious, more faithful poet for whom Christianity offered a way of reflecting on and venerating the entangled specificities of the natural world. Like many nineteenth-century British writers, Clare understood Christianity as necessarily ecological given its basis in care for and towards all species. His much-quoted lines from his 'Autobiographical Fragments' – 'we heard the bells chime but the fields was our church' – is not a rejection of religion: it is rather a trope familiar to nineteenth-century readers wherein the devotional space of the church is extended into the commons of the fields, heaths, and meadows (*JCBH*, p. 40).

To explore the connection between Christianity and ecology in Clare's work, this chapter first discusses Clare's early Christian faith, his relationship to Wesleyan Methodism and the Ranters, his distrust of some forms of organized religion, and his divine ecology as an expression of rural Christianity. The second part of the essay considers Clare's biblical paraphrases, especially Job, Psalms, Matthew, and Revelation, as well as two tree poems that illustrate his religious focus. While it is not the purpose of this chapter to assign a particular set of denominational beliefs to Clare, especially as his views were various and changing, it will nevertheless confront the critical refusal to call Clare a Christian. When he writes to a correspondent 'o take me as I am & like a good christian', he does so teasingly, but also because the word, and the language of Christianity more broadly, meant something significant to him (*Letters*, p. 505). In the Peterborough Museum and Art Gallery manuscript appears an even more idealized portrayal of Christianity:

> No religion upon earth deserves the epithet of divine so well as the Christian human blood never reeked upon its alters ... it owns the history of no wars to inforce or spread its doctrines its beautiful instruction was peace and earth & good will towards men its founder had no power to demand converts for he was of low station.[3]

Sympathetic to many denominations, movements, and faiths – Anglican, Independents, Methodists, Unitarians, Quakers, Catholics, Jews, and Muslims – Clare owned many religious books and referred to them throughout his prose writings and letters. He believed that religion was central to a functioning society, but that the particularities of doctrines and beliefs were inferior to a shared sacred commitment to 'truth & love':

> A religion that teaches us to act justly to speak truth & love mercy ought to be held sacred in every country – & what ever the differences of creeds may be in lighter matters they ought to be overlookd & the principle respected.[4]

No doubt Clare held prejudices towards certain religious groups, and he was sometimes critical of Catholicism as histrionic and superstitious. But little angered him more than those who misused or exploited Christian ideas, whom he charged with hypocrisy. As Sarah Houghton-Walker wisely remarks in the preeminent study of his religion: 'Clare's disenchantment with contemporary Christianity is always rooted in the lack of worthy followers of the religion, rather than the faith itself.'[5]

Clare is not a theological writer like Barbauld or Coleridge, nor did he develop his own reading of Christianity like Blake or Wordsworth. Yet his poetry and prose collectively reveal a Christian writer for whom the biblical vision of creation was an explicit call to listen to and so defend the particularities of the natural world. More than the pastoral Christianity of Bloomfield or Cowper in whose work the reader is encouraged to discern

Clare and Religion

God buried in discrete flowers or stones, Clare's divine ecology comprises relationships and correspondences between things founded on a mutual and inclusive love of God. The multiplicity of matter that defines Clare's work – wildflowers, pooties, caterpillars, badgers, wagtails, elm trees, hedgehogs, water lilies, bees, ravens – constitutes a creation that is at once various and singular but always interwoven. It lays bare what Clare called God's 'sacred design', one that eclipses his denominational indecision and spiritual melancholy but confirms that the joy he found in nature is always mediated by his Christian faith (*Prose*, p. 109).

Clare's interest in faith, the Bible, and Christian teachings is inseparable from his relationship with the natural world. As his friend Eliza Emmerson wrote to him, the phrase 'religion of nature' is inadequate to describe the more complex assertion of Christian ecological thinking and feeling in his writing. Clare wrote back to Emmerson to confirm that he was indeed more dependent on the gospels than such a phrase suggested, but that 'My creed is yours – but still the grave is terrible.'[6] This indication of a faith embedded in a profound fear of death is part of a larger spiritual crisis with which Clare struggled as young man in the 1820s. Only recently free of dependence on poor relief and having left his job as a limeburner, Clare was suddenly an up-and-coming author and married man: 1820 was both the year *Poems Descriptive of Rural Life and Scenery* was published and of his marriage to Martha Turner in the thirteenth-century Anglican Church of St Peter and Paul in Great Casterton. Clare was born into and identified as an Anglican for much of his early life and recalled that his father 'was brought up in the communion of the church of England, and I have found no cause to withdraw myself from it'.[7] He confirmed that the Anglican church was one for which he felt 'reverence' and did 'from my soul as much as any one curse the hand thats lifted to undermine its constitution' (*JCBH*, p. 30). At the same time, Clare turned away from the elitism of Anglicanism in the late 1810s towards Methodism. Mark Minor suggests that Clare was attracted to the Methodists because they favoured a form of worship held outdoors and punctuated by music and singing.[8] And yet he soon tired of the Methodists too, perhaps because they developed into a branch of the Church of England rather than a challenge to it. If the Anglicans were little more than hypocrites who 'mocked' God by claiming virtue even as they 'fleece the poor', as he wrote in *The Parish*, then the Methodists, and Dissenters more broadly, were extremists, a 'set of upstarts late from darkness sprung' and 'inspired to rave and not to preach' (EP II 747; 717).

Readers interested in Clare's views on religion are often directed to *The Parish* as his fullest exploration of religion in relation to community and the church. *The Parish* is widely acknowledged as a furious and satirical poem written just after his rise to fame following the publication of *Poems Descriptive of Rural Life and Scenery* (1820) but left unpublished in his lifetime. Aimed at the 'dirty' rich, Clare's poem is a sharp critique of the magistrates, farmers, land and store owners who exploited the poor, the same group who also damned Clare's ambitions as a poet (EP II 714). Villains like Farmer Cheetum and Bumtagg the bailiff are demonically depicted in the poem, malevolently eager to claim 'fresh taxes from the needy poor' or herd them into the workhouse, 'A makeshift shed for misery' (EP II 745; 747). As Eric Robinson argues, the main targets of *The Parish* are religious extremism, hypocrisy, and intolerance of other beliefs rather than specific creeds.[9] A more benevolent Christianity is embodied by the older generation, not least the 'good old Vicar' of an idealized church now lost to an imagined, rural past. Notably, the description of the old Vicar in lines 1584–1725 was already extant as a separate poem called 'The Vicar' when Clare started *The Parish*. His portrait is not only sympathetic, but also reverent, and depicts a good Samaritan who embodies charity and love for his parishioners, refuses to hunt, and serves as a beacon in the wilderness 'to cheer the weak' and 'rest the weary and relieve the poor' (EP II 761). Enclosure destroys the vicar's churchyard as it does his community, and the poor are left without spiritual or financial support when the old man dies. While Clare's targets were as much those who failed to reform those laws that penalized the poor (such as the authorities behind the Speenhamland system), he was similarly critical of new dissenting Christians whose faith he considered performative and superficial. His commitment to Anglicanism may have been nostalgic, but it motivated what would become a profound familiarity with several books of the Bible and attendance at Sunday worship. The fields might have been one of his churches, but he also sought to be part of his local parish: 'like many more I have been to church [more] often then I have been seriously inclined to recieve benefit or put its wholsome and reasonable admonitions to practice' he wrote, but 'still I reverence the church' (*JCBH*, p. 30).

How might we square Clare's written expressions of fervent despair at the state of Christianity in his own community with his devout allegiance to faith, the church, and the Bible? For Mark Minor, Clare's horror at the affected piety of some religious denominations was intensified by his belief in faith as a practice of compassion and kindness now destroyed by greed and self-interest both in church and society. Clare acknowledged that this was not always the case: he considered the Ranters 'a set of simple sincere & communing christians with more zeal then knowledge earnest & happy in their devotions'.[10] He wrote to the publisher James Hessey that he had 'joind the Ranters' because of their 'affection for each other their earnest tho simple extempore prayers' and 'preachings & manners', which to him appear 'real & not affected' (*Letters*, p. 294). Religion was at its most effectual and compelling when it directed people to the world around them not in the name of grand gestures or deep feelings but as a constant reminder of those with whom we share the world around us. Reading Genesis, Clare rejects literalist interpretations of the Bible to embrace its literary rules of conduct:

> it is a harmless & universal propensity to magnify consequences that appertain to ourselves & woud be a foolish thing to try the test of scriptures upon these groundless assertations – for it contains the best Poetry & the best morality in the world.[11]

These lines indicate both the Bible's significance as a model of art and virtue, and, as Minor affirms, its decentring of the human in creation. Out of Clare's spiritual crisis came a renewed belief in the relationship between nature and the divine understood within a Christian framework. Yet many who write about Clare appear to be allergic to the word 'Christian'. As Houghton-Walker argues, critics who reject Clare's work as Christian often do so because they either focus solely on the absence of references to Christ and ignore countless allusions to God, or because they are unable to register the connections between Clare's accounts of Christianity and his personal faith.[12] But his very refusal to instrumentalize and classify the world into capital or resources is at one with his affirmation of the more-than-human world as 'evidence of divinity, of a maker'.[13] Clare brings together his love of God with his love of nature not to subsume the former into the latter but because they are continuous and congruous.

To understand why this correspondence is ecological, it is helpful to contextualize Clare not in early Romantic expressions of pantheism or the 'one life', but in nineteenth-century readings of the Church as growing from and with the natural world. For example, here is the Victorian clergyman, Francis Kilvert, recording the details of his daily walk to church in his diary:

> I went to church early, soon after ten o'clock, across the quiet sunny meadows ... The ivy-grown old church with its noble tower stood beautiful and silent among the elms with its graves at its feet. Everything was still. No one was about or moving and the only sound was the singing of birds. The place was all in a charm of singing, full of peace and quiet sunshine. It seemed to be given up to the birds and their morning hymns. It was the bird church, the church among the birds.[14]

As he wanders around the graveyard, Kilvert pays his respects to the 'dewy grass-grown graves and picturesque ivy and moss-hung tombstones', consciously drawing on a familiar elegiac trope of the country churchyard. Yet this is not a trope for Kilvert; as its incumbent, he has dedicated himself to this church and recognizes those buried there: 'Under the elm on the north side of the church I found Jane Hatherell's grave – some withered wreaths lay upon the turf.' The vitality of the natural world set against overgrown tombstones might evoke Thomas Gray's elegiac country churchyard, but Kilvert's writing is representative of a turn towards creation as divinity in the period, heaven joined with earth. This is not quite an argument about design (that the things of the world are evidence of God as its designer) or natural theology (that we have knowledge of God that is separate from divine revelation), nor is it deism (in which a creator God has no interest in intervening in the universe). These perspectives are in different ways dependent on one in which the spiritual and physical are differentiated either in hierarchical terms (one is elevated over the other) or dissociative terms (the religious is split from the material). An ecological approach to the divine, however, allows the observer to see the world in harmony with itself, at once spiritual and material.

Clare, like Kilvert, strived to see his environment in this continuous way, an Eden in which heaven and nature, church and world, are one fabric. Human attempts to tear this fabric – either tangibly by felling or enclosing the land and the things that live on it, or philosophically by thinking outside of it through secular explanations of existence and being – are as much self-destructive as they negate other life forms. As Clare wrote in his natural history prose passage, 'Autumn':

> there is the beautifull Spire of Glinton Church towering high over the grey willows and dark wallnuts still lingering in the church yard like the remains of a wreck telling where their fellows foundered on the ocean of time.
>
> (*JCBH*, p. 273)

The image is a revealing one. The church is interwoven with the willow and walnut trees: the church spire reaches beyond the trees, but its cloistered garden holds them, as leaves, roots, nuts, and branches 'linger' there. Their connection is worldly and in time not only because the passage is called 'Autumn', but also because the reader learns that the fallen walnuts are 'dark', indicating their readiness to drop following the shedding of their lighter yellow-green colour earlier in the year. But it is also spiritual in that the church trees reveal back to the human the consequences of misreading oneself as separate from a divine ecology in which all things are entwined. The trees, embraced by the beauty of the church spire, masquerade as a shipwreck marking the spot where its sailors drowned. The dead sailors are an epitaph to humans who 'flounder' in real time because of a spiritual blindness to the coalescence of heaven and nature, church, and world. Thus when Clare writes that the fields are his church, he means both that they offer him a sacred alternative to the local chapel, but also that they are hallowed in the same way as the church, offering the faithful a holy place for quietude and worship:

> & now the church spire looking rather large dimensions catches the eye like a jiant overtopping trees & houses ... yonder is Maxey Tower church looking as if it was lighting up with sunshine when the Autumn sky is as gloomy as summer twilight & on the right peeping between the trees may be seen West Deepings crocketed spire (*JCBH*, p. 273)

This convergence of the trees and church embodies a mutual care between world and spirit, one that liberates the observer whose gaze is directed in all directions. For Clare, writing 'Autumn' between his two periods of incarceration first in Dr Matthew Allen's asylum at High Beach, Epping and then in Northampton General Lunatic Asylum, the vision released him from an intruding modern world. 'More interesting', he wrote, than a 'flight of arches' in a manicured park or 'bridges in a great city', the spires springing through and around their foliage kin are part of creation, not a ruinous adjunct to it.

'Autumn' appears in a foolscap volume of texts written in 1841, which includes several natural history passages, the 'journey from Essex', Clare's reworkings of Byron, and his biblical paraphrases. Even when he expressed suspicion about organized religion, Clare remained committed to what he called 'a religious feeling of faith in the Gospel', and there are many notes in his letters and journals in which he records reading specific parts of scripture (*Letters*, p. 414). In his autobiographical sketches, he immediately recalls his father reading 'a bible or testament' alongside superstitious penny tales, and he rails at the school system for diminishing the Bible as a textbook rather than a divine poem (*JCBH*, p. 2). He was rewarded from an early age for 'getting a Chap[ter] of Job I think the 3rd' and presented with '6d and praises of the Master' for his accomplishments (*JCBH*, p. 33). Following his early crisis of faith, Clare wrote to Hessey that the Bible was 'an antidote to my deepest distresses' and 'the one book that makes the carnallitys of life palatable & the way to eternity pleasant ... that supplys soul & body with happiness' and is 'poetry in perfection' (*Letters*, p. 515). 'Greater then Homer', he wrote, the Bible offered him aesthetic as well as religious guidance: he claimed that he could recite an 'abundance of passages by heart' from the Psalms and was personally drawn to 'the fine Hebrew Poem of Job' (*Letters*, p. 515; *JCBH*, p. 5). The Bible did not always equate to church attendance: he recalled that the father of his first love, Elizabeth Newbon, read the Bible in search of interesting stories and 'thought him self a religious man tho he never went to church and he was so for he was happy and harmless' (*JCBH*, p. 89). On the Sundays that he listened to the church bells from the fields, he recalled 'a religious feeling in our haunts' while 'some old shepherd sat on a mole hill reading aloud some favour[i]te chapter from an old fragment of a Bible which he carried in his pocket for the day a family relic' (*JCBH*, p. 40). From the fields, the church bells call back to the birds' songs while also preparing the listener for a period of reflection in which to recite, memorize, perhaps even illustrate their Biblical texts.

Clare was also nervous that he might appear 'ignorant' of the Bible, and his numerous verse paraphrases of Exodus, Numbers, Judges, 1 Kings, Job, Psalms, Isaiah, Lamentations, Habakkuk, Matthew, and Revelation show how keen he was to prove his exegetical credentials (*JCBH*, p. 89). Biblical paraphrase was regarded as an assertion of literary skill in the period, and an avenue for the critique of power via the translation of the Bible's radical condemnation of slavery, wealth, poverty, and inequity. While Clare's manuscript paraphrases might not have been intended for publication, they nevertheless reveal a poet who yearns to meditate on and in doing so assuage his suffering in relation to Job, David, Solomon, Matthew, and John. Consistent with Clare's other religious writing, the paraphrases emerge from his belief in the contiguity of God and nature, the divine and the material. For example, Clare relates going for 'a walk about the fields a deep mist in the morning hid every thing till noon', after which he is ready to read his Bible. Opening to the Song of Solomon, Clare finds an 'overstraind far fetchd and conjectural' 'eastern love poem' to 'our Saviour', the narrative of which runs counter to his perception of the Bible as a prophetic text that connects the divine to the material (*JCBH*, pp. 175–6). Clare's 'Solomons Prayer &c &c' is thus not a paraphrase of the Song of Solomon, but rather a retelling in rhymed couplets of 1 Kings 8, in which Clare explicates the 'thick darkness' of 'nature' in which God both resides and transforms into a 'grand habitation' for his created world (LP 1117). The prayer also adopts the word 'father' to denote both the creator poet God and Psalmist David, Solomon's actual father, to ally divinity with poetry. The repetition of words such as 'dwelling', 'house', 'mercy', and 'forgive' focus the reader on a world in which God speaks through both prophets (like David and Solomon) and the landscape, promising a marriage of spirit and matter, heaven and earth.

The notion of the landscape or nature as prophet also appears in Clare's paraphrase of Revelation 21, 'The New Jerusalem', in which John relates the coming together of heaven and earth in one new creation. Clare makes some significant amendments to John's text to bring out the vision's radical implications for the disenfranchised human and more-than-human alike. Like

John, Clare sees a 'new heaven / & earth on the bosom of day / For the first earth was fled with its deeds unforgiven' (Rev. 21.1); but where John expounds the dimensions of the New Jerusalem – 'And he that talked with me had a golden reed to measure the city, and the gates thereof, and the wall thereof. And the city lieth foursquare' and the 'length and the breadth and the height of it are equal' (Rev. 21.15–16) – Clare recalibrates the uniformity of John's measurements to mean equality of all beings:

> Twelve foundations the walls of the city upheld
> & twelve names thereon – the apostles of God
> & he that talked with me a golden reed held
> An emblem of justice & truth not his rod
> To measure the city the gates & the wall
> In kindness & love doing equal by all   (LP I 153)

For Clare, the equivalence of the new city's infrastructure attests to God's commensurate forgiveness to all: 'The length & the breadth & the height of the plan / Are equal – like God in his mercey to man' (LP I 153). He stresses redemption further in his paraphrase of Revelation 22, 'The River of the Water of Life', which for John conjures the purity of the new Jerusalem as an echo of the garden of Eden, both bringing together water and life as a counter to the contaminated waters of the tribulation. In Revelation 8, the earth is hit by a 'great star' called 'Wormwood', which pollutes and desecrates the waters, 'and many men died of the waters, because they were made bitter' (8.12). The river of life offers a correction to this environmental devastation just as our perception of the world as holy and divine reforms our relationship to it. As such, Clare's paraphrase recalls *The Shepherd's Calendar* (1827), in which he celebrates the interdependence between the church year and cultural traditions, rituals, festivals, and feasts. But he also reveals his confidence as an exegete by rewriting the very lines in which John warns others of editing or distorting his text: 'if any man shall take away from the words of the book of this prophecy, God shall take away his part out of the book of life' (22.19). Clare changes 'book of life' (God's list of the redeemed) to 'volume of life' (LP I 158) to intimate that those who disregard the prophecy's commandment to love creation are synonymous with the nescient reader. Employing the word 'volume' to mean at once quantity of sound and the format in which his poetry was published, Clare suggests that those who cannot attentively listen to or comprehend language are most in need of God's mercy. As Stephanie Kuduk Weiner argues, Clare paraphrased the most poetic books of scripture to speak in the voices of their narrators, the Psalmist David and the prophets Job and Isaiah, and based his translations on the distinctively poetic King James Bible.[15] Literary ignorance thus leads to a kind of homelessness in creation as well as in the new Jerusalem, an adversity God redresses in response to prayer. John's 'Even so, come, Lord Jesus. The grace of our Lord Jesus Christ be with you all. Amen' (22.20–1) becomes 'The power of Gods love be with all – now – & then / & the grace of christ jesus be with you – Amen' (LP 1158).

The final 'Amen' at the end of Clare's Revelation paraphrases accentuates their status as encounters with God and interpretive acts through which humans learn to understand their place within creation. The play of this divine ecological consciousness in Clare's work, one that mindfully registers the smallest details and patterns in the world as evidence of God, erases the distinction between his 'nature' and 'religious' poetry. Words like 'mystic', 'spirit', 'bless', 'spell', 'peace', and 'glory' recur alongside references to the Bible, Eden, the Sabbath, church spires and bells, and all are entwined with an eerie vocabulary of ghosts, witches, fairies, will-o'-the-wisps, and jack-o'-lanterns. Houghton-Walker's book includes a captivating discussion of Clare's negotiation of the supernatural, superstition, belief, and faith, one in which he wavered between asserting his scepticism as a safeguard against a diagnosis of neurosis and his genuine affection for a rural Christianity that united folklore, song, scripture, and doctrine.[16] I conclude by examining his invocation of rural Christianity in poems usually divided into 'secular' and 'religious'. For example, a comparison of Clare's much-cited tree elegy, 'The Fallen Elm', and his prayer-like 'This leaning tree with ivy overhung', both written in the 1820s, reveals that both poems explore the sanctity of the natural world with recourse to the Bible. The former poem is a wail of horror at the felling of an old elm tree, a 'music making' being who once sang the 'sweetest' anthems in tune with the song thrush ('mavis'), who made his home in branches that in turn offered shade to the community (MP III 440–1). As the landowning tyrants sink their 'vile unsatiated maws' into the root of the tree, they devour the 'weak' elm, who is cast into silence by the cleave of the axe (MP III 443). Like those Clare indicts for religious hypocrisy, the land-owners too betray creation as a common home, enclosing and parcelling out a landscape that belongs to God and so with all of creation. As Clare writes in his paraphrase of Matthew 25. 44–5, those who fail to 'administer comfort' to the 'poorest & least' do the same to Christ (LP 1150). Matthew features again in Clare's paraphrases of Psalms 91 and 97, wherein God 'delivers' his creation from 'the fowlers snare' to foreshadow Christ's Sermon on the Mount (LP 1134–6, ll. 5–7). Here, Christ declares that the poor, grieving, weak, and peaceful are deemed the most blessed, and the 'fowls of the air' and 'lilies of the field' exemplars of Christian being (Matt. 6.25–32). While the redemption Christ offers to the powerless cannot expiate Clare's anger at the brutal murder of a friend in 'The Fallen Elm', it nevertheless grants him a language to redirect his grief into a poem that consecrates the tree and voices its desire for 'pity' and compassion (MP III 442).

'The Fallen Elm' makes few explicit religious references, but the perceptive reader might note the presence of scriptural allusions that are plainer than those of the more overtly religious 'This leaning tree with ivy overhung'. The latter poem suggests that God 'writes' and sounds out creation in a voice only the attentive listener can hear:

> There is a language wrote on earth & sky
> By Gods own pen in silent majesty ...
> The voice of nature as the voice of God
> Appeals to me in every tree & flower
> Breathing his glory magnitude & power
> In natures open book I read & see ...
> I hear rich music where so eer I look   (MP II 212)

By the end of the poem, Clare has returned to God's universal unfolding in nature as a common home, one in which 'all may read & meet with joy again' (MP II 213). Reading, writing, seeing, and, above all, listening: these are the ways to secure faith in God and nature for Clare, one confirmed through a religious and emotional experience of the world. Without this, observers of creation misread and mishear in a confusion of senses wherein they 'look' for 'sound' and are insensible to the silence through which God speaks:

> I pause & hear a voice that speaks aloud
> Tis not on earth nor in the thunder cloud
> The many look for sound tis silence speaks
> & song like sunshine from her rapture breaks
> I hear it in my bosom ever near
> Tis in these winds & they are every where   (MP II 213)

Clare does not vocalize the more-than-human here. Rather, he describes what happens when he stops to listen to the more-than-human and hears their songs to God. As Isabel Karremann argues, Clare reads creation as a web of autonomous animals and birds with agency to meaning-make beyond human analysis.[17] But Clare was also engaged with many Christian writers who appeared in his library, letters, and diaries – Milton and Bunyan, Barbauld and Cowper, Coleridge and Hannah More – not to mention a number of lesser-known sermon writers and theologians.

Clare makes sense, then, in a lineage of religious poets for whom matter is evidence of God and their verse an endeavour to vocalize the sound of its worship.[18] Like Christopher Smart before him, who heard music in sunflowers, globe-thistles, oysters, and crocodiles, and Christina Rossetti after him, who perceived creation as a choir in which all things join in one song of divine praise, Clare experienced rapture and joy in the microscopic particulars of nature because they, like him, love God.[19] This does not mean he never questioned his faith. Clare struggled with the idea of God like all Christian writers do, but, as one of his verse fragments confirms, his faith always broke through any 'clouding doubts' to 'bless' him once again with religion's 'Sweet mystery' (MP II 189–90). In his unfinished 'Essay on Religion', Clare defines religion as 'the grand aspiration to live well & die happy':

> Do unto others as ye would others should do unto you was the creed of the divine founder of christianity & this creed is so beautifully simple that it impresses its truth on the slightest mind & so simply true that the weakest capacity can understand & retain it[20]

These are the words of a writer familiar with scripture and its claims for the 'weak' things of creation, a word that associates them not with acquiescence and deference but with the 'divine founder', at once lowly and the highest of all beings. The idea that the 'last shall be first' (Matt. 19.30) might have appealed to the suffering Clare, who identified not only with Christ's trials, but also with Job's afflictions: 'I am like Job broke out in b[o]ils from head to foot', he wrote to John Taylor in 1821 (*Letters*, p. 211). Yet he also discerned that such sorrow was part of the atoning value of faith, and his paraphrases of Job focus solely on the latter part of the book, chapters 38–41, in which God speaks out of the whirlwind. By moving past Satan's review of Job's piety, Job's lament, and his friends' monologues, and then omitting Job's concluding atonement, Clare gives priority to God. And yet Clare's two significant changes to Job 41 are indicative: first, he added the word 'brutes' to the description of God's children; and second, he located God, as he did the infamous chaos monsters Behemoth and Leviathan, in a rural landscape of 'shady trees' and mountain views (LP I 127, 130). As Clare wrote in 'The Village Minstrel', God 'unfurls' creation as an always 'new' and 'revealing world', a paradise in which, 'Joying to listen', we can learn to hear nature's song (EP II 130; 147).

Notes

1. Janet Todd, *In Adam's Garden: A Study of John Clare's Pre-Asylum Poetry* (Gainesville: University of Florida Press, 1973); John Barrell, *The Idea of Landscape and the Sense of Place 1730–1840: An Approach to the Poetry of John Clare* (Cambridge: Cambridge University Press, 1972); Paul Chirico, 'Writing Misreadings: Clare and the Real World', in John Goodridge, ed., *The Independent Spirit: John Clare and the Self-taught Tradition* (Helpston: The John Clare Society and the Margaret Grainger Memorial Trust, 1994), pp. 125–38.

2. Erica McAlpine, 'Keeping Nature at Bay: John Clare's Poetry of Wonder', *Studies in Romanticism*, 50.1 (2011), 79–104 (p. 99).
3. Peterborough Museum Collection, A46, vol. 2, p. 75; p. 68, qtd in Sarah Houghton-Walker, *John Clare's Religion* (Farnham: Ashgate, 2009), p. 204; p. 208.
4. See Eric Robinson, 'Introduction' to *John Clare: The Parish, A Satire* (Harmondsworth: Penguin, 1985), pp. 9–25 (p. 18fn2), Peterborough Museum Collection, B 4–136.
5. Houghton-Walker, *John Clare's Religion*, p. 204.
6. Mark Minor, 'John Clare and the Methodists: A Reconsideration', *Studies in Romanticism*, 19.1 (1980), 31–50 (p. 41), British Library Egerton Manuscripts, no. 2246, folio 123.
7. Robinson, 'Introduction', p. 18, quoting Clare's statement in *Drakard's Stamford News*, 7 January 1820.
8. Minor, 'Methodists', p. 45.
9. Robinson, 'Introduction'.
10. To J. A. Hessey, 20 April 1824, *Letters*, p. 294; see Minor, 'Methodists', p. 44.
11. Minor, 'Methodists', p. 49, Northampton Public Library MS 15.
12. Houghton-Walker, *John Clare's Religion*, p. 205.
13. Simon Kövesi, 'Introduction' to *John Clare: Flower Poems* (Bangkok: M&C Services, 2001), pp. ix–xxii (p. xvii; p. xxi).
14. *Kilvert's Diary: Selections from the Diary of the Rev. Francis Kilvert*, ed. William Plomer, 3 vols. (Hay on Wye: O'Donoghue Books, 2006), I, 328–9.
15. Stephanie Kuduk Weiner, 'John Clare's Manuscript Translations of Byron and the Bible', *Studies in English Literature 1500–1900*, 58.4 (2018), 877–97 (p. 880).
16. See Houghton-Walker, *John Clare's Religion*, chapter 3.
17. Isabel Karremann, 'Human / Animal Relations in Romantic Poetry: The Creaturely Poetics of Christopher Smart and John Clare', *European Journal of English Studies*, 19.1 (2015), 94–110.
18. See the 'Clare's Library' section of *Catalogue of the John Clare Collection in the Northampton Public Library* (Northampton: John Dickens and Co, 1964).
19. Christopher Smart, *Jubilate Agno* (1759–63); Christina Rossetti, 'All Thy Works Praise Thee, O Lord: A Processional of Creation' (1880).
20. Peterborough Museum Collection, A46, vol. 2, p. 75; p. 68, qtd in Sarah Houghton-Walker, *John Clare's Religion* (Farnham: Ashgate, 2009), p. 204; p. 208.

13

BRIDGET KEEGAN

John Clare and the British Labouring-Class Tradition

In their essay, 'John Clare: The Trespasser', John Goodridge and Kelsey Thornton offer a compelling analysis of Clare's account of his early encounter with James Thomson's *The Seasons*.[1] After purchasing a copy, Clare dares to climb over a wall into the patrician domain of Burghley Park to indulge in reading and making his first attempts in verse. His breach of aristocratic space is emblematic of other forms of breaking and challenging boundaries enacted throughout Clare's poetry. However, Clare's description of his literary awakening is as much about the nascent poet's potentially transgressive relationship to *time* as it is to *place*. Because the bookshop was closed on Sunday, Clare's only day free from work, he 'plannd a scheme in secret to obtain my wishes by stelth, giving one of the boys a penny to keep my horses in my absence, with an additional penny to keep the Secret' (*JCBH*, p. 11). Even at the age of thirteen, Clare understands that time is money and that, during the working week, his time is not his own. He must not only buy it back but also pay to conceal his actions from the surveillance of the master. His trespass into Burghley Park, moreover, is prompted by his awareness that he 'did not like to let any body see me reading on the road of a working day' (*JCBH*, p. 11). Clare had already internalized 'work-time discipline': because of his class, his time was under scrutiny.

E. P. Thompson's landmark essay on the concept of work-time discipline foregrounds the work of two poets who are typically identified as 'the first' British labouring-class poets: Stephen Duck (1705–56) and Mary Collier (c. 1688–1762). Thompson argues that their poems, 'The Thresher's Labour' (1730) and 'The Woman's Labour' (1739), memorialize a transitional moment in notions of work: from 'task orientation' to 'timed labor'; from 'natural' agrarian temporality (linked to the seasons and the sun) to 'abstract' industrial 'clock time'. Time becomes a commodity, a currency, 'it is not passed, but spent'.[2] While critics from John Barrell forward have discussed Clare's accomplishments as an innovative poet of place, I contend that his representations of time further establish his importance within eighteenth- and nineteenth-century labouring-class poetry. We have evidence, based upon Clare's copy of Robert Southey's *The Lives and Works of the Uneducated Poets* (1831), that Clare knew of Duck; moreover, much recent criticism, notably Goodridge's *John Clare and Community*, emphasizes the importance of Clare's relationships to several literary networks, including his 'brother bards and fellow labourers' such as Robert Bloomfield (1766–1823). In the context of eighteenth- and nineteenth-century labouring-class writing, Clare's thematic and stylistic experimentation with temporality demonstrates his pivotal contribution to the development of that tradition.

William J. Christmas identifies Clare's poetry as a decisive moment in the evolution of labouring-class literary identity. He elaborates upon 'Merryn and Raymond Williams's sharp observation that "John Clare was not the first, but in effect, the last, of the English 'peasant poets'"'.[3] For Christmas, Clare's work is distinctive in its rejection of cultural frameworks imposed on labouring-class poets from Duck forward. Notably, Clare unequivocally claims a right to his vocation as a writer. Christmas sees Clare 'at the beginning of a new, more overtly politicized and independent breed of plebeian poet',[4] emerging more fully, for instance, in the Chartist poetry of the 1830s. As Clare's trespassing narrative reveals, any claim to his vocation depends upon having control of his time, underscoring how a fundamental precondition for labouring-class poets to create is *simply having time to write*. Such time was never guaranteed. Literacy and access to literary texts, along with historical and socio-cultural developments, including the vogue for natural genius or changing ideas of the countryside, were also contributing factors. But finding, having, and protecting time to write – asserting writing as an activity (whether conceived of as 'work' or as a pastime) for which one could have or take the time – was fundamental for Clare, his predecessors and successors, to publish at all.

Perhaps for this reason, the titles of Clare's poems are replete with temporal indicators: times of day (evening, noon, morning); seasons; specific days or months; holidays; and abstractions of time, such as reflections upon the concept of eternity. Many other untitled or generically titled ('Song' or 'Sonnet') poems also depict temporality as early as the first or second line. Most poems referencing times are not occasional poems, although Clare produces his share of these, such as 'Sorrows for a Favourite Tabby Cat who left this Scene of Troubles Friday Night Nov. 26 1819' (EP II 225) or 'The Hail Storm in June 1831' (MP IV 226). Not only are Clare's poems 'time-stamped', but they also represent timekeeping and timepieces. In an early sonnet, 'To an hour glass', from *The Village Minstrel*, Clare reimagines the significance of this famously polysemous symbol:

> Old fashiond uncooth measurer of the day
> I love to watch thy siltering burthen pass
> Tho some there is that lives woud bid thee stay
> But those view reasons thro a different glass
> To him times meter who addresses thee
> The world has joys which they may deem as such
> The world has wealth to season vanity
> & wealth is theirs to make their va[i]ness much
> But small to do worlds joys & fortunes fee
> Wi him times cronicler who welcomes thee
> So jog thou on thro hours of doomd distress
> So haste thou on the glimpse of hopes to come
> As every sand grain counts a trouble less
> As every draind glass leaves me nearer home (EP II 320)

By the early nineteenth century, the hourglass was one of the most common instruments for measuring time and was often represented as a device used primarily by those of the lower orders.[5] However, recent historians of time, such as Jonathan Martineau or Paul Glennie and Nigel Thrift, have stressed that long before the late eighteenth century, rural inhabitants like Clare understood a wide and sophisticated range of temporal orders and methods of telling time. Their relationship with time was not simply 'natural' or driven solely by agricultural cycles but would have included familiarity with a range of concepts and technologies. Clare's poem further demonstrates his understanding of the class-based relativity of time – wealth here distinguishing one's response to its passage.

The poem opens with an apostrophe: 'Old-fashioned uncooth measurer of day'. In the 1820s, the homes of labourers like Clare might have possessed a clock or watch; however, hourglasses continued to be prevalent. Although Clare calls it 'old fashioned', the device likely came into widespread use at the same time as mechanical clocks.[6] Nevertheless, Clare calls it 'uncooth', simple and rustic and thus more closely affiliated with those of Clare's class.[7] While sandglasses might seem archaic, like clocks they too impose abstract temporal regularity. Clare often portrays himself as rejecting time-based obligations, for example, slipping off on the Sabbath to wander the woods. Yet instead of expressing disdain for an instrument that imposes time consciousness, in the second line he asserts, 'I love to watch thy siltering burdens pass.' Clare typically employs the phrase 'I love' when observing nature or reminiscing about childhood. Here, he admires an object that measures the linear passage of time. Time is 'siltering' – an unusual word that naturalizes the movement of the sand, likening it to the silt that accumulates in waterways. Addressing the hourglass, moreover, he does not 'bid thee stay'. Halting time is a privilege of the affluent, the 'world' of 'wealth' and 'vanity'. The speaker, having 'small to do' with the world of fortune instead celebrates the passage of time. As 'times cronicler', the hourglass signals not death, as in traditional iconography, but 'hopes to come' – the end of 'hours of doomd distress'. The speaker yearns for home; however, his nostalgic ache is located not in the mists of the past but in a future symbolized by the falling sand.

Not every labouring-class poet before or after Clare demonstrates equal attention to time or reflects upon it in as nuanced or persistent a way. Listed among John Goodridge's catalogue of labouring-class poets are a handful of clock- and watch-maker poets, including Clare's friend, Thomas Inskip. Regrettably, none produced a georgic poem in the vein of 'The Clock-maker's Labour'. Nevertheless, many other poets consider how time determines their vocation as a writer. Thompson and others have analysed the tension between writing and manual labour in Duck's and Collier's foundational poems. Almost every subsequent poet, regardless of primary occupation, describes how time awareness and time anxiety impact their artistic self-fashioning. Occupational spaces less open to surveillance or employments which permitted greater task autonomy tended to produce more poets. Handloom weavers, for instance, working primarily from home, are among the most prolific.

Shoemaking was also generally conducive to reading and writing.[8] Bloomfield's older brother narrates how young Robert was selected to read to his fellow workers when he first arrived in London 'because his time was of least value' as the most inexperienced craftsman (George Bloomfield to Capel Lofft, 1 March 1800).[9] Beginning in the early nineteenth century, the abandonment of guilds and the rise of factories led to more explicitly political poems about workers' rights to protect their time, with shoemakers at the forefront.

Surveying labouring-class poems about time, the word 'hour' predominates. Workers were not usually paid by the hour until the late nineteenth century. Wages were calculated by the day, week, or, in some professions such as domestic service, annually. However, debates about the number of hours to be worked per day and daily starting and stopping hours were sources of contention from the mid eighteenth century forward. Notably, in labouring-class poems, 'hour' is frequently modified by the word 'leisure'. Reading and writing poetry are typically activities for 'leisure *hours*' – indicating that poets eschewed any claim to writing as their primary occupation. The word 'hour', furthermore, is sonorous and metrically flexible (it can be one or two syllables). The preponderance of the term underscores that even for primarily rural workers, more precise abstract quantifications of time complemented broader natural divisions of time. In a later sonnet, 'An Idle Hour' (MP IV 155), Clare describes his '[s]auntering at ease' across a bridge, observing the river flowing beneath him. Rivers symbolize the passage of time, and the poet also delights in 'the sunshine dancing on the arch / Time keeping to the merry waves beneath' (ll. 5–6). He then notes the flowers on the banks, thirsting for water '[w]hile water flowers more than their share recieve' (l. 11) – perhaps an allusion to inequalities of time as a resource. Elsewhere, in his more explicitly vocational poems, Clare depicts the tensions between time devoted to 'productive' labour and poetic pursuits, often unfavourably scrutinized by his peers, such as in 'The Fate of Genius a Tale' (EP II 666). The sexton who remembers the now-departed poet reminisces about the genius's preference for wandering in nature, which makes others question 'if his mind was right' (l. 54). His artistic aspirations are kept 'secret' (l. 86). When he does finally publish, his efforts are judged harshly, subjected to 'slander' (l. 91). First made suspect for the unusual use of his leisure time, the poet ultimately perishes from despair, unsympathetically surveilled and judged first by his fellow villagers and then by the literary world.

Clare does not specify what type of manual work his ill-fated genius performs. Among the occupations whose hours were most scrutinized are household servants. Servants had the least freedom to control their time, often living with their employers and signing an annual contract for work. A servant had to be available at every hour. While he is rarely identified as one of the 'founders' of the tradition, Robert Dodsley (1703–64) is an important but overlooked contributor to the labouring-class canon. His earliest publications focused on his role as a London footman, offering an urban perspective on working-class life and balancing Duck's and Collier's rural focus. His first publication, *Servitude* (1729), contains moral and practical advice for his brothers in livery. The section on 'Diligence' describes 'Jack Swift' as an exemplary steward of his time: 'One Hour for this, and one for that ordains, / Nor lets the appointed Time slip idly thro' his Hands' (ll. 110–11). The speaker recommends staying ahead of one's tasks, as, 'We thus for all Contingencies prepare, / Whatever happens we have Time to spare' (ll. 118–19). However, that 'spare' time is not for personal pursuits but for the master's unexpected demands. Dodsley's second publication, *A Muse in Livery, or the Footman's Miscellany* (1732) includes a response to 'The Thresher's Labour': 'The Footman. An Epistle to my Friend Mr. Wright', an hour-by-hour inventory of a servant's day in an aristocratic household.

Clare and the British Labouring-Class Tradition

Unlike Duck and Collier, who feel their Master's eye upon them, Dodsley's situation allows him time to observe his master and his master's family. During dinner, once everyone has begun to eat, the poet states:

> This is the only pleasant Hour
> Which I have in the Twenty-four;
> For whilst I unregarded stand,
> With ready Salver in my Hand,
> And seem to understand no more
> Than just what's call'd for, out to pour;
> I hear, and mark the courtly Phrases,
> And all the Elegance that passes;
> Disputes maintain'd without Digression,
> With ready Wit, and fine Expression;
> The Laws of true Politeness stated,
> And what Good-breeding is, debated   (ll. 46–57)

While they dine, the servant becomes invisible to them. After waiting on them, Dodsley must wait *for* them, his time still at their disposal. He knowingly 'plays dumb', standing ready to perform his duties. Unlike Clare several generations later, Dodsley's access to elite culture is a trespass in plain sight: he listens and learns from the refined language. Unobserved, he educates himself, in one of the few moments when his duties permit sustained proximity to his superiors. In ways more remarkable than described in the poem, Dodsley exploited the vogue for natural geniuses, leveraging his household's literary connections to become the most important publisher of poetry in the mid eighteenth century. His success allowed him to 'write himself out' of any association with Duck, eventually becoming a patron to other labouring-class poets. The ability to 'stand on my own bottom as a poet without any apology' (*Critical Heritage*, p. 218), as Clare wrote to Eliza Emmerson in 1832, would remain the goal of many subsequent writers.

Until he published, Dodsley concealed his poetic proclivities from his employers and fellow servants. Servants who made their aspirations known, particularly female servants, subjected themselves to harsh judgements. In her brief career, Mary Leapor (1722–46) produced poems parodying polite and plebeian responses to her literary pursuits. Addressing her middle-class patron, Bridget Freemantle, in 'An Epistle to Artemesia. On Fame', she mocks those who would police her time and require 'Mira' (Leapor's neoclassical pseudonym) to use her time in manual rather than creative labour:

> *Parthenia* cries, "Why, *Mira,* you are dull,
> 'And ever musing, till you crack your Skull;

> 'Still poking o'er your What-d'ye-call – your Muse:
> 'But pr'ythee, *Mira*, when dost clean thy Shoes?"
>   Then comes *Sophronia*, like a barb'rous *Turk*:
> 'You thoughtless Baggage, when d'ye mind your Work?
>   . . .
> 'Go, ply your Needle: You might earn your Bread;
> 'Or who must feed you when your Father's dead?'
>
>   (ll. 149–54; ll. 156–8)

Not only do elite women monitor Leapor's use of her time, but also, just as with Clare's 'genius', those of her own class condemn her pursuits. Leapor humorously mimics her neighbour in 'The Epistle of Deborah Dough'. Deborah gossips about:

> Our neighbour Mary – who, they say,
> Sits scribble-scribble all the Day,
>   . . .
> She throws away her precious time
> In scrawling nothing else but Rhyme   (ll. 11–12; ll. 17–18)

Mary's activities are negatively compared to those of Deborah's daughter who cooks and knits. Underscoring her practical time consciousness, Deborah concludes,

>   'Tis One o'Clock, as I'm a Sinner,
> The Boys are all come home to Dinner,
> And I must bid you now farewell   (ll. 63–5)

Even as she criticizes her neighbour, Deborah frets about devoting her time to letter writing. 'As I'm a sinner', while a turn of phrase, signals how time anxiety informs the moral framework for judging women and the lower classes.

Leapor's use of the trope of dream visions also stresses time consciousness.[10] Labouring-class poets were often depicted as writing solely in the 'hours stolen from sleep'. Writing and sleeping are reprieves from work, which, while not precisely leisure, are also subject to moral accounting. In 'Epistle to a Lady', Leapor describes clock time directly impacting her creativity. Although she 'dreams, as slumbring Poets may, / And rolls in Treasures till the breaking Day: / While Books and Pictures in bright Order rise' (ll. 21–3), all is interrupted when 'the shrill Clock impertinently rings' (l. 25) and forces her 'to Business and to Woes, / To sweep her Kitchen, and to mend her Clothes' (ll. 31–2). Unlike Mary Collier, who wrote 'Our Toil and Labour's daily so extreme, / That we have hardly ever Time to dream' ('The Woman's Labour', ll. 133–4), Leapor has at least a brief respite. A clock also appears in Leapor's celebrated satirical country-house poem, 'Crumble Hall', found in the deserted 'brown Parlour' that is 'For nothing famous, but its leathern Chairs' (l. 60; l. 61). Here, 'the dull Clock beats audible and slow' (l. 63), announcing its banality as another empty status symbol. Locating the clock in a rarely used space, with no impact on the lives of the gentry, Leapor suggests that their ability to ignore time is a luxury. While Leapor can only dream of reading, the master ignores the books in his library, dozing rather than studying there, never disturbed by a clock. Leapor thus derides class and gender double standards: the master wastes time that could be spent in literary pursuits, while the clock prevents her from sleeping and reading. Clare's recollections of his relationship to his early patron Lord Milton or of being a gardener at Burghley House reveal similar judgements about how precious resources are wasted on the privileged. Clare was far more cautious of publicly criticizing patrons in his verse, but his letters and autobiographical prose express more candid perspectives regarding the literary tastes of the wealthy and the books they recommended to him.

Like Clare, James Woodhouse (1735–1820) was first solicitous but later highly censorious of his polite supporters. Woodhouse's relationship to time is in many ways exemplary of a wide range of late eighteenth-century and Romantic labouring-class poets. The 'Advertisement' to Woodhouse's first volume, *Poems on Several Occasions* (1764), links his creative activities to his manual labour as a shoemaker, underscoring his virtuous dedication to both:

> He generally sits at his work with a pen and ink by him, and when he has made a couplet he writes them down on his knee; so that he may not, thereby, neglect the duties of a good husband and kind father; for the same reason his hours for reading are often borrowed from those usually allotted to sleep.[11]

An independent craftsman, Woodhouse could pause to compose; however, even if he is not answering directly to a master for his trade, the advertisement implicitly places refined readers in the position of 'masters' to Woodhouse's poetic work. *They* expect an account of his time and reassurances that his literary aspirations do not endanger the welfare of his family. Notably, among Woodhouse's earliest supporters, listed first among the names at the conclusion of the Advertisement, is Robert Dodsley.

Woodhouse's talents attracted the attention of bluestocking Elizabeth Montagu, who hired him to serve for nearly two decades as her house steward. The relationship ended poorly. Woodhouse's posthumous verse autobiography, *The Life and Lucubrations of Crispinus Scriblerus* (1896), stands as an inventory of grievances against his erstwhile patron. Woodhouse's conversion to Methodism adds religious dimensions to commentary about the value of his time and what was owed to his mistress and to

God. He embodies the denomination's obsession with time accountability (Wesley himself touted his habit of early rising at 4 a.m.). In an early letter to Montagu, Woodhouse describes his daily schedule, organized predominantly by clock time. The passage is worth quoting in full, as it elaborates upon the picture painted by the Advertisement, documenting his additional role as a schoolteacher:

> I generally rise, in the Summer about Five: in the three seasons, with the sun – I immediately apply myself to my Labour, of Shoemaking; &, as has always been my Custom, to Study; if I have any Suit to Muses I always address them in that Manner: in my leathern doublet, with my Tool in my Hand; & always receive them like a King sitting on my four-legg'd throne; for I never made many Verses in my Life, but in that Manner – Thus I employ myself till the Business of my School calls me aside, which is commonly about Nine o'clock, & continues till Twelve – I then ply again to my Occupation, and generally eat my Dinner sitting on my stall – but One o'clock or soon after School begins again, lasts till Four – Then to my Trade; &, if Occasion requires, to the Muses, till Seven, or Eight; tho' in former years till Dark; or in the Winter till about Eleven o'Clock – I then read till about nine, and when I am in Bed, let the Hour be what it will, if I am in Health; which, (I heartily return thanks to the dispenser [?] herself & of every good thing) is generally my happy lot; I always read till I can understand no longer, for the Influence of Stupid Morpheus; whose power I am sometimes so great an Enemy to; that, was I not convinced human nature was created, and is directed by a Being infinitely powerful & wise; I could wish my Powers had so been fram'd, as to make sleep absolutely needless; because it reduces Man to a Level with the brute Creation: for we perceive that in sleep, the Brutes have their Dreams & Vagaries as well as we[12]

The letter is a tour-de-force performance of the poet's virtuous industry and meticulous time management. Woodhouse multitasks, pursuing manual and intellectual labour simultaneously. His reading and study are, as expected, 'stolen from hours of sleep', and he resents sleep for preventing him from working more. Woodhouse's religious commitments and his understanding that his literary ambitions could be misinterpreted, inform his exacting stewardship of the hours allotted him.

Given such exceptional time conscientiousness, it is not surprising that Woodhouse would have possessed a timepiece. Demonstrating what might be seen as an even more extreme level of time anxiety, early in his employment for Montagu he feels obliged to justify to her why he owns a watch, worrying that such ostentatiousness would expose her to criticism:

> I bought the watch, foolishly enough perhaps, when I was last in London, at second-hand, for my own Use, as I had no Watch, & One in my Case is necessary, tho' it was not necessary to have such an One, but I thought it cheap.[13]

Woodhouse's friend gave him an ornamental watch chain, which he later removed, as it further drew attention to the timepiece. By the late eighteenth century, someone of Woodhouse's rank was more likely to own a clock or watch.[14] However, the letter's tone indicates his apprehensions. Attempting to make the watch appear modest and linking time to his moral self-monitoring, he reassures Montagu that the object is no indication of pretentions to appear above his station.

Although Woodhouse was initially solicitous of Montagu's approbation, his autobiographical poem reveals his eventual rejection of such deference, scathingly condemning Montagu's conduct and intellect. More acerbically than Leapor, he excoriates Montagu and others of her class for their profligacy. In chapter 6, he employs the moral symbolism of the sandglass:

> Will Pleasure's Daughters, Dissipation's Wives,
> As nicely scrutinize their careless lives?
> Will Folly's fashionable Sires, and Sons,
> Engage their talents while Time's hour-glass runs?
> Turn the same end of telescopic glass
> And watch their faults, and foibles, while they pass?
> Inspect their Souls with microscopic sight,
> And read what Act was rash? what Habit right?   (ll. 201–08)

While written in thousands of lines of neoclassical couplets, his poem evokes the earliest modern form of labouring-class writing, namely, spiritual self-reckonings. Primarily produced by dissenters, these narratives shaped early novels such as *Robinson Crusoe*. Centred on individual conversions, they focus on sinners' (mis)use of their time. Often because of a fear of death (here and elsewhere symbolized by an hourglass), justifying the use of one's mortal time is an organizing theme.

We do not have evidence that Clare knew Woodhouse's work, but he did own a copy of another exemplary eighteenth-century labouring-class writer about time, sailor-turned-poet William Falconer (1732–70). Falconer's best-selling work, *The Shipwreck* (1762), remained immensely popular into the mid nineteenth century. Falconer combines epic and georgic elements to represent an occupation where time was strictly regulated. For sailors, sandglasses structured the watch system that organized their daily routines. Prior to the invention of a reliable marine chronometer in 1761, moreover, hourglasses were also used for navigation, to determine a ship's speed and location. Describing the destructive power of the storm at sea in Canto ii, the damage to these devices signals the sailors' doom, underscoring the futility of human efforts to control nature. The hull breaks and 'compasses and glasses strew'd the deck' (ii.244), their navigational purposes dramatically ended.

Like the hourglass, the shipwreck was a potent metaphor. Indeed, Clare's well-known poem 'I Am' mourns 'the vast shipwreck of my life's esteems' (LP 11 396–7, l. 10). Falconer's poem, however, may have appealed to Clare because of its depiction of the sailor's ability to read the signs of nature, which in Falconer's case could be a matter of life and death.

Among other labouring-class poets in Clare's library was his near contemporary, Bloomfield, with whom he corresponded. Like Woodhouse, Bloomfield rose to fame while a shoemaker. However, his first publication, *The Farmer's Boy* (1800), describes his time as a servant in husbandry on his uncle's farm. Foregrounding the seasonal cycle of tasks given to Bloomfield's alter ego, Giles, the poem depicts the joys and hardships of his assignments, supporting the farm and tending livestock. Giles's work is a source of pleasure and suffering: in the vivid description in 'Spring', his initial delight in the frolicking spring lambs is shattered when they are violently slaughtered. Driven by the needs of the animals he tends as much as his Master, Giles works irregular hours, especially when bad weather threatens. Lest he complain about lack of control of his time, his master cautions that the boy's burdens are slight compared to 'The Sea-boy, less fortunate than thou' ('Winter', l. 115):

> His labours cease not with declining day,
> But toils and perils mark his wat'ry way;
> And whilst in peaceful dreams secure *we* lie,
> The ruthless whirlwinds rage along the sky,
> Round his head whistling ('Winter', ll. 121–5)

Due to relentless bad weather, the young sailor's work is without respite, a theme that Clare addresses in several of his poems. 'The Sailor Boy' (LP 11 1001) describes a rural lad like Giles who leaves his home, his 'honest parents the church clock & the village' to 'plough the briny ocean'.

Like Clare, Bloomfield did not always see time consciousness as negative. 'The Widow to her Hour-Glass' from *Rural Tales* (1802) also portrays the device as a solace, not a threat. Naming it her 'friend', the speaker apostrophizes it as 'Companion of the lonely hour!' (l. 2). The hourglass accompanies her throughout her married life and during the birth of her children. More than just a marker of significant events, it prompts philosophical reflection:

> I've often watch'd thy streaming sand
> And seen the growing Mountain rise,
> And often found Life's hopes to stand
> On props as weak in Wisdom's eyes:
> > Its conic crown
> > Still sliding down

> Again heap'd up, then down again;
> The sand above more hollow grew,
> Like days and years still filt'ring through,
> And mingling joy and pain.   (ll. 11–20)

The widow's observations juxtapose the tedium of her life's routines with the transience of great and small events. Although a rustic object owned by a humble widow, the hourglass is an apt vehicle for larger moral concepts. Bloomfield, like Clare, revises its iconography (and may have influenced Clare's sonnet). Since the early Renaissance, hourglasses had often been included in paintings of intellectuals and in didactic 'vanitas' imagery imparting lessons about the ephemeral nature of human concerns;[15] however, Bloomfield's hourglass is a consolation rather than a warning.

The hourglass regulates the widow's workday, reminding her to pause her spinning at noon. Notably, the timepiece is silent. Conventional histories describe early modern rural time as primarily aural, marked most often by church bells, like those on Clare's landmark Glinton Spire. In 'Sabbath Bells' (EP II 499), Clare describes his reposing 'among the new mown hay / To listen distant bells / That beautifully flung the sound' (ll. 3–5), here associating the sound with leisure not labour. Although the visual cues of the sandglass guide the widow's tasks, the rural agricultural calendar still holds sway as she remarks: 'But when I glean the sultry fields, / When Earth her yellow Harvest yields, / Thou get'st a Holiday' (ll. 28–30). Daily timekeeping is supplemented by seasonal duties, and the personal timekeeping of the hourglass is replaced by communal ringing of the church bells that, prior to 1788, would have indicated to the widow that gleaners like herself were free to go to the fields to gather the remains from the harvest. Although her existence may be economically precarious, the accuracy of the hourglass provides encouragement. 'Steady as Truth' (l. 31) and 'Meditation's constant friend' (l. 33), it 'strik'st the Heart without a Bell' (l. 34), bringing comfort and inspiring contemplation. Bloomfield's hourglass is no 'memento mori', but a reassurance of continuity and predictability. Much like the speaker in Clare's early sonnet, the object brings pleasure rather than time anxiety.

For poets who were Clare's nearer contemporaries and successors in the labouring-class tradition, a world where natural and clock time peacefully coexisted was harder and harder to evoke, and the boundaries between work and leisure became starker. While Victorian-era labouring poets still write movingly of rural life and nature, the impact of industrialization and the role of organized labour movements become more prominent in their work. Clare's work stands as a point of transition. Increased opportunities for publication, particularly in the regional, trade-based, political periodicals (such as *The Northern Star*), exposed more workers to the powers of poetry and provided easier venues for publication. Scholars such as Kirstie Blair have begun to survey the rich archive of more ephemeral labouring-class poetic publications beyond the volumes that have been the focus of efforts to recover the labouring-class tradition. The poetry of the Chartist movement as well as the writings of women workers and 'factory girls' often explicitly address time in poems written in support of the initiatives for legislating working-day hours, especially the hours for children. An 1839 poem by 'E.H., A Factory Girl of Stalybridge', which appeared in the Chartist's periodical, *The Northern Star*, is a poignant example. Entitled 'On Joseph Rayner Stephens', it explores the impact of the Methodist preacher, who expounds 'the Gospel, and the Ten Hours Bill'. E. H. ironically reveals how those for and against labour reform marshal scripture to support their cause. Mentioning that she was not able to attend school because she was sent to work at the age of eight, she wryly notes that 'If they had sent us to school, better rhyme could we make / And I think it is time we had some of that cake'. With a potentially revolutionary allusion to Marie Antoinette's infamous declaration, the poet identifies herself as a 'Stephenite' and concludes with an apology for her uncouth style: 'We factory lasses have but little time / So I hope you will pardon my bad written rhyme'. While the working conditions they document may have changed, the lack of time for creative endeavours remains constant from Duck and Collier into the late nineteenth century. Fanny Forester's 1873 poem 'To The Lowly Bard' describes an author who

> tunes his lyre where busy wheels are grinding,
> And flying straps are never, never still
> Where rigid toil the buoyant limbs is binding
> That fail would wander from the dusty mill.   (ll. 9–12)

Unable to fulfil his true calling because he must 'Toil, toil to-day, and toil again tomorrow' (l. 25), he perishes while still asserting 'I've much to do, and precious time is fleeting' (l. 69). Mourning the loss of artistic potential caused by limited time, as Clare does in poems such as 'The Fate of Genius', is a theme uniting two centuries of authors.

Clare's poetry stands as a fulcrum, his work repeatedly voicing the labouring-class poet's struggles with time for and in poetry. In a moving sonnet from the Northborough period, Clare describes the anxiety of a shepherd boy, caught between different temporal registers. A traditional rural occupation, shepherding's rhythms typically follow the course of the sun, conventionally offering moments of pastoral leisure. Presumably, the boy has yet to master the ability to read time from natural signs – perhaps signifying knowledge lost due to the modern 'improvements' that brought enclosure.

Clare and the British Labouring-Class Tradition

Both the boy and the adults who regularly pass by rely primarily on abstract clock time:

> He waits all day beside his little flock
> & asks the passing stranger whats o clock
> But those who often pass his daily task
> Look at their watch & tell him before he asks
> He mutters stories to himself & lies
> Where the thick hedge the warmest house supplys
> & when he hears the hunters far & wide
> He climbs the highest tree to see them ride
> He climbs till all the fields are blea & bare
> & makes the old crows nest an easy chair
> & soon his sheep are got in other grounds
> He hastens down & fears his master come
> & stops the gap & keeps them all in bounds
> & tents them closely till its time for home (MP v 272–3)

A figure of a nascent poet, like the fated genius, the boy 'mutters stories to himself'. He is pulled between tending his flock and seeking comfort or amusement. His inability to tell clock time evokes his loneliness, abandonment, and alienation. Losing track of time, he also loses track of his herd, his primary occupation. He is called back from his musings to the work at hand by his internalized fear of his master's gaze. For poets from Duck to Clare to the Chartists and beyond, the master's imagined presence instils an apprehensive awareness of work-time discipline. Clare's shepherd boy, like Clare himself, navigates contrasting temporal demands: from the seasonal agricultural demands driven by 'natural' time to the abstract impositions of timepieces that set the servant's schedule to factory clocks depicted by Victorian labouring-class poets. Clare's work remains pivotal for understanding how plebeian poets shaped their artistic identities within and against evolving temporal constraints over which they had little influence.

Notes

1. John Goodridge and Kelsey Thornton, 'John Clare: The Trespasser', in *John Clare in Context*, ed. Hugh Haughton, Adam Phillips, and Geoffrey Summerfield (Cambridge: Cambridge University Press, 1994), pp. 87–129.
2. E. P. Thompson, 'Time, Work-Discipline, and Industrial Capitalism', *Past & Present*, 38 (1967), 56–97 (p. 61).
3. William J. Christmas, *The Laboring Muses: Work, Writing, and the Social Order in English Plebeian Poetry, 1730–1830* (Newark: University of Delaware Press, 2001), p. 268.
4. Christmas, *Laboring Muses*, p. 295.

5. See Marcus Tomalin, '"An Invaluable Acquisition": Sandglasses in Romantic Literature', *European Romantic Review* 28.6 (2017), 729–49.
6. Gerhard Dohrn-van Rossum, *History of the Hour: Clocks and Modern Temporal Orders*, trans. Thomas Dunlap (Chicago: University of Chicago Press, 1998), p. 271.
7. See Tomalin, 'Invaluable Acquisition', p. 732.
8. See Bridget Keegan, 'Cobbling Verse: Shoemaker Poets of the Long Eighteenth Century', *The Eighteenth-Century: Theory and Interpretation* 42.3 (2001), 195–217.
9. 'The Letters of Robert Bloomfield and His Circle', ed. Tim Fulford and Lynda Pratt, *Romantic Circles* https://romantic-circles.org/editions.
10. See Donna Landry, *The Muses of Resistance: Laboring-Class Women's Poetry in Britain, 1739-1796* (Cambridge: Cambridge University Press, 1990), p. 106.
11. *Poems on Several Occasions* (London: printed for the author, 1764), p. xiv.
12. James Woodhouse to Elizabeth Montagu [Rowley], September 1764. This is a transcript taken from National Library of Wales MS 5433C. The author is grateful to Dr Adam Bridgen for generously sharing his transcription of this material.
13. James Woodhouse to Elizabeth Montagu, 4 May [1769–71]. This is a transcript taken from National Library of Wales MS 5433C. The author is grateful to Dr Adam Bridgen for generously sharing his transcription of this material.
14. See Thompson, 'Time', p. 66.
15. See Dohrn-van Rossum, *History of the Hour*, pp. 270–1.

14

TIM FULFORD

The Politics of Nature

There was no nature in John Clare's England, if by 'nature' we mean a pristine, untouched wilderness. The rural world that Clare inhabited, a world of fields, heaths, fens, and woods, was the product of centuries of human cultivation and management, a worked landscape in which almost everything that grew and lived had a use for humans. It was a world in which he and those around him – people, animals, plants – were deeply rooted where and as previous generations had been. It was a timebound place that was measured in one's own lifespan and in the lifespans of one's peers and ancestors, human and nonhuman. A way of life – a habitat and habitus – now rapidly changing as a result of increasingly capitalist intensive agriculture.

If 'nature' does not exist as an entity separate from human activity in Clare's writing, that writing is nevertheless an effort to saturate language with his habitat, as it was experienced from within in all its variety. Likewise politics: these hardly feature in Clare's work if we mean by 'politics' formal discourse about government. Unlike his contemporaries Thomas Spence and William Cobbett, who campaigned for major changes to the ownership of land, to the agricultural economy, and to the exploitation of rural labourers, Clare published no public proposals for wholesale reform of the political system that benefited a few at the expense of people like himself. He was not a speechmaker at public meetings; he did not run a radical newspaper; he did not organize a democratic club or a land-sharing association. He did, however, sometimes publish in the local press letters objecting to policies that heavily affected the rural poor (the malt tax, the corn laws, the tithes) and verses satirizing the people who benefited from these policies. Yet it is not in these occasional protests but in the great body of his poetry that his originality as a political writer is to be found. In Clare's poems, place, people, nature, and selfhood are all revealed to be political because the very language on which knowledge depends is conditioned by what is said, and what is done on the ground as a result of what is said, by people of power. Clare, that is, counts the cost for his habitat and habitus of the capitalist ideologies that, from the early nineteenth century onwards, increasingly exploited nature – the rural community of people, plants, animals, water, earth, and air. He registers, with terrible pathos and stirring anger, how it is to be 'enslaved', as he put in in a deliberate allusion to what capitalism was doing in Africa and the Caribbean. He writes out the experience of having one's rights expropriated, one's land degraded, one's community impoverished – its customs waning, its dialect decaying, its local knowledge lost. Uprooted from the selves they had grown into over lifetimes, both people and places (principally Clare himself as witness but also the landscapes that he brings to voice) undergo alienation, destruction, and grief. Thus Clare is not, as sometimes he is claimed to be, a poet of place and of nature; he is a poet of dislocation and denaturing. Now, in the twenty-first century, as the global effects of the myriad local exploitations of the earth become ever more apparent in habitat destruction, climate change, and the creeping genocide of Indigenous peoples, Clare is more than ever relevant. His work is not a pastoral retreat from the political but a prophetic warning about the most urgent political issues of all.

Clare's identity as a person and poet was forged in the village of Helpston, but between 1809 and 1820 enclosure (the process that divided the large open fields traditionally worked by villagers in common) and engrossment (the taking of common grazing heaths into cultivation) degraded his environment. These changes, which were driven, in the name of efficiency and increased profit, by the large landowners and the farmers who paid rent to those landowners, had the effect of denuding the landscape and of imposing property lines where none had been marked. Lanes, trees, ponds, bushes, heaths, and commons were all eradicated and a new rectilinear geography imposed. The consequences were the removal of a habitat – a place embodying a way of working and living – that left villagers barred from their traditional walks, pastures, and playgrounds. Enclosure and engrossment were accompanied by a rigging of the agricultural market at rural labourers' expense. Grain prices went up during the Napoleonic Wars (1803–15), meaning that every scrap of land was planted for wheat and barley, depriving villagers of places to graze their cattle and sheep and thus leaving them wholly dependent on wage labour. But wages were steadily reduced – especially in the post-1815 depression, while taxes and tithes remained high. So did the grain price, which was propped up by the Corn Laws, passed in parliament by the oligarchy of landowners for their own benefit. The result for labourers was work at starvation rates: they reaped the corn and threshed the grain but could not afford bread. Food 'riots' swept the area around Helpston in 1830 and 1831 as desperate labourers sabotaged threshing machines and burned hayricks to encourage farmers to employ them at a living wage. Clare deplored the violence but expressed his sympathy with the grievance.

In his poems, Clare weighed the effects of these changes on his emplaced self – and on the enselved place. In many instances, there comes to be no clear separation between the poet and the place that he writes into verse. In 'The Mores' (early–mid 1820s), his great hymn to what it was to live in the land- and skyscape of vast, unenclosed fields, Clare attacks the enclosure and enclosers directly:

> These paths are stopt – the rude philistines thrall
> Is laid upon them & destroyed them all
> Each little tyrant with his little sign
> Shows where man claims earths glows no more divine
> On paths to freedom & to childhood dear
> A board sticks up to notice 'no road here'
> (MP II 347–50, ll. 65–70)

In context, it is apparent that Clare's protest in these lines is not only angrily expressed but also politically coded. To indict the enclosers as tyrants and to claim that 'freedom' is destroyed is, in terms of nineteenth-century political ideology, to say that the landowners have betrayed the paternalist duty to protect liberty and represent the powerless that they claimed to exercise on behalf of English people in general. Since the 1688 'Glorious Revolution', which supposedly saved Britain from tyrannical monarchy, they had claimed that this duty was a justification of their monopoly of power. Now, however, they were no longer 'friends of the people' protecting those who worked on their vast estates – the rural poor who were unable to vote. They had enclosed as their exclusive domain not just fields but also the liberty that was supposedly the Englishman's birthright. Here, Clare implies a political critique that had been made explicitly by his poetical hero William Cowper in *The Task* (1785) as well as by Burke, Wordsworth, and Southey, who all attacked the corruption of the governing classes by commercial capitalism.

Clare's protest is loud, but his targets are unidentified. Who the tyrants are and who sticks up the 'no trespassing' sign is implied but not announced. For a man of his class, identifying the perpetrators was dangerous. William Cobbett was charged with sedition in 1831 when his speeches and writings encouraged rural labourers to see their poverty as the result of farmers' and landowners' greed. When Clare had ventured to publish even a mild critique of profiteering enclosers in 1821, his self-appointed patron, the newly made aristocrat Lord Radstock, had called it 'radical slang' and demanded its removal.[1] Most of Clare's most vehement protests were then left unpublished. He concentrated instead on demonstrating enclosure's effects on place and person. In these lines from 'The Mores', to be forbidden access to one's native place is to lose access to 'childhood dear' – to find one's identity cut off from its roots. It is to be marooned in a detached present. Clare's tracing of the alienation that results from this loss – spatial restriction felt as temporal excision – is what makes his poetical voice unique. He transforms the Wordsworthian lament for lost innocence into a cry in which the political is heard as the personal: the enclosure of Helpston becomes an enclosure of the self.

Time and again, Clare mourns his lost childhood; it seems all the more golden – a period of total presence in the moment – as he confronts his new, adult severance from the places he worked, played and dreamed in as a boy. In 'Remembrances' (c. 1832), enclosure stands for the irreparable depredation of time on the self, cutting off the childhood spacetime in which the self was present to itself and leaving the adult regretful, fretful, and exiled:

> O I never thought that joys would run away from boys
> Or that boys would change their minds & forsake such summer joys
> But alack I never dreamed that the world had other toys
> To petrify first feelings like the fable into stone
> Till I found the pleasure past & a winter come at last
> Then the fields were sudden bare & the sky got over cast
> & boyhoods pleasing haunts like a blossom in the blast
> Was shrivelled to a withered weed & trampled down & done
> Till vanished was the morning spring & set that summer sun
> & winter fought her battle strife & won
>
> By Langley bush I roam but the bush hath left its hill
> On cowper green I stray tis a desert strange & chill
> & spreading lea close oak ere decay had penned its will
> To the axe of the spoiler & self interest fell a prey
> And cross berry way & old round oaks narrow lane
> With its hollow trees like pulpits I shall never see again
> Inclosure like a Buonaparte let not a thing remain
> It levelled every bush & tree & levelled every hill
> & hung the moles for traitors – though the brook is running still
> It runs a naker brook cold & chill.   (MP IV 130–4, ll. 51–70)

It is not just that the present self is barred from entering the old self / old places; in many cases, the old places are destroyed, leaving Clare to revive them in poetry, knowing that they no longer live on the ground. He names the lost places as if making a roll-call of the dead (the unusually long fourteen-foot lines and couplet rhymes make the names resound, as if the poem were a mnemonic). Here, enclosure is shown to destroy a whole tradition and an entire habitat – human, animal, botanical – as well as severing identity spatially, effectively unplacing Clare. As the analogy with Napoleon ('Enclosure like a Buonaparte') suggests, it is a petty despotism where everyone not thought to be contributing to the new order of profitable productivity is a traitor – even creatures as insignificant as moles. An absolutism of this kind, the comparison hints, is profoundly unEnglish. Most Britons agreed that Britain had been at war with Napoleonic tyranny to defend political liberty at home and across Europe. Thus, the erasing of Clare's birthplace is shown to have larger political implications than the local.

Once severance has occurred, Clare finds his identity deracinated. As he explains in 'Childhood' ('The past it is a majic word'), in this situation it is impossible to sustain oneself by dwelling on the spots that have escaped enclosure. The self, radically disturbed, no longer has the bearings needed to find its way back to its former, rooted, nature.

> Ponds where we played at 'Duck & Drake'
> Where the ash with ivy grew
> Where we robbed the owl of all her eggs
> & mocked her as she flew
> The broad tree in the spinney hedge
> Neath which the gipseys lay
> Where we our fine oak apples got
> On the twenty ninth of may
>
> There all remain as then they were
> & are not changed a day
> & the ivys crown's as near to green
> As mine is to the grey
> It shades the pond oerhangs the stile
> & the oak is in the glen
> But the paths to joy are so worn out
> I cant find one agen
>   (MP III 228–52, ll. 353–68; written 1831)

The worn-out paths are real before they are metaphorical; in poem after poem, Clare simultaneously relives childhood adventures in local places while lamenting that they revive only as ghosts of themselves, revenants of the lost and inaccessible. He sometimes gives these laments a bitterly ironic, self-cancelling turn when he speaks in the voice of an erased place, so that a spot comes into being verbally only to grieve its disappearance from the landscape. It's a rhetorically powerful but logically impossible move – poetry restoring something lost as lost. So, in 'The Lamentations of Round-Oak

Waters' (written 1818, pub. 1935), the speaker is a spring that had been denuded of the oak trees and bushes that once surrounded it:

> 'But sweating slaves I do not blame
> 'Those slaves by wealth decreed
> 'No I should hurt their harmless name
> 'To brand 'em wi' the deed
> 'Altho their aching hands did wield
> 'The axe that gave the blow
> 'Yet 't'was not them that own'd the field
> 'Nor plan'd its overthrow'
>
> 'No no the foes that hurt my field
> 'Hurts these poor moilers too
> 'And thy own bosom knows & feels
> 'Enough to prove it true
> 'And o poor souls they may complain
> 'But their complainings all
> 'The injur'd worms that turn again
> 'But turn again to fall'
>
> 'Their foes and mine are lawless foes
> 'And L–ws thems—s they hold
> 'Which clip-wing'd Justice cant oppose
> 'But forced yields to G–d
> 'These are the f—s of mine & me
> These all our Ru–n plan'd
> 'Alltho they never felld a tree
> 'Or took a tool in hand'
>
> 'Ah cruel foes with plenty blest
> 'So ankering after more
> 'To lay the greens & pastures waste
> 'Which profitted before
> 'Poor greedy souls – what would they have
> 'Beyond their plenty given?
> 'Will riches keep 'em from the grave?
> 'Or buy them rest in heaven?'   (EP 1 228–34, ll. 165–96)

Here, the water voices its solidarity with the 'slaves' – the poor workers – whose toil destroyed it. In a proto-Marxist recognition, Clare shows that ecological degradation and human exploitation go hand in hand, that profit, abstracted from labour, turns both place and people into commodities to be translated into money-value (what he calls 'riches'). In this process, the capitalists in charge do not themselves labour; nor are they on the spot.

The Politics of Nature

Their 'work' is to manipulate the law in their favour – by, for example, passing Enclosure Acts – so that justice is a class-controlled game. The lamenting spring expects no earthly remedy for what it shows as a biased system, hence its rhetorical question as to whether the capitalists will, after death, find a place in heaven. But this suggestion that they may pay for their greed in the next world is no more than a gesture: the poem is not a thoroughgoing Christian warning in the manner of the Calvinist Methodists of the hellfire and damnation awaiting sinners (Clare remained suspicious of such preachers, suspecting them of self-aggrandizement and hypocrisy). Instead, the spring speaks in ballad form, its voice thereby affiliated to the songs and stories that villagers played and sang – a tradition by which they entertained each other and set out shared beliefs and communal values (Clare, a fiddler in his youth, could perform scores of ballads and reckoned his father knew above a hundred).

Renewing the ballad tradition of village communities was to affirm its moral and critical vitality just as it was being threatened by the same forces that degraded villagers to wage slaves. Losing touch with one's place, as it was transformed under enclosure, meant losing touch with its traditions. Clare grieves for this process, while fighting against it, in another poem in which the earth itself speaks – 'The Lament of Swordy Well' (mid 1830s). The bitterness of this poem's attack on the supposed social superiors who control rural England reflects Clare's increasing alienation and disturbance. Swordy Well was a local wetland hollow that had never formerly been exploited, was a habitat for wildflowers, and was one of the few pieces of unowned land where villagers could graze a donkey or gypsies set up camp. But Clare makes it complain that it is now gutted by greedy landlords who quarry its stones, fell its trees, and plant it for grain. There is now no 'nature'; there are only resources to be taken for short-term gain.

> When war their tyrant prices got
> I trembled with alarms
> They fell & saved my little spot
> Or towns had turned to farms
> Let profit keep an humble place
> That gentry may be known
> Let pedigrees their honours trace
> & toil enjoy its own
>
> The silver springs grown naked dykes
> Scarce own a bunch of rushes
> When grain got high the tasteless tykes
> Grubbed up trees banks & bushes

> & me they turned me inside out
> For sand & grit & stones
> & turned my old green hills about
> & pickt my very bones
> . . .
>
> There was a time my bit of ground
> Made freemen of the slave
> The ass no pindard dare to pound
> When I his supper gave
> The gipseys camp was not affraid
> I made his dwelling free
> Till vile enclosure came & made
> A parish slave of me   (MP v 105–15, ll. 49–64; 225–32)

The transfer of voice from person to place shows with startling irony that the rural place is like the rural poor: like them, it is required in the new commercial regime to demonstrate its profitability or lose the right to independence. Swordy Well is, in the then-used colloquial phrase for people supported by social security, 'on the parish'. In this local system of poor relief, those unable to earn a living – typically the infirm, aged, or unemployed, but also increasingly workers whose wages were below subsistence level – were given money and goods in return for work on public projects. Clare's crippled father, for instance, received a dole and worked mending the roads. But being on the parish is now a cheat. Not only does it require one to justify one's existence, but it also leaves one enslaved, in poverty, to the will of the farmers and landowners who pay for, but ultimately profit from, the system that depends upon land and labour being at their command as inexpensively as possible. The place and person on the parish is not so much helped, or just allowed to be, as reduced to the cheapest and most easily exploitable resource to enrich those who do not themselves work.

> In parish bonds I well may wail
> Reduced to every shift
> Pity may grieve at troubles tale
> But cunning shares the gift
> Harvests with plenty on his brow
> Leaves losses taunts with me
> Yet gain comes yearly with the plough
> & will not let me be
>
> Alas dependance thou'rt a brute
> Want only understands
> His feelings wither branch & root

The Politics of Nature

> That falls in parish hands
> The muck that clouts the ploughmans shoe
> The moss that hides the stone
> Now Im become the parish due
> Is more then I can own   (ll. 25–40)

By giving this speech to a place rather than a person – and an eradicated place at that – Clare ensures it does not appear like the grasping self-pity of a beggar's hard-luck tale. He objectifies the voice so that it possesses unbiased authority that cannot be ignored as the self-interested whingeing of a single individual. We have to listen – so startled are we to hear a place speak – and we are admonished because it speaks a truth we would rather not hear, a truth that prevents us coping with changes by compartmentalizing or marginalizing their bad effects. Clare's brilliance, here, is to find a form that cuts through, bringing home to readers a realization that what was going on in their country was neither accidental nor temporary but a wholesale exploitation of land and impoverishment of villagers that was part of one new system.

But there were no readers – at least till a century or so after the poem was written. 'The Lament of Swordy Well', like most of Clare's most challenging work, remained unpublished – too radical for contemporary publishers to risk. Indeed, some of its radicalism stems from the fact that it became increasingly hard for Clare to get books published. He had been marketed as a 'peasant poet' in the wake of the phenomenal success on the newly expanded book market of the 'farmer's boy' poet Robert Bloomfield, whose collections had sold over 30,000 copies by the time Clare's first book appeared. Clare's publisher, just beginning editing a magazine and running a bookselling venture, had previously worked for Bloomfield's publishers, Vernor and Hood. John Taylor thus knew at firsthand what money was to be made if an editor experienced in book production could shepherd a labouring-class poet into acceptable print. He did for Clare as others had done for Bloomfield – spruced rough manuscripts into a form that polite taste might enjoy. Pastoral scenes whose simplicity betokened the sincerity of their 'peasant' author were preferred. Laments at change were acceptable, as were mild, generalized exclamations against enclosure. Attacks on the gentry, aristocracy, and clergy as hypocritical exploiters of the poor were not. This recipe made Clare's first book a considerable commercial success, changing his life. But that success diminished with his second and third collections, and Clare, with Taylor facing bankruptcy, found it impossible to get further volumes published in London. Thus, he had painful personal experience of being manufactured for the market – his words dressed for sale, his selfhood turned into a brand – only to be dropped when the public wanted something new. If the radical voice of his later poems represents his liberation from the need to avoid offending the reading public, it also embodies his bitter experience of being, like Swordy Well, commodified until his own nature was exhausted or no longer wanted by consumers.

Both his fame and its passing affected Clare's articulation of himself in nature. Suspicion that booksellers were taking advantage of him while he was profitable was followed by resentment that they took less notice of him when he was not. His perspective that rural labourers were slaves to a commercialized agriculture from which others benefited was related to his uneasiness about his own position as commercial property in the book market. There were effects on the ground too, in the form of well-to-do visitors who came to see the peasant poet and thus took him away from his work. While some of these visitors did benefit Clare materially, others promised gifts that did not arrive, gave condescending advice, showed him off to neighbours they wanted to impress, or pried into his private life. Clare had less and less peace in his own landscape. At the same time, the success, and the fact that he was known to be writing, isolated him from his fellow villagers. He was no longer one of them; he was a semi-detached reporter of their life and labour in terms they did not share (very few were readers of poetry or could afford to buy books of verse). Meanwhile, his own perspective was changed by the trips to London and the literary friendships that a career as an author made possible; these lapsed as his income waned and as the circle of writers associated with Taylor's *London Magazine* broke up. Clare was left in Helpston feeling socially and intellectually isolated; nature in his poems increasingly configured a solitary refuge rather than a communal workplace – and as a refuge it was often available only in memories of childhood before enclosure and before his adult career alienated him from the companions he shared it with. This process was only exacerbated by a well-meant attempt to help by setting him up as a smallholder in a cottage at Northborough, a few miles from Helpston. Clare found that the move unmoored him from the emplacedness that his identity depended upon; the new place's unfamiliarity was disturbing; his tendency towards depression intensified:

> Strange scenes mere shadows are to me
> Vague unpersonifying things
> I love with my old home to be
> By quiet woods & gravel springs
> Where little pebbles wear as smooth
> As hermits beads by gentle floods

> Whose noises doth my spirits sooth
> & warms them into singing moods
>
> Here every tree is strange to me
> All foreign things were eer I go
> There's none where boyhood made a swee
> Or clambered up to rob a crow
> No hollow tree or wood land bower
> Well known when joy was beating high
> Where beauty ran to shun a shower
> & love took pains to keep her dry
>
> ('The Flitting' (1832), MP III 479–89, ll. 89–104)

The word 'swee' in this poem is more significant than it first appears. A colloquial dialect term, it marks the lost boyhood occasions as parts of a local speech community: it is the term that boys would have used when they went on a spree together, bird's-nesting (an activity Clare records in many poems). It evidences Clare's linguistic affiliation to that community and shows his determination that, as Wordsworth put it, rustic speech was the 'best part of language' for poetry in that it is directly derived from a deep, reliable relationship between ordinary folk and the place they inhabit.² Place, in these dialect terms, is not translated into polite language but expressed as the knowledge of people who live in and work on it daily. And this is political in the sense that it upsets the linguistic hierarchy that positions the speech of the educated, 'polite' classes as superior to the speech of the poor. It aligns poetry not with its genteel readership but with the poet's labourer community – here, though, only in a single word redolent of long-gone childhood games. Elsewhere, words such as 'soodle', 'prog', 'crumping', and 'moozing' are precise terms for activities or states derived from the speech of people who regularly practise those activities and experience those states.

The questions of who speaks for the labourers, who speaks for a place, and how the poet speaks come to a head in 'The Fallen Elm' (1830). One of Clare's masterpieces, this poem details the intended felling of the elms that shaded Clare's cottage. It does so by staging a verbal and pre-verbal contest. The poet addresses the tree, voicing its soundscape as he does so. He assembles in it, in effect, a choir of the disregarded: the sounds of children, birds, leaves, wind, and rain are concentred there. These voices are too small for men of power to notice but collectively constitute a community, a habitat – at least when brought together by Clare's own voice and pen. He is the listening witness, the familiar friend, and the vocal interpreter:

> Old elm that murmured in our chimney top
> The sweetest anthem autumn ever made

> & into mellow whispering calms would drop
> When showers fell on thy many coloured shade
> & when dark tempests mimic thunder made
> While darkness came as it would strangle light
> With the black tempest of a winter night
> That rocked thee like a cradle in thy root
> How did I love to hear the winds upbraid
> Thy strength without – while all within was mute
> It seasoned comfort to our hearts desire
> We felt thy kind protection like a friend
> & edged our chairs up closer to the fire
> Enjoying comforts that was never penned
> Old favourite tree thoust seen times changes lower
> Though change till now did never injure thee
> For time beheld thee as her sacred dower
> & nature claimed thee her domestic tree
> Storms came & shook thee many a weary hour
> Yet stedfast to thy home thy roots have been
> Summers of thirst parched round thy homely bower
> Till earth grew iron – still thy leaves was green
> The childern sought thee in thy summer shade
> & made their play house rings of stick & stone
> The mavis sang & felt himself alone
> While in thy leaves his early nest was made
> & I did feel his happiness mine own (MP III 440–3, ll. 1–27)

The tree marks out affiliations: Clare aligns his relationship with it with that of birds, plants, and children, the owner's with that of men who seek money and power at others' cost. Clare makes the tree a selfmark as well as a landmark. He describes himself in words normally applicable to it and it in words normally applicable to himself: 'Thou owned a language by which hearts are stirred / Deeper then by a feeling cloathed in words / & speakest now whats known of every tongue' (ll. 31–3). The poet's communication is grounded on his perception of the inarticulate language that shapes his habitat – its soundscape.

Alongside that language – now doomed because the tree will be felled for profit – the languages of property and politics are hollow and hypocritical. Clare rejects not just the capitalist language of landowners exploiting land for profit but also the democratic language of the agitators who try to stir up the villagers against the landowners. He suspects the radical speech-makers of hypocrisy rather than a sincere adherence to the cause of liberty. The poor are fodder for their self-advancement, as is the local place. But the tree stands by, an unswerving witness, sheltering all, despite human betrayal:

> Thoust heard the knave abusing those in power
> Bawl freedom loud & then opress the free
> Thoust sheltered hypocrites in many a shower
> That when in power would never shelter thee
> Thoust heard the knave supply his canting powers
> With wrongs illusions when he wanted friends
> That bawled for shelter when he lived in showers
> & when clouds vanished made thy shade amends
> With axe at root he felled thee to the ground
> & barked of freedom – O I hate the sound
> Time hears its visions speak & age sublime
> Had made thee a deciple unto time   (ll. 41–52)

'The Fallen Elm' is a narrative of imprisonment. Clare reveals in it his sense of being trapped in corrupted languages: the elm, for all its strong indifference to the 'wrongs illusions' that it hears, cannot survive their power to effect change; nor, therefore, can the heart-stirring language 'deeper than ... the atribute of words' (see note to l. 32) which the poet derives from it. And neither the cant of popular agitators nor the language of property owners with its self-serving justification of the tree felling can be trusted. Neither is adequate to the needs of the self for a verbal source of truth and honesty. Yet neither can be avoided. Clare's literary form aligns him willy-nilly with property owners (the polite classes who buy books and patronize poets); his status as a rural labourer draws him towards popular agitators ('knave abusing those in power'). And since the ancient trees he so loved were being felled, he no longer had a home ground from which he could derive himself and for which he could speak with an untainted authority of love. Clare anticipates a linguistic as well as physical destruction, a mental as well as agricultural enclosure:

> – It grows the cant term of enslaving tools
> To wrong another by the name of right
> It grows the liscence of oerbearing fools
> To cheat plain honesty by force of might
> Thus came enclosure – ruin was its guide
> But freedoms clapping hands enjoyed the sight
> Though comforts cottage soon was thrust aside
> & work house prisons raised upon the scite
> Een natures dwellings far away from men
> The common heath became the spoilers prey
> The rabbit had not where to make his den

> & labours only cow was drove away
> No matter – wrong was right & right was wrong
> & freedoms bawl was sanction to the song
> – Such was thy ruin music making elm
> The rights of freedom was to injure thine
> As thou wert served so would they overwhelm
> In freedoms name the little that is mine (ll. 53–70)

In face of the power of a perverted language in which 'wrong was right and right was wrong', Clare can protest but cannot win. His own source of verbal and moral authority may remain, but it is likely to be obscured by the overwhelming language of men of power – left to speak from a human / animal / vegetable community that no longer exists. The experienced meaning of freedom will, in the poem's last grim phrase, be devoured in 'freedom's' name. What is apparent in this sad poem is Clare's ability to find a language able to anticipate its own destruction, to prophesy its own silence. It operates according to an aesthetics of weakness – an intimation of loss, dismemberment, and oblivion.

By 1841, the fracturing of Clare's identity that this poem heralds had led to his confinement in Northampton General Lunatic Asylum. There, he continued writing poetry about nature. In one fragment, time itself, now approaching its end as universal doom nears, has been captured by the kind of 'creative accountancy' – financial cheating – that enriched capitalists while impoverishing farmhands. The earth is betrayed and used up by such crooked discourses:

> False time what is it but a rogues account
> Of books wrong kept – times keystone is the sun
> True natures wronged – & what is the amount
> But deaths diseases – that their circuit run
> Through error & through deeds that faith has done
> (LP I 208, ll. 1–5)

Here, nature's measure – the sun that holds all things together as a keystone does an arch – is subjected to the fraudulent measure of bookkeepers. Clare could no longer counter such false accounts with his own books containing poetic measures: in the madhouse, he had very limited access to publication. The earth, having been commercialized at the root, ends in disease and death without restoration of past losses, without justice.

In much of the asylum poetry, nature is no longer an inhabited, local, named place. It appears instead as a set of general images indicating a universal destruction, with Clare taking the rhetorical position not of a dweller in a particular spot but of the biblical prophet of Apocalypse.

The Politics of Nature

The contest between the languages of power – capitalist landowners, popular radicals, villagers' speech community, Clare's individual apprehension – is superseded. Nature is now political in a different sense: Clare's voice acts as a warning of a total ecological breakdown brought about by the kinds of exploitation of place and people that, we now acknowledge, are responsible for globally destructive environmental degradation and climate change. Clare's remaining poetic power, borrowing biblical imagery, is to be a prophet of the earth's – and therefore his own – doom, as in this draft, borrowing from both biblical Revelation and Byron's 'Darkness':

> There is a day a dreadfull day
> Still following the past
> When sun & moon are past away
> & mingle with the blast
> There is a vision in my eye
> A vacuum oer my mind
> Sometimes as on the sea I lye
> Mid roaring waves & wind
>
> When valleys rise to mountain waves
> & mountains sink to seas
> When towns & cities temples graves
> All vanish like a breeze
> The skyes that was are past & oer
> That almanack of days
> Year chronicles are kept no more
> Oblivions ruin pays
>
> Pays in destruction shades & hell
> Sin goes in darkness down
> & therein sulphurs shadows dwell
> Worth wins & wears the crown
> The very shore if shore I see
> All shrivelled to a scroll
> The Heaven's rend away from me
> & thunders sulphurs roll
>
> Black as the deadly thunder cloud
> The stars shall turn to dun
> & heaven by that darkness bowed
> Shall make days light be done
> When stars & skys shall all decay
> & earth no more shall be
> When heaven itself shall pass away
> Then thou'lt remember me   (LP I 175–6)

The proposition made in the final two lines implies that personal relationships (and / or poetic reputation) are so distant and so fractured that they are only renewable, even in memory, when the universal destruction that Clare prophesies happens. This is a desperate hope, or threat – self-justification *in extremis*. It indicates the sheer degree of Clare's dislocation from the people and places of his past, and from himself. Yet it is not the distracted rambling of a broken mind; for all its expression of despair and destruction, it is a fully crafted artistic achievement. It is a terrible, prophetic culmination of the insight that is Clare's most original achievement and most pressing legacy to us today – the insight, realized in even the quietest of his sonnets, ballads, and lyrics, that in pursuit of power and profit we destroy our world and, in the process, destroy ourselves.

Notes

1. The marginal note stating this is in the hand of Clare's editor John Taylor, reporting Radstock's sentiment.
2. *The Prose Works of William Wordsworth*, ed. W. J. B. Owen and Jane Worthington Smyser, 3 vols. (Oxford: Clarendon Press, 1974), I, 112.

15

ERIN LAFFORD

Clare's Health

In March 1821, John Clare was so distraught at the prospect of losing his 'two favourite Elm trees' at the back of his garden that he wrote to his publisher, John Taylor. His letter is as much a questioning of his own despair as it is an impassioned description of it:

> I have been several mornings to bid them farewell ... a second thought tells me I am a fool was People all to feel & think as I do the world coud not be carried on – a green woud not be ploughd a tree or bush woud not be cut for firing or furniture & every thing they found when boys would remain in that state till they dyd – this is my indisposition & you will laugh at it ... I am in that muddy mellancholy again my ideas keep swimming & shifting in sleepy drowsiness from one thing to another – this letter will denote the crazy crackd braind fellow it has left behind – I do think from my soul that this comical complaint will carry me off ere long – but god knows best – perhaps before thursday I may be another thing fancying myself as far from death as doomsday
> (*Letters*, pp. 161–62)

The elms were felled, eventually, and Clare's grief consolidated into his elegy 'To a Fallen Elm' (1830). The tree in that poem is a bastion of strength and security, comforting in its capacity to endure harsh, changeful conditions: 'Storms came & shook thee many a weary hour / Yet stedfast to thy home thy roots hath been / Summers of thirst parched round thy homely bower / Till earth grew iron – still thy leaves was green' (MP III 441). Reading the letter that preceded this work offers insight into why Clare, who had much to endure in his own internal weather, might have so dreaded its removal. He describes a state of profound mental and physical upheaval; unlike the 'stedfast' elm, and the steadying rhythm and rhyme of his elegy, Clare's prose captures a more erratic 'swimming & shifting' state of thinking and feeling as he tries to communicate his condition. This shiftiness is both style and symptom. An inability to settle is one of the main presentations of the poet's disorder, yet it also shapes his experience and writing. For someone who professes to be almost pathologically resistant to change in this passage, Clare is remarkably changeful from moment to moment. Led continuously by the turn of 'second thought', he never rests in one state but rather makes an initial diagnosis only to inhabit another situation immediately; the slow stasis of 'muddy mellancholy' and 'sleepy drowsiness' transform quickly into being 'crazy' and 'crackd braind', a state in itself that Clare infers will not outlast the moment of writing – the letter has already left that version of himself 'behind'. This could all feel unbearably unsettling were it not for the fine line that Clare treads between helplessness and control, perhaps best expressed in the fluctuation between his fear of being laughed 'at' and more confident embrace of his 'comical complaint'. The latter carries with it a tantalizing sense of performance – of the 'fool' entertaining at court – so that although the poet suspects this complaint will 'carry me off' and hands himself over to the workings of divine providence, he cannot completely relinquish the prospect of a new guise: 'perhaps before thursday I may be another thing'.

Clare writes here as someone well acquainted with forms of mental, physical, and emotional upset, his remark that what he calls his 'mellancholy' having returned 'again' being just one signal of recurrent bouts of disorder. But as a window onto how his writing handles the task of representing such episodes, and onto what condition it was that the poet might have suffered from, the letter is anything but transparent. Mental illness of some kind has been an inescapable part of Clare's biography since his early reception; the story of the labouring-class poet who spent the second half of his life in asylums is a compelling one, and many attempts to diagnose Clare's 'madness' have followed. Deemed 'most likely of manic-depressive temperament'[1] by his early biographers, John and Anne Tibble, this suggestion has coloured much of the discussion around Clare's fluctuating moods and symptoms. Thomas Tennent offered cyclothymic disorder (a mood disorder analogous with bipolar disorder), and Jonathan Bate agrees, arguing that bipolar is a convincing assessment, albeit an insufficient retrospective diagnosis.[2] Other possibilities abound: seasonal affective disorder, post-traumatic stress disorder, malaria, and even cerebral syphilis (the poet often feared he had contracted venereal disease) all jostle for room as tentative conclusions about what it might have been that left Clare so prone to 'sickly sensibilitys' (*Letters*, p. 175).[3] Yet even the initial brief example of his letter above shows that such categoric approaches to the poet's psychophysiological life are unsatisfactory. Clare's disorder, much like his idiosyncrasy, refuses to be systematized. The term that he opts for as he attempts to articulate his singular pain is 'indisposition', a word both multitudinous and diffuse, and thus an apt term to guide a discussion of the poet's health and its relationship to his writings.

Meaning variously and historically the 'want of adaptation to some purpose', 'unfitness', 'unsuitableness', 'want of apt arrangement or orderly placing', 'displacement or misplacement', 'disorder', 'chaotic condition', 'disordered bodily condition', 'illness', 'disinclination', and 'unwillingness', indisposition captures the many-faceted quality of the disruptions Clare experienced to his mental and physical well-being, as well as the slippages between the somatic, the psychic, and the social that can be held in mind when thinking about what these disruptions were and what they mean. We get an especially significant insight into the work that the word might do for Clare in the early pages of his autobiography. In 'Sketches in the Life of John Clare' (1821), he outlines the circumstances that pushed him to consider 'revealing the Secret of my poetry': 'I my self was of a week const[i]tution and a severe indisposition keeping me from work for a twelvemonthe ran us in debt' (*JCBH*, p. 19; p. 18). As his increasingly frail father turned to the parish system for aid due to 'rumatics' (rheumatism) and 'infirmitys', Clare had to contend with his own 'dilemma of Embaresment' whilst grappling with the mental and physical pressures of supporting his family:

> my indisposition, (for I cannot call it illness) origionated in fainting fits, the cause of which I always imagined came from seeing when I was younger a man name Thomas Drake after he had fell off a load of hay and broke his neck   the gastly paleness of death struck such a terror on me that I coud not forget it for years ... every spring and autum since the accident happend my fears are agitated to an extreem degree and the dread of death involves me in a stupor of chilling indisposition as usual   (*JCBH*, pp. 18–19)

Writing in retrospect, Clare seeks an origin story for a set of chronic symptoms that have persisted since childhood but halts at the edge of 'illness', which seems too definitive a term. He demands to be allowed to inhabit the flexibility of his own experience which, as this attempt to articulate it shows, is highly elusive. It is emotional, rooted in fear and 'dread'; it is physical, manifest in lazy 'stupor', as well as fits and faintings; it is located in memory yet painfully present with each seasonal cycle. It is also wrapped up in the pain of feeling constitutionally unsuited to the labouring work his family is dependent upon, and the burning ambition to leave labour behind to pursue poetry. To insist on a distinction between 'indisposition' and 'illness' might seem like splitting hairs given that the former contains the latter in its capacious definition, but the distinction remains important to Clare and to us as readers of him because of its dislocating and indecisive potential. This essay explores Clare as a poet periodically 'indisposed', finding in that term a rich way of approaching his unsettled position within the medical and literary culture in which he lived as well as the relationship he had with his own psychic and somatic experience. Broadening the range of his medical encounters and vocabulary beyond the narrow context of the asylum, it considers his symptoms as entangled with his mobility across, and unstable status within, different places, social worlds, and identities, and how his poetry registers these mental, physical, and cultural forms of displacement.

Clare wrote within a Romantic climate that drew connections between poetry and illness, and between poetry and mental disorder especially. His admission papers to Northampton General Asylum in 1841 recorded assuredly that his 'insanity' was preceded by 'years addicted to poetical prossing'.[4] Having insanity and poetry stamped together onto his personal medical records has certainly shaped Clare's reception and the forms of suffering for which he is predominately known. Writing in the twentieth century, the Scottish poet William Soutar, for example, exclaimed that 'the troubles of the mind are not so distracting to an artist as the aches of the body ... Christopher Smart and [John] Clare could write poetry from a madhouse – but who can write at all when suffering from influenza, say, or severe toothache?'[5] A poet as steeped in Scottish literary tradition as Soutar was unlikely to be ignorant of Robert Burns's 'Address to the Tooth-Ache' (?1797), a poem that finds comedy in making this mundane ailment the subject of lyric apostrophe. His remark is perhaps a playful articulation of his own frustration (Soutar suffered from spondylitis, a form of chronic arthritis that impacts the spine) rather than a sincere thesis. Nevertheless, it crystallizes a prevalent image of the Romantic poet as having a special affinity with madness, and of Clare as an uncomplicated example of the mad Romantic poet, that warrants further attention. Soutar's division between mind and body was, for example, a boundary challenged by developments in eighteenth-century medicine. Whereas the earlier, medieval model of the humours offered a theory of health and illness as rooted in the balance, or imbalance, of four physical fluids (blood, phlegm, yellow bile, and black bile), revolutionary developments from the seventeenth century onwards uncovered the vital role of the nervous system as a network that connected body and mind.[6] Scottish physicians such as Robert Whytt (1714–66), William Cullen (1710–90), Alexander Monro (1733–1817), and John Brown (1735–88) ventured specific connections between mental and physical faculties and sparked attention to a live relationship between literature and medicine that captivated Romantic-period writers, contributing to conceptions of the Romantic poet as vulnerable to both psychic and somatic suffering.[7] Brown's Brunonian system of medicine especially conceived of nerves as vulnerable to both over- and under-stimulation, so that finding a balance in one's nervous excitement was the key to good health. This generated the idea that the overly sensitive individual prone to intense emotional responses to the world opened themselves up to dangerous levels of stimulation that could produce a range of illnesses, including mental illness which came to be considered a form of nervous disease and a disorder of an embodied mind.[8]

We need not go as far as the 'mad-house' to appreciate Clare's participation in this vocabulary of nervous illness. Whilst he appreciated a connection between nervous stimulation and insanity ('I am very nervous that is to say very crazey' (*Letters*, p. 199)), he groped for an understanding of the relationship between his body and mind long before he entered the asylum. Some of his more interesting engagements come less from any secure tie to madness as a defined state, and instead from a scrutiny of a more diffuse sensitivity – 'I am in such a tottering trembling state of nerves' – as well as from an exasperation with not knowing the cause behind his varied sufferings: 'If I coud get my head right I shoud do for if I coud read or write or even remember what I have done or know & feel as my self I shoud do ... I am certain its somthing more then nervous' (*Letters*, p. 175; p. 298). The exciting continuity between thinking and feeling offered by discourses of sensibility and the nerves is here shown by Clare to be equally disorienting, lost as he is between whether his 'self' is something he can do, know, or feel. He had perhaps good reason to feel hesitant towards this language of sensitive connection. As Richard C. Sha puts it: 'One major reason why the nerves had such cultural resonance was that they grounded notions of class and gender difference. Everyone had nerves, but few could control them.'[9] Regarding the nervous sensibility of the labouring classes, questions concerning the ability for self-control were matched by assumptions about the happily insensible nature of the labouring body. Debates about the relationship between creative 'genius' and unregulated states of mind, for example, emphasized this ambivalent gift as belonging exclusively to the learned and the quick-witted. The Scottish physician George Cheyne insisted that the range of 'nervous diseases' he explored in *The English Malady* (1733) 'never happens, or can happen, to any but those of the liveliest and quickest natural Parts, whose Faculties are the brightest and most spiritual, and whose Genius most keen and penetrating'.[10] In *Essays on Insanity* (1816), John Reid claimed it was 'men of letters' and 'artists' who had to be watched most carefully for the 'distresses of a refined and romantic sensibility' and segregated problems of the body and mind along class lines: 'The labor of the poor man relieves him at least from the burden of fashionable ennui, and the constant pressure of physical inconveniences, from the more elegant, but surely not less intolerable distresses of a refined and romantic sensibility.'[11] Many of Clare's verse explorations of genius show him to be a figure caught between the vital interest in subjective feeling that discourses of sensibility encouraged and the objective portrait of a class whose participation in this psychophysiological register was complicated or even denied.

Clare's first volume of poetry, *Poems Descriptive of Rural Life and Scenery* (published in 1820) celebrated him as an exciting new poetic genius. Taylor's introduction praises him as an 'extraordinary' talent, made all the more remarkable for his difficult origins: 'That passion must have been originally very strong and pure, which could sustain itself, for so many years, through want, and toil, and hopeless misery.'[12] A figure in whom 'Labour and the Muse ... kept alternate watch',[13] Clare straddled different sets of expectations, harbouring at once the 'natural irritability of the poetic temperament'[14] and, as debates around the irritating dangers of 'genius' would have it, an ostensibly simpler intellectual faculty free from the burden of enhanced sensibility. A poem from the volume that challenges such divided thinking head on is 'Dawning of Genius' (1817–19), which delights in errant states of thinking and feeling as disorderly as they are enjoyable. Genius is described as a 'pleasing rapture of the mind' (EP 1 451), suggesting an elated form of mental transport that is also sudden in its attack; it is 'wild' and comes in 'bu[r]sts of thought' that cannot be rationally tracked but rather 'Are bred one moment & are gone the next' (EP 1 452). What makes all the difference in this study of the mental pressures of genius, however, is that Clare is talking about the experience of a 'rough rude ploughman' (452). The poem on the one hand reclaims genius from the sole domain of 'Learning', demanding that the physical experience of labour be counted alongside 'arts Refinements' as a route into creative sensibility and its own revered forms of suffering; on the other hand, though, it presents the apparent rarity of rural genius as an almost pathological struggle towards successful expression, and as a fight between mind and body. The 'genius' in this poem is only just 'dawning', and the fate of the sensitive labourer lacking the means to articulate his thoughts is to undergo a painful short-circuiting of feeling with no outlet:

> Vain burns the soul & throbs the fluttering heart
> Their painfull pleasing feelings to impart
> Till by successles sallies wearied quite
> The memory fails & fancy takes her flight
> The wickett nipt within its socket dies
> Born down & smother'd in a thousand sighs   (EP 1 452)

Poems Descriptive ensures that the 'constant pressure of physical inconveniences' (to use Reid's phrase) is unignorable in its studies of labouring life; it introduces Clare as a poet of the body and the ways that it might hurt as well as a figure well versed in the ostensibly more 'elegant' distresses of the mind. 'Address to Plenty in Winter' (1817), for example, offers a litany of physical pains that labour and poverty bring about; Clare's speaker longs for a life free from 'Aching bones & heavy head / Worse than when one went to bed' (EP I 323), endures hunger felt as 'Empty guts that pines & frets' (317), and is subject to harsh weather conditions such as 'piercing snows' (321). Yet the volume also introduces Clare as a labouring-class poet in the midst of trying to figure out what kinds of pain might be special to him, and whether poetry introduces a kind of suffering that binds him to or sets him apart from his labouring community. The final lines of 'Dawning of Genius' share some remarkable resemblances, for instance, with a moment in his later quasi-autobiographical work 'The Progress of Ryhme' (1824–32), which depicts the emergence of the speaker's poetic inspiration as a thrilling experience of bodily disorder quite separate from the 'toiling care' (MP III 492) of agricultural labour: 'That instinct that would not be still . . . / . . . That heaved my bosom like my breath / That burned & chilled & went & came / Without or uttering or a name' (MP III 498). One poem charts the tormenting pressure of genius unexpressed, the other the restorative relief that poetry gives to a boy whose creative ambitions isolate him within his rural community (for all the imagery of physical distress contained in the lines above, 'poesy' is still welcomed as therapeutic, the speaker declaring 'when sick thy visions gives me health' (492)). Comparing the two for their embodied figurations of failure and inspiration shows Clare's immersion in the medical discourse of nervous sensibility to be a crucial vocabulary for expressing a perpetual conflict in his identity. As Mina Gorji shows, the association of the rustic poet with neglect, failure, and obscurity was an eighteenth-century tradition that Clare received primarily through Thomas Gray's 'Elegy Written in a Country Churchyard' (published in 1751), and a motif that he reworked frequently in his own verse.[15] The question of whether his genius would be 'smother'd' and follow the fate of the rural collective, or whether he could be a recognized poet in his own right, is one that nagged at the very fibres of Clare's being.

In exploring the resilience and failures of labouring bodies and minds, wondering over his own constitution, and feeling his way into poetry as something that might cure as much at it might necessitate mental and physical disorder, Clare also negotiated his place within his local therapeutic culture. Whilst his time in High Beach and, later, Northampton Asylum dominates critical attention on the poet's entanglements with nineteenth-century medical thought, practice, and the treatment of insanity, his experience, knowledge, and imaginative interpretation stretched far beyond this. Clare's much-discussed interest in botany, for example, was fuelled by a preference for earlier seventeenth-century practices in herbalism over the 'dark system' (*JCBH*, p. 61) of Latin taxonomy introduced by the Swedish botanist Carl Linnaeus (1707–78): 'when one turns to the works of Ray Parkinson and Gerrard were there is more of nature and less of Art it is like meeting the fresh air and balmy summer of a dewey morning after the troubled dreams of a nightmare' (*JCBH*, p. 62). A range of herbal texts influenced Clare's botanical sympathies – John Ray's *Historia Plantarium* (1686–1704), John Gerard's *Herball, or Generall Historie of Plantes* (1630), and John Parkinson's *Theatrum Botanicum* (1640). He was also familiar with Nicholas Culpeper's (1616–54) *The English Physician* (1652), which contained extensive catalogues of herbal remedies, via Joshua Hamilton's two-volume edition *English Family Physician* (1792). Clare's preference for the earlier herbals has been discussed predominately in the context of the significance of his love for wild, uncultivated flowers as a model of local poetic sensibility.[16] However, he explicitly frames these texts as reparative reading experiences that are surely rooted in their dedication to the therapeutic properties of plants. They offer relief from the 'dark system' of Latin taxonomy as a dry, unstimulating body of knowledge at the same time as they point the reader to the cures that surround them in their local environment. Clare embraced botany as a living practice that put him in touch with the materiality of nature, and with a rural community that spoke in the language of common names rather than artificial categories. His poem 'The Village Doctress' (1823) celebrates this local figure for her 'famous drinks & ointments made of flowers' (MP III 331) and insists, even though she owns copies of both 'Culpeppers Herbal' and 'Westleys Phisic', that her knowledge is more than can be learned in books, whose 'Puzzles' leave her 'sore vexed indeed' (MP III 332–3). She is instead one for whom 'Phisic seemed oozing from her finger ends' (334), and who exists in profound emotional communion with the nonhuman world: '& een when beetles neath her foot did fall / As bustling oer the foot path or the floor / It cost her many a sigh & grieved her heart full sore' (335). Clare's delight in the common names for plants extends to his interest in their curative properties. Plants such as 'self heal', 'scurvy grass', and 'eye brights' (MP III 337–8) offer at once an accessible shorthand of medical lore (he writes, for example, of how the eyebright is 'Infallable for weak short sighted eyes' (MP III 338)) and a rich poetic language that inscribes the body's intimate ties with its local flora.

A keen collector of plants himself, Clare was sensitive to how botany as an *activity* rather than a mass of textual information left him as open to threats as to remedies; one of his journal entries from April 1825 reads 'went a Botanizing after Ferns and Orchises and caught a cold in the wet grass which has made me as bad as ever' (*JCBH*, p. 232). There is a wonderfully ambiguous energy and sense of displacement to this sentence. Is the 'cold' he has 'caught' an illness that he has contracted, something that has breached his bodily boundary as he walked searching for plants? Or something held at more of a remove – a live specimen perhaps that he has collected along with his botanical samples? Clare's sense of the grass itself as a location where such a cold might be lurking, as well as his representation of the body and its potential ailments as distributed throughout an environment rather than as a discrete, self-contained entity, is suggestive of the rich importance of environmental medicine to his conceptions of physical and mental disorder. As Jan Golinski writes in *British Weather and the Climate of Enlightenment*, from the eighteenth century a 'prominent aspect of the age's deepening interest in the weather was the question of how it affected bodily and mental well-being.'[17] Weather and the seasons offered Clare a vocabulary that made his confusing 'indisposition' legible at the same time as it made his mind and body perhaps more inscrutable than ever. Writing to James Hessey in 1822, he lamented:

> I have been very poorly in fact very bad all this month but I hope ere long to be myself agen ... as soon as I loose this confounded lethargy of low spirits that presses on me to such a degree that at times makes me feel as if my senses had a mind to leave me   Spring & Fall such feelings it seems are doomd to be my companions
> (*Letters*, p. 234)

The seasons provide a way for Clare to map his interior suffering onto an exterior framework, offering some way out of his self-fixation towards a connection with natural rhythms. Even if those rhythms generate 'doomd' bouts of discomfort and distress, their regularity lends structure and temporality to these episodes. The 'low spirits' themselves, however, are more unsettling and amorphous, destabilizing the poet's hold on himself and the external world as they blur the boundary between inside and outside. The term 'spirits' encompasses mind, body, and atmospheric influences in a confusing mixture that recalls Robert Burton's *Anatomy of Melancholy* (1621), a text Clare's speaker enjoys poring over as he shelters indoors from the elements in 'The Winters Come' (1842–64): 'How pleasant on a feather bed to lie, / Or sitting by the fire, in fancy soar, ... / ... Or read fresh volumes we've not seen before, / Or o'er old Bartons "melancholy pore"' (LP 11 929). Burton's *Anatomy* still had one foot in the earlier humoral model of medicine; his discussion of 'air' as one of the causes of melancholy observes 'if it be impure and foggy, it dejects the spirits, and causeth diseases by infection of the heart ... Such as is the air, such be our spirits; and as our spirits, such are our humours.'[18] Burton's axiomatic phrasing unites the infectious matter of climate with affectivity: his 'infection of the heart' is at once physiological and emotional, as is the dejection of spirits. Whilst the vocabulary of nervous sensitivity already gave much to Clare as a means of thinking about his mind and body as bewilderingly entangled, his immersion in the earlier humoral framework of medicine, via Burton, is a rich influence, too, and informs his insecure relationship to his 'senses' as not fully his own, but subject to the whims of environmental influence.

Clare had perhaps more reason than most to fear the 'impure' and 'foggy' air that Burton tied to disease, melancholy, and dejection. Describing his Helpston home as 'a gloomy village in Northamptonshire, on the brink of the Lincolnshire fens' (*JCBH*, p. 2), he was all too aware of the long-standing associations between wetlands and mental and physical illness. Dr Fenwick Skrimshire, one of the physicians who later signed Clare's admission papers to Northampton asylum, wrote in his *Village Pastor's Surgical and Medical Guide* (1838) of chronic and remittent fevers as the 'Proteus of the fens';[19] his phrase captures at once the shape-shifting nature of fens as a mixture of land and water, and the disorienting symptoms that their infectious airs and stagnant pools were thought to cause. For all of Clare's celebration of the fens as a sanctuary for shy wildlife in poems such as 'To the Snipe' (1832), where 'in these marshy flats these stagnant floods / Security pervades' (MP IV 575), much of his poetic representation of this landscape is energized by an alertness to its dangers. In '[The Fens]' (1832–5), for example, the speaker declares how they 'love to rustle through the sedge', only to recoil from what they find there:

> Yet turning quick with shudder chill
> As danger ever does from ill
> Fears moment ague quakes the blood
> While plop the snake coils in the flood   (MP v 27–30, ll. 5–8)

A frightening encounter with a snake (once prevalent in British wetlands) is here couched in a language of both emotional and physical disarray. Fear is figured as an 'ague', an acute or high fever that causes fits of shivering and was often associated with malaria (one of the diagnoses, we recall, on offer as a source of Clare's confusing chronic 'indisposition'). Clare handles this experience in such a way as to make it all encompassing and yet also to dislocate it from a defined subject; the 'moment ague' belongs to fear itself, 'quakes the blood' as it visits the speaker, and vanishes again as quickly as the snake that sparked it. Later in the poem, experiences that one might expect to find as symptoms of both physical and mental illness are attributed to the landscape of the fens itself, such as 'Large grounds bethronged with thistles brown / Shivering & madding up & down' (ll. 109–10). Clare finds in the language of fever and mental disorganization an enlivening form of natural description, as well as a means of expressing the protean forms of disorientation such a landscape might produce.

Whilst Clare may have given his mind and body over to the vagaries of atmospheric 'spirits' and lurking agues, he was also anxious for the reassuring authority of medical advice. In his preferred choice of physician, he again found himself torn between the offerings of his rural community and the promise of what might lie beyond it. Clare was often mistrustful of the doctors available to him in Helpston, claiming either doubt about their level of expertise or seeing them as little better than quacks out to exploit the rural poor by peddling bogus cures. Doctors do not tend to fare well in Clare's verse, being often the subject of satirical attack; his long poem *The Parish* (1820–7), for instance, includes a description of the 'mighty doctor' who exploits the community's need for healthcare: 'For every mouth is puckered with his skill / So sing his patients & so say his bill' (EP II 723). Describing, too, the illness of his youngest daughter in 1825, he wrote 'if I had called in one of our docters they woud as likely have made her worse for I have no opinion about them since they handled me so roughly' (*Letters*, p. 355). The one physician he did trust, and implored frequently for advice and prescriptions, was Dr George Darling, a London doctor who also treated John Keats during his increasingly serious bouts of consumptive illness. Darling was an important tie to London's literary circles for Clare and, as a prose account of a visit to the capital between February and March 1828 suggests, a means of accessing a plethora of alternative therapies; for all of his reliance on Darling's advice, we can see in the following that Clare revelled in straying from this trusted source, too. The poet was in London ostensibly to seek advice from 'a celebrated scotch phisic[i]an Dr Darling' (*JCBH*, p. 149) for what he described as an ongoing 'complaint ... in my head and chest' (although Eric Robinson glosses this as 'depression' in his chronology of the poet's life, adding to the confusing elusiveness of his condition).[20] The account itself is, by design, 'observations of men and things thrown together in a myscellaneous manner' (*JCBH*, p. 150) and strays immediately from the focused intent that brought him there. Clare shares no detail of the encounter with Darling, even though he recalls having 'gradualy recievd benefit' (*JCBH*, p. 150) from his counsel. Instead, he digresses into an array of alternative treatments and diversions. Travelling to London from rural Helpston, he is immersed in the comparatively giddy pace of metropolitan life. He writes how he 'amusd my illness by catching the most beautiful women[s] faces in the crowd as I passd on in it till I was satiated as it were with the variety' (*JCBH*, p. 150). He visits

James DeVille, the prominent phrenologist, where he sees his 'collection of heads' and agrees sceptically to have a cast taken of his own – a 'stifling' procedure he swears never to repeat (*JCBH*, p. 153). The painter Edward Villiers Rippingille, whom Clare had become friends with on an earlier visit to London, comes from Bristol to meet him in the capital. Insistent on his own cures – 'he was always for thinking that constant exercise taking all weathers rough and smooth as they came were the best phisic for a sick man and a glass of Scotch Ale only seemed to strengthen his notions' (*JCBH*, p. 152) – Rippingille takes Clare on a varied tour of the city and its cultural offerings; they attend various theatrical performances, a boxing exhibition at the Fives Court, which inspires in Clare a 'mania' for the sport, and pay a visit to Sir Thomas Lawrence (then president of the Royal Academy) to take a tour of his gallery (*JCBH*, pp. 152–4). Described aptly by Clare as their 'brancing about the town', it is in many respects a whirlwind of a visit that may not immediately seem in keeping with the recuperation he is there for. 'Brancing' appears to be a word of his own invention, perhaps an amalgamation of 'branching' and 'prancing' which, with its suggestions of springing out in a new direction or path and of gambols and capers, captures well the joyful exposure to new experiences and opportunities that come to be their own kind of remedy.

Herbalism and environmental medicine lend new resonances to the prevalent reception of Clare as a poet dependent on his local bounds for both his creative inspiration and his sense of well-being. They offered him a vocabulary for thinking about the psychophysiological effects of being in place, which included pervasive sensations of disorientation and dislocation, and inspired a dedication to rural bodies of therapeutic knowledge that were becoming marginalized as medicine became increasingly professionalized and regulated in the eighteenth and nineteenth centuries. Yet Clare's constant desire to feel well and to get back to 'himself' also turned him into a poet frequently on the move. With its raucous sense of perpetual motion, his recollection of his London visit is an important reminder of the reach of Clare's encounters with his contemporary medical culture, and of what he perceived as the best kinds of medicine. His 'indisposition' was not a one-way ticket to the asylum, although that was the sobering end to a long struggle with physical, emotional, and financial pressures that he could no longer cope with. It was also a self-conscious project in trying to know, and test, the bounds of his own body and mind, and in trying to figure out what room there was for a labouring-class writer in both the live conversations between Romantic literature and medicine and the freedom of the Romantic poet to choose sickness over health.

Notes

1. J. W. Tibble and Anne Tibble, *John Clare: A Life*, 2nd ed. (London: Michael Joseph, 1972), p. 201.
2. Thomas Tennent, 'Reflections on Genius', *The Journal of Mental Science*, 99 (1953), 1–7; Jonathan Bate, *John Clare: A Biography* (London: Picador, 2003), p. 412.
3. See Bate, *John Clare*, pp. 404–18; Arthur Foss and K. L. K. Trick, *St Andrew's Hospital, Northampton: The First 150 Years (1838–1988)* (Cambridge: Granta, 1989), pp. 137–9; Sean Haldane, 'John Clare's Madness', *PN Review* 30.6 (2004), 42–6.
4. Bate, *John Clare*, p. 466.
5. Irene Taylor and Alan Taylor, eds., *The Assassins Cloak: An Anthology of the World's Greatest Diarists* (Edinburgh: Canongate, 2000), p. 348. See also Peter Fifield, *Modernism and Physical Illness: Sick Books* (Oxford: Oxford University Press, 2020), p. 5, who explores this quotation within modernism's reclaiming of physical illness as a site of literary imagination.
6. See George S. Rousseau, *Nervous Acts: Essays on Literature, Culture and Sensibility* (Basingstoke: Palgrave Macmillan, 2004), pp. 157–84.
7. See, for example, Clark Lawlor's discussion of 'Wasting Poets' in *Consumption and Literature: The Making of a Romantic Disease* (Basingstoke: Palgrave Macmillan, 2006), pp. 111–52.
8. See Allan Ingram, 'Mental Illness: Locking and Unlocking the Stereotypes', in Clark Lawlor and Andrew Mangham, eds., *Literature and Medicine: The Eighteenth Century* (Cambridge: Cambridge University Press, 2021), pp. 91–112.
9. Richard C. Sha, 'Only Connect: Romantic Nerves, Pleasure, Aesthetics, and Sexuality', in Clark Lawlor and Andrew Mangham, eds., *Literature and Medicine: The Eighteenth Century* (Cambridge: Cambridge University Press, 2021), pp. 161–85 (p. 167).
10. George Cheyne, *The English Malady: or, A Treatise of Nervous Diseases of All Kinds* (London: Wisk, Ewing, and Smith, 1733), p. 262.
11. John Reid, *Essays on Insanity, Hypochondriasis, and Other Nervous Affections* (London: Longman, Hurst, Rees, Orme, and Brown, 1816), pp. 3–6.
12. *Poems Descriptive of Rural Life and Scenery* (London: John Taylor, 1820), p. xxi.
13. *Poems Descriptive*, p. xxii.
14. *Poems Descriptive*, p. xxvii.
15. Mina Gorji, *John Clare and the Place of Poetry* (Liverpool: Liverpool University Press, 2008), pp. 32–56.
16. See, for example, 'Clare's Commonable Plants', in Theresa M. Kelley, *Clandestine Marriage: Botany and Romantic Culture* (Baltimore: Johns Hopkins University Press, 2012), pp. 126–58, and 'John Clare: Bard of the Wild Flowers', in M. M. Mahood, *The Poet as Botanist* (Cambridge: Cambridge University Press, 2008), pp. 112–46.
17. Jan Golinski, *British Weather and the Climate of Enlightenment* (Chicago: University of Chicago Press, 2007), p. 137.

18. Robert Burton, *Anatomy of Melancholy*, ed. Holbrook Jackson, 3 vols. (London: The Folio Society, 2005), 1, 257.
19. Fenwick Skrimshire, *The Village Pastor's Surgical and Medical Guide* (London: John Churchill, 1838), p. 240.
20. *John Clare: The Major Works*, ed. Eric Robinson and David Powell (Oxford: Oxford University Press, 1984), p. xxxi.

16

MINA GORJI

Clare among the Poets

> all I aspire to is that I may win a nitch among the minor bards in the memory of my country.
> (John Clare to James Montgomery, 13 January 1828
> (*Letters*, p. 412))

On 13 June 1989, Ted Hughes unveiled a memorial to John Clare in Poets' Corner, Westminster Abbey. To mark the occasion, Hughes read 'The Nightingale's Nest', a poem which reveals the tactile intimacy of Clare's writing:

> & where these crimping fern-leaves ramp among
> The hazels under boughs – Ive nestled down
> & watched her while she sung – & her renown
> Hath made me marvel that so famed a bird
> Should have no better dress then russet brown
> (MP III 457, ll. 17–21)

The russet-brown nightingale is both emphatically herself, a small bird singing in the hazel branches, and a symbol of poetry with whom Clare felt a particular affinity, since russet was a colour traditionally associated with rural labourers. From the publication of *Poems Descriptive of Rural Life and Scenery* in 1820, Clare's social identity was firmly part of his appeal as a poet. On the title page of that first collection, he was described as a 'Northamptonshire Peasant'. Clare was keenly aware that his humble rural circumstances brought him attention, but that this was circumscribed: as a Northamptonshire Peasant Poet, he could only hope for a place at the margins of the polite world of letters, a 'nitch among the minor bards'.

Clare's Influence

Clare's later reputation has, in part, resulted from his being perceived as a poet of the margins. Recent and contemporary poets such as Seamus Heaney, Tom Paulin, David Morley, Simon Armitage, and Paul Farley have been inspired by his commitment to the local and provincial. For these writers, Clare's appeal lay not only in his celebration of local landscape, flora, and fauna, but also in his use of local vernacular. In an essay first given as a lecture in 1989, Heaney praised what he termed Clare's wilful and intelligent refusal, in his mature writing, to ventriloquize the polite voice of literary tradition, and to speak, instead, in his own local accent and idiom:

> The story of his career, in other words, can be expressed as follows: once upon a time, John Clare was lured to the edge of his word-horizon and his tonal horizon, looked about him eagerly, tried out a few new words and accents and then, wilfully and intelligently, withdrew and dug in his local heels.[1]

Not only did Clare's example inform Heaney's own playful and sophisticated use of local language, it also, as Sidney Burris has suggested, encouraged him to celebrate his own native region, South Derry, at a time when it was marginalized. Clare was also a formative influence because, as Florian Gargaillo has argued, 'he showed Heaney how to position himself, as a lyric speaker, towards the world he wished to transcribe in verse, and played a key role in the formation of the mature poet of *North* (1975) and *Field Work* (1979)'.[2]

Clare's influence can also be felt in *Wintering Out* (1972), in 'A Backward Look', for instance, which centres on a hunted snipe:

> A stagger in the air
> as if a language
> failed, a sleight
> of wing.
>
> A snipe's bleat is fleeting
> its nesting ground
> into dialect,
> into variants,
>
> transliterations whirr
> on the nature reserves –
> *little goat of the air,*
> *of the evening*
>
> *little goat of the frost.*
> It is his tail feathers

> drumming elegies
> in the slipstream³

These lines call to mind one of Clare's finest poems, 'To the Snipe', first published in J. W. Tibble's 1935 edition of Clare's poetry, and then in the *Selected Poems and Prose of John Clare* edited by Eric Robinson and Geoffrey Summerfield in 1967. The rhythmic hesitancy of Heaney's poem recalls Clare's delicately awkward and uneven quatrains, its lines growing out in length before shrinking back to a short final line, a halting movement that expresses the snipe's trepidation:

> Lover of swamps
> The quagmire overgrown
> With hassock tufts of sedge – where fear encamps
> Around thy home alone
>
> The trembling grass
> Quakes from the human foot
> Nor bears the weight of man to let him pass
> Where he alone & mute
>
> Sittest at rest
> In safety neath the clump
> Of huge flag forrest that thy haunts invest
> Or some old sallow stump   (MP IV 574, ll. 1–12)

The poem shifts delicately between a sense of being 'at home' in the marshy landscape of the swamp, a sanctuary which won't bear the weight of human invaders, and a feeling of uneasiness experienced not only by the hunted birds, but also by the 'trepid air', startled by the sound of 'cracking guns', and 'the trembling grass' that 'quakes from the human foot'. Trembling grass is a species of grass, a vernacular name for *Briza media*, but here in Clare's lines, the word 'trembling' also attributes feeling to the grass, a sense of fear.

Of course, Heaney takes his own poem in a different direction, but there's a sense of Clare's sponsoring presence not only in the deft and uneven movement of the lines but also in its celebration of dialect. Although no dialect appears in 'To the Snipe', Clare's use of vernacular language throughout his writing represents, for Heaney, a linguistic version of the utter 'at home-ness' the poem celebrates:

> From dangers reach
> Here thou art safe to roam
> Far as these washy flag grown marshes stretch
> A still and quiet home   (MP IV 576, ll. 69–72)

For Heaney, Clare's finest writing reveals this quality of 'at home-ness in the district' or 'in placeness',[4] because of its local language.

Poet and critic Tom Paulin describes 'To the Snipe' as 'one of the greatest nature poems in the language', celebrating its artful literary allusions.[5] But for Paulin, it is above all as a vernacular poet that Clare is to be valued and admired; he includes a number of Clare's poems in his anthology, *The Faber Book of Vernacular Verse* (1990). Clare, he argues, 'wrote before the long ice age of standard British English clamped down on the living language and began to break its local and vernacular energies'.[6] In his own poem, 'The Writing Lark' (a letter to Clare written in May 1997 and first published in the *John Clare Society Journal* in 1988), Paulin celebrates Clare's dialect, focusing on one word in particular, 'pudge', a Northamptonshire term for puddles:

> Dear Mr Clare
> Dear John Clare
> I'll start with pudge –
> pudge not budge
> pudge because
> pudge is a smashed puddle
> A muddy puddle on a track
> Or a whole clatter
> Scattered like broken plates –
> shiny plates
> on scoggy scroggy marshland –
> each pudge is like piss
> cupped in a cow-clap
> so I imagine a boot[7]

In these lines, the repeated word *pudge* gathers force and emphasis as its *u* sound is repeated in *budge* and then *puddle* and *muddy puddle*. We hear the *c* in *clatter* echo in *scatter . . . broken* and *cupped in a cow-clap*. Paulin creates an image of and in sound, a feature of Clare's writing which he singles out for admiration. According to Paulin, Clare is one of the 'great sound poets';[8] 'Writing Lark' is a tribute to Clare's acoustic art.

Paulin admires the clatter of sound in Clare's poetry – 'the toltering bustle of a blundering trot', the crawking cry of a woodpecker, or the cranking, jarring noise of a heron flying overhead. His own poetry reveals a similar fascination for the rebarbative and discordant, for example, in the harsh, 'schisty flight-call' described in 'Of difference does it make' (published in *Liberty Tree*, 1983), which has a Clarean quality:

> Among the plovers and the stonechats
> protected by the Wild Birds Act
> of nineteen-hundred-and-thirty-one,
> there is a rare stint called the notawhit
> that has a schisty flight-call, like the chough's.
> Notawhit, notawhit, notawhit
> - it raps out a sharp code-sign
> like a mild and patient prisoner
> pecking through granite with a teaspoon. (ll. 1–9)

On one level, of course, this is a political poem about the Troubles, something that's made clear in the poem's epigraph: '*During the 51-year existence of the Northern Ireland Parliament only one Bill sponsored by a non-Unionist member was ever passed.*' But it is also about a bird and its 'schisty-flight call': the repeated cry, 'notawhit', is both a political joke and also a plausible representation of the bird's call, the kind of onomatopoeic or sound symbolic representation of bird sound we often find in Clare's poetry, for example in these lines from one of the Northborough sonnets:

> The pewet hollos chewsit as she flies
> & flops about the shepherd where he lies
> But when her nest is found she stops her song
> & cocks [her] coppled crown & runs along
> Wrens cock their tails & chitter loud & play
> And robins hollo tut & flye away (MP v 247, ll. 9–14)

In these lines, and elsewhere in his writing, Clare catches at the jerky and abrupt quality of birds' sounds and movements. This is part of a larger aesthetic of dissonance, a delight in the rebarbative Paulin celebrates both in his critical writing and in his own poetry. Clare pays attention to the harsh, the rough and the broken, to those 'desolate neglected' places celebrated in 'Shadows of Taste', the 'rut gulled wagon road' in 'The Pettichaps Nest', muddy pudges (puddles), and the cesspools which, in Clare's poem about a mouse's nest, 'glitter in the sun' (MP v 246, l. 14). Celebrating what others perceived as distasteful, rude, or uncouth, he stakes a claim for poetry that's not metropolitan or polite. 'Sand Martin' offers another example of this characteristic aesthetic, with its description of a 'wild', 'desolate' landscape, a 'rude waste' in which the bird, with 'strangest taste', prefers to make its home, its nest 'more like the haunts of vermin than a bird' (MP IV 309–10, ll. 1–7).

Writing in the Introduction to *Poems Descriptive of Rural Life and Scenery* in 1820, John Taylor also noted Clare's fondness for what others might consider ugly or rebarbative, those 'scenes which no other poet has thought of celebrating', 'The swampy falls of pasture ground, and rushy spreading greens', 'plashy streams', and 'weed-beds wild and rank'.[9] Almost a century later, Edward Thomas praised Clare's 'lowly fidelity', and his love 'not only of the wild, but of the waste places', explaining:

> Though he did call the henbane 'stinking', he half loved it for the places, like Cowper's Green, where he found it, with bramble, thistle, nettle, hemlock,
>
>> And full many a nameless weed,
>> Neglected, left to run to seed,
>> Seen but with disgust by those
>> Who judge a blossom by the nose.
>> Wildness is my suiting scene,
>> So I seek thee Cowper Green.[10]

What some perceive as disgusting, Clare celebrates here. Throughout his writing, he calls for a rethinking of aesthetic and social categories of worth and value: 'And weeds that bloomed in summer's hours / I thought they should be reckoned flowers', he declares in 'The Progress of Rhyme' (MP III 495, ll. 85–6).

Thomas's own poem, 'Tall Nettles' takes inspiration from Clare's championing of the neglected and uncultivated:

> Tall nettles cover up, as they have done
> These many springs, the rusty harrow, the plough
> Long worn out, and the roller made of stone:
> Only the elm butt tops the nettles now.
>
> This corner of the farmyard I like most:
> As well as any bloom upon a flower
> I like the dust on the nettles, never lost
> Except to prove the sweetness of a shower.   (ll. 1–8)

Like Clare, Thomas discovers beauty in unlikely places: the delicacy of dust on nettles; the sweetness of the shower. Clare's attention to what was usually considered ugly, unpoetical, or 'beneath notice' has also inspired a number of more recent poets. Heaney is one example: his poem 'Nettles', in which both Clare and Thomas are kindred sponsoring presences, takes pleasure in the discarded and uncultivated. Michael Longley is another: in 'Flora', for instance, he turns his attention to the 'outcasts', plants which grow in 'waste places':

> These pictures of me
> In waste places
> Naming the outcasts . . .

> Blue periwinkles,
> Meadowsweet,
> Tansy[11]

Or, in 'Gardening in Cardoso', Longley celebrates the wildflowers and weeds in Garfagnana, familiar from his home in Northern Ireland:

> herb robert,
> Spurge, wall-devouring
> Valerian, garlicky
> Ramsons, dead nettles.
> What about oregano
> No higher than dogs' piss,
> And pennywort protecting
> The lizard's hideaway?[12]

There's a relish to the description of the exuberant and what might be considered repellent here, the 'wall-devouring' oregano, measured by the height of a dog pissing. There is also a tender intimacy in these lines which name and particularize, a quality of attention in Longley's writing Heaney described as 'the intent, close-up numbering and savouring of each tiny identifying mark, the cherishing and lingering name laid upon the thing itself'.[13]

Longley's poetic homage to Clare, 'Journey out of Essex', centres around an act of naming:

> I dissolve in a puddle,
> My biographies of birds
> And the names of flowers[14]

In these lines and elsewhere, Longley associates 'the names of flowers' with Clare, and this attention to the act of naming is a characteristic of Clare's writing previously noted by Edward Thomas, another sponsoring presence in Longley's poetry:

> To enumerate the flowers was a pleasure to him [Clare], and he did so in a manner which preserves them still dewy, or with summer dust, perhaps, on 'an antique mullein's flannel-leaves'.[15]

Thomas's words themselves echo Arthur Symons's terms of praise: writing in the introduction to his own early edition of Clare's poems, Symons explained how Clare, 'enumerates, which means a friendly knowledge'. That word 'friendly' marks an important distinction: Clare's is not a forensic particularity, but a tender and companionable form of attention. Later, Symons notes, Clare 'enumerates'; he will 'count over aspects, one by one, as upon his fingers, saying them over because he loves them, not one more than another'.[16] The phrase 'counting on his fingers' senses the intimate, tactile quality of Clare's observation.

Clare's attention to the natural world, including those creatures and plants not usually celebrated in poetry, has inspired poets from Edmund Blunden reading Clare in the trenches, to Hughes and more recent poets including Longley, Farley, Morley, Armitage, John Burnside, Seán Hewitt, Kathleen Jamie, and Alice Oswald. In 'The Bounty', Derek Walcott remembers Clare's compassion for the tiniest creature, a poet who 'wept for a beetle's loss, for the weight / of the world in a bead of dew on clematis or vetch'.[17] Jamie praises Clare for being above all a noticer, a poet who, as she puts it in a 2005 interview, *attends*.[18]

Clare's attention to sound has inspired Oswald's own poetry. In her sonnet 'Wood Not Yet Out', for instance:

> I love
> to stand among the last trees listening down
> to the releasing branches where I've been –
> the rain, thinking I've gone, crackles the air
> and calls by name the leaves that aren't yet there[19]

Here, the cadence and rhythm of 'I love / to stand among the last trees listening down' sounds Clarean: Clare has at least forty-six poems which begin 'I love', including 'I love to hear the evening crows go by', 'I love to hear the nightingale', and 'I love to hear the uproar of the wind'. Clare loved to listen, and many of his poems record his pleasure in the act of listening:

> I love it well oercanopied in leaves
> Of crowding woods to spend a quiet hour
> & where the wood bine weaves
> To list the summer shower
>
> (MP III 425, ll. 1–4)

In these lines, Clare locates the speaking 'I' in space and time, in a sheltered bower, 'where the woodbine weaves', during a 'quiet hour'. Using this particular form of the verb *list*, a transitive form of the verb *listen* without the article, creates the impression of an intransitive verb, and a feeling of reverie, so that the act of listening is abstracted.

One of the most distinctive things about Clare's listening is the way it imagines and responds to other forms of listening: his awareness that when we listen to the birds, they are listening back. Like Clare, Oswald often extends her ear and her imagination beyond the human perspective. In a 2012 *Guardian* interview, she explains: 'I exert incredible amounts of energy in trying to see things from their own point of view rather than the human point of view.'[20] This quality of auditory empathy is an aspect of the ecological imagination at play. But it was not only to the natural world that Clare listened; he also tuned in to the voices, cadence, and rhythm of poets before him.

Clare and the Poets: Influence and Allusion

When Heaney declared that Clare was at his best when being authentic, speaking in his own regional voice, a 'monoglot' genius who tried out 'poet speak', didn't like it, and instead 'dug in his local heels', he was, perhaps unknowingly, echoing Clare's first editor, John Taylor. Introducing *Poems Descriptive*, Taylor remarked that Clare 'has a great delight in trying to run races with other men, and unluckily this cannot always be attempted without subjecting him to the charge of imitating; but he will be found free from this imputation in all the best parts of his poetry'.[21] And yet Clare troubles the notion of a singular authentic voice, not only because he wrote in and between so many voices, from Burns, Byron, and Cowper to a tiny clock-a-clay (or ladybird) hidden in a cowslip during a storm, but also because the very idea of an 'authentic voice' outside the world of influence is questionable. Clare may have had distinctive cadences, but these were developed in conversation with and response to his wide reading and also to the poetry he heard. Brought up in an oral culture, Clare was used to songs and ballads being passed on and modified through the generations; his communal experience of oral poetry resists the idea of an individual original voice, and this is something which inflects the way he draws on and transforms other forms of poetry in his own writing.

Not only is the idea of an authentic voice problematic, and especially so for Clare, but to separate the vernacular from the literary, the local from the poetic, is an artificial distinction. As Taylor himself pointed out, many of Clare's 'provincial expressions' could also be found in the works of 'our earliest authors' as well as floating 'on the popular voice', 'part of a large number which may be called the unwritten language of England'. They were once, he explains, 'perhaps, as current throughout the land'.[22] Reading through Keats's copy of Chaucer, lent to him by Taylor, Clare was 'astonied' (astonished) to find words that 'are very common now in what is called the mouths of the vulgar' (*Letters*, p. 547). We are reminded that 'vulgar' language could also be literary and was used by early writers. The linguist Barbara Strang also observed this in an essay on Clare's language, explaining that words such as '*Arrivance, pismire* and *puddock* ... are common to

Shakespeare and to later Northamptonshire dialect'. She emphasizes that Clare is not, however, a dialect poet, and that dialect words are 'By far the smallest group [of words]' in his poetry.[23] When he uses dialect, it can be startling and artful; more often, and just as artfully, he draws on the literary word-hoard.

Clare was widely read: his extant library, much of which is still housed in its original oak bookcase in Northampton Central Library, contains over 400 works, and this doesn't account for all the books he borrowed, nor for those he was forced to sell, nor for the journals and newspapers he read, which were full of poetry. In his writing, Clare often gives a distinctive accent and inflection to literary language. A number of critics (including myself, John Goodridge, Adam Rounce, and James McKusick) have challenged the view that Clare is at his best when he breaks from the constraints of literary tradition and writes in his own voice, celebrating instead his deft and artful allusions and transformations of literary modes and models.

In the third of his 'Natural History Letters', Clare offers a 'list of favourite Poems & Poets who went to nature for their images', which reveals the range of his poetic reading:

> Chaucer is one Passages in Spencer Cowleys grasshopper & Swallow Passages in Shakspear Miltons Allegro & Penseroso & Parts of Comus the Elizabethian Poets of glorious memory Gays Shepherds week Greens Spleen Thompsons Seasons Collins Ode to Evening Dyers Grongar hill & Fleece Shenstones Schoolmistress Greys Ode to Spring T. Wartons April Summer Hamlet & Ode to a friend Cowpers Task Wordsworth Logans Ode to the Cuckoo Langhorns Fables of Flora Jagos Blackbirds Bloomfields Witchwood Forest Shooters hill &c with Hurdis's Evening Walk in the village Curate & many others that may have slipt my memory
>
> (*Natural History*, pp. 39–40)

These authors and many more inspired Clare's poetry. Sometimes, the use of familiar vernacular appealed, or the rhythms of popular songs and ballads, but he also called artfully on the polished, Latinate idiom and formal cadences of eighteenth-century landscape poetry and a wide range of literary forms, including Spenserian Stanza, *ottava rima*, rhyming couplets, ballad stanzas, rhyming tetrameter, and different kinds of sonnet. Generically, much of his writing is descriptive, pastoral, and lyric, but he could also write satire (*The Parish*), romance, and elegy. Throughout his poetry, he skilfully crafted borrowed languages and modes into startling new forms of expression and feeling.

Clare is an artfully allusive poet, transplanting words from his favourite authors and giving them new life and resonance. For example, in an early poem, 'Evening', he calls on these lines from Collins's 'Ode to Evening' (1746):

> Now air is hushed, save where the weak-eyed bat
> With short shrill shriek flits by on leathern wing,
> Or where the beetle winds
> His small but sullen horn,
> As oft he rises midst the twilight path,
> Against the pilgrim borne in heedless hum;[24]

Clare tunes his own listening against the sound of Collins's beetle in a journal entry for 27 January 1825, explaining that he'd 'heard the buzz of the black beetle or cockchaffer that flyes about in the autumn evenings & early in spring', and that 'it is different to the brown or summer beetle which is described by Collins', which 'winds / His small but *sullen* horn'. Clare italicizes '*sullen*', drawing attention to the difference between the sound of the cockchafer he hears and Collins's beetle (*Natural History*, p. 219). The word 'sullen' conveyed gloom and was connected with a sense of melancholy, 'Of a sound or an object producing a sound: Of a deep, dull, or mournful tone. Chiefly *poetic*' (*Oxford English Dictionary*, 3b). But when Clare was writing, it also carried the sense now obsolete, 'Of animals and inanimate things: Obstinate, refractory; stubborn, unyielding' (*Oxford English Dictionary*, 1b).

In his own poem 'Evening', Clare transforms one kind of 'sullen' music to another, from the decorous and mournful tones of Collin's beetle to something more stubborn and disruptive:

> Now buzzing with unwelcome din
> The heedles beetle bangs
> Agen the cowboys dinner tin
> That oer his shoulder hangs
> & on he keeps in heedless pat
> Till quite enrag'd the boy
> Pulls off his weather-beaten hat
> Resolving to destroy   (EP 1 388, ll. 5–12)

Clare's beetle is 'heedles' (i.e., 'heedless'); it 'bangs' against the tin, producing a percussion out of accident, in contrast to the more solemn music of Collins's beetle with its 'sullen horn'. And yet, translating this 'sullen' music into another key, Clare is also responding to and amplifying a quality he hears in 'Ode to Evening'. Clare's word 'heedles' is itself borrowed from Collins, who describes the beetle's 'heedless hum'; doing so, he suggests that the beetle is inattentive to its surroundings and indecorous. Clare is tuning in to the irregular music of Collins's 'Ode', which he amplifies and transposes to a new, demotic key. In Collins's lines, the sound of the bat, 'with short shrill shriek', creates a frisson of disorder and surprise, disrupting the poem's established metrical pattern with its four stresses in a row. Reading Collins in conversation with Clare, we hear both poets afresh.

Another eighteenth-century poet who inspired Clare was William Cowper. In 'Lines on Cowper', Clare celebrates the domestic, familiar muse of *The Task*:

> Cowper the Poet of the field
>   Who found the muse on common ground
> The homesteads that each Cottage shields
>   He loved and made them Classic ground
>
> (LP II 871, ll. 1–4)

Clare admired Cowper's informality of style and delighted in the sense of intimacy evoked in *The Task*; his sonnet 'Winter Fields' conveys something of these qualities:

> O for a pleasant book to cheat the sway
> Of winter – where rich mirth with hearty laugh
> Listens & rubs his legs on corner seat
> For fields are mire & sludge – & badly off
> Are those who on their pudgy paths delay
> There striding shepherd seeking driest way
> Fearing nights wetshod feet & hacking cough
> That keeps him waken till the peep of day
> Goes shouldering onward & with ready hook
> Progs oft to ford the sloughs that nearly meet
> Accross the lands – croodling & thin to view
> His loath dog follows – stops & quakes & looks
> For better roads – till whistled to pursue
> Then on with frequent jump he hirkles through
>
> (MP IV 341–2, ll. 1–14)

Cowper's influence can be felt in the conversational cadences and homely details of these lines, but Clare adds his own accent and inflections, using dialect terms such as 'progs' (to 'prod, poke, stir up'), 'croodling' (to 'crouch, shrink from the cold'), or 'hirkles' ('to crouch down against cold winds'). Casting his poem in more diminutive, cosy form, as a rhyming sonnet, he offers a vignette or miniature glimpse of the world of Cowper's *Task*, with its experiences of snug intimacy set in a long blank verse poem.

When we read Clare among the poets, it both allows us to hear what is distinctive in his writing and invites us to listen afresh to the poets he calls into conversation, reconfiguring both our sense of Clare's place in literary tradition, and of the tradition itself. For instance, the poem about a mouse's nest, which Heaney celebrates as an example of Clare's vernacular excellence, was surely informed by Clare's familiarity with Burns's famous poem of encounter between man and mouse, 'To a Mouse'. Both poems are enriched if we read them in conversation. Where Burns turns the occasion into a meditation on human and animal consciousness and the relationship between them, Clare offers a drama of perception, celebrating the beauty of what appears to be 'grotesque': a mouse crawling with her young 'hanging at her teats' and the cesspool / sexpool, the grimy puddle which 'glittered in the sun' (MP v 246, l. 6; l. 14).

James Thomson was another favourite: reading and imitating *The Seasons* was part of Clare's apprenticeship as a young poet. However, John Barrell argues that Clare was at his best when he moved away from Thomson's early example and offered something more distinctive, 'because he decided that Thomson's descriptive procedures could not be used to represent his own sense of place, his own consciousness, and the mutually constitutive relations of the two'.[25] Barrell contrasts Thomson's formality and abstraction with Clare's intimate particularity. And yet this claim doesn't do justice to Thomson's range and art, nor to the extent of his influence on Clare. Reading Thomson alongside and through Clare offers a fresh perspective; we see different features of Thomson's writing emerge. Throughout *The Seasons*, Thomson shifts scale, between the movement of a tiny wasp in flight and the planets and the 'empire of the sky'. But he also pays close attention to the tiniest particulars of texture and colour of the natural world, picking out details like the 'velvet Leaves' or 'yellow Wall-Flower, stain'd with iron Brown' ('Spring'). There is a delicacy and precision in these attentions to textures and surfaces which appealed to Clare, and which belie attempts to distinguish between an abstract and distant poet of the prospect view.

Clare found in *The Seasons* numerous examples of close, particular attention; Thomson described not only wide vistas and distant prospects but also textures and sounds – the pattering and dimpling of rain on water in these lines from 'Spring', for instance:

> The clouds consign their treasures to the fields;
> And, softly shaking on the dimpled pool
> Prelusive drops, let all their moisture flow,
> In large effusion, o'er the freshened world.
> The stealing shower is scarce to patter heard,
> By such as wander through the forest walks,
> Beneath the umbrageous multitude of leaves.
>
> ('Spring', *The Seasons*, ll. 172–8)

The formality of Thomson's Latinate idiom and syntax here is distinct from Clare's characteristic vernacular ease. However, the delicate precision of attention in *The Seasons* is something we recognize in Clare's poetry. For example, he draws on Thomson's image of water drops shaking onto water and dimpling its surface in an early poem, 'Summer Morning':

> Brisk winds the Lightend Branches shake
> By pattering plashing drops confest
> & where oaks dripping shade the lake
> Prints crimpling dimples on its breast
>
> (EP I 554, ll. 117–20)

Clare's alliteration suggests the sound of the water drops in the row of repeated *p* sounds in *pattering plashing drops*, picked up in *dripping* in the next line and then again in *Prints crimpling dimples*, creating an image of and in sound, so that the alliteration enacts and describes the sound pattern at once. Clare is picking up and amplifying a sound effect in Thomson's lines, where the alliteration of the *p* sound from 'dimpled' carries into 'Prelusive drops' and later into 'patter'.

Reading Clare alongside *The Seasons*, we see how Clare's attention to the way things move and change draws on Thomson's interest in process and movement. In another early poem, 'Recollections after a Ramble', Clare focuses again on the pattern of raindrops forming on the water surface:

> Rain drops how they dimpt the brook
> Falling fast & faster still
> While the gudgeons sturting bye
> Cringd neath water grasses shade
> Startling as each nimble eye
> Saw the rings the dropples made   (EP II 192, ll. 147–52)

In these lines, Clare captures the drama of perception: the fish is startled by the water pattering and patterning the water's surface. What's distinctive and surprising here is the perspective: Clare is describing water rings forming from below the water's surface, from a fish's perspective; the patterns appear as a gudgeon sees them, looking up from the bottom of the brook. Doing so, Clare draws on a feature of Thomson's attention and does something fresh and unexpected.

Clare also admired Thomson's sensitivity to the sounds of the natural world, revealed in these lines from 'Winter' (1726), for example:

> Then list'ning Hares forsake the rustling Woods
> And, starting at the frequent Noise, escape
> To the rough Stubble, and the rushy Fen.   ('Winter', ll. 23–5)

Not only does he describe the rustling, he describes it from the perspective of the 'list'ning Hares'. This attention to how animals perceive the world around them is something we also find in Clare's poetry. In 'Summer', for instance, it is not 'list'ning Hares' but the 'listning foxes' that leave their 'startld lare' at the sound of the 'woodman's axe' (MP II 299, l. 7); in 'Childhood', 'the chaffinch in the hedgerow thorn / Cries "pink pink pink" to hear / My footsteps' (MP III 247, ll. 333–5). In 'The Nightingale's Nest', it's not only the nervous bird that hears humans trampling near its nest: the forest itself seems enraptured by the sound of the nightingale; the trees have 'listening leaves' (MP III 460, ll. 72–5). Reading *The Seasons* through Clare's eyes and ears reminds us of particular aspects of Thomson's poetry which have been overlooked. Seeing Clare alongside Thomson, and among other poets he read and admired, not only reveals what is distinctive about his poetry but also what it has in common with these writers. Doing so both enriches our sense of Clare and offers new perspectives on other poets.

In early March 1820, Clare visited Westminster Abbey; it was, by the early nineteenth century, a national literary pantheon, containing monuments to Shakespeare, Milton, Gray, Johnson, and Thomson among others. And yet for Clare, it was not only the poets commemorated in stone and published in books that he admired, but also the anonymous songs and ballads 'of two thousand years' that offered examples of true poetry, and of lasting fame: it was to these songs and ballads too that he turned for energy and inspiration, like many poets had done before him, and it was to the condition of these songs, to be among these 'melodies', that he aspired:

> What is songs eternity
> Come & see
> Melodys of earth & sky
> Here they be
> Songs once sung to adams ears
> Can it be
> – Ballads of six thousand years
> Thrive thrive
> Songs awaken with the spheres
> Alive
>
> (MP v 3–5, ll. 11–20)

Notes

1. Seamus Heaney, 'John Clare: a Bi-centenary Lecture', in Hugh Haughton, Adam Phillips, and Geoffrey Summerfield, eds., *John Clare in Context* (Cambridge: Cambridge University Press, 1994), pp. 130–47 (p. 131).

2. See Sidney Burris, *The Poetry of Resistance: Seamus Heaney and the Pastoral Tradition* (Athens: Ohio University Press, 1990), pp. 59–60, and Florian Gargaillo, 'John Clare and the Early Poems of Seamus Heaney', *Essays in Criticism*, 67.2 (2017), 175–94 (p. 175).
3. Heaney, *Wintering Out* (London: Faber & Faber, 1972), p. 29, ll. 1–16.
4. Heaney, 'John Clare: a Bi-centenary Lecture', p. 134.
5. Paulin, *The Secret Life of Poems* (London: Faber & Faber, 2011), pp. 87–93 (p. 89).
6. Paulin, 'John Clare in Babylon', in *Minotaur: Poetry and the Nation State* (London: Faber & Faber, 1992), pp. 47–55 (p. 47).
7. Tom Paulin, 'The Writing Lark', *John Clare Society Journal*, 17 (1998), 5–15 (p. 5).
8. Tom Paulin, 'The Despotism of the Eye', in Larry Sider, Diane Freeman, and Jerry Sider, eds., *Soundscape: The School of Sound Lectures 1998–2001* (London: Wallflower Press, 2003), pp. 35–48 (p. 37).
9. John Taylor, 'Introduction' to *Poems Descriptive of Rural Life and Scenery* (London: Taylor and Hessey, 1820), pp. i–xiii (p. xvi).
10. Edward Thomas, *A Literary Pilgrim in England* [1917] (Oxford: Oxford University Press, 1980), pp. 216–27 (p. 225).
11. Michael Longley, *Collected Poems* (London: Jonathan Cape, 2006), p. 93.
12. *The New Yorker*, 85 (26 October 2009), 75.
13. 'Place and Displacement: Recent Poetry from Northern Ireland', in *Finders Keepers* (London: Faber & Faber, 2002), pp. 112–33 (p. 130).
14. Longley, *Collected Poems*, p. 37, ll. 56–7.
15. Thomas, *A Literary Pilgrim*, p. 26.
16. Arthur Symons, 'Introduction' to *Poems by John Clare*, ed. Symons (London: H. Frowde, 1908), pp. 3–24 (p. 19).
17. Derek Walcott, *The Bounty* (New York: Farrar, Straus, and Giroux, 1997), p. 5.
18. Kathleen Jamie, interview with Kirsty Scott, *The Guardian* (18 June 2005), www.theguardian.com/books/2005/jun/18/featuresreviews.guardianreview15.
19. Alice Oswald, 'Wood Not Yet Out', in *Woods etc* (London: Faber & Faber, 2005), p. 9, ll. 9–14.
20. Alice Oswald, interview with Madeleine Bunting, *Guardian* (13 July 2012), www.theguardian.com/books/2012/jul/13/alice-oswald-devonshire-landscape.
21. John Taylor, 'Introduction', p. xxiv.
22. John Taylor, 'Introduction', p. xvi.
23. Barbara M. Strang, 'John Clare's Language', in *John Clare: The Rural Muse*, ed. R. K. R Thornton (Ashington: Mid Northumberland Arts Group, 1982), pp. 159–73 (p. 165; p. 162).
24. Collins, 'Ode to Evening', in *The Poems of Gray, Collins and Goldsmith*, ed. Roger Lonsdale (London: Longman, 1969), p. 464, ll. 9–14.
25. John Barrell, 'Being Is Perceiving: James Thomson and John Clare', in *Poetry, Language, Politics* (Manchester: Manchester University Press, 1988), pp. 100–36 (p. 134).

FURTHER READING

The following lists contain a selection of texts for further reading. Suggestions for editions of Clare's work, some biographies, and a more general list of critical texts are followed by specifically focused lists, intended to accompany each chapter within this volume. Where texts appear in the general and in a specific list, readers can assume that they are relevant in both general and more specific contexts.

Scholarly Editions of Clare's Poetry

John Clare: The Major Works, ed. Eric Robinson and David Powell, with an introduction by Tom Paulin (Oxford: Oxford University Press, 2004)

The Early Poems of John Clare 1804–22, ed. Eric Robinson, David Powell, and Margaret Grainger, 2 vols. (Oxford: Clarendon Press, 1989)

John Clare: Poems of the Middle Period 1822–37, ed. Eric Robinson, David Powell, and P. M. S. Dawson, 5 vols. (Oxford: Clarendon Press, 1996–2003)

The Later Poems of John Clare 1837–1864, ed. Eric Robinson, David Powell, and Margaret Grainger, 2 vols. (Oxford: Clarendon Press, 1984)

Scholarly Editions of Clare's Prose

John Clare, A Champion for the Poor: Political Verse and Prose, ed. P. M. S. Dawson, Eric Robinson, and David Powell (Ashington: MidNAG; Manchester: Carcanet, 2000)

John Clare by Himself, ed. Eric Robinson and David Powell (Ashington: MidNAG; Manchester: Carcanet, 1996)

The Letters of John Clare, ed. Mark Storey (Oxford: Clarendon Press, 1985)

The Natural History Prose Writings of John Clare, ed. Margaret Grainger (Oxford: Clarendon Press, 1983)

The Prose of John Clare, ed. J. W. Tibble and Anne Tibble (London: Routledge & Kegan Paul, 1951)

Biographies

Bate, Jonathan, *John Clare: A Life* (London: Picador, 2003)
Martin, Frederick W., *The Life of John Clare* (London: Macmillan, 1865)
Sales, Roger, *John Clare: A Literary Life* (Basingstoke: Palgrave, 2002)

Critical Works

The *John Clare Society Journal* is published annually by the John Clare Society and represents an excellent range of critical and creative approaches to Clare. An index of volumes 1–41 (1982–2022) is available at https://johnclaresociety.files.wordpress.com/2022/06/jcsj-cumulative-index-2022.pdf.

Beyond this resource, a list of some of the most important works on Clare might include the following:

Barrell, John, *The Idea of Landscape and the Sense of Place 1730–1840: An Approach to the Poetry of John Clare* (Cambridge: Cambridge University Press, 1972)
Brownlow, Timothy, *John Clare and Picturesque Landscape* (Oxford: Clarendon Press, 1983)
Chilcott, Tim, *A Real World and a Doubting Mind: A Critical Study of the Poetry of John Clare* (Pickering: Hull University Press, 1985)
Chirico, Paul, *John Clare and the Imagination of the Reader* (Basingstoke: Palgrave Macmillan, 2007)
Clare, Johanne, *John Clare and the Bounds of Circumstance* (Kingston: McGill–Queen's University Press, 1987)
Crossan, Greg, *A Relish for Eternity: The Process of Divinisation in the Poetry of John Clare* (Salzburg: Institut für Englische Sprache und Literatur, University of Salzburg, 1976)
Deacon, George, *John Clare and the Folk Tradition* (London: Sinclair Browne, 1983)
Goodridge, John, *John Clare and Community* (Cambridge: Cambridge University Press, 2012)
Goodridge, John, ed., *The Independent Spirit: John Clare and the Self-Taught Tradition* (Helpston: John Clare Society and the Margaret Grainger Memorial Trust, 1994)
Goodridge, John, and Simon Kövesi, eds., *John Clare: New Approaches* (Helpston: John Clare Society, 2000)
Gorji, Mina, *John Clare and the Place of Poetry* (Liverpool: Liverpool University Press, 2008)
Guyer, Sara, *Reading with John Clare: Biopoetics, Sovereignty, Romanticism* (New York: Fordham University Press, 2015)
Haughton, Hugh, Adam Phillips, and Geoffrey Summerfield, eds., *John Clare in Context* (Cambridge: Cambridge University Press, 1994)
Houghton-Walker, Sarah, *John Clare's Religion* (Farnham: Ashgate, 2009)
Kövesi, Simon, *John Clare: Nature, Criticism and History* (London: Palgrave Macmillan, 2017)
Kövesi, Simon, and Erin Lafford, eds., *Palgrave Advances in John Clare Studies* (Cham: Palgrave Macmillan, 2020)

Kövesi, Simon, and Scott McEathron, eds., *New Essays on John Clare: Poetry, Culture and Community* (Cambridge: Cambridge University Press, 2015)

Martin, Philip, 'Authorial Identity and the Critical Act: John Clare and Lord Byron', in John Beer, ed., *Questioning Romanticism* (Baltimore: Johns Hopkins University Press, 1995), pp. 71–91

Storey, Mark, *Clare: The Critical Heritage* (London: Routledge & Kegan Paul, 1973)

Storey, Mark, *The Poetry of John Clare: A Critical Introduction* (London: Macmillan, 1974)

Strang, Barbara, 'John Clare's Language', in John Clare, *The Rural Muse*, ed. R. K. R. Thornton (Ashington: MidNAG, 1982)

Taylor, John, 'Introduction', in John Clare, *Poems Descriptive of Rural Life and Scenery* (London: Taylor and Hessey, 1820), pp. i–xiii.

Vardy, Alan, *John Clare, Politics and Poetry* (Basingstoke: Palgrave Macmillan, 2003)

Weiner, Stephanie Kuduk, *Clare's Lyric: John Clare and Three Modern Poets* (Oxford: Oxford University Press, 2014)

White, Adam, *John Clare's Romanticism* (Cham: Palgrave Macmillan, 2017)

Works Related to Specific Chapters within This Volume

Chapter 1: On Clare and Lyric Song

Cronin, Richard, 'John Clare and the *London Magazine*', in Simon Kövesi and Scott McEathron, eds., *New Essays on John Clare: Poetry, Culture and Community* (Cambridge: Cambridge University Press, 2015), pp. 209–27

Deacon, George, *John Clare and the Folk Tradition* (London: S. Browne, 1983)

Gorji, Mina, *John Clare and the Place of Poetry* (Liverpool: Liverpool University Press, 2008)

Helsinger, Elizabeth, 'Poem into Song', *New Literary History*, 46 (2015), 669–90

McAlpine, Erica, 'Keeping Nature at Bay: John Clare's Poetry of Wonder', *Studies in Romanticism*, 50.1 (2011), 79–104

Weiner, Stephanie Kuduk, *Clare's Lyric: John Clare and Three Modern Poets* (Oxford: Oxford University Press, 2014)

Weiner, Stephanie Kuduk, '"Sea Songs Love Ballads &c &c &c": John Clare and Vernacular Song', in Simon Kövesi and Erin Lafford, eds., *Palgrave Advances in John Clare Studies* (Cham: Palgrave Macmillan, 2020), pp.61–85

Chapter 2: Clare's Forms

Cronin, Richard, 'In Place and Out of Place: Clare in *The Midsummer Cushion*', in John Goodridge and Simon Kövesi, eds., *John Clare: New Approaches* (Peterborough: John Clare Society, 2000), pp. 133–48

Gorji, Mina, 'Clare's Awkwardness', *Essays in Criticism*, 54.3 (2004), 216–39

Gorji, Mina, *John Clare and the Place of Poetry* (Liverpool: Liverpool University Press, 2008)
Heaney, Seamus, 'John Clare: A Bi-centenary Lecture', in Hugh Haughton, Adam Phillips, and Geoffrey Summerfield, eds., *John Clare in Context* (Cambridge: Cambridge University Press, 1994), pp. 130–47
Haughton, Hugh, 'Progress and Rhyme: "The Nightingale's Nest" and Romantic Poetry', in Hugh Haughton, Adam Phillips, and Geoffrey Summerfield, eds., *John Clare in Context* (Cambridge: Cambridge University Press, 1994), pp. 51–86
Hodgson, Andrew, 'Clare's Late Styles', in Norbert Lennartz, ed., *The Lost Romantics: Forgotten Poets, Neglected Works, and One-Hit Wonders* (Cham: Palgrave Macmillan, 2020), pp. 151–68
Hodgson, Andrew, 'John Clare's Ear: Metres and Rhythms', in Erin Lafford and Simon Kövesi, eds., *Palgrave Advances in John Clare Studies* (Cham: Palgrave Macmillan, 2020), pp. 111–36
Lodge, Sara, 'John Clare's Landforms', in Erin Lafford and Simon Kövesi, eds., *Palgrave Advances in John Clare Studies* (Cham: Palgrave Macmillan, 2020), pp. 87–110
Stafford, Fiona, 'John Clare's Colours', in Simon Kövesi and Scott McEathron, eds., *New Essays on John Clare* (Cambridge: Cambridge University Press, 2015), pp. 17–37
Storey, Mark. *The Problem of Poetry in the Romantic Period* (Basingstoke: Macmillan, 2002)

Chapter 3: On Clare's Translation of Perception to Poetry

Bate, Jonathan, *The Song of the Earth* (London: Picador, 2000)
Falke, Cassandra, 'Thinking with Birds: John Clare and the Phenomenology of Perception', *Romanticism*, 2.26 (2020), 180–90
Houghton-Walker, Sarah, 'Forms of Repetition in "The Robins Nest"', *Romanticism*, 2.26 (2020), 139–52
McAlpine, Erica, 'Keeping Nature at Bay: John Clare's Poetry of Wonder', *Studies in Romanticism*, 50.1 (2011), 79–104
McKusick, James, 'The Ecological Vision of John Clare', in *Green Writing: Romanticism and Ecology* (New York: Palgrave Macmillan, 2010), pp. 77–94

Chapter 4: Clare and the Sublime

Ashfield, Andrew and Peter de Bolla, eds., *The Sublime: A Reader in British Eighteenth-Century Aesthetic Theory* (Cambridge: Cambridge University Press, 1996)
Ferguson, Frances, *Solitude and the Sublime: The Romantic Aesthetics of Individuation* (London: Routledge, 1992)
Houghton, Sarah, '"Enkindling Ecstacy": The Sublime Vision of John Clare', *Romanticism*, 9.2 (2003), 176–95
Ness, Richard M., 'Song of Experience: John Clare's Empirical Taste', *John Clare Society Journal*, 38 (2019), 13–31

Storey, Mark, 'Clare and the Critics', in John Goodridge and Simon Kövesi, eds., *John Clare: New Approaches* (Helpston: John Clare Society, 1994), pp. 28–50

Strickland, Edward, 'John Clare and the Sublime', *Criticism*, 29 (1987), 141–61

Chapter 5: Clare and Animals

Albernaz, Joseph, 'John Clare's World', *European Romantic Review*, 27 (2016), 189–205

Bate, Jonathan, *The Song of the Earth* (London: Picador, 2000)

Barton, Anne, 'Clare's Animals: The Wild and the Tame', *John Clare Society Journal*, 18 (1999), 5–21

Bewell, Alan, 'John Clare and the Ghosts of Natures Past', *Nineteenth-Century Literature*, 65 (2011), 548–78

Castell, James, 'John Clare's Dynamic Animals', in Simon Kövesi and Erin Lafford, eds., *Palgrave Advances in John Clare Studies* (Cham: Palgrave Macmillan, 2020), pp. 157–77

Castellano, Katey, 'Moles, Molehills, and Common Right in John Clare's Poetry', *Studies in Romanticism*, 56 (2017), 157–76

Castellano, Katey, 'Multispecies Work in John Clare's "Birds Nesting" Poems', in Simon Kövesi and Erin Lafford, eds., *Palgrave Advances in John Clare Studies* (Cham: Palgrave Macmillan, 2020), pp. 179–97

Falke, Cassandra, 'Thinking with Birds: John Clare and the Phenomenology of Perception', *Romanticism*, (2020), 180–90

Kövesi, Simon, *John Clare: Nature, Criticism and History* (New York: Palgrave Macmillan, 2017)

Mackenney, Francesca, 'John Clare: Undersong', *Romanticism*, 26 (2020), 168–79

McAlpine, Erica, 'Keeping Nature at Bay: John Clare's Poetry of Wonder', *Studies in Romanticism*, 50 (2011), 79–104

McKusick, James C., *Green Writing: Romanticism and Ecology* (Basingstoke: Macmillan, 2000)

Miller, Eric, 'Enclosure and Taxonomy in John Clare', *Studies in English Literature, 1500–1900*, 40 (2000), 635–57

Morton, Timothy, 'John Clare's Dark Ecology', *Studies in Romanticism*, 47 (2008), 179–93

Nicholson, Michael, 'Unheard Swarms: John Clare and Romantic Entomology', *The Wordsworth Circle*, 51 (2020), 338–59

Oerlemans, Onno, *Poetry and Animals: Blurring the Boundaries with the Human* (New York: Columbia University Press, 2018)

Perkins, David, *Romanticism and Animal Rights* (Cambridge: Cambridge University Press, 2003)

Rowney, Matthew, 'Music in the Noise: The Acoustic Ecology of John Clare', *Journal of Interdisciplinary Voice Studies*, 1 (2016), 23–40

Thomas, Keith, *Man and the Natural World: Changing Attitudes in England, 1500–1800* (London: Penguin, 1984)

Washington, Chris, 'John Clare and Biopolitics', *European Romantic Review*, 25 (2014), 665–82

FURTHER READING

Chapter 6: John Clare's Plants

Bate, Jonathan, *Romantic Ecology* (London: Routledge, 1991)
Bate, Jonathan, *The Song of the Earth* (London: Picador, 2000)
Grigson, Geoffrey, *The Englishman's Flora*, new ed. (Oxford: Helicon, 1996)
Hess, Scott, 'Biosemiosis and Posthumanism in John Clare's Multi-Centred Environments', in Simon Kövesi and Erin Lafford, eds., *Palgrave Advances in John Clare Studies* (Cham: Palgrave Macmillan, 2020), pp. 199–220
Heyes, Robert, 'John Clare's Natural History', in Simon Kövesi and Scott McEathron, eds., *New Essays on John Clare: Poetry, Culture and Community* (Cambridge: Cambridge University Press, 2015), pp. 169–88
Mabey, Richard, *Flora Britannica* (London: Sinclair-Stevenson, 1996)
Mabey, Richard, 'Foreword', to M. M. Mahood, *A John Clare Flora* (Nottingham: Trent Editions, 2016), pp. xv–xvi
Mabey, Richard, 'Guest Editorial: Clare and Ecology', *John Clare Society Journal*, 14 (1995), 5–6
Mabey, Richard, *The Cabaret of Plants: Botany and the Imagination* (London: Profile, 2015)
Mahood, M. M., *A John Clare Flora* (Nottingham: Trent Editions, 2016)
Mahood, M. M., *The Poet as Botanist* (Cambridge: Cambridge University Press, 2008)
McKusick, James, *Green Writing: Romanticism and Ecology* (New York: St Martin's Press, 2000)
Phillips, Bill, 'When Ploughs Destroy'd the Green', *John Clare Society Journal*, 21 (2002), 53–62
Reno, Seth, 'John Clare and Ecological Love', *John Clare Society Journal*, 35 (2016), 59–76
Stafford, Fiona, *The Long, Long Life of Trees* (New Haven, CT: Yale University Press, 2016)
Stafford, Fiona, *The Brief Life of Flowers* (London: John Murray, 2018)

Chapter 7: John Clare and the Community of Naturalists

Bellanca, Mary Ellen, *Daybooks of Discovery: Nature Diaries in Britain, 1770–1870* (Charlottesville: University of Virginia Press, 2007)
Brownlow, Timothy, *John Clare and Picturesque Landscape* (Oxford: Clarendon Press, 1983)
Cash, James, *Where There's a Will There's a Way! Or, Science in the Cottage: An Account of the Labours of Naturalists in Humble Life* (first pub. London, Robert Hardwicke, 1873; new ed. Cambridge: Cambridge University Press, 2011)
Curry, Helen Anne, Nicholas Jardine, James Andrew Secord, and Emma C. Spary, eds., *Worlds of Natural History* (Cambridge: Cambridge University Press, 2018)
Jardine, Nicholas, James Andrew Secord, and Emma C. Spary, eds., *Cultures of Natural History* (Cambridge: Cambridge University Press, 1996)
Klonk, Charlotte, *Science and the Perception of Nature: British Landscape Art in the Late Eighteenth and Early Nineteenth Centuries* (New Haven, CT: Yale University Press, 1996)

MacGregor, Arthur, ed., *Naturalists in the Field: Collecting, Recording and Preserving the Natural World from the Fifteenth to the Twenty-First Century* (Leiden: Brill, 2018)
Mahood, M. M., *A John Clare Flora* (Nottingham: Trent Editions, 2016)
Mahood, M. M., *The Poet as Botanist* (Cambridge: Cambridge University Press, 2008)
Thomas, Keith, *Man and the Natural World: Changing Attitudes in England 1500–1800* (London: Allen Lane, 1983)

Chapter 8: Clare and Ecocriticism

Clark, Timothy, *The Value of Ecocriticism* (Cambridge: Cambridge University Press, 2019)
Davies, Jeremy, 'Romantic Ecocriticism: History and Prospects', *Literature Compass*, 15.9 (2018), 1–15
Garrard, Greg, *Ecocriticism*, 2nd ed. (London: Routledge, 2012)
Kövesi, Simon, *John Clare: Nature, Criticism and History* (London: Palgrave Macmillan, 2017)
Morton, Timothy, 'John Clare's Dark Ecology', *Studies in Romanticism*, 47.2 (2008), 179–93
Morton, Timothy, *The Ecological Thought* (Cambridge, MA: Harvard University Press, 2010)
Poetzsch, Markus, 'Plumbing the Depths of Wildness: From the Picturesque to John Clare', in Markus Poetzsch and Cassandra Falke, eds., *Wild Romanticism* (Abingdon: Routledge, 2021), pp. 43–58

Chapter 9: Self-Identity in a World of Influence

Barrell, John, *The Idea of Landscape and the Sense of Place 1730–1840: An Approach to the Poetry of John Clare* (Cambridge: Cambridge University Press, 1972)
Bate, Jonathan, *John Clare: A Biography* (London: Picador, 2003)
Chilcott, Tim, *A Publisher and His Circle: The Life and Work of John Taylor, Keats's Publisher* (London: Routledge & Kegan Paul, 1972)
Chilcott, Tim, *'A Real World & Doubting Mind': A Critical Study of the Poetry of John Clare* (Hull: Hull University Press, 1985)
Chirico, Paul, *John Clare and the Imagination of the Reader* (Basingstoke: Palgrave Macmillan, 2007)
Deacon, George, *John Clare and the Folk Tradition* (London: Sinclair Browne, 1983; repr. London: Francis Boutle, 2002)
Goodridge, John, *John Clare and Community* (Cambridge: Cambridge University Press, 2013)
Houghton-Walker, Sarah, 'John Clare's *The Shepherd's Calendar* and Forms of Repetition', in Simon Kövesi and Erin Lafford, eds., *Palgrave Advances in John Clare Studies* (Cham: Palgrave Macmillan, 2020), pp. 137–156

Kövesi, Simon, *John Clare: Nature, Criticism and History* (London: Palgrave Macmillan, 2017)
Kövesi, Simon and Scott McEathron, eds., *New Essays on John Clare: Poetry, Culture and Community* (Cambridge: Cambridge University Press, 2015)
Sales, Roger, *John Clare: A Literary Life* (Basingstoke: Palgrave Macmillan, 2002)
Storey, Edward, *A Right to Song: The Life of John Clare* (London: Methuen, 1982)
Storey, Mark, *The Poetry of John Clare: A Critical Introduction* (London: Macmillan, 1974)
Tibble, J. W. and Anne Tibble, *John Clare: A Life*, rev. ed. (London: Michael Joseph, 1972)
White, Adam, *John Clare's Romanticism* (London: Palgrave Macmillan, 2017)

Chapter 10: 'Leading Strings': Editing and Revision in Clare's Poetry

Chilcott, Tim, *A Publisher and His Circle: The Life and Work of John Taylor, Keats's Publisher* (London: Routledge and Kegan Paul, 1972)
John Clare: The Rural Muse, ed. R. K. R. Thornton (Ashington: MidNAG and Carcanet, 1982)
John Clare: The Shepherd's Calendar, ed. Tim Chilcott (Manchester: Carcanet, 2006)
John Clare: The Living Year 1841, ed. Tim Chilcott (Nottingham: Trent Editions, 1999)
Houghton-Walker, Sarah, 'John Clare's *The Shepherd's Calendar* and Forms of Repetition', in Simon Kövesi and Erin Lafford, eds., *Palgrave Advances in John Clare Studies* (Cham: Palgrave Macmillan, 2020), pp. 137–56
Leader, Zachary, *Revision and Romantic Authorship* (Oxford: Oxford University Press, 1996)
Pearce, Lynne 'John Clare's *Child Harold*: a Polyphonic Reading', *Criticism*, 31 (1989), 139–57
Robinson, Eric and Geoffrey Summerfield, 'John Taylor's Editing of Clare's *The Shepherd's Calendar*', *Review of English Studies*, 14.56 (1963), 359–69
Storey, Mark, *The Problem of Poetry in the Romantic Period* (Basingstoke: Macmillan, 2000)

Chapter 11: Constructed Image: Portraits of Clare

Bates, Tom, 'On the Portrait of John Clare by Henry Behnes', *John Clare Society Journal*, 27 (2008), 45–58
Holmes, Richard, David Crane, Stephen Hebron, and Robert Woof, *Romantics & Revolutionaries: Regency Portraits from the National Portrait Gallery London* (London: National Portrait Gallery, 2002)
McEathron, Scott, 'John Clare, William Hilton, and the National Portrait Gallery', *John Clare Society Journal*, 32 (2013), 5–25

FURTHER READING

Chapter 12: Clare and Religion

Crossan, Greg, 'A Relish for Eternity': The Process of Divinization in the Poetry of John Clare (Salzburg: Universität Salzburg, 1976)
Dixon, George E., 'Clare and Religion', John Clare Society Journal, 1 (1982), 47–51
Houghton-Walker, Sarah, John Clare's Religion (Farnham: Ashgate, 2009)
Minor, Mark, 'John Clare and the Methodists: A Reconsideration', Studies in Romanticism, 19.1 (1980), 31–50
Robinson, Eric, 'Introduction' to John Clare: The Parish, A Satire (Harmondsworth: Penguin, 1985), 9–25

Chapter 13: John Clare and the British Labouring-Class Tradition

Barrell, John, The Idea of Landscape and the Sense of Place, 1730–1840: An Approach to the Poetry of John Clare (Cambridge: Cambridge University Press, 1972)
Blair, Kirstie, The Poets of the People's Journal: Newspaper Poetry in Victorian Scotland (Glasgow: Association for Scottish Literary Studies, 2016)
Boos, Florence, Working-Class Women Poets in Victorian Britain: An Anthology (Peterborough: Broadview Press, 2008)
Dohrn van-Rossum, Gerhard, History of the Hour: Clocks and Modern Temporal Orders, trans. Thomas Dunlap (Chicago: University of Chicago Press, 1996)
Glennie, Paul and Nigel Thrift, Shaping the Day: A History of Timekeeping in England and Wales 1300–1800 (Oxford: Oxford University Press, 2009)
Goodridge, John, John Clare and Community (Cambridge: Cambridge University Press 2013)
Goodridge, John, ed., A Catalogue of British and Irish Labouring-Class and Self-Taught Poets c. 1700–1900, https://hcommons.org/deposits/item/hc:38629/
The Works of Mary Leapor, ed. Richard Greene and Ann Messenger (Oxford: Oxford University Press, 2003)
Keegan, Bridget, 'Cobbling Verse: Shoemaker Poets of the Long Eighteenth Century', The Eighteenth Century, 42.3 (2001), 195–217
Keegan, Bridget, 'The Poet as Laborer', in Jack Lynch, ed., The Oxford Handbook of British Poetry, 1660–1800 (Oxford: Oxford University Press, 2016), pp. 162–78
Martineau, Jonathan, Time, Capitalism, and Alienation: A Socio-Historical Inquiry into the Making of Modern Time (Chicago: Haymarket, 2016)
Solomon, Harry, The Rise of Robert Dodsley: Creating a New Age of Print (Carbondale: Southern Illinois University Press, 1996)
Tomalin, Marcus, '"An Invaluable Acquisition": Sandglasses in Romantic Literature', European Romantic Review, 28.6 (2017), 729–49

Chapter 14: The Politics of Nature

Barrell, John, The Idea of Landscape and the Sense of Place 1730–1840: An Approach to the Poetry of John Clare (Cambridge: Cambridge University Press, 1972)

Bate, Jonathan, *John Clare: A Life* (London: Picador, 2003)
Cronin, Richard, 'In Place and Out of Place: Clare in the Midsummer Cushion', in John Goodridge and Simon Kövesi, eds., *John Clare: New Approaches* (Peterborough: John Clare Society, 2000), pp. 133–48
Goodridge, John, *John Clare and Community* (Cambridge: Cambridge University Press, 2013)
Goodridge, John, and Bridget Keegan, eds., *A History of British Working Class Literature* (Cambridge: Cambridge University Press, 2017)
Kövesi, Simon, *John Clare: Nature, Criticism and History* (Houndmills: Palgrave Macmillan, 2017)
Kövesi, Simon and Scott McEathron, eds., *New Essays on John Clare: Poetry, Culture and Community* (Cambridge: Cambridge University Press, 2015)
Kövesi, Simon, and Erin Lafford, eds., *Palgrave Advances in John Clare Studies* (Cham: Palgrave Macmillan, 2020)
Nicholson, Michael, 'The Itinerant "I": John Clare's Lyric Defiance', *ELH*, 82 (2015), 637–69
Lodge, Sara, 'Contested Bounds: John Clare, John Keats, and the Sonnet', *Studies in Romanticism*, 51 (2012), 533–54
Swann, Karen, 'John Clare: The Sonnet "Ill at Rest"', *The Wordsworth Circle*, 52 (2021), 200–16
Swann, Karen, 'The Butter Bump, a Magpie, John Clare', *Romanticism on the Net*, 72–3 (2019), https://ronjournal.org/s/5317
Vardy, Alan, *John Clare, Politics and Poetry* (Houndmills: Palgrave, 2003)
Weiner, Stephanie Kuduk, *Clare's Lyric: John Clare and Three Modern Poets* (Oxford: Oxford University Press, 2014)
Williams, Raymond, *The Country and the City* (London: Chatto & Windus, 1973)

Chapter 15: Clare's Health

Bate, Jonathan, *John Clare: A Biography* (London: Picador, 2003)
Burwick, Frederick, *Poetic Madness and the Romantic Imagination* (University Park: Pennsylvania State University Press, 1996)
Cope, Jonas, 'Autumnal Affect in the Poetry of John Clare', *Studies in English Literature 1500–1900*, 58.4 (2018), 855–75
Gaull, Marilyn, 'Clare and "the Dark System"', in Hugh Haughton, Adam Phillips, and Geoffrey Summerfield, eds., *John Clare in Context* (Cambridge: Cambridge University Press, 1994), pp. 279–94
Golinksi, Jan, *British Weather and the Climate of Enlightenment* (Chicago: University of Chicago Press, 2007)
Keegan, Bridget, '"And All Is Nakedness and Fen": John Clare's Wetlands', in *British Labouring-Class Nature Poetry, 1730–1837* (Basingstoke: Palgrave Macmillan, 2008), pp. 148–71
Lawlor, Clark and Andrew Mangham, eds., *Literature and Medicine*, 2 vols. (Cambridge: Cambridge University Press, 2021)
Mahood, M. M., *The Poet as Botanist* (Cambridge: Cambridge University Press, 2008)

Porter, Roy, '"All Madness for Writing": John Clare and the Asylum', in Hugh Haughton, Adam Phillips, and Geoffrey Summerfield, eds., *John Clare in Context* (Cambridge: Cambridge University Press, 1994), pp. 259–78

Whitehead, James, *Madness and the Romantic Poet: A Critical History* (Oxford: Oxford University Press, 2017)

Chapter 16: Clare among the Poets

Barrell, John, 'Being Is Perceiving: James Thomson and John Clare', in his *Poetry, Language, Politics* (Manchester: Manchester University Press, 1988), pp. 100–36

Goodridge, *"John, Clare and Community"* (Cambridge: Cambridge University Press, 2013)

Gorji, Mina, *John Clare and the Place of Poetry* (Liverpool: Liverpool University Press, 2009)

Gorji, Mina, 'John Clare and the Language of Listening', *Romanticism*, 26.2 (2020), 153–67

Jamie, Kathleen, *Findings* (London: Sort of Books, 2005)

Heaney, Seamus, 'John Clare: A Bi-centenary Lecture', in Hugh Haughton, Adam Phillips, and Geoffrey Summerfield, eds., *John Clare in Context* (Cambridge: Cambridge University Press, 1994), pp. 130–47

Kövesi, Simon, 'Interview with David Morley: The Gypsy and the Poet', *John Clare Society Journal*, 32 (2013), 49–72

McKusick, James, 'Beyond the Visionary Company: John Clare's Resistance to Romanticism', in Hugh Haughton, Adam Phillips, and Geoffrey Summerfield, eds., *John Clare in Context* (Cambridge: Cambridge University Press, 1994), pp. 221–37

McKusick, James, *Green Writing: Romanticism and Ecology* (Basingstoke: Palgrave Macmillan, 2010)

Paulin, Tom, 'John Clare in Babylon', in *Minotaur: Poetry and the Nation State* (London: Faber & Faber, 1992), pp. 47–55

Paulin, Tom, *Liberty Tree* (London: Faber & Faber, 1983)

Paulin, Tom, 'Strinkling Dropples: John Clare', in *Writing to the Moment: Selected Critical Essays* (London: Faber & Faber, 1996), pp. 161–70

Paulin, Tom, 'The Writing Lark', *John Clare Society Journal*, 17 (1998), 5–15

Paulin, Tom, 'To the Snipe', in *The Secret Life of Poems* (London: Faber & Faber, 2011), pp. 87–93

Rounce, Adam, 'John Clare, William Cowper and the Eighteenth Century', in Simon Kövesi and Scott McEathron, eds., *New Essays on John Clare: Poetry, Culture and Community* (Cambridge: Cambridge University Press, 2015), pp. 38–56

Strang, Barbara, 'John Clare's Language', in John Clare, *The Rural Muse*, ed. R. K. R. Thornton (Ashington: MidNAG and Carcanet New Press, 1982), pp. 159–73

Thacker, Jack, 'The Thing in the Gap-Stone Style: Alice Oswald's Acoustic Arrangements', *The Cambridge Quarterly*, 44.2 (2015), 103–18

Weiner, Stephanie Kuduk, *Clare's Lyric: John Clare and Three Modern Poets* (Oxford: Oxford University Press, 2014)

INDEX

Africa, 113, 212
Albernaz, Joseph, 81–2, 127
All Saints' Church, Northampton, 174
Allen, Matthew, 164, 189
Anglicanism, 184, 185, 186
Aristotle, 132
Armitage, Simon, 242, 248
Artis, Edmund, 107, 108–10, 117
   Antediluvian Phytology, 109–10
   The Durobrivae of Antoninus, 110
Ashbery, John
   'For John Clare', 82
Ashfield, Andrew, 65, 66
Australia, 125

Barbauld, Anna Letitia, 184, 193
Barrell, John, 6, 86–7, 183, 196, 253
   The Idea of Landscape and the Sense of Place, 97
Barton, Anne, 87
Bate, Jonathan, 57, 99, 122, 228
Bates, Tom, 171
Bainton, 111
Behnes, Henry, 167, 170–2, 173, 179
Bentham, Jeremy, 142
Berkeley, Miles Joseph, 113
Berry, G[eorge] D[uval], 173, 179
Bible, 186, 187, 189–92
Blair Adam, 107, 110–11
Blair, Kirstie, 208
Blake, William, 183
   Songs of Innocence
      'Introduction', 28
Bloomfield, George, 199
Bloomfield, Robert, 139, 184, 197, 199, 207, 219
   'Lines, Occasioned by a Visit to Whittlebury Forest, Northamptonshire, in August, 1800', 250
   Rural Tales, 206
   'Shooter's Hill', 250
   The Farmer's Boy, 206
   'The Widow to her Hour-Glass', 207
Blunden, Edmund, 5, 248
Blythe, Ronald, 99
Boothstown Botanical Society, 113
Bosch, Hieronymus, 145
Bracton, Henry de, 142
Bristol, 116, 238
British Museum, 108–9, 111–12
British Ornithologists' Union, 110
Brotero, Félix de Avelar, 113
Brown, John, 230–1
Brown, Robert, 110
Brownlow, Timothy, 118
Brunonian system, 230
Buckland, William, 109
Buell, Lawrence, 120, 121, 124, 128
Bullock's Museum, 106
Bump, Jerome, 118
Bunyan, John, 139, 193
Burghley House, 203
Burke, Edmund, 62, 68, 70, 213
   A Philosophical Enquiry into the Origin of our Ideas of the Sublime and Beautiful, 4, 61, 63, 69
Burns, Robert, 28–9, 249
   'Address to the Tooth-Ache', 230
   'Despondency, An Ode', 103–4
   'Humble Petition of Bruar Water, to the Noble Duke of Athole', 103–4
   'Man was Made to Mourn, A Dirge', 103–4
   'To a Mouse', 253
Burnside, John, 248
Burris, Sidney, 242

INDEX

Burton, Robert
   Anatomy of Melancholy, 235–6
Byron, Lord, 7, 17, 127, 147, 164, 189, 249
   Childe Harold's Pilgrimage, 27
   'Darkness', 225
   Don Juan, 27
   The Corsair, 27

Caribbean, 212
Cary, Henry Francis, 141
Castell, James, 13
Castor, 109, 110
Catalogue of the Centenary Exhibition of Portraits, Books, Manuscripts, Letters and other Things, Belonging to or Connected with John Clare, 117
Catholicism, 184
Champollion, Jean-François, 110
Chartism, 197, 208, 209
Chaucer, Geoffrey, 249, 250
Cheyne, George
   The English Malady, 231
Chilcott, Tim, 160
Chirico, Paul, 126, 183
Christmas, William J., 197
Clare, Ann (Clare's mother), 107, 137
Clare, Charles (Clare's son), 148
Clare, Eliza Louisa (Clare's daughter), 237
Clare, Elizabeth (Bessy) (Clare's twin sister), 138
Clare, John
   poetry
      'A Rustic's Pastime, in Leisure Hours', 2
      'A Scene', 67–8
      'A Spring Day', 155
      'A Spring Morning', 155
      'A Vision', 20–1, 28, 43, 148
      'Address to Plenty in Winter', 233
      'Adventures of a Grasshopper', 88
      'An Idle Hour', 200
      'An Invite to Eternity', 43
      'Autumn' ('Syren of sullen moods & fading hues'), 43–4, 161, 162
      biblical paraphrases, 6, 150n8, 183, 184, 189, 190
         Exodus 15, 190
         Habakkuk 3, 145–6, 190
         Isaiah 47, 190
         Job 38, 190, 194
         Job 39, 190, 194
         Job 40, 190, 194
         Job 41, 184, 190, 194
         Judges 5, 6–31, 190
         Matthew 23, 190
         Matthew 25, 184, 190, 192
         Numbers 23, 21–30, 190
         Numbers 24, 190
         Psalm 19, 190
         Psalm 51, 190
         Psalm 56, 190
         Psalm 91, 184, 190, 192
         Psalm 92, 184
         Psalm 97, 190, 192
         Psalm 102, 1–17, 190
         Psalm 104, 20–26, 190
         Psalm 137, 190
         Psalm 148, 190
         Psalm 150, 190
         Revelation 21, 184, 190–1
         Revelation 22, 184, 190, 191–2
      'Birds in Alarm', 245
      'Birds Nesting', 85, 97, 118
      'Birds Nests' ('How fresh the air the birds how busy now'), 21–2, 84–5, 87
      'Birds Nests' ('Tis Spring, warm glows the South'), 84
      'Burthorpe Oak', 100
      'By Clare – to be Placed at the Back of his Portrate', 95
      Child Harold, 7, 17, 27, 34–5, 145–6, 165, 189
         'My hopes are all hopeless', 39
         'Song' ('Did I know where to meet thee'), 39–40
         'Song' ('Dying gales of sweet even'), 40
      'Childhood', 215
      'Childhood' ('The past it is a majic word'), 255
      'Clock a Clay', 249
      'Cottage Tales', 159, 160
      'Dawning of Genius', 156, 232–3
      'Death' ('Why should mans high aspiring mind'), 153
      'Death of Dobbin' ('At days mid hour when weary labour stops'), 80
      'Decay, a Ballad', 143, 163–4
      'Dolly's Mistake', 156
      Don Juan a Poem, 5, 7, 27, 145–6, 164, 189
      'Emmonsails Heath in Winter', 26
      'Enclosure', 97, 100
      enclosure elegies, 122
      'Ere I had known the world & understood', 30–1

Clare, John (cont.)
  'Evening' ('Now grey ey'd hazy eve's begun'), 252
  'False time what is it but a rogues account', 224
  'First Love', 20–1, 27, 28
  'Good & substantial painter merits raise', 176–7
  'He waits all day beside his little flock', 208–9
  'Hedge Sparrow', 32
  'Helpston Green', 95
  'Helpstone', 60, 67, 122, 139, 156–7
  'High overhead that silent throne', 50–1, 53, 54
  'I am', 7, 43, 53, 72, 147, 206
  'I found a ball of grass among the hay', 245, 253
  'I love to hear the evening crows go by', 248
  'I love to hear the uproar of the wind', 248
  'I walked with poesy in the sonnets bounds', 32
  'I wish I was a little bird', 83
  'In the hedge I pass a little nest', 48–9
  'Is nothing less than naught – nothing is naught', 147
  'Jealousy', 155
  'Labourers Soliloquy on Dead Dobbin', 80
  'Langley Bush', 100
  'Little Trotty Wagtail', 78
  'Mary' ('It is the evening hour'), 43
  'My Mary', 156
  'My Matey', 156
  'My Rover', 156
  'Noon', 6, 91–2
  'Nothingness of Life', 104
  'O' come to my arms i' the cool o' the day', 148
  'Obscurity', 70–1, 104
  'Old times forgetfull memories of the past', 70
  'On seeing two Swallows late in October', 52–3, 55
  'One day across the fields I chancd to pass'/'One day accross the fields I chancd to pass', 32–3, 47
  'One day when all the woods where bare & blea', 50
  'Pastoral Affections', 164
  'Petitioners are full of prayers', 98
  'Pewits Nest', 24
  'Pleasant Places', 66
  'Pleasures of Spring', 154–5
  Poems Descriptive of Rural Life and Scenery, 1, 4, 17, 43, 54, 77, 107, 140, 154, 155–7, 158, 168, 185, 186, 219, 232, 241
  'Recollections after a Ramble'/'Reccollections after a Ramble', 60–1, 92, 254
  'Remembrances', 143, 162–3, 214–15
  'Sabbath Bells', 207
  'Sand Martin', 21, 86, 245
  'Shadows of Taste', 65, 67, 125, 245
  'Sighing for Retirement', 3, 49, 58, 141, 151, 165
  'Solomons Prayer &c &c', 190
  'Some keep a baited badger tame as hog', 87
  'Song' ('A seaboy on the giddy mast'), 38–9
  'Song' ('The daiseys golden eye'), 41–2
  'Song Last Day', 148
  'Songs Eternity', 19–20, 29, 255
  'Sonnet, I am', 71, 147
  'Sorrows for a Favourite Tabby Cat who left this Scene of Troubles Friday Night Nov. 26 1819', 197
  'Spring (a)' ('Welcome gentle breathing Spring'), 153–4
  'Spring (b)' ('Welcome gentle breathing Spring'), 153–4
  'Spring' ('How beautiful the spring resumes its reign'), 154–5
  'Spring' ('Pale sun beams gleam'), 43
  'St Martins Eve', 158
  'Summer' ('The wood mans axe renews its hollow stroke'), 255
  'Summer Evening', 26, 77–80, 81, 82
  'Summer Images', 160–2
  'Summer Morning', 154
  'Summer Morning' ('The cocks have now the morn foretold'), 254
  'Summer Shower', 248
  'Sunday Evening', 155
  'Sweet mystery that comes to bless', 194
  'The Ants', 6
  'The Author's Address to his Book', 3
  'The Autumn Robin', 19, 21
  'The badger grunting on his woodland track', 87
  'The Blackcap', 32, 97
  'The Crab Tree', 100
  'The crowing coks the morns for told', 154

INDEX

'The Death of Dobbin' ('Old Dobbin dead . . . '), 80
'The Eagle and the Crow', 88
'The Evening Walk', 139
'The Fallen Elm', 97, 184, 192–3, 221–4, 227; *see also* 'To a Fallen Elm'
'The Fate of Genius', 208, 209
'[The Fens]', 47, 54–7, 236–7
'The fire tail tells the boys when nests are nigh', 24–5, 26, 27
'The Flitting', 53, 144, 163, 164, 221
'The Gipsies Evening Blaze', 139–40
'The Gipsy Camp', 7
'The Hail Storm in June 1831', 197
'The happy white throat on the sweeing bough', 32–3
'The Heath', 65
'The Hollow Tree', 100
'The Lament of Swordy Well', 7, 37–8, 98, 100, 122, 217–19
'The Lamentations of Round-Oak Waters', 7, 103–4, 122, 215–17
'The Land Rail', 130
'The Last of March, Written at Lolham Brigs', 66
'The Maple Tree', 100
The Midsummer Cushion, 102, 161, 162
'The Mores', 7, 97, 122, 213
'The Morning Walk', 139
'The Nightingales Nest', 22–3, 36, 50, 129–31, 241, 255
'The Old Willow', 100
The Parish, 5, 6, 35–6, 159, 183, 185–6, 237, 250
The Peasant Boy, 158
'The Peasant Poet', 19
'The Pettichaps Nest', 3–4, 21–2, 97, 245
'The Primrose', 95
'The Progress of Rhyme' ('The Progress of Ryhme'), 19, 69, 151, 233, 246
'The Robins Nest', 50, 51–2, 53
The Rural Muse, 4, 22, 102, 160, 162, 164
'The Sailor Boy', 206
'The sharp wind shivers', 43
The Shepherd's Calendar, with Village Stories, and Other Poems, 4, 13, 28, 34, 84, 100, 141–2, 157–8, 159–60, 170–1, 191, 219
  'January', 149–50, 157–8
  'July', 160
  'June', 34, 144
  'March', 158
  'May', 30
  'November', 34, 85
  'October', 160
'The Shepherds Tree', 100
'The Skylark' ('Although I am in prison'), 83–4
'The Spindle Tree', 102–3
'The Surrey Tree', 100
'The Sycamore Tree', 100
'The Thrushes Nest', 21
'The Vicar', 186
'The Village Doctress', 234
The Village Minstrel, and Other Poems, 3, 4, 27, 94, 97, 157, 158–9, 168, 194, 198, 219
  'The Village Minstrel'
  'Lubin's Song', 159
  'Lubins sigh For the pauper', 159
  'Woodcroft Castle The Netherds tale', 159
'The Wild Flower Nosgay', 92–4
'The Winters Come', 235
'The Woods', 43
'The Wrynecks Nest', 32
'The Yellowhammers Nest', 22, 36, 47, 87
'This leaning tree with ivy overhung', 192, 193
'To a Bower', 92
'To a Fallen Elm', 36–7, 122; *see also* 'The Fallen Elm'
'To a Favourite Tree', 95
'To a Winter Scene', 68
'To An Angry Bee', 88
'To an April Daisey', 91
'To an hour glass', 197–9, 207
'To an Insignificant Flower, obscurely blooming in a lonely wild', 46, 47, 48, 49–50
'To John Clare', 149
'To the Nightingale' ('I love to hear the nightingale'), 248
'To the Snipe', 36, 97, 236, 243–4
'To the Violet', 92
'Walcott Hall and Surrounding Scenery', 11–13
'Where the broad sheep walk', 98
'Wild Bees', 88
'Winter' ('From huddling nights embrace how chill'), 157–8
'Winter' ('The small wind whispers through the leafless hedge'), 157
'Winter Evening', 80–3

271

INDEX

Clare, John (cont.)
  'Winter Fields', 26, 252
  'Winter Rainbow', 157
  'Written in a Thunderstorm July 15th 1841', 71
  'Written in Prison', 83, 91
  prose
    autobiographical writings, 6, 57, 87–8, 107, 127, 140–1, 142, 152, 183, 186, 189–90, 196, 203, 229, 237–8
    'Autumn', 145–6, 188–9
    comments on the beautiful and sublime in poetry, 61–2
    'Essay on Landscape', 27, 31–2
    'Essay on Religion', 194
    journal, 85, 101–2, 111–12, 116, 153, 190, 234–5, 251
    'Journey out of Essex', 91, 146, 189
    natural history writings, 85, 95–7, 102, 189, 250
    on herbals, 234
    'On Lying', 106
    on the Bible, 187
    on trifles, 4
    'Self Identity', 146–7
Clare, Martha (Patty) (Clare's wife), 6, 138, 144, 177, 185
Clare, Parker (Clare's father), 137, 189, 217
Clark, Timothy, 121, 122, 123, 126
Clarke, George, 173–4
Cobbett, William, 211, 213
Cochrane, John Dundas
  Narrative of a pedestrian journey through Russia and Siberian Tartary, from the frontiers of China to the frozen sea and Kamtchatka, 106
Colebrook, Claire, 121
Coleridge, Samuel Taylor, 30, 66, 94, 184, 193
  conversation poems, 27
  'Frost at Midnight', 18, 24, 26
  'Hymn before Sun-rise, in the Vale of Chamouni', 64–5
  lectures, 26
Collier, Mary, 199, 200, 201, 208
  'The Woman's Labour', 196, 202
Collins, William, 162
  'Ode to Evening', 44, 161, 250, 251–2
Cook, James
  The Three Voyages of Captain Cook Round the World, 106
Cowley, Abraham
  'The Grasshopper', 250
  'The Swallow', 250

Cowper, William, 139, 184, 193, 249, 252
  'My Mary', 156
  The Task, 213, 250, 252
Crabbe, George, 35
Crowland, 107
Cullen, William, 230
Culler, Jonathan, 53–4
Culpepper, Nicholas, 234
  The English Physician, 234
Curtis, John, 115
  British Entomology, 110, 115, 116
Cuvier, Georges, 110

Dale, James, 115
Darling, George, 237
Darwin, Charles, 98, 112
Davies, Jeremy, 122, 124, 127–8
De Bolla, Peter, 65, 66
De Quincey, Thomas, 141
De Wilde, G. J., 177, 178
De Wint, Peter, 10, 27, 31–2
Defoe, Daniel, 139
  Robinson Crusoe, 205
Dennis, John, 68
DeVille, James, 238
Dissenters, 185, 186, 205
Dodsley, Robert, 200–1, 203
  A Muse in Livery, or the Footman's Miscellany, 200
  Servitude, 200
  'The Footman, An Epistle to my Friend Mr. Wright', 200–1
Dorset, 115
Drakard's Stamford News, 109
Drury, Edward, 152, 153, 156, 158
Duck, Stephen, 197, 199, 200, 201, 208, 209
  'The Thresher's Labour', 196, 200
Dupere, Dr, 107
Dyer, John
  'Grongar Hill', 250
  'The Fleece', 250

E.H., A Factory Girl of Stalybridge
  'On Joseph Rayner Stephens', 208
East Asia, 125
Edinburgh, 107, 108
Edinburgh Botanic Garden, 110
Edwards, Sydenham, 113
  Edwards's Botanical Register, 113
Egypt, 110, 152
Elton, Charles Abraham, 116
Ely, 108

272

INDEX

Emmerson, Eliza, 153, 155, 159, 160, 164, 185, 201
   'Lines on Receiving the Bust of the Northamptonshire Poet, Executed by Henry Behnes, Esq', 171
Emmerton, Isaac
   A Plain and Practical Treatise on the Culture and Management of the Auricula, Polyanthus, Carnation, Pink, and the Ranunculus, 96
   The Culture & Management of the Auricula, Polyanthus, Carnation, Pink, and the Ranunculus, 113
Epping Forest, 91, 144, 164, 189
Essex, 7, 146

Falconer, William
   The Shipwreck, 205–6
Farley, Paul, 242, 248
Fitzwilliam family, 108, 110, 111
Fitzwilliam, Earl, 7, 108, 109
Fives Court, 238
Forester, Fanny
   'To the Lowly Bard', 208
Freemantle, Bridget, 201
Friedrich, Casper David
   'The Sea of Ice', 68
Fulford, Tim, 7, 99

Gargaillo, Florian, 242
Garrard, Greg, 122
Gay, John
   The Shepherd's Week, 250
Gentleman's Magazine, 84
Gerard, John
   Herball, or Generall Historie of Plantes, 234
Germany, 109
Gilpin, William, 10
Glanville's Wootton, 115
Glinton, 207
Glorious Revolution, 213
Glotfelty, Cheryll, 120
Goddard, Henry, 179
Goddard, Joe, 178–9
Goldsmith, Oliver, 139
   'The Deserted Village', 156
Golinski, Jan
   British Weather and the Climate of Enlightenment, 235
Goodridge, John, 49, 199, 250
   John Clare and Community, 197
Goodridge, John and Kelsey Thornton
   'John Clare the Trespasser', 196
Gorji, Mina, 88, 127, 233, 250
Gouger, Robert, 106
Grainger, Margaret, 113
   ed. *The Natural History Prose Writings of John Clare*, 95–6
Gray, Thomas, 255
   'Elegy Written in a Country Churchyard', 188, 233
   'Ode to Spring', 250
Great Casterton, 185
Greece, 1
Green, Matthew
   The Spleen, 250
Grigson, Geoffrey, 5, 144
Grimshaw, Thomas, 172–4, 176, 178
Grosvenor Square, 110
Guardian, 249
Guyer, Sara, 46, 71–2

Habakkuk, 146
Hamilton, Joshua
   English Family Physician, 234
Hardy, Thomas, 30
Haughton, Hugh, 30
Haworth, Adrian, 108
   Lepidopterorum Britannicorum, 108
Hazlitt, William, 141
Heaney, Seamus, 37, 54, 242–4, 247, 249
   'A Backward Look', 242–4
   Field Work, 242
   'John Clare, A Bi-centenary Lecture', 242–4
   'Nettles', 246
   North, 242
   Wintering Out, 242
Heise, Ursula, 126
Helpston, 6, 7, 55, 60, 91, 94, 96, 97. 103, 107, 108, 126, 129, 137, 139, 140, 141, 143, 148–9, 162, 212, 214, 220, 236, 237
Henderson, Joseph, 108–9, 110–17
Henslow, John Steven, 112
Herbert, George, 30
Hess, Scott, 99
Hessey, James Augustus, 96, 141, 153, 157, 158, 159, 168, 169, 171, 186, 189, 235
Hewitt, Seán, 248
Hewlett, Maurice, 86
Heyes, Robert, 13, 96, 125
High Beach, 7
High Beech Asylum [High Beach Asylum], 7, 40, 49, 91, 167, 144, 164, 189, 233

INDEX

Hilton, William, 167, 168–71, 172, 173
Hobson, Edward, 114–15, 116
   Musci Britannici, 114, 115
Homer, 189
Hone, William
   Every-day Book, 153
Houghton-Walker, Sarah, 70, 184, 187, 192
Hughes, Ted, 241
Hulme Field Naturalists Society, 113
Hurdis, James
   'The Evening Walk', 250
   'The Village Curate', 250

Illustrated London News, 170
Independents, 184
Inskip, Thomas, 199
Irvine, Richard, 127
Islam, 184

Jago, Richard
   'The Blackbirds', 250
Jamie, Kathleen, 248
Jenkins, Edward, 114
Jerom, William, 178
John Clare Society Journal, 99, 244
Johnson, Samuel, 255
   A Dictionary of the English Language,
      61, 63
Joyce, Mary, 6, 40, 42, 138, 148
Judaism, 184

Kant, Immanuel, 68, 70, 71
   Critique of Judgement, 62–3
Karremann, Isabel, 193
Keats, John, 17, 151, 169, 237, 249
   'La Belle Dame sans Merci', 35
   'Ode to a Nightingale', 18
   'Ode to Autumn', 43
Keegan, Bridget, 122
Kilvert, Francis, 187–8
Kinross, 107, 110
Knight, W. F., 83
Kövesi, Simon, 100, 122–3, 124

Lamb, Charles, 141
Lancashire, 113
Langhorne, John
   The Fables of Flora, 250
Latin America, 125
Law, Edmund Francis, 178
Law, William Wilby, 173, 177–8
Lawrence, Sir Thomas, 238
Leapor, Mary, 201–3, 205

'An Epistle to Artemesia, On Fame', 201–2
'Crumble Hall', 202–3
'Epistle to a Lady', 202
'The Epistle of Deborah Dough', 202
Leeds, 172
Lilford Hall, 110
Lilford, Lord
   Notes on the Birds of Northamptonshire and Neighbourhood, 110–11
Lincoln, 169
Lindley, John, 113
Linnaeus, Carl, 234
Linnean Society, 111, 112
Logan, John
   'Ode to the Cuckoo', 250
London, 7, 106, 109, 110, 140–1, 143, 167, 169, 171, 219, 220, 237–8
London Magazine, 31, 107, 169, 220
'Longinus', 65, 68
   On the Sublime, 63
Longley, Michael, 246–7, 248
   'Flora', 246–7
   'Gardening in Cardoso', 247
   'Journey out of Essex', 247
Loudon, John Claudius, 113
Lowe, Richard Thomas, 113
Lower Mosley Street Natural History Society, 113
Lucas, John, 36
Lynch, Dierdre, 53

Mabey, Richard, 95, 99, 101
   Flora Britannica, 95
Madeira, 113
Magazine of Natural History, 113
Mahood, M. M., 85
   A John Clare Flora, 95–6
   The Poet as Botanist, 94, 95
Maine, George, 174–7
Mallarmé, Stéphane, 54
Manchester, 114
Marie Antoinette, 208
Marsh, George, 117
Marsh, Herbert, 117
Marsh, Marianne, 117
Marvell, Andrew, 9, 43
   'The Garden', 153–4
Mary Joyce, 8
McAlpine, Erica, 183
McKusick, James, 79, 86–7, 99, 122, 250
Methodism, 183, 184, 185, 203, 208, 217
Middle East, 125
Middleton Botanical Society, 113

INDEX

Milton Hall, 108–9, 110, 111, 112, 113, 114, 115, 116, 117
Milton, John, 1, 2, 32, 63, 69, 139, 193, 255
  Comus, 250
  'Il Penseroso', 250
  'L'Allegro', 250
  Paradise Lost, 63, 71
Milton, Lord, 113, 203
Minor, Mark, 185, 186
Monro, Alexander, 230
Montagu, Elizabeth, 203–5
Montgomery, James, 241
Moore, Thomas, 28–9, 142
  Irish Melodies, 28
More, Hannah, 193
Morley, David, 242, 248
Morton, Timothy, 69, 121, 125
  The Ecological Thought, 132
Murry, John Middleton, 54, 77, 85–6

Napoleon, 147, 215
Napoleonic Wars, 61, 212
National Portrait Gallery, 167, 168, 170
Natural History Society of Edinburgh, 108
Nelson, 147
Nersessian, Anahid, 121
Ness, Richard M., 67
Newark, 106
Newbon, Elizabeth, 189
Nicholson, Michael, 71, 88
Noehden, George Henry, 108, 110, 112
Norfolk, 107
Norfolk Broads, 115
Northampton, 172, 173, 174, 176, 178
Northampton Central Library, 167
Northampton General Lunatic Asylum, 7, 77, 91, 95, 164, 173, 174, 178, 189, 230, 233, 236
Northampton Mercury, 173, 177
Northampton Militia, 61
Northampton Museum, 178
Northamptonshire, 109
Northamptonshire Natural History Society, 110
Northborough, 7, 33, 86, 129, 143–4, 146, 162, 220, 245
Northern Star, 208

Oerlemans, Onno, 77, 87
Oswald, Alice, 248–9
  'Wood Not Yet Out', 248
Oundle, 110
Oxford Museum of Natural History, 115

Paris, 110
Parkinson, John
  Theatrum Botanicum, 234
Paulin, Tom, 242, 244–5
  Liberty Tree, 244
  'Of difference does it make', 244–5
  The Faber Book of Vernacular Verse, 244
  'The Writing Lark', 244
Perkins, David, 87
Peterborough, 7, 107, 109, 111, 115, 117
Peterborough Museum and Art Gallery, 178, 184
Poe, Edgar Allan
  'The Raven', 51
Poets' Corner, 241, 255
Poetzsch, Markus, 13
Portugal, 113
Posthumus, Stephanie, 124
Powell, David, 54, 57
Peakirk, 111

Quakers, 184
Quarterly Review, 85

Radstock, Lord, 155–7, 159, 213
Ranters, 183, 186–7
Ray, John
  Historia Plantarium, 234
Redding, Cyrus, 167
Reid, John, 232
  Essays on Insanity, 231
Reresby, Thomas
  A Miscellany of Ingenious Thoughts and Reflections, 63
Reynolds, John Hamilton, 141
Rippingille, E. V., 171, 238
River Nene, 110
Robinson, Eric, 54, 57, 99, 155, 174, 186, 237
Robinson, Eric and Geoffrey Summerfield
  Selected Poems and Prose of John Clare, 243
Rogers, Thomas, 114
Rome, 1, 60, 171
Rossetti, Christina, 193
Rounce, Adam, 250
Royal Academy, 238
Royal Society, 112
Royce Wood, 96, 129, 143

Salzmann, Philipp, 113
Scharf, George, 170
Scotland, 7
Scots Musical Museum, 28

INDEX

Scriven, Edward, 168, 170
Selvamony, Nirmal, 120
Sha, Richard C., 231
Shakespeare, William, 1, 255
  Henry IV, Part II, 39
  Sonnet 73, 103
  Sonnet 92, 1
Shelley, Percy Bysshe, 31, 66, 86, 151
  'Mont Blanc', 64–5
  'To a Skylark', 84
Shenstone, William
  'The Schoolmistress', 250
Sinclair, Stéfan, 124
Sisyphus, 142
Skrimshire, Fenwick, 107–8, 115, 116
  A Series of Essays Introductory to the Study of Natural History, 108
  Village Pastor's Surgical and Medical Guide, 236
Skrimshire, Thomas, 107
Skrimshire, William, 107–8, 116
Smart, Christopher, 193, 230
Smith, James Edward
  Flora Britannica, 107
Smith, William
  Dionysius Longinus on the Sublime, 63
Soutar, William, 230
South Australia, 106
South Derry, 242
Southey, Robert, 213
  The Lives and Works of the Uneducated Poets, 197
Speenhamland system, 186
Spence, Thomas, 211
Spenser, Edmund, 27, 34, 35, 159, 250
St Peter and Paul, Great Casterton, 185
Stafford, Fiona, 13
Stamford, 107, 152, 179
Stamford Mercury, 84
Stephens, Joseph Rayner, 208
Storey, Mark, 8
Strang, Barbara, 249–50
Suzuki, Renichi, 126
Swordy Well, 96, 98, 217, 220
Symons, Arthur, 5, 247–8

Talbot, Edward Allen
  Five years residence in the Canadas including a tour through part of the United States of America, in the year 1823, 106
Tangier, 113

Taylor, John, 4, 13, 32, 61, 62, 85, 94, 96, 107, 108, 141, 142, 143, 151–3, 155–7, 158–60, 162, 166, 168–71, 194, 219, 220, 227, 249
  'Introduction' to Poems Descriptive of Rural Life and Scenery, 4, 43, 232, 245–6, 249
Taylor, John (of Northampton), 177–8
Tennent, Thomas, 228
Thomas, Edward, 246, 247
  'A Literary Pilgrim in England', 246, 247
  'Tall Nettles', 246
Thompson, E. P., 199
  'Time, Work-Discipline, and Industrial 'Capitalism', 196
Thompson, Lady Mary, 111
Thomson, James, 2, 253–5
  The Seasons, 83, 138–9, 196, 250, 253–5
  'Spring', 138–9, 253–4
  'Winter', 254–5
Thornhaugh, 112
Thorpe Hall, 114
Tibble, J. W.
  The Poems of John Clare, 243
Tibble, J. W. and Anne Tibble, 228
Todd, Janet, 183
Troy, 60
Tucker, Herbert F., 61
Turnill, John, 107
Turnill, Richard, 138
Tyldesley Botanical Society, 113

Unitarianism, 184
University of Cambridge, 112

Vardy, Alan, 86
Vernor and Hood, 219
Vesey-Fitzgerald, Brian, 170

Walcott, Derek
  'The Bounty', 248
Walton, Isaac, 139
Wark, Mackenzie, 125
Warton, Thomas
  'Ode on the Approach of Summer', 250
  'Sent to a Friend, on his leaving a favourite village in Hampshire', 250
  'The First of April', 250
  'The Hamlet, Written in Whichwood Forest', 250
Weiner, Stephanie Kuduk, 79, 191
Wellington, 148

INDEX

Wentworth Woodhouse, 109, 110, 111, 113
Wesley, John
   Primitive Physic, 234
Wesleyan Methodism, 183
West Riding, 109
Westminster Abbey, 241, 255
Westminster Review, 142
White, Gilbert, 122
   The Natural History of Selborne, 96
Whittaker, Joseph, 177–8
Whittlesea Mere, 115–16
Whytt, Robert, 230
Williams, Merryn, 197
Williams, Raymond, 197
Wisbech, 107
Woodhouse, James, 203–5, 206
   Poems on Several Occasions, 203
   The Life and Lucubrations of Crispinus Scriblerus, 203–5
Wordsworth, Dorothy, 122
Wordsworth, William, 17, 32, 48, 66, 86, 127, 183, 213, 214, 221, 250
   'Composed upon Westminster Bridge', 35
   'Lines Written a few Miles above Tintern Abbey', 18, 24, 26, 52, 57
   'Ode. Intimations of Immortality', 94
   'Preface' to *Lyrical Ballads*, 18
   The Prelude, 64–5
Wordsworth, William and Samuel Taylor Coleridge
   Lyrical Ballads, 27

Yorkshire, 109

Cambridge Companions To ...

AUTHORS

Edward Albee edited by Stephen J. Bottoms
Margaret Atwood edited by Coral Ann Howells (second edition)
W. H. Auden edited by Stan Smith
Jane Austen edited by Edward Copeland and Juliet McMaster (second edition)
James Baldwin edited by Michele Elam
Balzac edited by Owen Heathcote and Andrew Watts
Beckett edited by John Pilling
Bede edited by Scott DeGregorio
Aphra Behn edited by Derek Hughes and Janet Todd
Saul Bellow edited by Victoria Aarons
Walter Benjamin edited by David S. Ferris
William Blake edited by Morris Eaves
Boccaccio edited by Guyda Armstrong, Rhiannon Daniels, and Stephen J. Milner
Jorge Luis Borges edited by Edwin Williamson
Brecht edited by Peter Thomson and Glendyr Sacks (second edition)
The Brontës edited by Heather Glen
Bunyan edited by Anne Dunan-Page
Frances Burney edited by Peter Sabor
Byron edited by Drummond Bone (second edition)
Albert Camus edited by Edward J. Hughes
Willa Cather edited by Marilee Lindemann
Catullus edited by Ian Du Quesnay and Tony Woodman
Cervantes edited by Anthony J. Cascardi
Chaucer edited by Piero Boitani and Jill Mann (second edition)
Chekhov edited by Vera Gottlieb and Paul Allain
Kate Chopin edited by Janet Beer
Caryl Churchill edited by Elaine Aston and Elin Diamond
Cicero edited by Catherine Steel
J. M. Coetzee edited by Jarad Zimbler
Coleridge edited by Lucy Newlyn
Coleridge edited by Tim Fulford (new edition)
Wilkie Collins edited by Jenny Bourne Taylor
Joseph Conrad edited by J. H. Stape
H. D. edited by Nephie J. Christodoulides and Polina Mackay

Dante edited by Rachel Jacoff (second edition)
Daniel Defoe edited by John Richetti
Don DeLillo edited by John N. Duvall
Charles Dickens edited by John O. Jordan
Emily Dickinson edited by Wendy Martin
John Dronne edited by Achsah Guibbory
Dostoevskii edited by W. J. Leatherbarrow
Theodore Dreiser edited by Leonard Cassuto and Claire Virginia Eby
John Dryden edited by Steven N. Zwicker
W. E. B. Du Bois edited by Shamoon Zamir
George Eliot edited by George Levine and Nancy Henry (second edition)
T. S. Eliot edited by A. David Moody
Ralph Ellison edited by Ross Posnock
Ralph Waldo Emerson edited by Joel Porte and Saundra Morris
William Faulkner edited by Philip M. Weinstein
Henry Fielding edited by Claude Rawson
F. Scott Fitzgerald edited by Ruth Prigozy
F. Scott Fitzgerald edited by Michael Nowlin (second edition)
Flaubert edited by Timothy Unwin
E. M. Forster edited by David Bradshaw
Benjamin Franklin edited by Carla Mulford
Brian Friel edited by Anthony Roche
Robert Frost edited by Robert Faggen
Gabriel García Márquez edited by Philip Swanson
Elizabeth Gaskell edited by Jill L. Matus
Edward Gibbon edited by Karen O'Brien and Brian Young
Goethe edited by Lesley Sharpe
Günter Grass edited by Stuart Taberner
Thomas Hardy edited by Dale Kramer
David Hare edited by Richard Boon
Nathaniel Hawthorne edited by Richard Millington
Seamus Heaney edited by Bernard O'Donoghue
Ernest Hemingway edited by Scott Donaldson
Hildegard of Bingen edited by Jennifer Bain
Homer edited by Robert Fowler
Horace edited by Stephen Harrison
Ted Hughes edited by Terry Gifford

Ibsen edited by James McFarlane
Henry James edited by Jonathan Freedman
Samuel Johnson edited by Greg Clingham
Ben Jonson edited by Richard Harp and Stanley Stewart
James Joyce edited by Derek Attridge (second edition)
Kafka edited by Julian Preece
Kazuo Ishiguro edited by Andrew Bennett
Keats edited by Susan J. Wolfson
Rudyard Kipling edited by Howard J. Booth
Lacan edited by Jean-Michel Rabaté
D. H. Lawrence edited by Anne Fernihough
Primo Levi edited by Robert Gordon
Lucretius edited by Stuart Gillespie and Philip Hardie
Machiavelli edited by John M. Najemy
David Mamet edited by Christopher Bigsby
Thomas Mann edited by Ritchie Robertson
Christopher Marlowe edited by Patrick Cheney
Andrew Marvell edited by Derek Hirst and Steven N. Zwicker
Ian McEwan edited by Dominic Head
Herman Melville edited by Robert S. Levine
Arthur Miller edited by Christopher Bigsby (second edition)
Milton edited by Dennis Danielson (second edition)
Molière edited by David Bradby and Andrew Calder
Toni Morrison edited by Justine Tally
Alice Munro edited by David Staines
Nabokov edited by Julian W. Connolly
Eugene O'Neill edited by Michael Manheim
George Orwell edited by John Rodden
Ovid edited by Philip Hardie
Petrarch edited by Albert Russell Ascoli and Unn Falkeid
Harold Pinter edited by Peter Raby (second edition)
Sylvia Plath edited by Jo Gill
Plutarch edited by Frances B. Titchener and Alexei Zadorojnyi
Edgar Allan Poe edited by Kevin J. Hayes
Alexander Pope edited by Pat Rogers
Ezra Pound cdited by Ira B. Nadel
Proust edited by Richard Bales
Pushkin edited by Andrew Kahn
Thomas Pynchon edited by Inger H. Dalsgaard, Luc Herman and Brian McHale
Rabelais edited by John O'Brien
Rilke edited by Karen Leeder and Robert Vilain
Philip Roth edited by Timothy Parrish
Salman Rushdie edited by Abdulrazak Gurnah
John Ruskin edited by Francis O'Gorman
Sappho edited by P. J. Finglass and Adrian Kelly
Seneca edited by Shadi Bartsch and Alessandro Schiesaro
Shakespeare edited by Margareta de Grazia and Stanley Wells (second edition)
George Bernard Shaw edited by Christopher Innes
Shelley edited by Timothy Morton
Mary Shelley edited by Esther Schor
Sam Shepard edited by Matthew C. Roudané
Spenser edited by Andrew Hadfield
Laurence Sterne edited by Thomas Keymer
Wallace Stevens edited by John N. Serio
Tom Stoppard edited by Katherine E. Kelly
Harriet Beecher Stowe edited by Cindy Weinstein
August Strindberg edited by Michael Robinson
Jonathan Swift edited by Christopher Fox
J. M. Synge edited by P. J. Mathews
Tacitus edited by A. J. Woodman
Henry David Thoreau edited by Joel Myerson
Thucydides edited by Polly Low
Tolstoy edited by Donna Tussing Orwin
Anthony Trollope edited by Carolyn Dever and Lisa Niles
Mark Twain edited by Forrest G. Robinson
John Updike edited by Stacey Olster
Mario Vargas Llosa edited by Efrain Kristal and John King
Virgil edited by Fiachra Mac Góráin and Charles Martindale (second edition)
Voltaire edited by Nicholas Cronk
David Foster Wallace edited by Ralph Clare
Edith Wharton edited by Millicent Bell
Walt Whitman edited by Ezra Greenspan
Oscar Wilde edited by Peter Raby
Tennessee Williams edited by Matthew C. Roudané

William Carlos Williams edited by Christopher MacGowan

August Wilson edited by Christopher Bigsby

Mary Wollstonecraft edited by Claudia L. Johnson

Virginia Woolf edited by Susan Sellers (second edition)

Wordsworth edited by Stephen Gill

Richard Wright edited by Glenda R. Carpio

W. B. Yeats edited by Marjorie Howes and John Kelly

Xenophon edited by Michael A. Flower

Zola edited by Brian Nelson

TOPICS

The Actress edited by Maggie B. Gale and John Stokes

The African American Novel edited by Maryemma Graham

The African American Slave Narrative edited by Audrey A. Fisch

African American Theatre edited by Harvey Young

Allegory edited by Rita Copeland and Peter Struck

American Crime Fiction edited by Catherine Ross Nickerson

American Gothic edited by Jeffrey Andrew Weinstock

The American Graphic Novel edited by Jan Baetens, Hugo Frey and Fabrice Leroy

American Horror edited by Stephen Shapiro and Mark Storey

American Literature and the Body edited by Travis M. Foster

American Literature and the Environment edited by Sarah Ensor and Susan Scott Parrish

American Literature of the 1930s edited by William Solomon

American Modernism edited by Walter Kalaidjian

American Poetry since 1945 edited by Jennifer Ashton

American Realism and Naturalism edited by Donald Pizer

American Short Story edited by Michael J. Collins and Gavin Jones

American Travel Writing edited by Alfred Bendixen and Judith Hamera

American Women Playwrights edited by Brenda Murphy

Ancient Rhetoric edited by Erik Gunderson

Arthurian Legend edited by Elizabeth Archibald and Ad Putter

Australian Literature edited by Elizabeth Webby

The Australian Novel edited by Nicholas Birns and Louis Klee

The Beats edited by Stephen Belletto

Boxing edited by Gerald Early

British Black and Asian Literature (1945–2010) edited by Deirdre Osborne

British Fiction: 1980–2018 edited by Peter Boxall

British Fiction since 1945 edited by David James

British Literature of the 1930s edited by James Smith

British Literature of the French Revolution edited by Pamela Clemit

British Romantic Poetry edited by James Chandler and Maureen N. McLane

British Romanticism edited by Stuart Curran (second edition)

British Romanticism and Religion edited by Jeffrey Barbeau

British Theatre, 1730–1830 edited by Jane Moody and Daniel O'Quinn

Canadian Literature edited by Eva-Marie Kröller (second edition)

The Canterbury Tales edited by Frank Grady

Children's Literature edited by M. O. Grenby and Andrea Immel

The City in World Literature edited by Ato Quayson and Jini Kim Watson

The Classic Russian Novel edited by Malcolm V. Jones and Robin Feuer Miller

Comics edited by Maaheen Ahmed

Contemporary African American Literature edited by Yogita Goyal

Contemporary Irish Poetry edited by Matthew Campbell

Creative Writing edited by David Morley and Philip Neilsen

Crime Fiction edited by Martin Priestman

Dante's 'Commedia' edited by Zygmunt G. Barański and Simon Gilson

Dracula edited by Roger Luckhurst

Early American Literature edited by Bryce Traister

Early Modern Women's Writing edited by Laura Lunger Knoppers

The Eighteenth-Century Novel edited by John Richetti

Eighteenth-Century Poetry edited by John Sitter

Eighteenth-Century Thought edited by Frans De Bruyn

Emma edited by Peter Sabor

English Dictionaries edited by Sarah Ogilvie

English Literature, 1500–1600 edited by Arthur F. Kinney

English Literature, 1650–1740 edited by Steven N. Zwicker

English Literature, 1740–1830 edited by Thomas Keymer and Jon Mee

English Literature, 1830–1914 edited by Joanne Shattock

English Melodrama edited by Carolyn Williams

English Novelists edited by Adrian Poole

English Poetry, Donne to Marvell edited by Thomas N. Corns

English Poets edited by Claude Rawson

English Renaissance Drama edited by A. R. Braunmuller and Michael Hattaway (second edition)

English Renaissance Tragedy edited by Emma Smith and Garrett A. Sullivan Jr.

English Restoration Theatre edited by Deborah C. Payne Fisk

Environmental Humanities edited by Jeffrey Cohen and Stephanie Foote

The Epic edited by Catherine Bates

Erotic Literature edited by Bradford Mudge

The Essay edited by Kara Wittman and Evan Kindley

European Modernism edited by Pericles Lewis

European Novelists edited by Michael Bell

Fairy Tales edited by Maria Tatar

Fantasy Literature edited by Edward James and Farah Mendlesohn

Feminist Literary Theory edited by Ellen Rooney

Fiction in the Romantic Period edited by Richard Maxwell and Katie Trumpener

The Fin de Siècle edited by Gail Marshall

Frankenstein edited by Andrew Smith

The French Enlightenment edited by Daniel Brewer

French Literature edited by John D. Lyons

The French Novel: From 1800 to the Present edited by Timothy Unwin

Gay and Lesbian Writing edited by Hugh Stevens

German Romanticism edited by Nicholas Saul

Global Literature and Slavery edited by Laura T. Murphy

Gothic Fiction edited by Jerrold E. Hogle

The Graphic Novel edited by Stephen Tabachnick

The Greek and Roman Novel edited by Tim Whitmarsh

Greek and Roman Theatre edited by Marianne McDonald and J. Michael Walton

Greek Comedy edited by Martin Revermann

Greek Lyric edited by Felix Budelmann

Greek Mythology edited by Roger D. Woodard

Greek Tragedy edited by P. E. Easterling

The Harlem Renaissance edited by George Hutchinson

The History of the Book edited by Leslie Howsam

Human Rights and Literature edited by Crystal Parikh

The Irish Novel edited by John Wilson Foster

Irish Poets edited by Gerald Dawe

The Italian Novel edited by Peter Bondanella and Andrea Ciccarelli

The Italian Renaissance edited by Michael Wyatt

Jewish American Literature edited by Hana Wirth-Nesher and Michael P. Kramer

The Latin American Novel edited by Efraín Kristal

Latin American Poetry edited by Stephen Hart

Latina/o American Literature edited by John Morán González

Latin Love Elegy edited by Thea S. Thorsen

Literature and Animals edited by Derek Ryan

Literature and the Anthropocene edited by John Parham

Literature and Climate edited by Adeline Johns-Putra and Kelly Sultzbach

Literature and Disability edited by Clare Barker and Stuart Murray

Literature and Food edited by J. Michelle Coghlan

Literature and the Posthuman edited by Bruce Clarke and Manuela Rossini

Literature and Religion edited by Susan M. Felch

Literature and Science edited by Steven Meyer

The Literature of the American Civil War and Reconstruction edited by Kathleen Diffley and Coleman Hutchison

The Literature of the American Renaissance edited by Christopher N. Phillips

The Literature of Berlin edited by Andrew J. Webber

The Literature of the Crusades edited by Anthony Bale

The Literature of the First World War edited by Vincent Sherry

The Literature of London edited by Lawrence Manley

The Literature of Los Angeles edited by Kevin R. McNamara

The Literature of New York edited by Cyrus Patell and Bryan Waterman

The Literature of Paris edited by Anna-Louise Milne

The Literature of World War II edited by Marina MacKay

Literature on Screen edited by Deborah Cartmell and Imelda Whelehan

Lyrical Ballads edited by Sally Bushell

Medieval British Manuscripts edited by Orietta Da Rold and Elaine Treharne

Medieval English Culture edited by Andrew Galloway

Medieval English Law and Literature edited by Candace Barrington and Sebastian Sobecki

Medieval English Literature edited by Larry Scanlon

Medieval English Mysticism edited by Samuel Fanous and Vincent Gillespie

Medieval English Theatre edited by Richard Beadle and Alan J. Fletcher (second edition)

Medieval French Literature edited by Simon Gaunt and Sarah Kay

Medieval Romance edited by Roberta L. Krueger

Medieval Romance edited by Roberta L. Krueger (new edition)

Medieval Women's Writing edited by Carolyn Dinshaw and David Wallace

Modern American Culture edited by Christopher Bigsby

Modern British Women Playwrights edited by Elaine Aston and Janelle Reinelt

Modern French Culture edited by Nicholas Hewitt

Modern German Culture edited by Eva Kolinsky and Wilfried van der Will

The Modern German Novel edited by Graham Bartram

The Modern Gothic edited by Jerrold E. Hogle

Modern Irish Culture edited by Joe Cleary and Claire Connolly

Modern Italian Culture edited by Zygmunt G. Baranski and Rebecca J. West

Modern Latin American Culture edited by John King

Modern Russian Culture edited by Nicholas Rzhevsky

Modern Spanish Culture edited by David T. Gies

Modernism edited by Michael Levenson (second edition)

The Modernist Novel edited by Morag Shiach

Modernist Poetry edited by Alex Davis and Lee M. Jenkins

Modernist Women Writers edited by Maren Tova Linett

Narrative edited by David Herman

Narrative Theory edited by Matthew Garrett

Native American Literature edited by Joy Porter and Kenneth M. Roemer

Nineteen Eighty-Four edited by Nathan Waddell

Nineteenth-Century American Poetry edited by Kerry Larson

Nineteenth-Century American Women's Writing edited by Dale M. Bauer and Philip Gould

Nineteenth-Century Thought edited by Gregory Claeys

The Novel edited by Eric Bulson

Old English Literature edited by Malcolm Godden and Michael Lapidge (second edition)

Performance Studies edited by Tracy C. Davis

Piers Plowman edited by Andrew Cole and Andrew Galloway

The Poetry of the First World War edited by Santanu Das

Popular Fiction edited by David Glover and Scott McCracken

Postcolonial Literary Studies edited by Neil Lazarus

Postcolonial Poetry edited by Jahan Ramazani

Postcolonial Travel Writing edited by Robert Clarke

Postmodern American Fiction edited by Paula Geyh

Postmodernism edited by Steven Connor

Prose edited by Daniel Tyler

The Pre-Raphaelites edited by Elizabeth Prettejohn

Pride and Prejudice edited by Janet Todd

Queer Studies edited by Siobhan B. Somerville

Renaissance Humanism edited by Jill Kraye

Robinson Crusoe edited by John Richetti

Roman Comedy edited by Martin T. Dinter

The Roman Historians edited by Andrew Feldherr

Roman Satire edited by Kirk Freudenburg

The Romantic Sublime edited by Cian Duffy

Science Fiction edited by Edward James and Farah Mendlesohn

Scottish Literature edited by Gerald Carruthers and Liam McIlvanney

Sensation Fiction edited by Andrew Mangham

Shakespeare and Contemporary Dramatists edited by Ton Hoenselaars

Shakespeare and Popular Culture edited by Robert Shaughnessy

Shakespeare and Race edited by Ayanna Thompson

Shakespeare and Religion edited by Hannibal Hamlin

Shakespeare and War edited by David Loewenstein and Paul Stevens

Shakespeare on Film edited by Russell Jackson (second edition)

Shakespeare on Screen edited by Russell Jackson

Shakespeare on Stage edited by Stanley Wells and Sarah Stanton

Shakespearean Comedy edited by Alexander Leggatt

Shakespearean Tragedy edited by Claire McEachern (second edition)

Shakespeare's First Folio edited by Emma Smith

Shakespeare's History Plays edited by Michael Hattaway

Shakespeare's Language edited by Lynne Magnusson with David Schalkwyk

Shakespeare's Last Plays edited by Catherine M. S. Alexander

Shakespeare's Poetry edited by Patrick Cheney

Sherlock Holmes edited by Janice M. Allan and Christopher Pittard

The Sonnet edited by A. D. Cousins and Peter Howarth

The Spanish Novel: From 1600 to the Present edited by Harriet Turner and Adelaida López de Martínez

Textual Scholarship edited by Neil Fraistat and Julia Flanders

Theatre and Science edited by Kristen E. Shepherd-Barr

Theatre History edited by David Wiles and Christine Dymkowski

Transnational American Literature edited by Yogita Goyal

Travel Writing edited by Peter Hulme and Tim Youngs

The Twentieth-Century American Novel and Politics edited by Bryan Santin

Twentieth-Century American Poetry and Politics edited by Daniel Morris

Twentieth-Century British and Irish Women's Poetry edited by Jane Dowson

The Twentieth-Century English Novel edited by Robert L. Caserio

Twentieth-Century English Poetry edited by Neil Corcoran

Twentieth-Century Irish Drama edited by Shaun Richards

Twentieth-Century Literature and Politics edited by Christos Hadjiyiannis and Rachel Potter

Twentieth-Century Russian Literature edited by Marina Balina and Evgeny Dobrenko

Utopian Literature edited by Gregory Claeys

Victorian and Edwardian Theatre edited by Kerry Powell

The Victorian Novel edited by Deirdre David (second edition)

Victorian Poetry edited by Joseph Bristow

Victorian Women's Poetry edited by Linda K. Hughes

Victorian Women's Writing edited by Linda H. Peterson

War Writing edited by Kate McLoughlin

Women's Writing in Britain, 1660–1789 edited by Catherine Ingrassia

Women's Writing in the Romantic Period edited by Devoney Looser

World Literature edited by Ben Etherington and Jarad Zimbler

World Crime Fiction edited by Jesper Gulddal, Stewart King and Alistair Rolls

Writing of the English Revolution edited by N. H. Keeble

The Writings of Julius Caesar edited by Christopher Krebs and Luca Grillo

Printed in the United States
by Baker & Taylor Publisher Services